THE CHRISTIAN FAITH

THE MACMILLAN COMPANY
NEW YORK · BOSTON · CHICAGO · DALLAS
ATLANTA · SAN FRANCISCO

MACMILLAN & CO., Limited
LONDON · BOMBAY · CALCUTTA
MELBOURNE

THE MACMILLAN COMPANY
OF CANADA, Limited
TORONTO

THE CHRISTIAN FAITH

A SYSTEM OF CHRISTIAN DOGMATICS

BY

JOSEPH STUMP, D.D., LL.D., L.H.D.

President of Northwestern Lutheran Theological Seminary

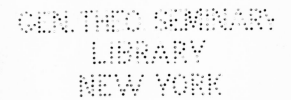

NEW YORK

THE MACMILLAN COMPANY

1932

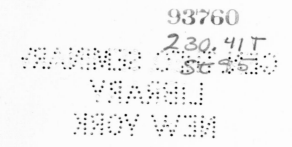

SET UP BY BROWN BROTHERS LINOTYPERS
PRINTED IN THE UNITED STATES OF AMERICA
BY THE FERRIS PRINTING COMPANY

TO

J. K. JENSEN

PREFACE

THE following pages are an endeavor to present the doctrines of our Church on the basis of the Holy Scriptures, in consonance with her confessions, and in the language of to-day. Such technical terms as have obtained a fixed place in dogmatics have been retained and defined. But unnecessary technical terms have been avoided, and the constant aim has been to present the doctrines as simply, clearly and intelligibly as possible. The work is intended primarily as a text-book, but it is hoped that the book will also be found useful by pastors who desire to review this important subject, and by intelligent laymen who desire to gain a connected and well-grounded knowledge of the Church's teaching.

J. S.

Minneapolis, Minn.

CONTENTS

ix

CONTENTS

PART III

THE WORK OF THE HOLY SPIRIT

PART IV

THE LAST THINGS OR THE CONSUMMATION OF REDEMPTION

THE CHRISTIAN FAITH

INTRODUCTION

In this introductory chapter we purpose to present a number of topics whose preliminary consideration is important for the proper study of dogmatics itself.

RELIGION

Universality of Religion. Man is distinctly a religious and moral being. His very nature as a person implies both the possibility and the necessity of religious and moral relationships. It is this fact which most clearly differentiates him from the brute. The latter has intelligence, which is sometimes of so high an order that it almost resembles reason. But no brute has ever given evidence of anything that resembles religion. He lacks the endowment for it. He does not possess self-consciousness and self-determination, without which the processes involved in religion are impossible. Man, on the other hand, wherever he is found and whatever his state of savagery or civilization, is a religious being. There has never been found anywhere a nation or a tribe without some kind of religion. The religious ideas and customs which prevail may be of the most degraded kind; but they are never altogether wanting. Atheism is not a natural state of man, but is one into which some persons endeavor to bring themselves by specious reasoning. The Scriptures tell us that "the fool hath said in his heart, There is no God" (Ps. 14:1). Whether he ever actually gets himself to believe it, as well as to say it, is a different matter.

In spite of the wide dissimilarity between the many religions found in the world, they all are marked by three underlying

1

characteristics; namely, the consciousness of a need which cannot be supplied by human power; the idea of a good which will satisfy the need; and the idea of a God who is able to supply that good. The explanation is found in the saying of Augustine, "Thou, O God, hast made us for Thyself; and our heart is restless until it rests in Thee." [1]

Origin of Religion. The origin of religion has been variously explained. Lucretius ascribed it to the fear of extraordinary events in nature. To this it may be replied, that before man could have ascribed such events to the gods, he must already have believed in the existence of gods. Bolingbroke and others ascribed it to the invention of rulers and priests for the purpose of holding the people in subjection. Others have regarded it as resulting from the consciousness of the need of a First Cause, or from reflections upon the many evidences of design in nature. Feuerbach ascribed it to self-deception, and Renan to poetic illusion.

The very universality of religion, however, shows that religion is native to man. He is constituted by nature a religious being. Religion is part of the very warp and woof of his nature, and he cannot cease to be a religious being unless he ceases to be a man. He may endeavor to crush out the religious tendencies in himself, and profess atheism; but he will never completely succeed in eliminating the religious factor from his nature.

The origin of religion, therefore, must be traced back to man's original constitution. He was made for a personal relationship with God, and was originally endowed with a personal integrity and a knowledge of God sufficient to enable him to remain in the right relation in which he was placed at creation. But with the fall into sin, the fellowship between man and God was broken off; and with the gradual but enormous growth and

[1] *Confessions,* par. 1.

development of sin in mankind, the original true knowledge of God became darkened and obscured, false elements became mingled with the true, the law written in the heart was largely erased, and men in their folly and blindness began to worship false gods (Rom. 1:18-23). Thus the natural religions of the world are not the result of a natural process of evolution by which man rose from animism and fetichism to ever higher stages of religious development, but are the attenuated and diluted remainder of man's original constitution and endowment. Profound study and a reverent mind enabled such men as Plato and Buddha to read from the blurred tablet of the mind much of the partially erased original law which has escaped other religious leaders, and which has remained utterly undecipherable to savage and barbarous tribes.

Subjective and Objective. The term religion may be used in a subjective and in an objective sense. In the subjective sense the term refers to the personal relation of man to God; in the objective sense it refers to the religious teachings, worship, ritual, ceremonies, etc. in which the subjective religion finds expression. In the former sense we say that a man has religion or is a religious man. In the latter or objective sense we speak of the Christian religion, the Jewish religion, the Mohammedan religion, etc. It is necessary to bear these two uses of the word in mind, so that we may distinguish between references to a man's personal religious state, and to the beliefs and teachings which characterize a certain community or organization of professedly religious persons.

Natural and Revealed. Heathen religions are classed as natural, because they are based solely on the natural revelation of God in conscience and in nature. The Christian religion is classed as revealed, because it is based on the supernatural revelation of God recorded in the Holy Scriptures. Although the natural religions contain much that is imperfect and false, they serve a useful purpose in keeping alive the consciousness of a Higher Being and the need of a right relation to Him; and they thus form the foundation of religious consciousness upon which Christianity may build. Were it not for this natural religiousness of man, Christianity, when it comes to him, would find no point of contact.

The Christian Religion

In the wide sense of the term, the word religion is used to describe the natural, inborn tendency of man to recognize the existence of a higher power, to feel the need of a right relation with it, and to proffer acts of worship for the purpose of establishing the right relation. Such a religion may be, and in some cases is, so compounded of ignorance and superstition, that little or nothing remains true in it but the consciousness of a higher power and the impulse to worship. As we advance upward in the scale, however, the natural religions of mankind embody more and more elements of truth; and some of them are worthy of great respect for their moral teachings, and for the effect produced upon their adherents. But the religious nature of mankind finds its true expression only in Christianity; for only in Christianity is there the knowledge of the true God and of the way in which man is to enter into and abide in the right relation with Him. The word religion in the strict sense of the term, therefore, is used to designate the Christian religion.

Definition. In this strict sense of the term religion may be defined as the communion or fellowship of man with God, mediated by Christ, and made ours by faith. It includes, indeed, other elements of importance, such as knowledge, prayer and worship, right conduct, the feeling of dependence on God, a satisfying view of the world, etc. But these other elements, important as they are, do not constitute its essence. True religion is an intensely personal matter, and concerns fundamentally the right relation of the soul to God. And this right relation is fellowship with God—a fellowship so full of trustful reliance upon God's love and power, that the soul which possesses it says to God, "Thou art mine, and I am Thine."

The definition once current in dogmatical circles, that religion is a mode of knowing and worshiping God, is defective, because it places too exclusive an emphasis on doctrine and ritual, and says nothing about the right relationship with God, which after all is the very essence of religion. It is true, genuine religion must include a true knowledge of God and a right mode of worshiping Him. But the essence of religion is found in fellowship or communion with God. Where this is wanting, knowledge and so-called worship do not constitute a man truly religious.

Religion, from the standpoint of Christianity, may be called life. To have religion means to be spiritually alive; and to have no religion means to be spiritually dead. Christ said, "I have come that they might have life, and that they might have it more abundantly (John 10:10). And John declares, "He that hath the Son hath life; and he that hath not the Son of God hath not life (1 John 5:12). True religion means to be born again, to receive a new, spiritual life from God, to be spiritually alive in Christ Jesus.

Christianity and Other Religions. It was long the custom simply to make a broad line of demarcation between Christianity and other religions, and to declare that Christianity is true, and that all the other religions are false. The fact that these other religions often contain much truth was wholly overlooked. In a certain sense, however, the distinction made was correct, because, while there are some elements of truth in all religions, and many elements of truth in some of them, all the

religions of mankind outside of Christianity lack the full truth
which has come by supernatural revelation, and consequently
lack the knowledge of the true and only way of obtaining fellowship with God, namely, through Christ. And while it is
true, that these natural religions still possess some remnants of
the original knowledge of God which was placed in man's heart
at creation, and the true elements in the natural religions are
the remainder of that original revelation, their devotees have
not only lost much of what was thus originally revealed, but
they also are ignorant of the revelation of God's redeeming
love. With all the elements of good which some of those
religions contain, they aim at attaining a right relation with
God by human efforts, sacrifices or virtues, while the only true
and possible mode is through the grace of God in Christ Jesus.
We are reconciled with God through faith in Christ, and not by
any works of our own.

The Absolute Religion. Christianity is the absolute religion,
because it is based on the full and final revelation of God as
recorded in the Holy Scriptures, and adequately meets the deepest needs of mankind. It is not, as some persons claim, the
product of natural evolution, and thus merely the most highly
developed among existing religions. On the contrary, it is the
one religion founded by direct divine supernatural revelation,
is true in all its parts, and is in no need of any addition or sub-
traction. It is the one true religion which is meant to be and
ought to be the universal religion of mankind.

The teachings of Christianity must be drawn from the record
of the divine supernatural revelation, namely, from the Holy
Scriptures; for these are the only rule and norm of faith and
life. The truth drawn from them approves itself in Christian
experience, according to the words of Christ, "If any man will
do His will, he shall know of the doctrine, whether it be of
God" (John 7:17). The Word of God has a self-evidencing
power all its own. Its truth is attested, also, by many external

evidences, whose consideration belongs specifically to Apologetics, and cannot be enlarged upon here.

THE ESSENCE OF CHRISTIANITY

We have defined true religion as fellowship or communion with God, mediated by Christ, and made ours by faith. It is possessed by him and only by him who has faith in Christ as his Redeemer. This faith is trust in or reliance upon Christ as our Savior. It might be supposed that since the time of the Reformation Protestants would be agreed upon this definition of faith. But in recent times the definition has been disputed,[2] and the claim is made that Christian faith is not faith in Christ as the Redeemer, but such faith in God as Christ Himself had. According to this view Christianity would not be the religion of redemption, but a code of ethics, with Christ as the Teacher and Example; and fellowship with God would be attained, not by trusting in the redemption which Christ has accomplished, but by taking Him as our example of religion.

A Religion of Redemption. The attempt is made, by raising the cries, "Back to Christ" and "Back to the Christianity of Christ," and by excluding the witness of all the Scriptures except the Synoptics, to show that Christianity is not the religion of which Christ is the center, but the religion which Christ practiced and exemplified. But even the Synoptics clearly indicate that Christ came to found a religion of redemption. It was, indeed, natural that during His public ministry Jesus should endeavor only in a preparatory and pedagogical way to lead His disciples into an understanding of His death, by which redemption and reconciliation were to be brought about. But at the same time He does not fail, even according to the Synoptics, to indicate its redemptive character. Thus He says, "The Son of Man came not to be ministered unto, but to minister, and to

[2] Harnack: *Wesen des Christentums.* 1908. *What Is Christianity?* Putnam, New York.

give His life a ransom for many" (Mark 10:45). And still more clearly He brings out its redemptive character in His words of Institution recorded by all the Synoptics. From those words, spoken when He instituted the Holy Supper, it is plain that He regarded His approaching death, not as a calamity which would put an end to all His work, but as the point of entrance upon a new dispensation of grace, which would bring the needed deliverance from sin. Thus it is evident, even from the Synoptics, that the Christian religion is the religion of reconciliation and redemption, and that the power which proceeds from Christ and is operative in the world to-day is something different from the religion which Christ Himself practiced.

That this is St. Paul's conception of Christianity is evident from his epistles. For him Christianity is the religion of redemption and reconciliation founded upon Christ's death and resurrection. For him the great central fact of Christianity is that "Christ was delivered for our offenses, and raised again for our justification" (Rom. 4:25); and the essence of the Gospel which he proclaims is that "God was in Christ, reconciling the world to Himself, not imputing their trespasses unto them" (2 Cor. 5:19). He "determined not to know anything" among the Corinthians "but Jesus Christ and Him crucified" (1 Cor. 2:2). And he gives this striking summary of his Gospel: "Moreover, brethren, I declare unto you the Gospel which I preached unto you, which also ye have received, and wherein ye stand; by which also ye are saved, if ye keep in memory what I preached unto you, unless ye have believed in vain. For I delivered unto you first of all that which also I received, how that Christ *died for our sins* according to the Scriptures, and that He was buried, and that *He rose again* the third day according to the Scriptures" (1 Cor. 15:1-4). Thus for Paul the content of the Gospel in its essence was, that Christ died for our sins and rose again.

This was the essence of the Gospel for the other apostles also. St. Peter tells us that we were "redeemed with the precious blood of Christ, as of a lamb without blemish and without spot" (1 Pet. 1:19). And St. John declares that Christ "is the propitiation for our sins; and not for ours only, but for the sins of the whole world" (1 John 2:2). And again he says, "Herein is love, not that we loved God, but that He loved us, and sent His Son to be the propitiation for our sins" (1 John 4:10).

It is only by the rejection of the plain testimony of the Holy Scriptures that men can come to the conclusion that the Christian religion is anything else than the religion of redemption and reconciliation through Jesus Christ, our Lord and Savior. And if some men claim that Christianity means to believe *as* Jesus believed, our reply is that their so-called Christianity is not the religion of the New Testament; and that it neither takes account of man's religious needs, nor sets before man the abundant provision which God has made in Christ for the salvation of his soul.

Christ came, not to exemplify the true religion, but to found it. He came, not simply to make known God's love, but to reveal it as a redeeming and reconciling love, which is ours in the true sense of the word when and only when we accept it by faith in Christ as our Savior. He came to establish man in a fellowship with God; but it is a fellowship which is not identical with that which He Himself has with the Father. On the contrary, it is a fellowship based on what He has done. And while He speaks to His disciples about His Father and their Father, He does not include Himself with them under the term "Our Father." His fellowship with the Father was unique, and was that of the only begotten Son who is in the bosom of the Father.

Christian faith, therefore, is not a believing as Christ believed, but is a personal trust in Christ our Savior, as the Son of God "who loved us and gave Himself for us" (Gal. 2:20) as a propitiation for our sins. And the essence of Christianity or true religion is fellowship with God, mediated by Christ, and made ours by faith in Christ as our Redeemer.

ROMANISM AND PROTESTANTISM

The Roman Catholic Church maintains that the Church is the source and judge of Christian doctrine. Her teachings must be accepted and her commands must be implicitly obeyed on pain of eternal condemnation. The pope is infallible when he speaks *ex cathedra*. The Church is built on the apostle Peter and his successors, the popes, whose legitimacy is secured by an unbroken succession. For the Roman Catholic the Church is not, as it is for the Protestant, the communion of saints or believers, but is the external organization with the pope at its head, and with a thoroughly articulated hierarchical system. In accordance with this doctrine the Roman Catholic Church has more and more put herself into the place of Christ the Mediator, and has arrogated to herself the place of mediator between God and men. Outside of her she claims there is no salvation; and inside of her there is salvation for all who conform to her outward requirements. Obedience to the Church is the *sine qua non* of salvation.[3] The Church has the sole right to interpret the Scriptures, and does it according to the tradition handed down in the Church. The priesthood is an order set over the laity, and its office is to administer the sacraments, in order by

[3] "Protestantism makes the relation of the individual to the Church dependent on his relation to Christ; Catholicism makes the relation of the individual to Christ dependent on his relation to the Church." Schleiermacher, *Der Christliche Glaube*, I, Sec. 24.

"Catholicism has developed itself into a great system of guarantees of Christianity; but Christianity, the thing itself, which was thus to be guaranteed, has been thrown into the shade. The opposition between genuine and spurious Christianity has been gradually reduced to the affirmation and negation of these guarantees. To attack the infallibility of the pope and of the Church is the prime heresy." Martensen, *Christian Dogmatics*, Engl. transl., Edinburgh, p. 30.

means of them to supply the Christians with influxes of grace which will enable them to obey the commandments of the Church and to perform the work necessary to salvation. Faith does not consist of confidence in Christ as our Savior, but in assenting to all the teachings of the Church. Salvation is by faith and works, and not by faith alone. Christ's office is not simply that of a redeemer, but that of a new lawgiver.[4]

The Roman Catholic Church has cast aside some of the abuses which prevailed in the Middle Ages. But in her opposition to the Reformation she has given official sanction to errors which were held by individuals in the Medieval Church but which had not previously obtained official recognition; and she has cast out the remnants of evangelical life which persisted through the Middle Ages. By the Canons and Decrees of the Council of Trent she has definitely set her seal upon errors and abuses against which the Reformation was a protest.[5]

In opposition to Roman Catholicism, Protestantism maintains the formal principle that the Holy Scriptures are the supreme and only rule of faith and life; and the material principle that justification is by faith alone, without works. It denies that the pope is the vicar of Christ or the successor of Peter. It declares that the Church is not an external organization, but the spiritual fellowship of all believers in Christ; that the Lord has done away with all mediating human priesthoods; that the only priesthood remaining is the spiritual priesthood of all believers;

[4] "If any one saith that Christ Jesus was given of God to men as a redeemer, in whom to trust, and not also as a legislator, whom to obey, let him be anathema." Canons and Decrees of the Council of Trent, Sess. VI, Can. 21.

[5] The Eastern Orthodox Church, often called the Greek Church, agrees in general with the principles and doctrines of the Roman Church. It maintains the authority of the episcopate, the validity of tradition as a source of religious teaching, and the infallibility of the General Councils, of which she recognizes, however, only seven. She rejects the primacy of the pope, the procession of the Holy Spirit from the Son, and the doctrines of purgatory and of indulgences. She accepts the same seven sacraments as the Roman Church, and teaches transubstantiation, but gives the communion in both kinds to the laity, including little children.

that Christ is the only Mediator between God and man; and that in Him we all have immediate access to the Father.

Protestantism split into two great branches, the Lutheran and the Reformed. For Lutheranism the determining principle was faith; for the Reformed or Calvinistic branch it was the absolute sovereignty of God. This principle of Calvin and the rationalizing principle of Zwingli, who sought to banish all mystery and to make every doctrine completely intelligible, explain the course taken by Reformed theology.[6]

LUTHERAN AND REFORMED PROTESTANTISM

Lutheran and Reformed Protestantism agree in maintaining the Formal and Material Principles of the Reformation; namely, the supreme authority of the Holy Scriptures, and the doctrine of justification by faith alone. The Lutheran Church is conservative and permits the retention of those traditions which are not contrary to the Scriptures; while the Reformed Church is inclined to reject all traditions which are not actually commanded in the Bible. Zwinglianism, being averse to the acceptance of mysteries and insisting on comprehending the doctrines of Scripture, seeks to explain away what it does not understand. Lutheranism, on the other hand, accepts the teachings of Holy Writ, even when it cannot comprehend them. Calvinism, basing all on the absolute sovereignty of God, lands in arbitrary divine predestination, and thus restricts the scope of the Gospel and the efficacy of the Means of Grace.[7] Reformed and Lutheran Protestantism differ more or less widely on the

[6] Some of the Reformed Churches have, however, rejected the Calvinistic position, e.g. the Arminians.

[7] The Reformed Churches separate the working of God from the Means of Grace, and conceive of God as working directly, or as adding His working to the Means—a thing which He is supposed to do, however, only in the case of the elect. The Lutheran Church, on the other hand, regards the Means of Grace as never disjoined or separated from the power of God, but as always accompanied by it, and as *the* means employed by God for the accomplishment of His gracious purposes.

doctrine of the Word of God, Predestination, the Person of Christ, Baptism and the Lord's Supper.

THEOLOGY

While subjectively religion is a personal relation between man and God, it involves certain beliefs and teachings concerning God and man and their relation to each other. It is with these beliefs and teachings that theology concerns itself. It is the science of religion.[8] It meets a demand of the human mind that our knowledge shall be systematized in the realm of the spirit as well as in the realm of nature. Such a system of truth results in a higher order of knowledge. It gives a clearer perception of the works of God, deepens our love for Him, and enables us to exhibit and teach the truth more satisfactorily to others. It is a progressive science; for while the objective facts and truths given in the divine supernatural revelation do not change, our understanding and exposition of them may grow. Its purpose is at once theoretical and practical; for it aims to give a scientific presentation of Christianity in all its aspects and departments, and at the same time by means of such a presentation to furnish material which is needful for training men to become preachers of the Gospel and shepherds of the flock.

Theology is usually divided into four departments,[9] namely, the Biblical or Exegetical, the Historical, the Systematic, and

[8] In the wide sense of the term any religion which is sufficiently developed in its teachings may have a theology. Thus we might speak of Mohammedan or Buddhistic theology. The term is used above in the sense of Christian theology. In this sense it may be more closely defined as the science of the Christian religion.

There are no fewer than five senses in which the word theology has been used, namely: 1. The scientific study of any religion. 2. The scientific study of the Christian religion. 3. Dogmatics. 4. The specific doctrine of God. 5 The doctrine concerning the deity of Christ.

[9] Theology was formerly classified as natural and revealed. But of late years the term natural theology has fallen into disuse, and what was once called by that name is now generally included under philosophy of religion.

the Practical. Of these the Systematic includes dogmatics, the subject which lies before us for study.

DOGMATICS

Definition. Dogmatics deals with the doctrinal teachings of the Christian religion. It is the systematic and scientific presentation of the doctrines of Christianity in harmony with the Scriptures and in consonance with the confessions of the Church. It is a science, because it employs a scientific method in dealing with its subject matter. The mere fact that its data belong to a sphere which transcends matter, and that the teachings of religion belong to the realm of faith rather than to that of knowledge in the ordinary sense of the term, does not prevent dogmatics from being a science. The term science has reference not to the nature of the subject matter, but to the nature of the method; and this can be as truly scientific in the sphere of religion as in that of physics.[10] Dogmatics takes the doctrinal results of exegetical and historical theology, formulates them, and weaves them into an organic whole.

Dogmatics aims not only to set forth the doctrines of Christianity, but to present them in a scientific manner as a well-articulated system. There is a "body of doctrine"; and the term implies that there exists something which may be called a doctrinal organism. Dogmatics deals with the Christian doctrines as a whole, and connects them in logical order. Each part has its place and use, just as an organ of the human body has. In this it differs from Biblical Theology, which aims to present only the characteristic teaching of Christ Himself or of the different authors of the Biblical books, and not to present a complete and well-rounded whole of Christian teaching. The latter is the distinct province of dogmatics.

Various names have been applied to this branch of theology.

[10] The old dogmaticians called theology a *habitus practicus.*

Melanchthon called his dogmatical work *Loci Communes*. Gerhard called his *Loci Theologici*. Baier called his work *Theologia Positiva*. Calvin's dogmatical treatise is known as *Institutes of the Christian Religion*. The name dogmatic theology was introduced in the seventeenth century. In the English-speaking world the names for this branch of theology have been "Systematic Theology," "System of Theology," "System of Christian Doctrine," "Christian Dogmatics," and "Doctrinal Theology."

Dogmatics and Ethics. Dogmatics and Christian ethics are closely related, and were formerly treated as one subject. Dogmatics is the science of the Christian faith; ethics is the science of the Christian life. Dogmatics deals with the objective truths of the Christian religion; ethics deals with the subjective disposition and conduct of the believer. The bond which unites them is faith: for faith as a receptive power accepts the grace of God exhibited in dogmatics; and faith as an operative power results in the Christian life as exhibited by Christian ethics. Among Lutheran theologians Calixtus was the first to treat ethics separately. With a few exceptions authors since his day have followed his example. If dogmatics and ethics are treated as one branch of theology, there is danger, either that ethics will receive insufficient treatment, or else that the ethical section of dogmatics will be out of proportion to the other sections.

Derivation of Name. The name dogmatics comes from the word dogma. This word, which is derived from the Greek *dokei moi* or *dedoktai,* came to mean an accepted teaching or truth, for example, in philosophy. In the usage of the Church a dogma means a doctrine which the Church has officially formulated and promulgated as her own.[11] It embraces all Christian truth so far as it exists as doctrines believed, confessed, and

[11] All dogmas are doctrines; but not all doctrines are dogmas. Doctrines become dogmas when the Church has officially formulated them, and sets them forth as its teaching.

taught by the Church. It includes the whole doctrine of the life in God as mediated by Christ: the nature of God, the relation in which we and the world around us stand to Him, the effect of sin upon that relation, the redemption effected by Christ, and the acts of God by which the communion of man with God is restored, maintained and perfected in Christ. As the science of dogmas, therefore, dogmatics has as its task the scientific presentation of Christian doctrine as a complete system.

Presuppositions. Dogmatics presupposes the existence of God, and does not undertake to prove it. The full consideration of the proofs of His existence belongs to apologetics and not to dogmatics. The usual philosophical proofs are the Ontological, the Cosmological, the Teleological, the Moral and the Historical. These proofs are not coercive. However convincing they may be to Christians, they may and often do fail to convince the enemies of the Christian religion.

Dogmatics also presupposes a supernatural revelation of God to man. Without a revelation of some kind by which God makes Himself known to us, we could know nothing about Him. Something of God may be learned from the natural revelation in conscience and nature; but, as we have already seen, this revelation is partial and incomplete. The revelation presupposed by Dogmatics is a supernatural one—the revelation which God gave of Himself in history through the prophets of old and through His own Son in the fullness of time.

Furthermore, dogmatics presupposes that there is in existence an inspired and authoritative record of this supernatural revelation; namely, that which is given in the Holy Scriptures; and that this record is an infallible source from which all the doctrines of the Christian religion must be drawn. These doctrines receive much corroboration from the natural revelation in conscience and nature. But the doctrines of dogmatics are not drawn from the natural revelation, as a source, but only from the Scriptures.[12]

Purpose and Method. The purpose of Dogmatics is to present in scientific form the truth which God has revealed for men's guidance and salvation. The form is not Biblical, but the content is. Dogmatics undertakes to present the very essence of Holy Scripture, especially as it relates to God and His gracious redemption in Christ, in a complete, systematic, orderly and intelligible way. The presentation must be clear, unmistakable, guarded against error, and fitted to give to those who study it a true and reliable knowledge of the truths which God has made known in His Word.

Such a work, unless it is to possess a purely objective, historical and confessional character, necessarily implies that the presentation of Scriptural doctrine will be based on Christian experience. Many of the doctrines of Scripture are unintelligible except on the basis of Christian experience, and cannot otherwise be adequately presented. At the same time, however, care must be taken that experience be made subject to Scripture, and not Scripture to experience. The presentation must remain objective in character and be true to its mission of setting forth clearly the teachings of Scripture, and those alone.

Works on Dogmatics naturally fall into certain classes according to the method pursued, though often they contain features which align them with more than one class. Biblical Dogmatics aims to set forth a systematic presentation of Christian doctrines as drawn from the Holy Scriptures. Symbolical or Confessional Dogmatics aims to present in a purely objective way the doctrinal system of the Church as recorded in her symbols. Positive Dogmatics aims to present the doctrines of Chris-

---

[12] Dogmaticians have sometimes distinguished between pure and mixed articles of faith: pure, comprising those which can be learned from the Word of God alone; and mixed, comprising those which may be learned from reason as well as from Scripture. But since dogmatics properly draws all its material from the Word of God alone, the distinction is useless for dogmatical purposes.

tianity as the result of the study of Scripture and of its interpretation by the Church. Speculative Dogmatics aims to present the doctrines in such a way as to make them and the questions connected with them as comprehensible as possible to the human mind. The present work comprises elements from each of these four classes.

A distinction has sometimes been drawn between fundamental and non-fundamental articles of faith. But when the effort is made to point out which doctrines are fundamental and which are not, a difficulty arises. The fact is that, while some doctrines are more necessary to salvation than others, no doctrines taught in God's Word dare be regarded as of no real consequence; and, furthermore, many doctrines which seem at first glance to be non-fundamental are found, when carried to their logical conclusions, to bear largely on doctrines which are unmistakably fundamental.

Dogmatics and Philosophy. Many of the questions dealt with in dogmatics are also dealt with by philosophy from a purely intellectual standpoint. There is, therefore, a close relation between dogmatics and philosophy. But philosophy is not equal to the task which it sets itself. It cannot on the basis of the intellect alone satisfactorily explain the universe. There are many questions which cannot be answered by philosophy, but which are answered by the Word of God. Any philosophy whose principles are in conflict with the teachings of God's Word must be rejected. There is a false philosophy which spoils men (Col. 2:8); but this implies that there is a true philosophy which is not vain deceit, but is "according to Christ."

REVELATION

Need of a Revelation. The source of dogmatics is the divine revelation, the record of which is given in the Holy Scriptures of the Old and New Testaments. The need of a supernatural revelation of God for man's sake may be shown on psychological and historical grounds. From the psychological standpoint a revelation is a need of man's nature; for he cannot truly find or know God as he should, unless God reveals Himself in a supernatural way. Reason and nature do, indeed, tell something of God; but they cannot give an answer to the deepest questions of life; they cannot show man any way of escape from the guilt and power of sin; and they cannot bring him the spiritual life and strength which he needs. From the historical standpoint the need of a supernatural revelation is evident from the career of natural religions. With nothing but the natural revelation to guide them, even the best of heathen religions have left their devotees in the bonds of ignorance and superstition; have been powerless to stem the tide of natural depravity; and have failed to satisfy the soul, because they failed to provide a remedy for sin and guilt. The necessity of a supernatural revelation cannot be proved to one who denies or ignores sin and the need of redemption. In the Eastern Church the necessity of such a revelation was based chiefly on man's intellectual need; in the Western Church it was based chiefly on his moral need.

Possibility of a Revelation. The possibility of a supernatural revelation is denied by Pantheism and Materialism, because according to these theories a God who is distinct from nature and is a person does not exist. It is denied by Deism on the basis of its claim, that God, having created the world, has nothing more to do with it except to look on while it runs its course. But since God is a person, a supernatural revelation is possible. Such a revelation is not inconsistent with the nature of God; for as a person He is distinct from and above the world, possesses infinite power to do as He chooses, and is moved by His infinite goodness to make Himself known to men for their salvation. The ability to make Himself known and to perform miracles is inseparable from the idea of a personal God. So far as man is concerned, such a revelation is possible, because man has the capacity to receive it.

Reason and Revelation. Reason is not related to revelation as an additional source of theological or religious knowledge; for the sole source is the Word of God. But reason has an instrumental use, and is, in this respect, indispensable. Brutes, having no reason, are incapable of experiencing religion or appreciating theology. God has given us our reason to use, and nowhere can we make a more important use of it than in the study of religion and its teachings. To speak of reason as if it had no place in theology is absurd. But its place, as has often been said, is not that of a master but of a handmaid of theology. It is perfectly within the province of reason to declare whether such and such a doctrine is clearly taught in God's Word or not. But it is not within the province of reason to sit in judgment on a doctrine taught in Holy Writ and to declare that it is not true, because reason cannot comprehend it.

Even as sources of religious knowledge reason and revelation are not necessarily opposed to each other; for reason also derives from God such true religious knowledge as it naturally possesses. But it must be remembered that much of its original knowledge has been obscured and lost through sin, and that thus reason has ceased to be a reliable source. And because spiritual darkness has come upon it, it is totally ignorant of many things which Scripture reveals and which are true in spite of reason's ignorance. We must also distinguish between reason before the fall and reason since the fall. Had there been no fall into sin and no consequent darkening and perversion of the mind, reason would have seen into many things which it cannot now comprehend; and in the case of those things which it could not comprehend, it would immediately have realized its own limitations and at once have concluded that the finite cannot expect to understand the infinite.

The position of those who undertake to reject doctrines of Scripture because they are "unreasonable" is not sound. What is reasonable? Is it not a fact that whatever we recognize as true and actual is reasonable? A hundred years ago the idea that man could fly or that his voice could be heard a thousand miles away was "unreasonable." But it is not unreasonable now. And why? Because we know that men do fly in aeroplanes and that men's voices can be heard by telephone or radio a thousand miles away. What the Word of God declares to be true is not to be rejected as unreasonable because it appears to be in conflict with experience or is beyond our comprehension.

It is the business of reason to acknowledge its limitations and to subject itself to revelation. If it does this and accepts the Word of God as true, the time comes when much which seemed at first unreasonable becomes the most reasonable thing in the world, because we know by experience that it is true. The Gospel seemed "to the Jews a stumbling-block and to the Greeks foolishness, but to them that are called, both Jews and Greeks, Christ the power of God and the Wisdom of God" (1 Cor. 1:23, 24).

THE HOLY SCRIPTURES

Definition. The Holy Scriptures of the Old and New Testaments are the inspired and inerrant record of the supernatural revelation of God to men. In them holy men, inspired by the Holy Ghost, have written down a correct and complete account of all the facts and truths which God desires us to know for the guidance and salvation of our souls. They are the only source of the true knowledge of God and of the way of salvation. Neither reason nor tradition nor creeds are in any true and real sense the source of that knowledge. The Holy Scriptures are the only rule and standard of faith and life.[13]

The Bible the Word of God. When the statements are properly understood, it may be said that the Bible is the Word of God, and that the Bible contains the Word of God: The Bible *is* the Word of God, because it is the divinely inspired record of the revelation given to men. But not every individual statement recorded in the Bible as part of the history of revelation is a statement of divine truth made by God to men. On the contrary, some of the statements contained in the record given in the Bible were made by wicked men and even by devils. On the other hand, the Bible *contains* the Word of God, because it contains the truth through which, as the Means of Grace, the Holy Spirit converts, sanctifies and saves men. But the statement that it contains the Word of God must not be interpreted to mean that it contains that Word in the same way in which a heap of chaff contains some wheat, or that men must sift its contents and in a subjective way decide which portions are the Word of God and which are not.

Revelation Progressive. The supernatural revelation which God made to men was progressive, with various stages of completeness, and was made known in part through the Old Testament prophets, and made known fully through His Son Jesus

---

[13] "We believe, teach and confess that the only rule and standard according to which at once all dogmas and teachers should be esteemed and judged are nothing else than the prophetic and apostolic Scriptures of the Old and of the New Testament, as it is written (Ps. 119:105), 'Thy Word is a lamp unto my feet and a light unto my path.' Other writings, of ancient or modern teachers, whatever reputation they may have, should not be regarded as of equal authority with the Holy Scriptures, but should altogether be subordinated to them, and should not be received other or further than as witnesses, in what manner and at what places, since the time of the apostles, the doctrine of the prophets and apostles was preserved." *Form. of Concord*—Jacobs', *Book of Concord*, p. 491.

Christ. Hence the record given to us in the Scriptures is the history of a gradually unfolding revelation. The incomplete revelation of the Old Testament must be interpreted and understood in the light of the full revelation given in the New Testament. The writings of the New Testament, and not those of the Old, are the last court of appeal in all matters of Christian doctrine. Proper interpretation of the Scriptures must always take into account the stages of revelation.

While the Holy Scriptures are primarily the record of God's revelation as given to men in the past, they are at the same time the means through which God reveals Himself to us now. They are, thus, at once a record of revelation and a revelation. The revelation which God made in times past through the prophets and through Christ and His apostles is called immediate; and the revelation by which He now makes Himself known to us through the writings of the prophets and apostles is called mediate revelation.

The Analogy of Faith. Since the Scriptures contain the revelation of God to men, they must be in harmony with themselves in all their parts, and cannot, when properly interpreted, teach contradictions. But not all passages are equally clear. The dark passages must therefore be interpreted in the light of the clear passages. Every article of faith is set forth clearly somewhere in the Holy Scriptures. Thus, for example, the doctrines of sin and grace and the relation of the Law and the Gospel are fully and clearly treated in the Epistle to the Romans. The full and clear passages, which are called the *sedes doctrinae* or seat of the doctrine, become the norm for the interpretation of those which merely allude to the doctrine or do not fully discuss it. This method of interpretation is called the analogy of faith.

The doctrine of inspiration, together with other questions

concerning the Holy Scriptures, will be treated at the proper place in the body of the work.

CREEDS AND CONFESSIONS

Their Nature. Confessions or symbols are official formulations of the common faith of the Church. They are public testimonies as to the manner in which the Church apprehends and teaches the doctrines of the Holy Scriptures. They have not been forced on the Church from without, nor are they the result of an arbitrary attempt on the part of some men to formulate the Church's teaching for her. They have grown out of historical conditions and necessities. The times and circumstances demanded that the Church let her voice be heard in no uncertain tones on doctrines which were in dispute; and the symbols and confessions are the result. They serve the twofold purpose of exhibiting what the Church believes and teaches, and of guarding against error and heresy.

Symbols possess a high value. They are a standing testimony of the experience of faith through which the Church passed in the formulation of the Scriptural doctrines. They are not authoritative as a norm of doctrine, but they record the definite conclusions to which the Church has come as a result of her activity in interpreting God's Word and defending it against error. They are useful also as criteria by which those who hold the same faith may know one another and join together in one organization.

The Lutheran Confessions are contained in the Book of Concord, and include the three Œcumenical Creeds, the Augsburg Confession, the Apology of the Augsburg Confession, the Schmalcald Articles, Luther's Small Catechism, Luther's Large Catechism, and the Formula of Concord. Bona-fide subscription to these Confessions is required of Lutheran ministers, because the Church must see to it that those who go forth in her name preach only the pure doctrines of the Gospel as she holds them. No one is compelled to subscribe. But if any minister refuses to do so, he thereby testifies that he is not in harmony with the doctrinal position of the Lutheran Church, and has no right to preach in her name. On the other hand, if he is a Lutheran in his convictions, he will be glad to subscribe to the Confessions and to preach the doctrines set forth in them.[14]

Value of Dogmas. The doctrines formally stated and set forth in the Creeds and Confessions are the dogmas of the Church. They possess large value for us, because they show how the Church understands and teaches the doctrines of Scripture, and are a help to our understanding of them.

It is asserted by some persons that dogmas and creeds have outlived their usefulness, and that they are really injurious to the cause of true religion. Some demand that they be reformulated in modern terms, and others demand that they be discarded entirely.

It is undoubtedly true that when the Church formulated the various dogmas, she employed the thought terms of that day. In the very nature of the case she was obliged to think and express herself in the modes and terms which the thought of the time employed, and to work with such categories as the philosophy of the day furnished. It is also true that in some cases the dogma is only an approximation of the full divine truth, because, at best, human speech is inadequate for the full expression of the divine mysteries. Thus the Ancient Church employed the term "essence" to define the unity of God and the word "person" to define the distinctions in the Trinity. They

---

[14] The two words *quia* and *quatenus* have been used to designate respectively a genuine and a non-genuine subscription to the confessions. A genuine subscription is *quia*, that is, *because* the confessions correctly exhibit the teachings of Scripture. To subscribe to the confessions *quatenus*, that is, *so far as* they correctly exhibit the teachings of Scripture, is not a real subscription at all.

were the nearest approach to the divine reality which the Ancient Church was able to make. Shall this dogma, for example, be reformulated in modern terms? If so, who shall do the formulating? Dogmas grow out of the historical conditions of the Church which compel their formulation, and not out of the arbitrary agreement of a few theologians to formulate them anew.

Others object not only to the form but to the content of the dogma. We are told in certain quarters that dogmas and dogmatics no longer have a right to exist, and that the Church will make a mistake if she insists on their retention. A prominent member of the liberal school tells us, "It is time to acknowledge that the day of dogma and of dogmatics as works on dogmas is definitely past. Dogmas in the old sense as ready formulated truths in which one must believe to show one's self a Christian are done away with." [15] Only the history of dogmas, he tells us, is important, because that shows us the answer which the Church found at different periods to the problem set by the New Testament.

To abolish the dogma, however, or to reject its content, would be to throw away the faith which is built, not indeed on the dogma, but on the truths of divine revelation which the dogma defends and safeguards. Dogmas cannot be thrust aside, but must abide, not as the norm of faith and life, but as the Church's interpretation of the norm of faith and life, which is the Holy Scriptures.

Dogma has large value for the Church, in that it gives expression to the truth which she believes and teaches. It underlies her preaching and instruction. It guards against erroneous teaching on the part of those whom she sends forth to preach, and provides a definite basis of instruction for the young in the

[15] Wernle: *Einführung in das theologische Studium*, pp. 298-9.

fundamentals of the Christian faith. It makes possible a common worship and common edification from the sermon. And it is a helpful guide to the student of Holy Scripture, because it points out an abundance of spiritual riches which unaided he would not discover.

PART I

GOD AND MAN, AND THE ALIENATION THROUGH SIN

CHAPTER I

THE BEING AND ATTRIBUTES OF GOD

Our Knowledge Based on Revelation. We can know God only to the extent to which He has revealed Himself to us. The Scriptures declare that "He dwelleth in the light which no man can approach unto; whom no man hath seen or can see" (1 Tim. 6:16). But, as we have seen in the introduction, He has revealed Himself to men in two ways: by a natural revelation, on the one hand, through conscience and nature; and by a supernatural revelation, on the other, through His dealings with men in history. He speaks to men in the voice of conscience (Rom. 2:14, 15), which tells them that there is a Higher Being to whom they are accountable; and in the voice of the universe in which we live (Rom. 1:19, 20; Ps. 19:1 seq.), which tells them that there is a Creator and Designer who has fashioned the world with wondrous power and wisdom. But He also speaks to us through the Holy Scriptures (2 Pet. 1:19), in which are recorded the words and deeds by which He has made Himself known to men in times past. The knowledge gained from conscience and nature supports and corroborates much of the knowledge gained from the supernatural revelation.

Natural Knowledge. Left to himself, that is, to the natural revelation, man has been able to know God only in a very limited way. He knows that God is, and cannot escape the consciousness of His existence. The idea of God is a constant in his thought along with that of self and the world. He knows that God is just and holy, because these attributes are impressed

31

upon him by his conscience. And he knows from the world in which he lives that God is a being of vast intelligence and power. The degree of this natural knowledge varies with different nations and individuals.

Even at best, however, the natural knowledge of God is defective and mixed with much error. And it is utterly insufficient, because it tells and can tell absolutely nothing concerning the way of salvation for mankind. God is the God of salvation and cannot be known apart from Christ. For "no man hath seen God at any time; the only begotten Son, which is in the bosom of the Father, He hath declared Him" (John 1:18). Only in Christ can the right conception of God and His saving love be obtained. The doctrine of God is to be viewed, therefore, from the standpoint of salvation; for only when we know Him as the God of saving love do we know Him as He is. The natural knowledge of God is useful, however, in that it stimulates men to seek after a fuller knowledge of Him and forms the foundation on which the supernatural revelation rests. Without the native conviction of God in the heart and the feeling of religious need of Him, the Gospel could make no appeal to men. If the idea of God had first to be put into the mind, and the existence of God had first to be logically and coercively demonstrated, the preaching of the Gospel would be a hopeless undertaking.

Proofs of God's Existence. The so-called proofs for the existence of God originated in the philosophy of the ancients, and at an early date were adopted into the theology of the Church. Much weight was once laid upon these proofs. They have been employed, not only by the scholastics but also by Protestant theologians, to combat unbelief and to establish the faith of believers. With the growing emphasis upon natural theology in the rationalistic period undue importance was attached to them, and they gradually supplanted the Christian certitude based upon the testimony of the Holy Spirit. Kant criticized these proofs and denied their validity on the basis of pure reason; but he accepted the belief in God as a postulate of the practical reason. These proofs are, however, not without some weight and use to-day.

The Ontological Proof argues from the existence of the idea of God in man to the actuality of His existence. This has value chiefly when the idea of God referred to is identified with the native intuition of God. The fact that a finite being conceives of an infinite being, and cannot think without positing God along with self and the world, certainly constitutes a strong probability that God exists.

The Cosmological Proof concludes that the world which exists must have a First Cause back of all the secondary causes seen to be operative in nature. Arguing from the consciousness that we as self-determining beings are real causes, the inference is that the first or real cause behind the world is a Person. Since the world presumably is a finite entity, however, the cosmological argument cannot prove that God is infinite, but only that He is inconceivably great and powerful.

The Teleological Proof argues from the evidences of design and purpose in nature. Everywhere in the world there is evidence not only of the adaptation of means to ends, but of the coördination of means to remote ends. A purpose is seen in the arrangement and functioning of the world, and this purpose cannot be ascribed to a blind process of nature, but must be ascribed to a Person.

The Moral Proof argues from the existence of a moral constitution in us to the existence of a higher moral being who has made us moral beings, and who imposes His will on us in the moral demands of conscience.

The Historical Proof draws the conclusion from the history of the world and particularly of man, that there is a governor and ruler who, without interfering with men's freedom as persons, is guiding the affairs of the world to an end which He has foreseen and foredetermined.

None of these arguments is actually demonstrative and coercive, though taken together they constitute a very respectable probable proof of God's existence. One who denies that there is a God cannot, however, by means of these arguments be compelled to acknowledge God's existence. He may declare that in spite of them all he is still unconvinced. The value of these proofs lies not so much in their use against atheists, as in corroborating the faith of the believer. They show that faith in God is natural and reasonable. And while it may be said that the believer needs no proof that God exists, these proofs are none the less serviceable to him in giving added strength to his intellectual convictions.

Supernatural Knowledge. While the fact that God exists is a native conviction of the human heart, what kind of God He is can be learned only from the revelation which is recorded in the Holy Scriptures. This revelation gives us an adequate knowledge of God. All that we need to know in order to come into the right relation with Him and to remain in it is there set forth. Beyond that which is contained in the Scriptures our knowledge of God in this world cannot go. The Bible does not aim to enable us completely to understand God; for we do not understand our own nature and many other things in this world. How then can we expect to understand God? How can the finite comprehend the infinite? But while God cannot be comprehended by the finite mind, He can nevertheless be known, and is known from His Word. In spite of the fall into sin with all its dire consequences, man still possesses the capacity to know God when the true knowledge is brought to Him by divine grace through the Holy Scriptures.

Definition. A definition of God in the strict sense of the term is impossible, because there is no genus to which He can be assigned. He is absolutely unique, the only Being of His kind in all the universe. All attempts to define Him result, therefore, simply in descriptions of Him. These descriptions can never be complete, since God is infinite. The Scriptures themselves, however, furnish us with several brief and pregnant descriptions. They tell us that God is a Spirit (John 4:24); He is Life (John 5:26); He is Light (1 John 1:5); He is Love (1 John 4:16). These are not definitions of God, but a presentation of certain fundamental aspects in which He may be regarded.

God has been variously defined during the course of the history of the Church as Pure Being, as The Independent One, as The Intelligent and Self-conscious One, as Love, as a Simple Essence, as an Independent Spirit, as an Infinite Spiritual Essence. The chief weakness of these definitions, considered from the modern viewpoint, is that they do not sufficiently bring out the idea of personality in God. In this respect the definition of God as "The Absolute Personality" is much better. But since even this definition may be criticized as too negative in character or too purely metaphysical, and as omitting the positive and moral elements in God, we define God as The Absolute and Perfect Personality. For the Christian the absoluteness, personality and moral perfection of God are fundamental presuppositions, without which the relation to God involved in the religion of salvation would be impossible.

The term absolute as applied to God does not signify unrelatedness, but the absence of necessary relation. God is related to the world which He has made, but it is a relation established by His own free will. He is the Absolute One, in that He exists in and by Himself, and is absolutely unconditioned and unlimited. He is the ultimate ground of His own being and of all that exists outside of Him.

The word "personality" is used here in the modern psychological sense, which signifies a being possessed of self-consciousness and self-determination, and not in the sense in which the word "person" is used in connection with the doctrine of the Trinity. In the latter sense God is three "persons," while in the former sense He is one person, the Absolute and Perfect Personality.

On the basis of the axiom that "every determination is a negation," pantheists maintain that the ascription of personality to the Absolute One does away with the absoluteness, and implies limitation. But the limitation which is found in our human personalities is not due to personality as such, but to the limited development of our finite consciousness. The real essence of personality is not to be found in the fact that it is separate from other personalities, but in the fact that it is identical with itself and is conscious of this identity.

The personality of God is an essential presupposition of personal fellowship with Him on man's part, and of the possibility of prayer. The universal all which forms the pantheist's God is utterly unfitted to be the God of a religion which involves ethical life and a relation of fellowship. For religion is a personal relation—a relation between a finite human person and an infinite divine person.

The Christian conception of God is theistic. God is a person, who is at once transcendent and immanent. He is transcendent over the world, not included in it nor identical with it, and is its Creator and Ruler. On the other hand, He is also immanent in the world; His are the living power and will that uphold and energize it every moment of its existence. For "in Him we live and move and have our being" (Acts 17:28).

Errors. The current errors which conflict with this theistic view of God are pantheism, deism, agnosticism and atheism. Pantheism denies personality in God, and identifies Him and the world. It is the antithesis of theism not only in its view of God, but in its view of the world and of all the ethical relations of life. By identifying God and the world, it not only takes away personality from God but also from man, and with it takes away from man all moral responsibility and all possibility of true ethical development. If everything that is is a manifestation and activity of God, there is no responsibility on the part of man for his actions, there exists no evil or sin, and there is no moral goal to be striven for. All is a necessary process of development over which man has no sort of control, and for which he is in reality unaccountable. Evil, then, does not exist, and what seems evil is only the good as yet imperfectly developed. Pantheism appears in two chief forms: the one, which may be called oriental pantheism, spiritualizes the world and identifies it with God; the other, which may be called occidental pantheism, materializes God and identifies Him with the world.[1]

Deism conceives of God as a person, but as one who has made the world, and then has retired to look on while it runs its course. All the forces of nature, having been once started by Him, are supposed to run of their own accord in accordance with certain fixed and immutable laws. Miracles would be an irruption into this fixed and unalterable order of nature, and are impossible because they would act as a wrench thrown into the machinery of the world. According to the deistic theory God is the slave of His own laws, and cannot in any way

[1] Pantheism was introduced into Greek philosophy by the Eleatics, and found its way into the Christian world through the Neoplatonic philosophy. It marks the mysticism of the Middle Ages. Its prominent place in modern thought is due primarily to Spinoza, and its fullest development is found in Hegel. The Eleatics and Spinoza represent what may be called the oriental type, in which the world is spiritualized and identified with God in such a way that there is no becoming, but only a being. In what may be called the occidental type, represented in essence by Heraclitus, the Stoics, Fichte, Schelling and Hegel, God is materialized and identified with the world in such a way that there is only a becoming, not a being. The Absolute is only in the process of becoming, and God is viewed as a developing God. This type leads to materialism and atheism.

change or modify their operation. Prayer is regarded as useless.

Agnosticism conceives of the world as matter, motion and force. What the power back of these is, if any, it professes not to be able to know. Agnosticism holds a sort of halfway position, from which man is bound sooner or later to be driven forward into theism, or backward into materialism.

Atheism denies the existence of any God at all. Materialism is that form of atheism which claims that matter is all that there is; that there is no such thing as spirit; and that what we conceive of as evidences of spirit are only the results of the functioning of matter. In its crassest form materialism maintains that the brain secretes thought as the liver secretes bile.

It is evident that the philosophical system of theism, which maintains that God is a person, and that He is both transcendent and immanent, is the only one compatible with the teachings of Christianity.

Names of God. The names ascribed to God in Holy Writ are of three kinds, essential, attributive and relative. The first kind aims to describe His essential nature, such as God, Elohim and Jahve. The attributive names are those which are drawn from some attribute of God, like The Omnipotent. The relative are those which express relation, like King of Kings or Lord of Lords.

The term Name of God is used, however, in a more comprehensive sense to refer to everything by which God is expressed to men. In this sense the Holy Scriptures, the Sacraments, etc., are included under the term. To pray, "Hallowed be Thy Name" means to pray for the hallowing of all that belongs to God and that expresses Him to men.

Attributes of God. The Attributes of God are those special features which characterize Him as God. They are different aspects under which God has revealed Himself, different angles

from which we contemplate Him. They are not accidents of
His being, but are unchangeable, and characterize Him at all
times and under all circumstances. They are invariable and
permanent. They have always characterized Him and always
will. Without any one of them God would not be God. A man
may be just or unjust, and still be a man. He may be truthful
or untruthful and still be a human being. But God is just and
truthful permanently and unalterably. His attributes are fixed
and never vary. They are not identical with the being of God
in the sense that an attribute can define Him. They are, however, part of His very nature, but not in the sense that the aggregate of parts constitutes the whole. For God is a simple essence,
and is not made up or compounded of parts.

The attributes are not to be confused with the personal peculiarities which mark the inter-Trinitarian relationship, or with
the predicates which designate the external acts of God, such
as Creation. It was generally held by the scholastics that the
difference of attributes exists only for our subjective thinking
of God, and that they do not possess objective reality in Him.
The Thomists and the Protestant dogmaticians, however, held
that the attributes are not purely subjective distinctions, but
correspond to an objective reality.

A knowledge of the attributes of God is essential to an
understanding of His nature. Without them we would not
know what kind of God He is, and our knowledge of Him
would therefore be fatally defective. A list of His attributes
may be drawn up both on a Biblical and on a philosophical
basis. Biblically they are obtained by noting what attributes are
ascribed to Him in Holy Scripture. Philosophically they are
obtained by a threefold process, namely, by Causation, by Negation and by Eminence. "By Causation" means, that since God is
the Creator of the world He must possess the attributes necessary for such a work. "By Negation" means, that all those

attributes which denote imperfection in men are to be subtracted from God; they cannot belong to Him, since He is a perfect being. "By Eminence" means, that all those attributes which we recognize as excellent in men are to be ascribed to God in the most eminent degree.

Classification of Attributes. The classification of the attributes of God and the lists given in each class vary somewhat with different authors. They may be best arranged under two heads; namely, as Absolute or Relative.[2] The Absolute attributes are those which belong to God irrespective of any relation into which He may have entered with created objects. They refer to God as He is in Himself. They are those which would be exhibited in Him even if He had never created the universe. The Relative attributes are those which refer to God in his relation to the world. Though as essentially characteristic of God as the others, they become exhibited only because God has entered into relation with a world outside of Himself.

The Absolute attributes consist of the following: 1. Independence. 2. Unity. 3. Simplicity. 4. Immutability. 5. Infinitude, including Eternity and Immensity.

The Relative attributes are: 1. Life. 2. Knowledge. 3. Wisdom. 4. Power. 5. Omnipresence. 6. Holiness. 7. Justice. 8. Truth. 9. Love, comprising both the love of Pity and the love of Complacency, and including Goodness, Mercy, Grace, Long-suffering and Patience.[3]

Absolute Attributes. The Absolute Attributes may be defined as follows:

1. Independence (Exod. 3:14; Ps. 90:2) is that attribute of God by reason of which He is independent of all other beings

---

[2] By some the Absolute attributes are called also Immanent or Negative; and the Relative are called also Transient or Positive. The nomenclature in the text is, however, to be preferred as more clearly descriptive and self-explanatory.

[3] By some dogmaticians the Relative attributes are subdivided into attributes of the intellect and attributes of the will. This additional classification adds cumbersomeness, and has no particular value.

either as to His existence or as to any necessary relations. All the relations which God sustains toward other beings and objects have been freely entered into by Him.

2. By Unity (Deut. 6:4; Isa. 44:6) we mean that God is one. He is *unus et unicus*. He is one in Himself, a single individual God; and He is the one and only God.

3. By Simplicity (John 4:24) we mean that God, being a Spirit, is a simple essence, not composed of parts or elements, and indivisible in any way.

4. By Immutability (Mal. 3:6; Ps. 26:27) we mean that there is no change or mutation in God with respect to His being, or attributes, or will. He is always exactly the same. He is capable neither of increase nor of diminution, neither of greater nor lesser perfection. Once knowing from His Word what God is, we know that He is always the same in every age of the world. The certainty of this unchangeableness on God's part is of fundamental religious value, because it enables us to rely on all God's attributes as ever the same. This immutability does not prevent God from entering into human history, as evidenced by the incarnation. Nor dare it be interpreted to mean lack of feeling or stony impassivity; for God is love, with all the feelings which love involves.

5. By Infinitude (Job 11:7; Ps. 145:3) we mean that God is without bounds or limitations of any kind. All His perfections are infinite. As an infinite God He transcends the bounds both of time and of space.

When considered with respect to time this infinitude results in the attribute of Eternity (Ps. 90:2). God is eternal, that is, a timeless being, without beginning and without end and without succession. For Him there is nothing but an eternal now; there is no past or future. He always was and He always will be, from eternity to eternity the same.

When considered with respect to space, infinitude results

in the attribute of Immensity (Jer. 23:24; 1 Kings 8:27). God transcends the bounds of space, filling all things, and completely present everywhere. Closely connected with this absolute attribute of immensity is the relative attribute of omnipresence.

Relative Attributes. The Relative attributes may be defined as follows:

1. By Life we mean that God not only has life in Himself (John 5:26) and is the everliving God (Jer. 10:10), but that He always shows Himself active and is the source of all the life that exists in the universe (Acts 17:28).

2. By Knowledge or Omniscience (Ps. 139:1, 2; 1 John 3:20) we mean that God knows all things—those that have been, those that are, and those that will be, as well as those which for any reason are possible. With respect to men, this knowledge of God means a knowledge not only of what is outwardly evident but of the innermost thoughts and desires of the heart (Ps. 139:1, 2). Being above the limitations of time and space, His knowledge is direct and intuitive, and not successive and discursive as human knowledge is. He sees all things past, present and future as an eternal present. And His knowledge is certain, true and infallible. He cannot be mistaken about anything. His knowledge of the future, or foreknowledge, is not causative. The things which He foreknows will surely happen. But the certainty of the happenings is the cause of their being foreknown; and not the being foreknown the cause of the happenings. Some things which God foreknows have been foreordained by Him, but not all; for much happens which God has not foreordained; for example, sin.

3. By Wisdom (1 Tim. 1:17; Isa. 55:8, 9) we mean that God always knows and always uses the best means for the best ends. He is all-wise. He never makes mistakes, but does all things well.

4. By Power or Omnipotence we mean that God possesses all possible power. He can do everything which He desires to do. With Him all things are possible (Mark 10:27). This does not mean that God can do all things in the sense that He can do two things which are contradictory to each other, such as to make one equal one and at the same time to make one equal two. He respects the laws which He has written into the mind and consciousness of man as a transcript of His own. Nor does it mean that He can do anything which is wrong or in conflict with His own nature and will, such as to lie or deceive or contradict Himself.

5. By Omnipresence (Ps. 139:7-10) we mean that God is present everywhere throughout the entire universe; also, that all of God and not a part of God is present in every place. But the omnipresence of God must not be conceived of as local. The infinite Spirit is above the requirements of space and locality.

6. By Holiness (Lev. 19:2; 1 Pet. 1:15) we mean that attribute of God which separates or sets Him apart from everything that contaminates, defiles or stains. He is a perfectly pure and stainless being, utterly untouched and untouchable by evil; and He requires holiness on the part of man.

7. By Justice (Ps. 145:17; Rom. 2:6; Gal. 3:10) we mean the divine rectitude of will by which He exhibits righteousness in all His acts, and demands righteousness of men and angels. He views the right with favor and the wrong with disfavor, and will measure out reward and punishment for right and wrong with absolute certainty and impartiality.

8. By Truth (Num. 23:19; 2 Tim. 2:13) we mean that attribute of God which constitutes Him absolutely trustworthy and faithful in all that He says and does. Whatever He says is infallibly true; and whatever He promises He will certainly perform.

9. By Love (1 John 4:16; John 3:16, 16:27) we mean that

characteristic attribute of God by which He is filled with absolute good will for all His creatures, and seeks only their good. So characteristic of God is this attribute and so fundamental is it in His dealings with men, that the apostle regards it as a description of God, and says that God is love. This love is universal and unlimited. There are no possible lengths to which it will not go. It prompted Him to give His only begotten Son to redeem and save men. It is a Love of Compassion for the lost (Luke 19:10), and prompts Him to seek their salvation. And it is a Love of Complacency (John 16:27; 14:21) for those beings who have remained in communion with Him, namely, the good angels, and for those men who have been reconciled to Him in Christ, namely, the believers.

This love of God takes the specific forms of Goodness, Mercy, Grace, Long-suffering and Patience.

By Goodness is meant, not goodness in the sense of holiness, but in the sense of kindness. God is absolutely kind in His attitude toward all. An evidence of His goodness is found in the fact that "He maketh His sun to shine on the evil and on the good, and sendeth rain on the just and on the unjust" (Matt. 5:45). The term Mercy (Luke 6:36) describes God's love and kindness to the wretched. The term Grace (Eph. 2:8, 9; Rom. 3:24, 25) describes His love and kindness to the unworthy. Long-suffering (2 Pet. 3:9) is that aspect of God's love by reason of which He bears long with the sinner, and withholds deserved punishment. Patience (Rom. 15:5) is that aspect of His love by reason of which He seeks the repentance and salvation of men in the face of their stubbornness and disobedience.

CHAPTER II

THE TRINITY

THE doctrine of the Trinity distinguishes the Christian religion from all others. The natural religions do not have it.[1] Mohammedanism and Judaism reject it. The natural reason can rise no higher than the conception of the unity of God; and philosophical speculations do not get beyond mental concepts. The doctrine of the Trinity is accepted and taught solely on the basis of the revelation which God has made of Himself in His Word. It is clearly taught in the Holy Scriptures, and is fundamental to the plan of salvation set forth in them.

Three in One. The Bible plainly teaches that God is one; but at the same time it ascribes deity to three, namely, to the Father, to the Son, and to the Holy Ghost. This doctrine is a mystery which the Scriptures reveal, but which they do not attempt to explain. But while the doctrine contains a mystery, it does not contain a contradiction; for truth cannot contradict itself. God is one and three; but He is not three in the same sense in which He is one. If He were said to be both one and three in the same sense, there would be a contradiction. But that is not said. As the Church has made clear in the formulation of her doctrine, God is one numerically; He is three hypostatically. He is one individual God; but He is three *hypostases* or subsistences or "persons." He is not one in the sense of a whole comprising three parts, but is a simple essence, uncompounded of parts, and indivisible.

[1] The triads of the Egyptians, Hindus and others are not trinities, but denote three individual gods.

The Word "Person." It is to be noted that the word "person" when employed by the Church to designate the Father, the Son and the Holy Ghost is not used in the modern psychological sense in which it means an individual being possessed of self-consciousness and self-determination. In this sense God is only one person, and is the Absolute and Perfect Personality. Self-consciousness and self-determination are predicated of the one divine essence, and not of the three "persons." If self-con-sciousness and self-determination were predicated of the three "persons" or *hypostases* in God separately, that would mean that there are three individuals or three Gods.

The word "person" is used by the Church in the doctrine of the Trinity in a sense in which the word is used nowhere else. It is not even the sense in which the word was currently used in the times when the doctrine of the Trinity was formulated. But the ancient Church took the word and gave it a meaning, taking care to see to it that that meaning was apprehended.[2] She employed it and meant it to be understood in the sense in which she used the Greek word *hypostasis* to describe the three-ness in God. *Hypostasis* means a foundation, a reality. And the intent and meaning of the word when employed by the Church to describe the threeness in God was and is that there is a threefold metaphysical foundation or reality in God, corre-sponding to the historical manifestation of God as Father, Son, and Holy Ghost. She maintains that, to the economic Trinity or the Trinity as revealed, there is an actual counterpart in the metaphysical being of God, and that God is an ontological as well as an economic Trinity. Not only has God shown and revealed Himself as Father, Son and Holy Ghost; but He is Father, Son and Holy Ghost in His very being and nature.

Reasons for Formulating the Doctrine. The word Trinity is not a Biblical term. It was first used by Tertullian to describe

---

[2] The Latin word *persona* originally meant a mask worn by an actor; then the rôle of the actor. The term also was used to designate a party at law.

the inner nature of God. The language in which the Church formulated the doctrine is also non-Biblical. She used and was obliged to use the language of philosophy. The language of the Bible was not suited to her purpose; for she needed to guard the true doctrine against errorists who used the language of Scripture, but gave it a false interpretation. The doctrine as presented in the Nicene and Athanasian Creeds is the result of a long struggle with error.

In formulating the doctrine the Church did not aim to fathom or to make comprehensible the mystery of the Trinity, but simply to state it in unmistakable terms. She knew that she was dealing with a doctrine which was far above the comprehension of the human mind; but she felt compelled to set it forth as well as she was able in the language at her disposal.

A Practical Doctrine. The doctrine of the Trinity is not merely a theoretical or speculative one. On the contrary, it is intensely practical. Our salvation is bound up with it. It was revealed to us historically in most intimate and vital connection with the redemption of our race, and not as an abstract theological or metaphysical conception. God the Father sent His Son into the world to save us; God the Son became incarnate and redeemed us; and God the Holy Ghost applies the redemption of Christ to our souls. If there is no Trinity, then we are not saved; for then there is no Father to send His Son, no Son to make atonement for our sins, and no Holy Ghost to bring us to living faith in Christ our Savior. It is, of course, from this practical side, and not from the metaphysical, that the doctrine is to be presented in the pulpit.

A New Testament Doctrine. The doctrine of the Trinity is not explicitly taught in the Old Testament. It is a New Testament doctrine. When it has been learned from the New Testament, traces and implications of it may be found in the Old. Divine revelation was progressive. It was not till the fullness of time had come and God sent forth His Son, that the truth of the Trinity was revealed. There are passages of the Old Testament, such as the Aaronic benediction, the Trisagion, and numerous other passages, which in the light of the New Testament may be regarded as intimations of a Triune God. But the attempt actually to find the doctrine explicitly stated in the Old Testament is futile.[3] The Jews never found it there. And if we had no revelation but that contained in the Old Testament, we should be in ignorance of the doctrine. The proof of the Trinity must be drawn from the New Testament.

A Unity. That God is one is the clear teaching both of the Old and of the New Testament. Besides Him there is no other God (Isa. 44:6). On this point there has been no controversy among the professed adherents of Christianity. On this point there is also philosophical agreement among all who believe in the existence of a personal God. There can be only one Supreme Being, one Absolute One.

A Trinity. That God is three "persons" is equally the clear teaching of the New Testament. The proof for the doctrine was drawn by the old dogmaticians from the theophany at Christ's baptism, from the baptismal command, from the New Testament benediction, and from the fact that in the Scriptures divine names, divine attributes, divine works, and divine worship are ascribed respectively to the Father, to the Son, and to the Holy Ghost.[4]

Since all who acknowledge the existence of a personal God acknowledge that the Father is God, the proof of the Trinity

---

[3] Quenstedt maintained that since this doctrine belongs to the fundamental doctrines necessary for salvation, it must have been known to the Old Testament saints, and hence must be clearly taught in the Old Testament. Calixtus was severely attacked, especially by Calovius, for asserting that it is only implicitly and not explicitly taught there. The correctness of Calixtus' position is generally recognized to-day. For the proofs of the Trinity cited by the old Dogmaticians from the Old Testament, see Schmid, *Doctrinal Theology of the Ev. Luth. Church,* trans. by Hay and Jacobs, pp. 176-7.

[4] I John 5:7, also quoted by them, has since their day been found to be spurious.

resolves itself into the proof of the deity of the Son and of the Holy Ghost.

The Deity of Christ. The proof of the deity of Christ is best gained from a consideration of the declarations of Christ concerning Himself and the declarations of the apostles concerning Him.

In the Synoptics Jesus emphasizes His transcendent relation to the world, rather than His relation to the Father. He declares, "All power is given unto me in heaven and in earth" (Matt. 28:18). But the possession of this power is to be traced back to the divine Sonship; for He also declares, "All things are delivered to me of my Father; and no man knoweth the Son but the Father; neither knoweth any man the Father save the Son and he to whomsoever the Son will reveal Him" (Matt. 11:27; Luke 10:22). Hence He will always be with His own, and will come again to judgment (Matt. 28:20; 25:24, 31).

In the Gospel of John, Jesus in many places emphasizes the intimate relation in which He stands to the Father. He is from eternity with the Father and came forth from Him (John 3:13; 6:38, 51; 8:42; 16:28). Before Abraham was He is (John 8:58), and He had a glory with the Father before the world was (John 17:5, 24). So closely is He united with the Father that He who has seen Him has seen the Father (John 14:9); for He and the Father are one (John 10:30), and He is in the Father and the Father in Him (John 10:38). As the Father has life in Himself, so has He given to the Son to have life in Himself (John 5:26, 27). Christ will answer the prayers of His disciples, that the Father may be glorified in the Son (John 14:13), and He will send the Holy Spirit unto them to guide them into all truth (John 16:7, 13). He calls Himself and is called by others the Son of God, not only in the theocratic and Messianic sense, but in the sense of personal relationship with the Father (John 1:49; Luke 4:41; Matt. 8:29; 4:3; 16:16; 26:63, 64).

The apostles declare that Jesus is the Son of God in the essential sense. John declares that in the beginning was the Word, and the Word was with God, and the Word was God (John 1:1 seq.), and that the Word was made flesh and dwelt among us (John 1:14). When Thomas saw the risen Lord, he said, "My Lord and my God" (John 20:28). Paul declares that the Son of God was made of the seed of David according to the flesh (Rom. 1:3), and this implies that He must have existed before the incarnation. In the fullness of time God sent forth His Son to redeem men (Gal. 4:4), and in these last days God has spoken unto us by His Son . . . by whom He made the worlds (Heb. 1:2, 3). In Him dwelleth all the fullness of the Godhead bodily (Col. 2:9), and He is God over all, blessed forever (Rom. 9:4).[5] The words of the Psalmist (Ps. 45:6, 7), "Thy throne, O God, is forever and ever," are quoted by the writer of Hebrews (Heb. 1:8) as an address to Christ. Stephen, when he was stoned to death by the Jews, called on Christ as God (Acts 7:59). And the disciples are described as those who call on Christ's name (Acts 9:14, 21; 1 Cor. 1:2). The preëxistence of Christ is implied in all those passages which describe the world as having been created by or through Him (John 1:3; 1 Cor. 8:6; Col. 1:16; Heb. 1:2, 10). His ontological relationship to the Father, with its essential equality and its hypostatical distinction, is expressed by Paul and by the writer of Hebrews, when we are told that Christ is "the image of the invisible God, the first-born before all creation" (Col. 1:15),[6] and that He is the brightness of

---

[5] The passages Eph. 5:5; 2 Thess. 1:12; Tit. 2:13; 2 Pet. 1:1; and I John 5:20 are also regarded by some as asserting the deity of Christ, but they do not necessitate such an interpretation.

[6] The translation given above is quite generally admitted by commentators, and is justified by verse 16 which follows.

God's glory and the express image of His person (Heb. 1:3).[7]

The Deity of the Holy Ghost. That the Holy Spirit has personal subsistence, and is not simply a power or influence of God, is evident from the fact that He is designated by the masculine pronoun (John 14:16, 26; 16:8, 13, 14), and is included by name in the baptismal command (Matt. 28:19). His relation to the believers is a personal one; for He bears witness with our spirit (Rom. 8:16), He helps our infirmities (Rom. 8:26), He speaks (Rev. 22:17), and He can be grieved (Eph. 4:30). His deity is expressly asserted by Peter in rebuking Ananias (Acts 5:3, 4), and follows from the very fact that He is the Spirit of God. His eternal existence follows from His deity. His procession from the Father is based on John 15:26, interpreted as referring both to His historical procession into the world and to His eternal procession in the metaphysical sense. The passage which declares that "the Holy Spirit was not yet" (John 7:39) refers, not to a question of His actual previous existence, but to His manifestation as the New Testament Spirit of grace.

The Three Persons. The three persons of the Trinity appear at the baptism of Jesus (Matt. 3:16; Mark 1:10; Luke 2:21, 22), and they are coördinated in the baptismal command (Matt. 28:19) and in the New Testament benediction (2 Cor. 13:14). There is a historical order of revelation, according to which the Father comes first, the Son second, and the Holy Ghost third. But this does not imply any subordination or any lack of equality. The passages in which Christ subordinates Himself to the Father (John 5:19; 8:28; 14:28; 20:17; Matt. 27:46) are to be interpreted in the light of His humanity, and not in

---

[7] The Logos of John 1:1 seq. has from the earliest times been interpreted in a Philonian sense as a self-revelation of God, and hence as indicating the ontological relation of the Son to the Father. It has also been interpreted as referring to the historical revelation of God, of which Christ is the essential content.

that of His essential deity. The same thing applies to similar expressions of His apostles (1 Cor. 11:3; Eph. 1:17). The passages in which Christ says, "Why callest thou me good? There is none good but one, that is, God" (Matt. 19:17; Mark 10:18), are to be explained by the fact that Christ purposed by these words, not to deny that He Himself was good, but to correct the low ideal of the good held by His interrogator, and to direct Him to God as the source and norm of all goodness.

The historical, though not the ontological, subordination of the Holy Spirit follows from the fact that He comes to carry on and complete the work of Christ (John 11:26; 15:26; 16:14).

On the basis of the declarations of Holy Scripture concerning Christ and the Holy Spirit, the Church formulated her doctrine of the Trinity. The substance of her doctrine is, that God is one in Essence, but that He has three modes of Subsistence. He is one God, but three persons. And this doctrine she designates by the term Trinity, or Three in One.

The Homo-ousia. God is one God, not three Gods. There is but one divine essence, and this is common to the Father, the Son and the Holy Ghost. Each possesses exactly the same essence and the entire essence of the deity. By essence is meant that which constitutes God: that which makes Him what He is. The three persons do not simply possess the same kind of essence, as we might say that three men have the same kind of essence; but one and the very same essence belongs to the three persons. The essence is not divided, so that each person possesses a part of it; but it belongs in its entirety to each person. The entire essence of God is in the Father, the entire essence of God is in the Son, and the entire essence of God is in the Holy Spirit. In this sense God is absolutely one. The Son is God just as the Father is God, and the Holy Ghost is God just as the Father and the Son are God: three persons, but only one God; not a triad, but a Trinity.

The unity of the divine essence was designated by the term *homo-ousia*. This term, which means that the three persons possess the identical essence, was adopted in opposition to the Arians, who maintained that the Son does not have the same essence as the Father, but a similar essence; and who described their doctrine by the term *homoi-ousia*. The controversy which raged on this doctrine in the early Church centered around the insertion or the rejection of a single letter of the alphabet, namely, the "i" (in the Greek, *iota*). The Church maintained that Christ does not possess an essence similar to that of the Father, so that He is a sort of demigod, but that He possesses the very same essence which the Father possesses, and thus is not subordinated but equal to the Father. Superficially it might have been argued that so small a difference as that represented by the smallest letter in the alphabet was not worth all the controversy that raged over it. But in reality the absence or presence of the *iota* signified the difference between having a Savior who is true God and thus able to save, and having a Savior who is only similar to God, and therefore not true God and not able to save. The Homo-ousians won, and the result is recorded in the Nicene Creed, in which the Church declares that Christ is "God of God, Light of Light, Very God of Very God, being of One Substance with the Father." A further and fuller formulation is given in the Athanasian Creed which was framed later.

The Perichoresis. God is Three Persons. He is one in essence, but is three in the sense that He has three modes of subsistence, namely as Father, as Son and as Holy Ghost. There are three distinctions in God, but not three individuals. The three persons or *hypostases* may be distinguished, but they cannot be separated, because they have exactly the same essence. This threeness of persons with the oneness of essence is further defined by the doctrine of the *perichoresis,* which means that the three persons of the Trinity do not exist separately alongside of one another, but that they permeate and interpenetrate one another, and exist in and through one another. This *perichoresis* is the inevitable result of the oneness of essence. The three persons are clearly distinct; but having the same essence they must and do exist in the mode which is described by the term *perichoresis* or mutual permeation.

The threeness of persons and the oneness of essence in the Trinity may be illustrated by means of the angles of an equilateral triangle. The angles, of course, are not only distinct but are separate angles and therefore do not illustrate properly the three persons in God. But they do illustrate the unity of essence and the perichoresis. Each angle includes exactly the same area, namely, the whole area of the triangle; and each angle permeates the other angles. In a similar way each person of the Holy Trinity includes in Himself the very same entire essence of the Deity, and each person permeates the other two. All illustrations break down at a certain point. And so this illustration of the triangle dare not be pressed beyond the two points referred to. It illustrates the oneness of essence, or the *homo-ousia* of the three persons, and the perichoresis.

Analogy from Human Personality. Among the many illustrations used to throw light on the doctrine of the Trinity, there is only one which can be regarded as in any real sense an analogy. It is the illustration drawn from personality as we know it in man. We are told in the first chapter of Genesis that God made man in His own image. This image distinguishes man from the brute. It is not a physical image; for God is a Spirit and has no body. Since the brute is not a person and man is a person, we conclude that the metaphysical image of God in which man was created consists in personality. God is the Absolute and Perfect Personality; and making man in His own image, He made him a finite personality. He made man to be on a finite scale the same kind of being that He Himself is on an infinite scale. It follows, therefore, that if God is the prototype and is Triune in the very constitution of His being, man, who is God's image, must in a finite way be triune also in the very constitution of his being.

That there is a triplicity or trinity in man is a fact which is involved in the very nature of personality. For in the processes of self-consciousness we discover in ourselves three "I's" or selves—three foci of consciousness which are the very foundation of self-consciousness, and which differentiate it from the simple consciousness of the brute. There is in us, first, the self which thinks of self; secondly, the self which is thought of; and thirdly, the self which is conscious that self is thinking of self. We are at one and the same time subject and object of thought, and conscious of subject and object.

This triplicity of selves which constitutes the one single personality becomes still clearer in those cases in which a man speaks to himself aloud, and then suddenly becomes conscious of himself speaking to himself, and quickly desists lest others overhear and smile at him.

With all this, however, the man is aware that each and all of these three "I's" or selves is he himself; that he is one individual or person, and not three separate ones; and that these three "I's" or selves have exactly the same essence or substance, and are each and all himself; that they interpenetrate and permeate one another, and together constitute him one person. Without this triplicity of "I's" or selves, personality would not and could not exist. It is this very triplicity which marks and characterizes self-consciousness, and hence personality.

The processes of conscience in which self reproves self, and self defends itself against the reproof, and in which self is conscious of this inner reproof and defense, furnish additional evidence of the triplicity referred to. They also make clear the further fact, that the second self in us is the incarnate and acting self, and that the first and third selves in us are purely spiritual; thus furnishing a further analogy which illustrates the possibility of the incarnation of the second person of the Holy Trinity without the incarnation of the first and the third.

It is not to be supposed that the triplicity of "I's" or selves in finite personality approaches the clearness and distinctness of the divine *hypostases* in the Holy Trinity; or that the use of such an analogy clears away the mystery connected with the doctrine of the Trinity. The very triplicity in ourselves which furnishes the analogy is itself a mystery beyond our comprehension. How much more is the Triunity in God sure to be a mystery which we cannot fathom! But since God is a self-conscious and self-determining Being, we find in human personality a triplicity which clearly meets the objection that the doctrine of the Trinity involves an impossibility or a contradiction. From the standpoint of personality, the Trinity is not only a possibility but a necessity inherent in the very nature of God as the Absolute and Perfect Personality. There are three "I's" or selves, or what the ancient Church called "persons," in God known to us through revelation as the Father, the Son, and the Holy Ghost. The Father begets the Son; the Son is begotten of the Father and is His express image; and the Holy Ghost proceeds from the Father and the Son. These three are One; they have the same essence or substance, and they permeate one another. The Father is not the Son or the Holy Siprit; the Son is not the Father or the Holy Spirit; and the Holy Spirit is not the Father or the Son. They are distinct yet not separate; they have three modes of subsistence, but they are one God—a Unity in Trinity, and a Trinity in Unity, Blessed forevermore.

Athanasian Creed. The following is an extract from the Athanasian Creed's full and unmistakable statement of the Church's doctrine of the Trinity: "We worship one God in Trinity, and Trinity in Unity; neither confounding the Persons nor dividing the Substance. For there is one Person of the Father, another of the Son, and another of the Holy Ghost. But the Godhead of the Father, of the Son, and of the Holy Ghost is all one; the Glory equal, the Majesty coeternal. Such as the Father is, such is the Son, and such is the Holy Ghost. The Father uncreate, the Son uncreate, and the Holy Ghost uncreate. . . . The Father eternal, the Son eternal, and the Holy Ghost eternal. And yet there are not three eternals, but one eternal. . . . The Father is God, the Son is God, and the Holy Ghost is God; and yet they are not three Gods, but one God. . . . In this Trinity none is afore or after another; none is greater or less than another; but the whole three persons are coeternal together, and coequal."

Errors. The doctrine of the Trinity was formulated by the early Church in order to state the truth as clearly as the limitations of the human mind and of human language permitted, and at the same time in order to guard against certain errors and heresies that prevailed. These errors were chiefly some forms of Monarchianism, and Arianism.

The Monarchians were of many kinds, but agreed in denying the deity of Christ and of the Holy Ghost, and maintained that the Father alone is God, and that there are not three persons or *hypostases.* One kind, the Dynamistic, regarded Christ as a creature. The other, the Modalistic or Sabellian, identified Christ with the Father, and regarded the Trinity as solely economic, and as simply three modes in which God the Father manifested Himself historically. Father, Son and Holy Ghost were supposed to denote the same divine person in different capacities. As the Father He created the world; as the Son He redeemed it; and as the Holy Ghost He works in the hearts and lives of men.[8] A natural deduction from this view was the

---

[8] Modalism reached its largest speculative development in Sabellius. He maintained that God is without distinction of persons, one God; that the silent God develops and broadens out into the speaking God, the Logos. The persons are simply the phases of His appearance. He reveals Himself as the Father in the giving of the Law, as the Son in the incarnation, and as the Holy Ghost in the application of salvation.

theory of the Patripassians, that the Father suffered on the cross for us.

Arianism maintained that Christ is of a similar but not of the same substance as the Father, and that He is an intermediate being between God and man, who was created by God before the existence of the world.[9] Other heresies, such as Ebionism, Docetism, Nestorianism, Eutychianism and Apollinarianism, belong more properly under the head of Christology, and will be considered there.

In the extensive controversies of the early Church the doctrine of the Holy Spirit received only incidental treatment. But the doctrine of the *homo-ousia* of the Son was followed, as an inevitable consequence, by the doctrine of the *homo-ousia* of the Holy Spirit. The Creed known as the Nicene declares of the Holy Ghost that He is "the Lord, the Giver of Life, who proceedeth from the Father and the Son,"[10] and who with the Father and the Son together is worshipped and glorified."

Opera ad Intra. In view of the three *hypostases,* certain activities in God, called *opera ad intra,* are predicated of Him. They belong respectively to each of the three "persons," and clearly distinguish them from one another. They are the two activities of Paternity or Generation, and of Spiration, both in their active and their passive significance. The Father begets the Son; and the Father and the Son spirate the Holy Ghost. Because of these *opera ad intra* there are five personal peculiarities of the Trinity; namely Unbegottenness, Paternity, Filiation, Spiration, and Procession. Two of these belong to the

[9] The great champion of orthodoxy against Arianism was Athanasius, who maintained the homo-ousia on the basis of the Scriptures; on the basis of tradition, namely, that Christ was worshiped; on the basis of the nature of Christianity, which is the restoration of fellowship with God through Christ; and on the basis of the Christian consciousness, which combines the Father and the Son in one act of faith, a thing which would be impossible if Christ were a creature.

[10] The words "and the Son," or the *filioque,* were inserted in the Nicene Creed by the Western Church (Synod of Toledo, A.D. 447 and 589), but were never accepted by the Eastern.

Father, namely Unbegottenness and Paternity; one belongs to the Son, namely Filiation; one belongs to the Father and the Son, namely Spiration; and one belongs to the Holy Ghost, namely, Procession.

The Generation of the Son and the Spiration of the Holy Ghost are an eternal generation and spiration. This means that the generation and spiration did not take place once for all, but that they are eternal in the sense of being eternally continuous. The Father eternally begets the Son, and the Father and the Son eternally spirate the Holy Ghost. The generation and spiration are without beginning and without end. If they had a beginning or an end, then the Son and the Holy Ghost would date their existence from that beginning or end, and would not be eternal. The Son and the Holy Spirit are, however, coeternal with the Father, one eternal Triune God.

The generation and the spiration must, of course, be distinguished. They are not identical. Generation belongs to the relation between the Father and the Son; and spiration belongs to the relation of the Father and the Son to the Holy Spirit. As observed above, the Nicene Creed in the form held by the Eastern Church declares that the Holy Ghost proceeds from the Father, while in that held by the Western Church it declares that He proceeds from the Father and the Son.

The three persons of the Trinity are coequal in majesty. There is no difference in rank or in origin; for none had an origin or beginning, and all are from eternity. There is, however, an order of subsistence necessitated by our thought and employed in the Scriptural grouping of the names of the three persons; so that we speak of the Father as the first person of the Holy Trinity, of the Son as the second person, and of the Holy Ghost as the third person.

The word "Father" as used in speaking of the first person of the Trinity has a specific meaning, and refers to His relation to the Son. He is the Father of our Lord Jesus Christ. When the word "Father" is used to address God in our prayers, as for example in the Lord's Prayer, the word refers, not to the first person of the Trinity, but to all three persons as one God. The Triune God is our heavenly Father.

Opera ad Extra. There are also three *opera ad extra* which are predicated of the Holy Trinity. They are Creation, Redemption and Sanctification. But unlike the several *opera ad intra* which are predicated of the three *hypostases* respectively, the *opera ad extra* are predicated of the entire essence of God. While the latter works are, indeed, often directly predicated of one person, they are not predicated of Him in such a way as utterly to exclude the other two persons. This is explained by the fact that they must, in the nature of the case, be regarded as proceeding from the essence of God, and this essence in its entirety is common to all three persons; and thus all three persons participate in the outward works. But since each person of the Trinity has manifested Himself in sacred history in a peculiar way, it follows that by preëminence Creation is ascribed to the Father, Redemption to the Son, and Sanctification to the Holy Ghost.

CHAPTER III

CREATION

THE work of creation is the first of the *opera ad extra* of the Holy Trinity. "In the beginning God created the heavens and the earth," and in six days He fashioned them into their present order and beauty.

Our Knowledge of Creation. The source of our knowledge of creation is the Holy Scripture. Without the account given in the Bible, we should have no knowledge of the manner in which creation took place. While many mythological accounts are found among the heathen, it is from Genesis alone that we can obtain the proper conception of the manner in which the world came into being. The accounts given in the first and in the second chapters of Genesis are not contradictory but complementary accounts. The one given in the second chapter does not aim to give an account of creation as such, but to begin a history of the world whose creation has just been described. In it man does not constitute the goal but the starting point. It is a history which begins with man and recapitulates the things which are necessary for the understanding of the fall into sin.

Compared with the heathen stories of creation—for example, the cosmogonies of the Orient and the theogonies of the Greeks—the Scriptural account is characterized not only by its simplicity and sublimity, but by its distinctly religious character. It is written from the religious standpoint, and emphasizes the great fundamental truth that God brought the world into existence by the act of His free will, and that the order and purpose everywhere apparent in it are the result of His almighty fiat.

The account of creation given in Genesis is accepted in the rest of the Holy Scriptures as literally true, and not as in any sense allegorical or symbolical. We have in it a real account of the manner in which the universe came into existence, and of the manner in which the earth in particular was made to take on its present form and order.

Neither in Genesis nor elsewhere does the Bible pretend to be a scientific book or to give a scientific explanation of things. It does not follow from this, however, that the results of scientific study will conflict with the Biblical account. All that science has so far discovered as actual truth may be harmonized with it, and all that she ever will discover will without doubt be harmonized with it also.

Meaning of Creation. The term creation is used in two senses: first, as the creation of something out of nothing; and secondly, as the fashioning of the raw material of the world into the present order of things. The first is called *immediate* creation, and is described in the first verse of Genesis. The second is called *mediate* creation, and is described as the six days' work. The *immediate* creation out of nothing, *ex nihilo,* is not to be conceived as though "nothing" were the negative material out of which God made the world. "Nothing" means here pure nothing—the complete lack of any existence outside of God. There was no antecedent world-stuff. Where nothing at all existed before, God brought the world into being by His creative act.

Definition. Creation may be defined as that act of the eternally existing Triune God by which at the beginning of time and out of nothing He brought the world into existence by His almighty power, and fashioned it in six successive days into its present order. It is the work of the one undivided Godhead, and not the work of the Father or of the Son or of the Holy Ghost alone or separately. The work of creation is ascribed to the essence of God, and not to any one of the three subsistences or *hypostases* in God. It is, indeed, ascribed in the Scriptures to each of the three persons: to the Father (1 Cor. 8:6), to the Son (1 Cor. 8:6; John 1:3), and to the Holy Ghost (Gen. 1:2). But the three persons are not to be regarded as separate causes nor as associated causes. For as the three persons are only one God, so there is only one cause of creation, the Triune God. Creation is, however, ascribed by preëminence to the Father. Thus we confess in the Apostles' Creed, that God is the Father Almighty, Maker of heaven and earth; and in the Nicene Creed, that He is the Maker of all things visible and invisible. The latter also declares that all things were made by or through the Son, and that the Holy Spirit is the Giver of Life.

Ex Nihilo. It appears from the account in Genesis first of all, that in the beginning God brought forth the world out of nothing. Where no matter at all existed, God called into existence all the matter that constitutes the universe. The world is the result of God's creative act. Matter did not exist alongside of God from all eternity. God did not fashion the world out of preëxisting material.

By God's Free Will. Having existed alone from eternity, God might have continued to exist alone, had He chosen to do so. But for His own wise and loving purposes He determined to bring the universe into being. Creation is thus the work of God's free will, and was not due to any inherent necessity of His nature. In this respect it differs from the *opera ad intra*. The world is not to be conceived of as something necessary to God's welfare, or as an emanation from God, or as an unfolding of what was from the first implicitly in Him. God and the world are not in any sense identical. The world is not a part of God; it is not that portion of Him which we see; but it is a work which He has made, and which exhibits His glory

(Ps. 19:1 seq.). It is a work done by a fiat: not by a thought of God: but by His Word. "He spake and it was done, He commanded and it stood fast" (Ps. 33:9). In the first chapter of John this word is described as the personal Word or Logos. While God is immanent in the world and His energy produced and maintains it, He is at the same time transcendent over it.[1]

Creation is the work of God alone, and not of God and the angels. There was no instrumental cause, but only the efficient cause, God, acting through His Word. Creation was by the Father, through the Son, and to the Holy Ghost. For of Him and through Him and to Him are all things" (Rom. 11:36).

The Beginning. The beginning of creation is the beginning of time. "In the beginning" God created the heavens and the earth. Before that there was only eternity. Time implies the successive happening of things in an existing world. Where no world exists nothing can happen, and there is no time, but only eternity, of whose absolute nature we are in complete ignorance. We can think only in terms of time and space, because of our finite limitations. Whether time be regarded as an actuality in the world or only as an intuition of the mind, in either case time or the conception of time dates from the creation of the world. For us that is the beginning. Time before the world would be a contradiction.

Extent of Creation. The extent of the creation described in Genesis includes the whole universe. The conception of the cosmos held by the writer of the Biblical account differs vastly from that which we have gained from modern astronomy. The world of being is enormously greater than the Old Testament saints conceived. But it is nevertheless the plain intention of

---

[1] Pantheism requires an eternal existence of matter, because it cannot conceive of *natura naturans* without the *natura naturata*. Fichte holds that the acceptance of a creation is the fundamental error of all false metaphysics and religions. Hegel regards the world as an emanation from God.

the writer of Genesis to describe God as the author of the whole range of existence. His account is not the only case in which an inspired writer included much more than he fully realized. Since other parts of his record show that the writer of Genesis had knowledge of the existence of angels, his statement that God created the heavens and the earth includes the creation of the spiritual world as well as of the natural. As the Nicene Creed puts it, God is "the Maker of all things visible and invisible." All the angels, together with all other spiritual or physical beings anywhere in the universe, if there be any such of whom we know nothing, are included in God's work of creation. The Biblical record divides that which was created into heaven and earth—a division unsuitable for science, but religiously the proper division of the world.

Chaos. The original state of the world immediately after the creation *ex nihilo* was one of chaos (Gen. 1:2). God first created the raw material of the world, and then as an almighty builder fashioned it into an orderly universe. The first verse of Genesis describes the actual creation in the *immediate* sense. The rest of the chapter is devoted to what is called the *mediate* creation, in which the only new thing brought into existence *de novo* is the soul of man created on the sixth day. The theosophical view that there was a previous world which was destroyed in the downfall of the angels, and that this ruin constituted what is described as a formless and void world, is unnecessary and untenable.[2] Equally untenable from the Scriptural point of view is the theory that the present universe is only one of many worlds which succeeded one another in existence. These theories are baseless speculations. According to the Scriptural account, the creation of the present world constituted the beginning. And there is no statement of Scripture

[2] This theory is held, for example, by Schofield's Bible and supported by fanciful interpretations of other parts of Scripture.

anywhere which by any legitimate interpretation teaches that a preceding world was thrown into ruin by a cataclysm.

The Six Days' Work. The fashioning of chaos into the cosmos was not the result of "the fortuitous concourse of atoms" [3] but was a divine work occupying six days. The world was, according to the second verse of Genesis, a mass of unorganized raw material, without form and void, a chaos. Then in the course of six days God made this raw material assume by successive stages its present form. Each day's work represents a definite advance over that of the previous day. The description of these six days' work is given from the standpoint of the earth, rather than from that of the universe as a whole. On the first day God created light; on the second He made the firmament appear overhead; on the third He divided the earth's surface into land and sea, and caused the earth to produce vegetation; on the fourth He made the sun, moon and stars appear in the sky; on the fifth He made the living creatures of the water and the air; and on the sixth He made the beasts and man.

A textbook of science which would undertake to describe these same events would be quite differently worded, but, if true, would describe the same essential facts. The writer of Genesis lacked, of course, such a knowledge of the vastness of the universe and of the nature of chemical and geological processes as the modern man possesses. But the aim of the writer of Genesis is quite different from that of the author of a scientific textbook. It is simply to declare that God created the world, and to give in outline an account of the order which He followed in bringing the world to its present state.

Much argument has been expended on the question whether the six days of creation were of twenty-four hours each, or whether the days represent long periods of time. The record in

[3] So Lucretius, "On the Nature of Things" (*De Rerum Natura*).

Genesis permits the holding of either theory. The word "day" is sometimes used in Scripture to designate a period of twenty-four hours, and sometimes it is used to denote a period of time, as for example, the "day of the Lord" (Isa. 2:12; 13:6). A thousand years are with the Lord as one day, and one day as a thousand years (2 Pet. 3:8). That God could, if He chose to do so, fashion the world into its present form and order in six days of twenty-four hours each is clear to everyone who believes in God's infinite power. On the other hand, it is equally clear that God was, if He so chose, perfectly at liberty to use a long period of time for bringing about the results specified under the head of each day's work. The Scriptural record does not define the length of the "day," and leaves us free to believe either that the days were periods of twenty-four hours or of millions of years.

At the present time God produces results in nature by means of second causes to which He gives ample time to bring about the results intended. He may have chosen to operate in this very gradual way during the six "days"; for He had unlimited time at His disposal. On the other hand, He was perfectly able to accelerate the operation of second causes, if He desired to do so, and to make them produce the purposed results within the compass of twenty-four hours. The essential thing is to recognize that God made the world, and that second causes, whether considered as operating now or as operating in the period of creation, do not produce their results by any inherent power of their own; but that they are simply the mode in which God operates. They produce the results which they do solely because of the activity of His will.

Objections. The account in Genesis has, of course, been frequently assailed by unbelievers. By some it is regarded as a fabled cosmogony similar to those of heathen nations, and based on them. But a comparison of those heathen accounts of the origin of the world with the Biblical account shows that they are very far removed from the sanity and consistency evident in the Scriptural record.

By others it is urged that the Biblical account gives to the earth an importance out of all proportion to its size in relation to the rest of the universe. But the importance of a planet destined by God to be the abode of creatures made in His own image cannot be judged by its material size. The objection that the light of the nearest fixed star traveling at the rate of one hundred and eighty-six thousand miles per second takes years to reach the earth, and that the light from remote stars takes thousands of light years to reach us, and that consequently the account of a creation completed in six days cannot be true, and that the universe must be vastly older than the Scriptural record implies, has no force if the six days of creation are conceived as days in the sense of long periods of time. The objection of geologists that it took extremely long periods to form the various strata of rocks is met by the consideration that the rate of geological changes was not necessarily as slow in the period of creation as now, and that even if it was the objection falls of its own weight if the six days represent long periods of time.

The chief opposition to the Scriptural account of creation comes from the advocates of a naturalistic evolution. Instead of an orderly process of creation by the will and word of God in six distinct and successive stages, naturalistic evolution would have us believe that from some primeval nebulæ, whose existence is not accounted for and which must therefore be supposed to have existed from eternity, the universe came to be what it is through the laws of condensation and gravitation; and that vegetable life spontaneously originated amid organic matter, and was followed by the spontaneous origination of conscious life in the brute and of self-conscious life in man. Further it would have us believe that the various species of animal life, including man, have developed from an original protoplasm, whose origin and vast potentialities it does not account for— higher species developing out of lower till the acme is reached in man; and all this, not by the will of God, but by reason of laws inherent in the material world. Evolution, however, is purely an hypothesis, vastly fascinating to many persons, but utterly unproved and, we are persuaded, unprovable.[4] The Biblical account of creation, on the other hand, is a divinely inspired record of fact.

The Reason for Creation. It has been said by some, that God created the world primarily for His own glory, and secondarily for the benefit of man. But in view of the fact that God is described by the apostle as Love, and hence that all His acts are to be attributed to love as the fundamental motive, it is better to say that God created the world in order that creatures might share in His life and love.[5]

The question why God created the world is not yet, however, sufficiently answered by the statement made above. In the

---

[4] The naturalistic evolution which is so popular to-day, and which would explain all forms of life without reference to God's activity, breaks down at three vital points. First, since nature cannot give what she does not have, inorganic matter cannot have given life to the vegetable world. Secondly, for the same reason, unconscious vegetable life cannot have given conscious life to the brute. And thirdly, the conscious life of the animal world cannot have given self-conscious life to man. In any case, nothing but the creative activity of God could have initiated vegetable, animal and personal life in turn. The theory of the differentiation of species breaks down in the face of the sterility of hybrids, notably the mule. The declaration in Genesis that each shall propagate after its kind holds good in the world of experience. Dogs breed varieties of dogs, but always and only dogs. Brutes remain on the same plane from age to age. Man alone shows progress and improvement in his history. This is due to the fact that he is endowed with self-consciousness and self-determination. But this growth of man in civilization, science, art, etc., is a development, not an evolution. Amid all the changes of time man has been and remains a man, with no new organs of body and no new faculties of mind. He is the same kind of being he always was, whether he be found in a state of savagery or in a high state of civilization. He has not evolved into any different or higher kind of being.

[5] Comp. Kahnis, Die luth. Dogmatik, I, 428: "The ground of creation is found in love; the purpose, not in the blessedness of God, but in the blessedness of the world."

minds of many men the question assumes the form, Why did God make man in particular, when He foreknew that man would fall into sin, and that the world would become the abode of sorrow, pain and death? To this it must be replied that an answer which will be satisfactory to all cannot be given, but that the following considerations should be taken into account.

First, if God desired to have in the world any creatures higher in the scale of being than the dog or the horse, in other words, if He desired to have in the world personal beings capable of living in fellowship with Him, it was necessary to create beings endowed with a freedom of will which they would be able to abuse as well as properly use. To make man incapable of choosing between right and wrong, and compulsorily to bind him to a certain course of action, would have been to create him as no man at all, but as a brute or a machine. Self-determination, if it was to exist in a creature, was inseparable from the possibility of a fall. Secondly, the creation of man dare not be separated from the redemption of man. Both belong to the eternal counsel of God. When from eternity He determined to create man, He also determined to redeem him (Eph. 1:4). And hence God's eternal contemplation of the fall was accompanied by the contemplation of the divine work of redemption which should undo the work of the devil, and bring man back to God. Thirdly, the fact that some men will be lost in spite of redemption is solely due to their own refusal to let God save them. Finally, the fact that some men will wickedly and pertinaciously refuse to accept God's proffered grace does not form an adequate reason why others who accept that grace should have been kept out of existence and excluded from all possibility of profiting by the unspeakable goodness of God and enjoying it forever.

While such considerations will not satisfy the minds of all, they satisfy the minds of the Christians. Knowing that God is a God of infinite love, they are sure that His creation is an act of love, and that, in a way which is well defined in His own mind, He will bring out of the welter and confusion which marks the world of mankind a result which will more than vindicate His creation of man.

The Dignity of Man. It is evident from the Biblical account of creation, as well as from the whole tenor of Scripture, that the earth and man are regarded as occupying a central place in God's mind. This will not appear unreasonable, in spite of the vastness of the universe, if we remember that a single personal being made in God's image is and must be in His eyes of greater value than a planet or a fixed star, indeed, than the entire material universe. Christ tells us that a single soul is of more value than the whole world (Matt. 16:26). The central character of the earth and man seems to find corroboration in astronomical studies which locate the earth practically in the center of the physical universe,° and which regard the earth as the only sphere in which the conditions necessary for the existence of physical life exist.

Quite evidently the Biblical account pictures man as the culmination of God's creative activity. Whatever may be man's relative significance with respect to the angels, he evidently was intended to be and is the highest of all earthly creatures. This is indicated not only by the fact that he was created as the last and crowning work after the world had been made ready for him, but particularly by the fact that he was made in the image of God. The beasts were made of the dust of the ground. Man also, as regards his body, is of the dust, and is akin to the brute creation. But on the spiritual side of his being he is separated from the brute by an impassable gulf, and is akin to God. He is a person as God is a person. He was made on a finite scale the same kind of being that God is on an infinite scale. This fact

° See Wallace, *Man's Place in the Universe*, N. Y., 1904.

not only gives to man himself a dignity and importance which outweigh all material considerations, but invests the earth with peculiar dignity and importance because it is man's abode.

The value which God sets on man appears from creation, but still more from redemption. For in order to redeem this creature whom He had made in His own image, God sent His only Son to become incarnate and to suffer and die on the cross.

Since man is so plainly the chief of God's earthly creatures, and the world is to be regarded as created for him, the question has been asked, whether everything in the world has been created for man's benefit. The reply is that the world in general has been made for man, as is indicated by God's command, "Be fruitful and multiply and replenish the earth and subdue it; and have dominion over the fish of the sea, etc." (Gen. 1:28); but that it is not possible to find in every existing thing or living creature a specific benefit for mankind. The usefulness of a mosquito and of countless other things in the world has not yet been discovered, and probably never will be. But it is evident that the world as a whole was made for man's benefit. And he is constantly making new discoveries and inventions which enable him to use for his own welfare and comfort objects which he had previously regarded as merely useless or even harmful.

Creation Very Good. At the end of the six days' work we are told that "God saw everything that He had made, and behold, it was very good" (Gen. 1:31). The world as it came from His hands was free from blemish or evil of any kind. It was the best possible world for the purposes which God intended.[7] Thus far the purest optimism is justifiable. But evil entered into the world with sin; and sin with its effects, together with God's

[7] The doctrine that the world is adapted to these purposes is called optimism, and in this sense, and not in the sense of a choice between various possibilities, the world is spoken of as the best possible world. This adaptedness of the world to the divine purposes remained after the corruption of the world had taken place through sin, but it requires a restoration, and can reach its goal only through Christ. Comp. Col. 1:16; Eph. 1:10.

plan of redemption, must be taken into account in any estimate of the present world.

The Origin of Evil. When the statement is made that everything that God had made was very good, the plain implication is that if evil is in the world to-day its presence must be traced to some other source, and not to God. He did not create sin and evil. Sin is not an entity existing by itself, but is a quality in a personal being: it is the antagonism of a finite will to God's. Since all that God had made was declared at the end of the sixth day (Gen. 1:31) to have been very good, all the personal beings created by Him were originally without sin. But the possession of free will on their part involved the possibility that they might abuse it. Thus through the temptation and the fall recorded in the third chapter of Genesis sin entered into our human world. Its entrance into the universe is referred to in those passages which describe Satan as the originator of sin (2 Pet. 2:4; Jude 6; John 8:44).

It is plain that if God desired to complete the world by placing in it the highest kind of creatures, namely, personal beings, then self-determination or freedom to sin or not to sin was necessarily a part of those creatures' endowment. Absolutely to bar the possible entrance of sin into the world would have been to bar the creation of personal beings, and to end creation with the formation of the highest kind of brutes. But what a world this would then have been, without a person in it to appreciate its beauty and grandeur or to adore its Creator, and with no inhabitant capable of voluntarily serving God or living in loving communion or fellowship with Him!

The Seventh Day. On the seventh day God rested from the work of creation. This is not to be understood as meaning that God retired from the world which He had made and let it run its course by reason of independent forces resident in it. The seventh day's rest is simply rest from the work of creation, and not a resting from all activity. God is immanent in the world, as well as transcendent above it. What He has made continues to exist because He perpetually sustains it. The seventh day's rest means that the heavens and the earth were finished, and that no new creatures were fashioned after that time. But God is unceasingly active in the work of Providence, continually preserving, sustaining and governing the universe which He has made. The seventh day is, therefore, not a day of twenty-four hours, but a long period of time. God is still resting from His work of creation.[8]

[8] It may be argued that if the seventh day mentioned in the account in Genesis is a long period of time, there does not seem to be any valid reason why the other six days may not be taken to represent long periods also.

CHAPTER IV

PROVIDENCE

GOD preserves, sustains and cares for the world which He has made. The universe is not a self-operating machine. It would not continue to operate or even to exist, were it not for the sustaining and energizing power and activity of Him who created it.

This providential care of God is the source of the greatest comfort to the Christian. A world which God made, but about whose further fate He did not concern Himself, would be a most disheartening world. But the Scriptures assure us that God's tender mercies are over all His works; that He cares for the greatest and the least; and that the Christian is to cast all his anxiety upon God.

God Transcendent and Immanent. In general the relation of God to the world is to be described as twofold: He is both transcendent and immanent. The transcendence is maintained in opposition to pantheism, which identifies the world and God, and robs God of personality. The immanence is maintained in opposition to deism, which, while it acknowledges the personality of God, separates Him from the world and regards all that occurs as due to the operation of natural laws which are resident in nature. Christianity maintains that God is at once a transcendent personal being who is above the world, and an immanent being who is present and operative in the world. If God ceased to sustain the world, it would cease to be. He operates ordinarily through second causes which He so accurately

75

adapts to His purpose, that there is no need of special intervention here and there in order to supplement them and keep the world in operation.

The Belief in Providence. The certainty of divine providence is a natural belief as well as a matter of supernatural revelation. The Epicureans, indeed, claimed that the gods do not care for human affairs; but apart from them the belief in Providence was practically universal among the ancients. It is a necessary implication of religious belief. The belief of the ancients was defective, however, in that it ranged fate alongside of Providence, and restricted Providence itself to major things, since it would be beneath the dignity of God to concern Himself with minor matters. Complete certainty concerning Providence is given only by the revelation of salvation, which makes known to us God's will of love. For that assures us that God would have all men be saved; and that in giving Christ for our sins, He gave the guarantee of every other needful gift (Rom. 8:32).

Providence not Continued Creation. The doctrine of Providence means that God continually sustains and cares for the world which He has made. But this continuous activity of providence is not to be regarded as continuous and unending creation. Creation and providence are two distinct activities of God. The creation of the world was definitely concluded on the sixth day. On the seventh day, which extends to the present time, God rested from the work of creation. This means that the order of nature was established, that its laws were in permanent operation, and that the species of vegetable and animal life were fixed at the end of the six days' work. It is assumed by many persons that the laws now operative in nature were operative during the period of creation; but this has not been proved. The creation of species recorded in Genesis is not identical with the propagation of the species. There is no actual evidence that any new species have come into existence since the conclusion of the six days' work and the appearance of man upon the scene. Providence and creation must, therefore, be clearly distinguished as different activities of God. Creation and providence are, indeed, often found together in Scriptural allusions to them. But this is only natural, when we remember that without the activity of providence in preserving them the things created would have fallen back into nothingness.

Proof of Providence. Divine providence is a reasonable assumption even from the standpoint of the natural knowledge of God and the world. The uniformity of the laws of nature argues for a controlling and directing power back of them. The marvelous adaptation of creatures to their environment shows a beneficent care for their welfare. And the history of the human race gives evidence of direction toward some definite end or goal.

The Scriptural proof of divine providence is plain and full. All things great and small are included in it. All the stages and events in man's life are objects of divine providence. God's solicitous care includes man's conception and birth (Job. 10:8; Ps. 137:15, 16; 71:6), the necessities of life (Ps. 145:15, 16; Matt. 6:25, 26), the troubles of life (Ps. 56:8), and protection from danger (Ps. 127:1) and disease (Ps. 91:3). The shortening (Ps. 55:23) and lengthening (Exod. 20:12; Prov. 3:1, 2) of man's days and the end of human life (Job. 14:5) are in His hands.

There is a substantial and immanent presence of God with His creatures. The world continues to exist and runs its course because of His continuous and omnipotent working. The second causes in nature are not forces operating independently of Him, but are sustained in their action by His continuous will. The apostle declares that "in Him we live and move and have our being" (Acts 17:28). Every created thing is every moment dependent on His sustaining will.

Definition. Providence is that activity of the Triune God by which He sustains, energizes and governs the universe, exercising loving care over all the things which He has made, and particularly over the believer. It is an *opus ad extra* of the Holy Trinity. It is ascribed to the Father (John 5:17), to the Son (John 5:17; Col. 1:17; Heb. 1:3), and to the Holy Ghost (Ps. 104:30), but, like creation, it is ascribed to the Father by preëminence.

The objects of God's providence are all created things from the greatest to the least. It includes the animal creation (Ps. 147:9) down to those considered by man to be insignificant (Matt. 6:26; 10:29; Luke 12:6); but especially man—mankind in general (Acts 17:26; Ps. 36:7, 8), the individual both good and bad (Matt. 5:45), and the believer in particular (Rom. 8:28). Providence is, therefore, usually classed as General, Special, and Most Special.

General Providence. The General Providence of God is His care for the universe as a whole, and for everything in it. He who made the heavens and the earth and all things that are therein preserves them all (Neh. 9:6). His providential care extends from the vast and complex stellar universe with its innumerable worlds and its inconceivable distances down to the birds of the air (Matt. 6:25) and the lilies of the field (Matt. 6:28, 29). Nothing from the greatest to the least lies outside its bounds.

Special Providence. The Special Providence of God is His special care for men as the earthly creatures made in His image. He sustains their being and powers, sends rain and sunshine on the evil and on the good (Matt. 5:45), and supplies their wants with liberal hand (Ps. 145:16). He is concerned not simply with their temporal but with their eternal welfare (1 John 4:9). His providential dealings with men cannot be understood apart from His desire to save them, and, hence, from His desire so to order their lives on earth that they may, if possible, be brought to life eternal.

Most Special Providence. The Most Special Providence of God is His particular care for the believer. Those who have been reconciled to Him in Christ have become His dear children (Gal. 3:26) and are regarded as the special objects of His fatherly affection (Rom. 8:32). He cannot overlook or forget them or in any sense be indifferent to what happens to them. So great and constant is His thought for them, that they are told to cast all their care upon Him, because He careth for them (1 Pet. 5:7). They are bidden not to be anxious or to worry, but confidently to intrust themselves to Him who feeds the birds of the air and clothes the lilies of the field (Matt. 6:25 seq.). Since not even a sparrow falleth without His knowledge (Matt. 10:29), believers should know that He watches still more closely over them, and that nothing can happen to them without His knowledge and permission (Luke 12:7). Even the very hairs of their heads are all numbered (Luke 12:7). If sorrow and pain are permitted to come upon them, it is for some wise and good purpose which God has in mind (Prov. 3:12; Rev. 3:19). For all things shall be made to work together for good to them that love Him (Rom. 8:25). Afflictions are designed to conduce to their eternal welfare, and, if received in the right spirit of loving submission to God's providence, they will work the peaceable fruit of righteousness (Heb. 12:11).

The goal of providence is the glory of God and the welfare of His creatures, particularly the eternal salvation of men.

Classification. In Providence God works in two ways: through second causes and through miracles. The former is called Ordinary Providence, the latter is called Extraordinary Providence.

Ordinary Providence is exercised in three ways, namely, by Preservation, by Concurrence, and by Government.

Preservation. By Preservation we mean that activity of God by which He sustains and preserves the world which He has made. Created things do not subsist by themselves nor by virtue of any inherent strength, but only because God continuously sustains them. As they came into being by His will, so with all their various powers and properties they remain in being by His will. Without His preserving power they would fall back into nothingness. So, also, second causes have not been created and set into independent operation apart from God, but are continuously kept in operation by His sustaining will. Preservation includes all inorganic matter with its powers and properties; the various species of the vegetable and animal worlds, as well as each individual composing the species; and the human race as a whole, as well as each individual, body and soul.

Concurrence. By Concurrence we mean that activity of God by which He concurs in the operation of second causes, and coöperates with living creatures in all their actions. Nothing happens independently of God. He is immanent in all things, and every power employed by the creature is one with which God supplies him. Without God's concurrence it would be impossible for us even to move a finger. Concurrence rests upon the omnipresence of God, a presence which is actual and operative everywhere. It does not mean simply that God conserves certain powers in nature as second causes, but that there is an immediate coöperation of God with the action and effects of second causes.

This doctrine of the divine concurrence [1] raises some difficulties in connection with the sinful acts of men. The solution of the dogmaticians was, that God concurs in the effect but not in the defect of the sinful act. The explanation of this state-

---

[1] The earlier dogmaticians did not teach concurrence as a separate mode of providence, but used only the two divisions, preservation and government. Beginning with Quenstedt, concurrence was added as a third mode.

ment is to be found in the peculiar nature of human personality and God's attitude toward it. God concurs, indeed, in every action of man, good or bad, or else man could not act. But in giving to man self-determination, God gave him a relative independence in matters of volition, so that by virtue of that independence man's volition is his own act; and he may and often does will in antagonism to God's will. While God concurs in the action of man's various faculties and organs, He does not concur in the volition itself. The volition is man's own act; and the power to perform it is sustained in man by God. This sustaining of the power of independent volition in man is essential to his continued existence as a personal being. Hence God concurs in the effect of man's actions, but not in their defect, that is, not in the wicked intention, because this latter comes from man's own self-determination.

Concurrence seems to be a term by which the dogmaticians sought to express what we believe is better expressed by the modern term immanence. Without the divine immanence or concurrence we should have a world which exists apart from God, and whose energies possess a certain independence of Him. This would approach if it did not coincide with the deistic theory of divine transcendence without immanence. God's share in the activity of the world would then be restricted to the work of sustaining from the outside, as it were, independent powers which He has given to nature, animate and inanimate. But according to the Scriptures God is an active participant in all that takes place in the world. His is the ultimate energy in all things.

There is in nature a certain necessity or determinism that goes back to God's will. And it is this necessity that gives stability to the world. The laws of nature are the mode of the working of God's will; and their uniformity is certain because His will is fixed and His energy constant. Without this constancy in

nature we should be helpless in the face of arbitrary and contradictory natural forces which might at any moment act in any
conceivable or inconceivable manner, and not according to any
rule or law deducible from experience.

But concurrence must be guarded against the misconception
that it involves necessity or determinism in the case of man,
or that God is in any way responsible for the evil which men
do. In all the realm of created things there is one sphere in
which God does not operate directly, and that is the sphere of
self-determination in a personal being. Here is an inner realm
from which God has voluntarily withdrawn as a determining
power, and which He has left to the creature made in His
image. This gives to the voluntary acts of man independence
of God's determination, so that they are man's and not God's
acts. The act is performed by God's concurrence, but the moral
direction or quality of the act is due to the self-determination
of man, and for it man is responsible.

Government. By Government we mean that divine activity
by which God controls and directs the world and its affairs,
particularly those of the human race, so that, without interfering with human freedom, He guides the world on to the goal
which He has set for it. This goal is the salvation of as many
as possible of the human race. And the aim of the divine government is so to direct and control the world that His gracious
divine will shall be accomplished in spite of the evil purposes
of wicked men and devils.

Divine Government may be regarded as exercised in four
ways; namely, by Permission, by Hindrance, by Direction, and
by Determination.

Permission. By Permission we mean that God permits many
things to be done which He does not desire nor will, and
which He actually forbids. He permits them, because He does
not desire to take away from men the self-determination or

freewill which characterizes them as personal beings. God's government must not be understood to mean that everything that happens takes place because God wills that it should. In creating man a person, He voluntarily restricted Himself to the use of other than compulsory methods of influencing man's acts. He seeks to persuade men to do right. Persuasion is the only method which can be applied if man's personality is respected. Hence, if men will not be persuaded to do right, but insist on doing evil, God permits them to do so. Thus men commit many sins, small and great, and are guilty of cruel murders and bloody wars. God does not desire that men should do these things, and has for centuries been seeking through His Word to persuade them not to do them, but to act toward Him and toward one another altogether according to the law of love. But if they will not heed Him, what shall He do? To compel them to do only what He wants would take away their self-determination and reduce them to the level of the brute. To slay them in order to prevent them from doing evil would bring the race to a speedy end. Hence he permits them to carry out their wicked purposes, even though these are contrary to His holy and loving will. But He holds them responsible for their actions, and will some day call them to account. This doctrine of God's permission of what He does not will, and, indeed, of what is completely in opposition to His will, is essential if God is not to be made the author of sin.

Hindrance. By Hindrance we mean that God frequently brings to naught the counsels and purposes of wicked men, either by putting an end to their lives or by limiting them in various ways, so that they do not possess the power to carry out their wicked intentions.[2]

Direction. By Direction we mean that God so regulates the

---

[2] Examples of God's hindrance are seen in Abimelech, Gen. 20:6; in Laban, Gen. 31:24; and in Balaam, Numb. 22:12 seq.

good actions of men as to guide them to the result intended by Him; and that He so overrules the evil actions of men that in spite of their evil intentions those actions result in the accomplishment of a purpose of God. Thus the wicked action of the Jews who crucified Christ was overruled for good, and Jesus by His death became the propitiation for the sins of the whole world. God frequently brings good out of evil and directs the actions of men to an unexpected goal.[3]

Determination. By determination we mean that activity of God by which on the basis of His own will alone He determines what shall be, and executes His will without fail. This determination is absolute in the material world, and works itself out through the forces of nature. In the realm of finite personality God attains His determined ends by withdrawing from men or devils the power to act or by holding their power within limits which they cannot transcend.

The Limit of Human Life. The limit of human life is determined by God's providence in the sense that no man can or will live beyond the time allotted by God. But in many cases God would undoubtedly have been willing that men should live longer than they did, if they had obeyed the laws of health ordained by Him. Care must be taken not to ascribe to the foredetermination of God that brevity of human life which is due to folly and sin in men. The ending of a human life by murder or suicide or foolhardiness or neglect must not be laid to the foreordination of God. When such a life has come to an apparently untimely end, the consolation to be given to the bereaved is not that God has willed it in the sense of having determined it beforehand, but that He permitted it for His own wise and good purposes and will overrule it for the good of His children. So far as such deaths may be ascribed to God's will,

---

[3] Another striking example of God's direction is seen in the case of the sale of Joseph by his brethren, Gen. 50:20.

it must be to His "will of permission," if we might use such a term, and not to His will of determination.

God's government of the world is one which constantly takes into account man's freedom of action. This makes it possible for God to answer prayer, and makes prayer a factor in the divine government of the world.

Opposing Theories. Theories in conflict with the Christian doctrine of Providence are numerous. Fatalism regards all events as the inevitable result of an immutable and resistless fate. Casualism ascribes all events to chance. Deistic determinism turns the affairs of the world over to invariable mechanical forces supposed to be resident in nature. Pantheistic determinism does away with personality, and regards all things and events as a necessary unfolding out of God, the All. Theological determinism ascribes every act and event to the sovereign and absolute decree of God.

The Old Testament. In the early stages of divine revelation all emphasis was laid upon God's sovereign power, while the distinction between His direct determination and His permissive act was reserved for a later period of revelation. Hence we find passages in the Old Testament which ascribe to God's direct efficiency what in the light of fuller revelation we know to be due to God's permission, or, as in the case of the hardening of Pharaoh's heart, the working out of the law that sin engenders sin.[4]

Miracles. By Extraordinary Providence we mean that which is exercised by God through miracles. God is a God of wonders; He possesses unlimited powers of operation, and is not bound to natural modes.[5] The actual sphere of miracles is the revela-

---

[4] Exod. 7:3,13. This passage should, however, be compared with Exod. 8:15, in which Pharaoh is said to have hardened his own heart. In 2 Sam. 24:1, God is said to have moved David to number Israel; but according to a later writer, in 1 Chron. 21:1, it was Satan who provoked David to do so.

[5] In the Old Testament the natural and the miraculous are often viewed together as the work of the God of wonders.

tion of the Old and New Testaments. The Biblical designations are: miracles, signs, prodigies (wonders), powers, works of God, works.

Miracles are to be regarded primarily as a constituent part of revelation. They were given in the days when the Church was founded, in order to guarantee its divine origin and nature. But now the Church itself takes the place of the miracles.[6] The latter do not of themselves, irrespective of attending circumstances, furnish the proof of the truth. They have apologetic value only as integral parts of revelation.

A miracle is an event produced by a direct act of God outside of the operation of the laws of nature. The underlying idea in it is that of the use of other than the natural means of operation. Hence we distinguish between miracles and *mirabilia*. The latter are wonderful simply because we are ignorant of the natural causes by which they are produced. Larger knowledge would dispel their wonderful character. The scholastic doctrine, that the miracles were preceded by a miraculous suspension of the laws of nature and were followed by a miraculous restoration of those laws, is based on a false conception of the nature of miracles.

The possibility of miracles is grounded in the transcendence of God, and their necessity in the need of revelation and redemption. Their actuality is a matter of historical evidence.

The laws of nature are our conception, based on experience, of the way in which God ordinarily accomplishes His purposes. So far as our "laws" are correct and not based on insufficient data, they are the mode in which the divine will ordinarily expresses itself. But God is not bound to these ordinary modes of action, and can, if He chooses, act in another and direct way. He is the master and not the slave of His ordinary

---

[6] Hence the Protestants polemicize against the "miracles" of the Roman Catholic Church.

modes of activity. The laws in nature are not laws in the sense of obligations or commands, but are modes of action. Hence miracles are not violations of the laws of nature. By an act of the human will the hand may hold a book in the air; but this is not a violation of the law of gravity. On the contrary, it is a case in which an effect ordinarily produced by the law of gravity is not produced, because the effect of that law has been temporarily prevented by the higher law of the human will.

The miracles are not arbitrarily performed wonders, but appear as integral parts of the divine supernatural revelation. No such revelation could be given without the use of the miraculous, that is, without the occurrence of events outside the operation of natural laws. Without the miraculous we could have no revelation but that which is contained in conscience and nature. The miracles of Scripture are abundantly vindicated when viewed in connection with the history of revelation.

The certainty of the miracles is found in the reality of the person of Jesus Christ. As the incarnate Son of God He is the miracle of miracles. On the basis of this fundamental miracle, those connected with His public ministry together with those of His resurrection and ascension follow naturally and inevitably. The constantly recurring regeneration of men is a miracle, because it takes place outside the laws of natural psychology, and can be explained only by the direct activity of God through the Means of Grace.

CHAPTER V

THE ANGELS

Their Existence. The existence of the angels cannot be known from reason or nature, but only from the Holy Scriptures. Both in the Old and in the New Testament their existence is clearly taught. They are actual beings, and not mere personifications of the attributes of God or of the forces of nature. They are not the spirits of departed men. They are beings of a particular kind. Their very existence is an evidence that they are creatures of God.

The time of their creation is not known. It evidently must fall somewhere within the period described in the first chapter of Genesis, and before the resting of God on the seventh day. But as that chapter describes creation from the standpoint of the earth, it does not mention the creation of the angels. Whether the angels were brought into existence before or during the six days' work cannot be shown. The Nicene Creed doubtless has the angels in view when it declares that God is the "Maker of all things visible and invisible."

With regard to the object of God in creating the angels, it is best to revert to the fundamental attribute of God, His love, referred to in connection with the creation of man, and to say that God created the angels in order that they might share in His life and love.

Their Nature. Angels, like men, are persons, possessing self-consciousness and self-determination. They think and feel and will. But unlike men, they have no bodies, and are pure spirits.

They are invisible, therefore, to human eyes. In the course of the history of revelation they have, however, assumed bodies in order to be visible to men and to converse with them. But those visible bodies were *human* bodies.[1] There are no angelic bodies. The ascription of wings to the angels is by a figure of speech.

The angels are not a race. In the case of mankind, God created the first pair, and commanded them to increase and replenish the earth. Thus Adam and Eve became the ancestors of all the other human beings who ever lived, and mankind constitutes a race, each member of which is related to the others. But the angels are an aggregate of individuals, each of whom must have been directly created by God. They are not male and female, and do not propagate their kind (Matt. 22:30).

Attributes. Being purely spiritual persons and not made up in any sense of matter, angels have the attributes of indivisibility, immutability, illocality and agility. They are indivisible, because as spirits they are simple entities. They are immutable and immortal, because there is in them no matter to undergo any process of change or decay. They are illocal and not subject to the limitations of space, because they are pure mind or spirit. They are agile, because as mind or spirit they can move with the greatest celerity. They are not, however, omnipresent. As creatures they are constantly dependent on God to sustain their being and their attributes. They possess according to the Scriptures much greater knowledge (Matt. 24:36) and much vaster power (2 Kings 19:35) than men, but they are nevertheless finite beings who are far removed from the omniscience and omnipotence of God.

There appear to be various ranks among the angels. There is mention in the Scriptures of archangels (1 Thess. 4:16; Jude 9), seraphim (Isa. 6:2), cherubim (Gen. 3:24), thrones,

---

[1] So the angels who appeared to Abraham and to Lot. Gen. 18; 19.

dominions, principalities and powers (Col. 1:16; Rom. 8:38; Eph. 3:10). But we have no definite knowledge concerning the nature of these ranks or gradations in the angelic hosts.

Good and Bad Angels. The angels at their creation were perfect and flawless beings. The statement that God saw everything that He had made, and behold, it was very good, includes the angelic creatures also. Endowed with freedom of will as personal beings, they were meant voluntarily to choose the service of God, and to persevere in it. Their original perfections were to be developed and increased by the practice of the right. Some of the angels used their freedom to serve God and do His will alone, thus fulfilling the purpose which God had in mind for them. Others, however, abused their freedom and acted in opposition to His will. As a result of this different attitude toward the will of God, the angels now find themselves in two widely different states. The good angels are in the state of glory, and the bad angels in the state of misery. If we take into account these two states together with their original condition, we may very properly consider the state of the angels under three heads: 1. The State of Innocence.[2] 2. The State of Glory. 3. The State of Misery.

The State of Innocence is that state in which all the angels found themselves immediately after their creation. The State of Glory is that state to which the good angels have attained by their persistent choice of the good. The State of Misery is that state into which the bad angels have plunged themselves by their antagonism to God.

[2] This state is usually called the State of Grace. But this nomenclature is unfortunate in view of the fact that the word "grace" must in that case be given a meaning entirely different from that which it bears elsewhere in theology, and particularly from that which it bears when the same term "State of Grace" is used with respect to man after he has been restored to God's favor by grace. In this case the angels had not yet fallen; and those who did afterwards fall never were and never will be received into a state of grace like man. It is better therefore to designate the original condition of the angels as the State of Innocence.

The relation of the angels in these various states to the matter of sin has been stated as follows: In the State of Innocence they were able to sin and able not to sin (*posse peccare et posse non peccare*). In the State of Glory the good angels are not able to sin (*non posse peccare*). In the State of Misery the bad angels are not able not to sin (*non posse non peccare*); that is, they are not able to do otherwise than sin.

The State of Innocence. In the State of Innocence all the angels were free to choose good or evil. They were endowed with a perfectly free will. They were all equally endowed with the ability to conform to God's will, and none of them had been fashioned with a bias toward evil. There was no defect of any kind in their nature which inclined them to sin or made it difficult to choose the right; nor was there any outward necessity compelling them to do wrong. The choice of good or evil was entirely within the power of the self-determination of each. The sin, therefore, which brought the first angel to a fall was entirely self-originated (John 8:44). Why such an angelic being as Satan originally was, who had no evil principle to tempt him from within and no evil person to tempt him from without, and who had every reason to choose God's service, nevertheless chose to do evil is the ultimate, unsolvable mystery of sin. Yet it is clear that not only Satan but a great number of other angels fell away from God. What their number is and what ratio it bears to the total number of angels created we do not know.

The State of Glory. In the State of Glory the good angels, in view of their constant choice of the good, have been advanced to a closer relationship with God than that which they possessed at the beginning, and they enjoy the beatific vision of God. (Matt. 18:10). They have also been so confirmed and established in righteousness that they are no longer able to sin, and cannot fall away from God. There is a law which God has established in connection with personality, and which therefore holds good in the angelic as well as in the human world, according to which repeated acts of good or evil engender habits which eventually become fixed. In accordance with this law God had bestowed upon the good angels the blessing of not being able to sin. This is no curtailment of their liberty, nor any interference with their self-determination. They are still able to choose what they will. But they never will choose anything but the good. This established bias of the mind toward the good is in reality the highest kind of freedom. Only he is truly free who is able to choose and always does choose to do that which he ought to do. Such is the freedom of God Himself.

Along with this advancement into the state of glory there has come to the good angels an increase in the powers of their original endowment. They are living examples of the happy results which follow from invariably using the divinely given powers and faculties in the manner which God intends. If their original knowledge was great, their present knowledge is far greater. If their original power of accomplishment was vast, their present power is still vaster. Through their persistence in the good all their glorious angelic endowments were made still more glorious.

The occupation of the good angels is that of worshiping and serving God (Dan. 7:10). They are sent out to minister to the godly (Heb. 1:14; Ps. 34:7) and to punish the wicked among men (Matt. 13:41). They will accompany Christ when He comes to judge the world (Matt. 25:31). They have no part, however, in carrying out the plan of salvation. The sphere of their activity is that of the natural world. Their appearance in human history has been especially prominent at crises in the revelation of redemption. That each human being has a special guardian angel, as some have assumed, cannot be proved from Scripture.

Angels are not to be worshiped (Rev. 19:10), since they are creatures as well as ourselves, and God alone is to be worshiped. The distinction made by the Roman and Greek churches between invoking the aid of angels and worshiping them is untenable, since such invocation assumes the possession by angels of attributes which belong to God alone.

The State of Misery. The State of Misery into which the bad angels have fallen is one of eternal persistence in sin and of eternal rejection by God. As we have seen, their fall was not due to any necessity from within or to any compulsion from without, but solely to a self-originated apostasy from God. What the nature of their sin was we are not told. It is surmised that it was some act of pride (1 Tim. 3:6). In any case it was an elevation of their own will against God's, and this necessarily involved pride of some kind.

The number of angels who fell appears to have been very great. When Satan sinned, he evidently persuaded many other angels to do likewise. For there is a real kingdom of evil spirits with Satan at their head. He is the prince of darkness, and under him are principalities, powers and rulers of the darkness of this world (Eph. 6:12).

It is evident from the temptation in Eden, that the apostasy of the evil angels preceded the fall of man; but by how much, we do not know. Apparently it took place at some time after the six days' work of creation; for at the end of the sixth day "God looked on all that He had made, and behold, it was very good." This statement seems to imply that the fall of the evil angels had not yet taken place.

By their fall the evil angels did not cease to be angels nor lose their angelic endowment. But their heavenly glory was lost, and the luster of their endowment was gone. Their knowledge is still great, but the keenness of their minds has suffered much as a result of their sin, and their reasoning is often defective. Thus the devil made a futile attempt to cause Christ to sin in the wilderness (Matt. 4:1 seq.) and apparently had a mistaken notion that he could wreck God's plan by crucifying Jesus (1 Cor. 2:7, 8). To conclude, however, as was sometimes the fashion in the Middle Ages, that the devil is stupid and can easily be outwitted and made a dupe is a great mistake. He is still possessed of great intelligence, cunning and resourcefulness (2 Cor. 11:3, 14), and our spiritual safety depends on constant vigilance against his wiles (1 Pet. 5:8).

The power of the bad angels is still very great, but God sets bounds which they cannot overpass. Hence, fiercely as they hate man and seek his destruction, they cannot harm him in temporal matters without God's permission (Job 1:12), and cannot hurt his soul without the consent of man's own will.

By their fall the bad angels have come under the enduring wrath and condemnation of God (2 Pet. 2:4), and will reap the full measure of their deserts at the judgment (Jude 6). They shall all be punished eternally (Matt. 25:41). No provision has been made for the salvation of any fallen angels. The Son of God took on Him the nature of man, but not that of angelic beings (Heb. 2:16). Since God is a God of infinite love, it is a fair inference that He would have sought to save the fallen angels, if they had been salvable. There must, therefore, be in the nature of their apostasy from God something radically different from the sin of man. For sinful, wicked, hostile to God, and indeed dead in trespasses and sins as man is by nature, he yet has the capacity for salvation, and is capable of being saved by divine grace. But the evil angels cannot be saved. Their sin was self-originated; man's came by temptation from without. Their sin is a choice of evil as evil; man's is a choice of evil for the sake of the good which he supposes he will gain in profit or pleasure. The devils are without a conscience; man still has a conscience, and the good can still make an appeal to him. The devils have as their motto, "Evil be thou my good; falsehood be thou my truth." If man ever becomes diabolical in his sin and chooses evil and falsehood for their own sakes, he is beyond all hope of salvation because he is then beyond all hope of repentance; his conscience is dead, and he has committed the unpardonable sin. This sin, which involves absolute deadness, not mere slumber or obtuseness, of conscience, is fortunately rare among men. It has not been committed by those who feel any compunctions for sin.

The disposition of the fallen angels toward God is one of absolute and persistent hatred and hostility. They are banded together in a kingdom of darkness whose purpose is to antagonize God in all things, and particularly to frustrate His gracious will toward men (Matt. 13:19; 2 Cor. 4:4). This malignant purpose of the evil angels finds its chief representative in Satan who stands at their head.

Satan. That Satan is a person and not an evil principle in man is evident from every mention of him in Scripture. It is expressly stated, for example, that it was Satan who tempted Peter to deny Christ (Luke 22:31), who put it into the heart of Judas Iscariot to betray Him (John 13:2), and who filled the heart of Ananias to lie to the Holy Ghost (Acts 5:3). Christ had no evil principle in Him; and yet He was tempted by the devil for forty days and forty nights in the wilderness.

On the one hand, Satan's attacks are aimed at the individual. We are therefore exhorted to put on the whole armor of God, that we may prevail against him (Eph. 6:11). He appears sometimes as an angel of light to delude (2 Cor. 11:14), and sometimes as a roaring lion to intimidate and overwhelm (1 Pet. 5:8). Safety is found only in constant vigilance and prayer. On the other hand, his attacks are also aimed at the Church and its Means of Grace. He seems at times to threaten its very existence. But the promise is, that the gates of hell shall not prevail against it (Matt. 16:18).

CHAPTER VI

MAN IN HIS STATE OF INTEGRITY

Man's Five States. Viewing the history of mankind as a whole, it is customary to recognize five states of man: 1. The State of Innocence or Integrity. 2. The State of Sin or Corruption. 3. The State of Grace. 4. The State of Glory. 5. The State of Misery.

The State of Innocence or Integrity is that state in which man was found immediately after his creation. The State of Sin or Corruption is the state into which he fell by his transgression of God's command. The State of Grace is that in which he is found when he has been brought to faith in the Redeemer. The State of Glory is that in which the believer will be found in the world to come. And the State of Misery is that in which the impenitent and unbelieving will be found in the next world.

Man's Original State. By the State of Innocence or Integrity we understand, then, the original state of man before sin entered into his life and blighted his nature. In this state he was in full possession of all his endowments, faculties and attributes in their original power and perfection (Gen. 1:31). His body was not only perfectly formed and exquisitely fashioned to be the organ of the soul, but there were in it no seeds of corruption, decay or mortality. His intellectual powers were perfectly adapted to the accomplishment of the purposes for which they were designed, and were not subject to the weaknesses and errors which characterize them in his fallen state. His sensibilities were keen, sensitive and normal, free from bias and

97

fault. His will was perfectly free, capable of acting, as it should, in complete harmony with God's.

Dichotomy and Trichotomy. Considerable difference of opinion has prevailed as to whether man is composed of two parts, body and soul, or whether he is composed of three parts, body, soul and spirit. Accordingly, we have what are called the dichotomist and the trichotomist theories.

The Trichotomists claim that man is made up of three parts: body, soul and spirit.[1] An endeavor is made to substantiate this theory from the Scriptures.[2] Soul and spirit are supposed to be distinct. God breathed the spirit into man, and the soul is the result of the union of the body and the spirit. But soul and spirit are treated in Scripture as being really identical.[3] The dividing asunder of soul and spirit spoken of in the Epistle to the Hebrews (4:12) is not an argument for the tripartite nature of man, but a figure of speech by which the author seeks to show the deep and searching power of God's Word. The fact that he also speaks of the Word as dividing asunder the joints and the marrow shows that his language is figurative.

The Dichotomists, on the other hand, hold that man is composed of body and soul, or of body and spirit. Soul and spirit are regarded as two words for essentially the same thing. In ordinary speech and in Scripture the two terms are generally used as synonyms, though they may be employed to emphasize two distinct aspects of man's nature. The word "soul" or "mind" refers more to the psychological aspect of man's spiritual nature, while the word "spirit" refers to his religious relation to God. We are conscious of our spiritual or psychic selves

[1] Comp. Plato's theory that man is composed of the νοῦς or reason, the θυμός or spirit, and the σῶμα or body.
[2] Among the modern defenders of this theory are Olshausen, Meyer, Delitzsch and others.
[3] See Matt. 10:28; 27:50; Eccl. 12:7; Acts 20:10; 1 Pet. 3:19; Rev. 6:9; 20:4; Heb. 12:23.

as a single entity. The soul cannot be distinguished from the spirit even in its religious relationships, since the same intellectual, emotional and volitional faculties are employed in religion as in other activities. Accordingly, the Lutheran theologians quite generally and with few exceptions accept the dichotomist theory.[4]

The Soul. The soul or spirit is the immaterial part of man, which inhabits and moves the body, and which constitutes man's real self. It is an entity created by God. It is not a part of God's Spirit, nor God's Spirit dwelling in man, nor God coming to consciousness in man. Nor on the other hand is it the result of the functioning of the matter of the brain, nor a heap of sensations, nor simply a stream of consciousness. It is a finite spiritual being made in God's image, and like Him possessed of self-consciousness and self-determination.

Self-determination on the part of man is denied by materialists, pantheists and agnostics. According to them man is not self-determining, but is determined just as is the brute. This contention, however, runs counter to the consciousness of men and to the methods of human speech. Human language really becomes practically unintelligible if freedom of will is denied. Man is conscious that he determines himself, and that he might or could have done differently in this case or that. Indeed, he often bitterly regrets that he did not act differently, and his regret would be utterly senseless if he were not conscious that he might have acted differently.

The possession of personality, with self-consciousness and self-determination, gives to man his peculiar dignity compared with all the other creatures of earth. It is this which gives him

[4] So Luther, the old dogmaticians, Harless, Thomasius, Kahnis, Tholuck, Luthardt, etc. It is the theory which underlies Luther's explanation of the first article of the Creed in the Small Cathechism: "I believe that God . . . has given to me my body and soul."

capacity for morality and religion. As a person he is capable of communion with God and of moral action, and is accountable to God for what he does.

The Body. While the body is in a sense only the abode of the soul, it is nevertheless an essential part of man. It is true, in the intermediate state between death and the resurrection, the soul exists without the body; but that state is abnormal, and will come to an end when the body is raised from the dead and reunited with the soul. The body is not to be regarded as a fetter from which the soul seeks release as a deliverance from sin; for sin lies not in the body, but in the soul. The body has a dignity all its own, because it is the creation of God, and is the object of His providential care; because it is a wondrously fashioned dwelling place for the soul; and because the Son of God assumed a body as well as a soul when He became man to redeem us. The body is not the seat of sin, and becomes an organ of sin only when so used by the soul. Sin is a defect, not in matter, but in the will. The body is marvelously adapted to be the natural organism through which the soul functions. How well adapted it is, we can realize best if we consider what a handicap it would be to the soul if it were furnished with the body of a horse or of some other beast.

According to the evolutionary theory the body of man was developed through that of lower animals by an age-long process from an original protoplasm, and the soul is merely the superior development of the intelligence of the brute. Man's intelligence is, however, of an entirely different and higher order; for man possesses mental powers and capacities of which the brutes possess not even the rudiments, notably the power of generalizing and forming concepts, and the moral and religious activities of the soul. Man is a new kind of being whom God created after the rest of creation had been finished and the world was ready for this superior order of creature.

The nature of the union between soul and body is a profound mystery which no theories have been able satisfactorily to explain. How, for example, a visual impression on the retina of the eye, which is a purely material thing, becomes translated into a mental idea, which is a purely spiritual thing, none can tell. The statement sometimes made that the presence of the soul in the body is not local but definitive is merely a confession of ignorance, and furnishes no real information as to the relation between the two.

The Origin of Souls. The question of the present origin of souls has been answered in a threefold way: by the theories of Preëxistence, Creationism and Traducianism.

The Preëxistence theory maintains that all souls were created by God in the beginning, and that these souls enter into the bodies propagated by human parentage.[5] It involves the necessity of a fall of all human souls in a preëxistent state, and thus stands in conflict with the account of the fall in Genesis 3, and with Romans 5:12-18.

Creationism maintains that only the body is propagated by the parents, and that a new soul is created by God for each new child. But according to this theory it would follow, either that there is no original sin, or that it inheres in the body, or else that God creates sinful souls and is thus the author of sin. Since sin inheres in the personality and not in the body, and since God cannot be Scripturally conceived of as the author of sin, the theory of Creationism is not tenable. In addition to these objections, the theory really stands in conflict with the unity of the race and its descent from the first pair.

Traducianism or Generationism holds that both the body and the soul of the child are propagated by the parents. This theory

[5] This theory has been advocated by Plato, Philo, Origen, Kant, Fichte, Schelling, Schleiermacher, Jul. Mueller, Coleridge, Wordsworth and others.

[6] This theory has been held by Aristotle, Ambrose, Jerome, the Greek and Roman Churches, by many Reformed theologians, and by a few Lutherans, as for example, by Brentz and Calixtus.

is in harmony with the implication of numerous Scripture passages that body and soul are derived from the parents,[7] and with the teaching of Scripture concerning the unity of the race and the universality of inherited sin. It is corroborated by the experience of the race, which shows that not only physical but mental characteristics are inherited by children from their parents. There is, of course, a sense in which God creates the child, soul and body; but it is a mediate creation through second causes.[8]

Mankind a Race. Mankind is a race, a brotherhood descended from the first pair. The great differences in physiognomy and color found in various races of men are difficult to account for in detail, but are to be explained in general as the result of different climatic conditions, modes of life, etc. The Scriptural teaching concerning the unity of the race is clear (Gen. 3:20), and finds corroboration in a number of factors common to all mankind, such as a common psychology with identical mental processes, general agreement in the principles underlying the various languages, the similarity of traditions current in various parts of the world, and the universal religiousness of mankind. These things make the unity of the race very probable.[9] The certainty of that unity is known from the clear teaching of Scripture not only with regard to the origin of mankind but also with regard to the universality of inherited sin and of the universality of divine redemption.

The Image of God. The Scriptural account of creation declares that God made man in his own image, after His own likeness (Gen. 1:26). Since God has no body but is pure spirit

[7] See Gen. 1:28; 5:3; Ps. 51:5; Job 14:4; Acts 17:21-26.
[8] In this sense the Formula of Concord is to be understood when it declares "that not only has God before the fall created human nature, but that also since the fall it is a creature and work of God." *Jacobs,* Book of Concord, p. 545. In this sense Luther also in his Small Catechism speaks of God as having given us body and soul.
[9] Hence the unity of mankind has been held by such men as Buffon, Cuvier, Blumenbach, Humboldt and many geographers and historians.

(John 4:24), the likeness referred to is not bodily but spiritual. What, then, is meant by the image of God? The term is used in two senses, which should be carefully distinguished. There are passages of Scripture which speak of the image of God as something which man still possesses (Gen. 9:6; James 3:9); and there are other passages which speak of it as something which must be restored, and hence as something which has been lost (Col. 3:10; Eph. 4:24). The image of God which has not been lost but is still retained by man refers to his very constitution as a man, and is called the metaphysical or substantial image. The image of God which has been lost by the fall and needs to be restored by divine grace refers to the moral perfection which characterized man in his original state, and is called the moral or accidental image. We distinguish, therefore, between the metaphysical and the moral image of God. The former is sometimes called the image of God in the wide sense; the latter, the image of God in the narrow sense.

The Metaphysical Image. By the metaphysical image of God we mean that man is a person, just as God is a person. God made man on a finite scale the same kind of being that He Himself is on an infinite scale. God is the Absolute and Perfect Personality; man is a finite personality. The fundamental difference between man, who was made in God's image, and the brute, who was not so made, consists in personality; man is a person, while the brute is not a person. And while man lost much by the fall into sin, he did not lose the metaphysical image of God; otherwise he would have ceased to be a person, would have sunk to the level of the brute, and would thus have become incapable of religion or morality.

The Moral Image and Its Loss. The Moral image refers to the concreated perfection which belonged to man in his original state. He was not only created a person, but he was created a morally perfect finite personality. He was morally the image of God because he was without fault or sin. The particular factors of which this original moral image consisted may be learned from the two classic passages of the New Testament which refer to the need of the restoration of that image (Col. 3:10; Eph. 4:24). Man needs to be "renewed in knowledge after the image of Him that created him," and he needs to "put on the new man which after God is created in righteousness and true holiness." The characteristic marks of the moral image of God possessed by man before the fall were, therefore, knowledge, righteousness and holiness. These constituted the image of God in the moral sense.

This moral image of God has been lost by the fall, and needs to be restored by divine grace. Once a good person, man has become by the fall a bad or sinful person. The purpose of the divine redemption in Christ is to restore in man the lost moral image of God. That restoration is begun in man's regeneration and sanctification here on earth, and is completed in his glorification and perfection in the world to come.

It is important to bear in mind these two senses in which the term image of God is used in Scripture and theology, in order to avoid confusion and misunderstanding. In his state of integrity man possessed both the metaphysical and the moral image of God. Since the fall he still possesses the metaphysical image and remains a person; but he has lost the moral image and has become an imperfect and sinful person. His knowledge, natural and spiritual, has become obscured. The righteousness and holiness which characterized his original state are gone. He has lost the freedom of will which originally enabled him to will in harmony with God's will. The love which characterized his relation with God is replaced by alienation.

The perfections denoted by the moral image which belonged to man in his original state were concreated. They were not added to him after his creation as a *donum superadditum* or supplementary gift, as the Roman Catholic Church maintains. In his original state those perfections were natural to him, and not a supernatural addition. When a circle is drawn, the true circularity is drawn at once with the circle, and not added to the circle afterwards. To regard the original perfection of man as a superadded gift minimizes the consequences of the fall and the seriousness of original sin.

The happy state of being, physical, mental and spiritual, denoted by the moral image of God is one which man would have transmitted to his descendants, if he had not fallen into sin. Like begets like. And when man had lost the excellencies which we have enumerated, he could not transmit them to his descendants. What he actually does transmit is a lack of those excellencies and a natural bent or inclination toward evil, which will be considered in the following chapter.

The importance of the doctrine of the original integrity of man and of a subsequent fall into sin is fundamental. It is because man has fallen from his original state of perfect communion with God that redemption is necessary and has been provided by God. If, instead of a fall from an original state of holiness, it is assumed, as it is for example by the evolutionists, that man's history has been one of continuous progress upward, then there is no need of redemption. For then there is no sin from which man needs to be redeemed; and final perfection will be reached by the human race when the natural process of evolution has been completed. Such a theory, of course, runs counter to the whole teaching of the divine Word, in which the great basic facts of religion are on the one hand the sin of man, and on the other hand the grace of God which saves him from his sin. "Where sin abounded grace did much more abound" (Rom. 5:20). This is the comforting message of the Gospel.

CHAPTER VII

MAN IN HIS STATE OF SIN

In contrast with man's original state of innocence and integrity, the human race now finds itself in a state of corruption or sin. This state is universal, and includes all the descendants of Adam and Eve except the Lord Jesus Christ, who was sinless because He had God alone for His Father.

The origin of sin, as we have already seen, is not to be traced to God as its author, but to the self-determination of the creature. God neither created sinful beings, nor decreed that any should sin. On the contrary He desired that all his personal creatures should live in perfect communion and fellowship with Him. And when sin made its appearance in the world, it was because the personal creature by his own voluntary act turned away from God. First came the self-originated sin of the devil, and then came the sin of man when he yielded to the temptation of the devil.

The First Sin. The record of man's first sin is given in the third chapter of Genesis. The story of the fall which it recounts has been familiar to us from childhood. God placed Adam and Eve in the Garden of Eden, and gave them permission to eat of the fruit of every tree but one. Of this one God said, "Thou shalt not eat of it; for in the day that thou eatest thereof thou shalt surely die." Man was in a position to obey this command, and should have done so. He had freedom of will, and that involved ability to obey or to disobey. But Satan entered upon the scene in the guise of a serpent, and tempted Eve, and she fell. Eve gave of the forbidden fruit to Adam, and he ate of it also. Thus sin entered into the world "with all our woe," because man abused his freedom and set up his own will instead of God's as his norm.

This record of the first sin is not a poetic fancy, a myth or an allegory, as some have maintained; nor an act marking the transition of man from the animal stage to reason; nor a step in the process of evolutionary development, a fall upward.[1] On the contrary, it is a record of fact, and is recognized as such in the New Testament.[2] Its historical character is corroborated by the fact that it accounts for sin in such a way as to trace it back to man's self-determination, and yet to a self-determination influenced from without. If man's sin had originated entirely in himself and not through temptation from without, his fall would have been like that of the devil, and, like him, he would have been unsalvable. But man after the fall was still capable of being saved; and his fall was followed immediately by the *protevangelion* with its announcement of divine redemption for him (Gen. 3:15).

The eating of an "apple" seems to some persons to have been entirely too trivial an act to have involved all the consequences that have been ascribed to it. But it was by no means a trivial act; for it was one by which Adam and Eve set up their own wills in opposition to God's; and such an act of the mind, no matter how trivial its outward expression may appear to be, is

[1] Philo, Clement Alexandrinus, Origen and others regard the account as true, but only in an allegorical sense. Others regard it as a myth which describes the manner in which man rose to the use of his free reason. Schiller called the fall the first adventure of reason, the first beginning of moral existence, the happiest event in human history. Hegel says in his *Philosophy of History*, "Paradise is a park where only brutes, not men, can remain. For the brute is one with God only implicitly. Only man's spirit has a self-cognizant existence. This existence for self, this consciousness, is at the same time separation from the Universal and Divine Spirit. The Fall is therefore the eternal Mythus of Man —in fact, the very transition by which he becomes a man."

[2] That Paul regarded the fall as an historical occurrence is evident from his references to it in Rom. 5:12; 2 Cor. 11:3; and 1 Tim. 2:14.

of the most tremendous significance. For by it man, in defiance of God, set out for himself on a path of his own choosing.

It has also been suggested by some persons that it was, to say the least, unkind in God to place that forbidden tree in the Garden, and that if He had left it out, all would have been well. But the placing of that tree there and the command not to eat of it were in reality acts of the greatest kindness on God's part. A personal being must make the decision for right or for wrong; he cannot escape the choice. If the choice had not been placed before man in the form in which it was, he could not have escaped the necessity of choosing in other ways. The tree represented essentially that which was forbidden as over against that which was allowed—a distinction which is bound to run all through the life of an ethical being. There is no conceivable test of the voluntary obedience of Adam and Eve which would have been easier to meet than the one which God placed before them. All the fruit of the garden was theirs except that of this one tree. The eating of this one fruit would bring death, and they were therefore commanded to refrain from eating it.[3] Was this a hard test of obedience? Is it difficult for a sane man to refrain from eating a substance labeled poison, when he is surrounded by an abundance of things which are good and harmless to eat? Yet Adam and Eve, surrounded by trees laden with fruit of which they were permitted to eat as much as they would, ate of the one tree of which a truthful God had told them that if they ate of it they would surely die.

The nature of the temptation which Satan brought to bear on Eve is worthy of notice, inasmuch as it is typical of his general method of approach. He appealed to the lust of the eye— the "food was pleasant to the eyes"; to the lust of the flesh —"it was good for food"; and to the pride of life—it was

---

[3] The forbidden fruit is supposed by some to have been literally poisonous, but there is no real occasion for such an assumption.

"desirable to make one wise." The devil's method of dealing with God's Word was also typical. He suggested a doubt of God's Word; he denied its truth; and he perverted it to suit his purposes.[4]

The Sin of Adam. The first sin is called in the Scriptures and in theology the sin of Adam. It is doubtless called so, because Adam was the head of the race. Furthermore, it must be borne in mind that Adam's sin was not committed in ignorance and as a result of deception, as was his wife's. Eve believed what the devil told her; she was deceived. But Adam was not deceived. He knew what he was doing when he accepted the fruit from Eve's hand (1 Tim. 2:14). His act is probably to be explained by the fact that he realized what Eve had done, and that rather than lose her he decided that he would share her fate by eating of the forbidden tree also. It was a case of loving Eve more than God.

It has been suggested that if Eve alone had sinned and not Adam, God would have created another wife for him to take Eve's place; or that if she had continued to live and to be his wife, his descendants would not have inherited sin, because he was sinless. But this is useless speculation, for the simple reason that Adam actually did sin.

The Punishment. The consequences that followed upon the first sin are indicated in the threat which God added to His prohibition. They are all included in the one word "death." This death which our first parents incurred was death in the whole extent and scope of the word—physical, spiritual and eternal.

Physical Death. By his sin Adam incurred physical death. Apparently death followed after a long interval; for he lived over nine hundred years. But as a matter of fact, it followed at once, because he became a dying man the very moment he

---

[4] Compare the temptation of Christ by Satan, Matt. 4:1-11.

ate of the forbidden fruit. It took him a long time to die; but the seeds of death were now in him. He who a moment before was immortal, now had become mortal. The process of decay set in at once. The many years which elapsed before the actual dissolution of soul and body took place may be explained by the fact that man's original constitution was perfect; that no long history of sin had weakened his powers of resistance to disease; and that no such development of disease germs and hurtful bacteria as has since then taken place existed at that time to endanger his health. But his body eventually succumbed to the forces of mortality and corruption which had taken root in him, and he died.

Spiritual Death. By his sin Adam incurred spiritual death. By his act of transgression he severed himself spiritually from God the source of life, and was involved in all the consequences of such an act. His communion or fellowship with God was broken off. As a branch that is severed from the tree is dead because the life of the tree no longer courses through it, and remains dead unless it is grafted back into the tree, so man severed from God by sin is spiritually dead and remains dead unless grafted back into God through faith in Christ Jesus. He does not and cannot live again spiritually until he is born again by the gracious operation of the Holy Spirit.

Eternal Death. By his sin Adam incurred eternal death; for eternal death is after all only the eternal continuation of spiritual death. In every case in which the spiritual death is not replaced by spiritual life, the spiritual death continues and becomes eternal. The unregenerate sinner is spiritually dead in this world and the next. It is the same death there as here, only eternally extended. In this world it is still possible for the sinner to be saved from death by divine grace; in the next world his salvation will no longer be possible, and his fate will be sealed forever.

Far-reaching Consequences. By the fall man, as observed in the preceding chapter, lost the moral image of God, that is, his original moral perfection. He still remained a person, and thus continued to possess the metaphysical image. But the moral image was gone; and the loss of it not only made man guilty and subjected him to punishment, but left him in a ruined and helpless state in which he could never by any efforts of his own regain what he had lost. The moral image of God is for mankind a lost treasure until the Holy Spirit graciously restores it by renewing man in knowledge, righteousness and holiness.

The far-reaching consequences of the fall are seen in man's entire nature and in all his relations. Physically he not only became mortal, but he became subject to sickness, pain and sorrow. Mentally his powers suffered deterioration and enfeeblement; for while the history of the world shows that man still possesses wonderful intellectual powers, these would have been vastly greater if they had not been dimmed by the fall. Morally and religiously man became alienated from God; he was no longer able by his natural powers to perceive spiritual things (1 Cor. 2:14); his sensibilities were perverted, so that his love was centered on the world and on self instead of on God (Rom. 8:7); and his will was helpless in spiritual matters, so that he was no longer able to do God's will (Rom. 8:8). Viewed with regard to man's inner state of well-being and comfort, the consequences of the fall were an evil conscience, inner contradiction, and the misery resulting from the introduction of a fundamental discord into his nature. Viewed with regard to his relation to God, the consequences were guilt and condemnation (Rom. 6:23), separation from God (Isa. 59:2), and the prospect of endless misery in the world to come (Matt. 25:46).

The Nature of Sin. Having considered the entrance of sin into the world, let us now inquire concerning its nature. Sin may be defined as the opposition of the human will to the divine. This opposition exists in man as a state of the will and also as particular acts of the will. Sin is found wherever a personal being is not morally the kind of being he ought to be, or does not do morally what he ought to do. There is such a thing as being in a wrong moral condition, as well as being guilty of wrong or sinful actions. To find sin only in words and deeds, and not in the state of the heart, is to ascribe a superficial and external character to morality which is utterly untrue and unscriptural (Matt. 15:19). There is an adultery of the eye (Matt. 5:28), and there is a murder of the heart (1 John 3:15), as well as of outward deeds. The sum and substance of the moral law is, not that we shall do or omit this or that outward act, but that we shall love God with all our heart and mind and strength, and our neighbor as ourselves (Matt. 22:37-39). And this love is a matter of the heart. When it is present, the good outward action will follow; but when it is absent, what seems like a good outward act is not a good act at all (1 Cor. 13:1-3).

Located in the Will. Sin can and does exist only in a personal being. The brute cannot sin, because he is simply a brute and has no moral constitution. In the last analysis sin is located in the self-determination or will. It is essentially the deflection of the will, so that it acts at an angle or at cross-purposes with God's will. Since man is a self-determining being and therefore the real author of his own acts, any antagonism on the part of his will against God's is sin.

The State of Sin, therefore, is that state in which man's will is in antagonism to God's, and the will of self instead of the will of God is the norm of action. Sin may and does exist where there is no conscious and deliberate purpose to disobey God. For where the will by nature is deflected, as it were, from the vertical plane, it is naturally in a state of disharmony and opposition to God; and when it acts, it is bound to act in opposition to Him, even when there is no deliberate purpose to do so. The very deflection of the will into a chronic state of opposition is a sinful state, and one which ought not to exist. Men utterly fail to apprehend the profound significance of sin when they fail to conceive of its nature as a state as well as an act. Original Sin is the term employed to designate the chronic state of antagonism of the will; and Actual Sin is the term employed to designate individual antagonistic acts of the will.

Sin, being located in the will and being found only in personal beings, is not an entity or substance, but an evil quality in a person. It is not a substance of which man now is composed; but it is, in the technical sense of the word, an accident in man. Though unchanged in substance, man became qualitatively a quite different person after the fall from what he was before.

Sin therefore is not something whose existence can be explained by supposing it to inhere in matter. Ascetic practices which aim to overcome sin by cruel treatment of the body miss the mark. Many sins, such as pride, envy and hatred are purely spiritual in kind. Sin is in the mind or soul, and the body is only the organ which the mind uses to carry out its sinful purposes.

The determinists would explain sin as the result of an inner necessity, and therefore as not really sin. Thus for the pantheist, sin is only a defect due to finiteness and hence unavoidable —a dissonance preparing the way for a sweeter harmony to follow. For the evolutionist the fall was a fall upward, and sin is a necessary and passing stage in the evolution of man toward perfection. For the theological determinist sin is the result of the divine decree of predestination. All these varieties of determinism take away from man that responsibility for sin which as a self-determining being he cannot escape. His sins are his own acts in opposition to God's will, and for this reason they are sin.

The New Testament names for sin throw much light upon its nature. Thus 'αμαϱτία denotes a missing of the mark; παϱάπτωμα, a fall; 'ανομία, lawlessness; παϱάβασις, transgression; 'αδικία, unrighteousness; κακία, wickedness. Each of these names emphasizes some particular feature inherent in sin.

It follows from the very nature of sin that it is displeasing to God and incurs his wrath and condemnation. For His will is the law for all His creatures. Sin is a breaking of that law and a setting up of self-will as the law of conduct—a law of conduct which can, in the very nature of the case, work only havoc and ruin in a moral world, and which God therefore must punish. The fact that sin brings guilt and deserves punishment is not only clearly taught in God's Word, but is attested by every man's own conscience.

Kinds of Sin. Sin is of two kinds, which are called respectively Original Sin and Actual Sin. The term Original Sin was used by the old dogmaticians in two senses, which they named Original Sin Originating and Original Sin Originated. By the former is meant the original or first sin committed by Adam and Eve in the Garden of Eden. By the latter is meant the sinful condition which we have inherited as a result of that first sin. For the sake of clearness, however, it will be better to call the former The First Sin, and to reserve the term Original Sin for the latter.

Original Sin designates the sinful state or condition which man inherits as a result of his descent from sinful ancestors. The term is useful, though not Biblical. Actual sin is a sin of act, performed with a greater or lesser participation of the will. By naming such sins "actual" we do not mean that they are the only real sins, or that original sin is not real sin. Both kinds are real sin. But we mean by the term "actual sin" simply that it is a sin which is committed by an act of mind or body.

Actual sins are not confined to sins of *action,* but include mental acts. There are sins of thought as well as of word and deed.

Original Sin. Original sin is the natural sinful condition of men inherited from Adam, and consisting of a lack of righteousness, a constant inclination to evil, and an inability to know or do the will of God. In the Augsburg Confession[5] the following definition of original sin is given: "Since the fall of Adam, all men begotten after the common course of nature are born with sin; that is, without the fear of God and without trust in Him, and with concupiscence; and this disease or original fault is truly sin, condemning and bringing eternal death now also upon all that are not born again by baptism and the Holy Spirit." This is an exceedingly illuminating definition, though one could wish that Melanchthon had added the word love to the fear and trust which he declares are wanting in the natural heart. For love is the fulfillment of the law, and the lack of love in the natural heart is the very essence of original sin. The word love is, however, implied in the word trust.

Negatively, therefore, original sin may be described as consisting of the absence of that fear, love and trust toward God which ought to be in the heart; and positively, as consisting of the presence of concupiscence or evil desire which ought not to be there. This concupiscence refers to evil desires of every kind, and not merely to carnal lusts.

Original Sin Inherited. The fall of Adam made him a sinner and left him in a state of moral alienation from God. The consequences of his sin made themselves felt in all parts of his nature, and particularly in what may be described as his moral and religious nature. His whole relation to God was reversed:

[5] Article II.

he was now in heart at enmity with God (Rom. 8:7), and being guilty was under God's wrath and condemnation (Ezek. 18:4). The change in Adam affected his descendants (Rom. 5:12, 19).⁶ A sinner cannot propagate sinless persons. "That which is born of the flesh is flesh" (John 3:6). Like produces like. Hence the first sin was of profound significance not only for Adam but for the race. As a result of the fall in Eden sin has been passed on as an inheritance to Adam's descendants (Rom. 5:19).

Original Sin is universal.⁷ It belongs, as the Augsburg Confession says, to all who are born after the common course of nature. Christ is the one exception, because He was not born after the common course of nature, but was born of a virgin, with God alone for His Father. All others are conceived and

---

⁶ The later dogmaticians, beginning with Calovius, distinguished between what they called the immediate imputation and the mediate imputation of Adam's sin (Schmid, *Doctrinal Theology of the Lutheran Church*, p. 263). By immediate imputation they meant that, antecedently to any question concerning inherited corruption, Adam's sin in Eden was directly imputed to his individual descendants, because they were all in him as the head of the race, and thus his act was their act. But Adam was an individual man, not a collection of individuals. The individuals of the human race were not actually but only potentially in him. There is no warrant in Scripture for this doctrine of an immediate imputation; and the confessions do not teach it.

Related to this doctrine is that of Cocceius of Leyden, who maintained that Adam was the federal head of the race; that God entered into a covenant with him, in which Adam should endure a moral probation as the representative of the race; and that his obedience or disobedience should be counted as that of all his descendants. But this theory also lacks Scriptural basis.

By mediate imputation the dogmaticians meant that Adam's sin is imputed to us through the original sin which we have inherited from him, and which constitutes us guilty before God. This teaching concerning a mediate imputation is Scriptural (Rom. 5:12 seq.; 1 Cor. 15:22).

The existence of original sin is to be explained as the inevitable result of our descent from sinful ancestors. And the guilt of original sin is to be explained by the fact that original sin is a wrong moral state.

⁷ The universality of sin is an established teaching of the Old and the New Testaments. See such O. T. passages as 1 Kings 8:46; Ps. 14:3; 143:2; Prov. 20:9; Job 14:4; Eccl. 7:20. The consciousness of sin finds expression in the rite of circumcision and the sacrifices of the Old Testament. See also such N. T. passages as Matt. 7:11; Rom. 3:23; 1 John 5:19. It is implied in the universality of redemption. Sin has its roots in the corrupt nature with which man is born, Gen. 6:3; 8:21; Ps. 51:5; Matt. 15:19; John 3:6; Rom. 5:12 seq.; 7:7 seq.

born in sin. Children are innocent when compared with adults. But the germs of sin are in them and manifest themselves as soon as the children become old enough to perform voluntary acts. The fact that children die is a proof that they are sinful beings (Rom. 5:12).

Original Sin Really Sin. Original Sin is really sin, because it constitutes a state of separation and alienation from God. Righteousness consists essentially in being what we ought to be; and Sin consists essentially in being what we ought not to be. Hence the question of sin is one of condition or state, rather than one of particular acts growing out of that state. Man's will and all his powers and faculties ought to be in harmony with God. But in man's natural state they are not; on the contrary they are set in opposition and antagonism to Him. In the very nature of the case, God cannot be pleased with nor look with complacency on a human being whose whole nature has been warped by sin into a state of crookedness and opposition to Him.

"This disease or original fault is therefore truly sin," and places every man as he is by nature under the wrath and condemnation of God. The lack of inner righteousness and the constant inclination and tendency to sin, leading inevitably to actual sin as soon as man is old enough to act, necessarily make man the object of God's displeasure, and render it necessary for man to be redeemed and regenerated before God can take any pleasure in him. Original sin is a deep corruption and not a superficial taint of man's nature. The Formula of Concord * thus describes its far-reaching blight: "It is a deep, wicked, horrible, fathomless, inscrutable and unspeakable corruption of the entire nature and all its powers, especially in the highest principal powers of the soul, in understanding, heart and will." It has not become man's nature; but it is in the true sense natu-

* *Jacobs;* Book of Concord, p. 542.

ral to him, inasmuch as every human being is born with it.[9] And man never becomes free from it as long as he dwells on earth. When he has become a new man through the grace of God in Christ Jesus, the reign of sin in him has been broken, and he has obtained power to resist his evil propensities; but he never in this world ceases to have the old evil nature dwell in him alongside of the new nature implanted by grace. And between these two natures there will in this world always be a strenuous and unceasing conflict, as St. Paul shows in the seventh chapter of Romans. Through Christ the Christian is freed from the guilt and punishment of original sin, as well as from that of actual sin; but the inclination to sin remains in him as long as he lives in this world, and must continually be fought against.

This deep corruption of nature is, as we have seen, common to all men.[10] But not all men are equally under its sway. The believers are not controlled by it, but by the Spirit of Christ, even though the old nature continually seeks to assert itself.

Absence of Moral Image. Original sin involves the absence in us, as in Adam after the fall, of the divine image in the moral sense of the term. Man now lacks the moral perfection

[9] Original sin, like original righteousness which it has replaced, is an accident and not the substance of human nature. It is a quality in man, and not his constitutive essence. The error of Flacius, who maintained that original sin is the substance of human nature, was one into which he fell in his intense desire to combat those who minimized original sin and its effects. But the far-reaching and destructive effects of original sin may be maintained on the correct basis that it is an accident or quality in man, and not his essence.

[10] Sometimes original sin is spoken of as the total depravity of man. In the sense in which this term is meant when so used and in the light of the statement of the Formula of Concord given above, it is true, and quite compatible with the fact that the natural man may and does from the earthly standpoint possess many virtues and do many good deeds. But we must bear in mind that the term total depravity expresses for many persons much more than this. It is a term quite commonly used to denote degrees and species of wickedness which involve degeneracy, and which are not common to men. The devil is totally depraved in this sense, and men are not born diabolical, though in a few cases they seem ultimately to become so. It will be better, therefore, not to use the term total depravity in connection with original sin, or else so to guard its use that it will not be misunderstood.

which Adam originally had. The passages in Colossians and Ephesians cited in the previous chapter (Col. 3:10; Eph. 4:24) indicate that this absence of the moral image involves the loss of knowledge, righteousness and holiness. There is not only an objective defect in man's relation to God, so that he is justly under God's disfavor (Rom. 1:18); but there is a great subjective defect in his nature which renders him unable by his own powers to reëstablish the right relation between himself and God, or to do anything which is really pleasing to God (1 Cor. 2:14; John 6:44). He has by nature a wrong attitude toward God and things divine and a bias toward evil, which he is unable by his own efforts to overcome. He not only does not love God with all his heart, but he is utterly unable so to love Him. The natural mind is not only not friendly to God but is actually hostile to Him (Rom. 1:28; 8:7). All man's psychological powers are defective in the spiritual realm. His intellect cannot know or understand the things of the Spirit of God (1 Cor. 2:14); his feelings are moved to love and fear by the wrong objects (Rom. 8:5, 8); and his will, while able to function in external and earthly matters, is unable to function in the higher spiritual sphere, and cannot will to serve God (Phil. 2:13).

Original sin results in a threefold disability with regard to God's will, so that the natural man does not do God's will, does not desire to do it, and is not able to do it. Only by the operation of divine grace in the heart is man enabled to do God's will, given the desire to do it, and brought to the actual doing of it. Without this operation of divine grace, the natural man would remain forever alienated from God and unable to desire to do or actually to perform His will. For it is God that worketh in us both to will and to do of His good pleasure (Phil. 2:13).

Denials of Original Sin. The reality of original sin is denied by evolutionists, pantheists, and materialists, in accordance with their theories of determinism. It was denied by Pelagius, and in modern times by the Socinians and the Arminians. According to Pelagianism sin has not corrupted man's powers, but has left him abundantly able by his own efforts to do God's will. Semi-pelagianism leaves man enough power to begin his conversion, but requires that God's grace should come to his assistance and complete it.

According to the teaching of the Roman Catholic Church man by the fall did not lose any of his original powers, but only what is called a superadded gift. According to this theory God made man originally in a morally neutral state, and made him good by adding the moral image of perfection; hence the loss of the moral image by the fall left him with all his original endowments unimpaired.

The Loss of Freedom of the Will. Intimately connected with the doctrine of original sin is the doctrine concerning the freedom of the will since the fall. Did man or did he not lose his freedom of the will, and is he to-day born with or without it? The answer is that man is still a self-determining being and possesses freedom of the will in certain respects, but no longer in all. Freedom in natural and earthly matters is still his. He can choose freely in temporal affairs, and attain a civil righteousness. But he cannot will freely in spiritual matters. He cannot by his natural powers do the will of God. He cannot love God with all his heart and mind and soul and strength, nor his neighbor as himself. Yet this is what he was created for—to do God's will and to live in perfect harmony with Him. No man is fully free unless he is able to do what he ought to do—what in accordance with the very constitution of his original nature he was created to do. Hence in the spiritual realm man is not free. Just as the arm that has been badly wrenched may be able to function perfectly below the level of the shoulder but cannot be raised or be made to function above that level, so man's will is able to function in the lower sphere of earthly morality, but is powerless to function in the higher or spiritual sphere. He cannot will to love God or serve Him until his will has been set free by grace.[11]

Actual Sins. Actual Sins are sins of act, performed with greater or lesser participation of the will. They include inward acts as well as outward actions. They are committed by thought as well as by word and deed. Wrong thoughts, feelings and purposes, even when they remain internal, and do not take form in external conduct, are sinful. Actual sins are the outcropping of an internal state, the outgrowth of original sin. They are the stream which flows from original sin as the fountain; the fruit, of which the original sin is the seed; the symptoms, of which original sin is the disease.

Much actual sin exists in the heart while there is no outward evidence of its existence. Pride, envy, hatred, malice and other sins may and often do exist as inner acts and states of the mind while no overt act makes known their presence. Sin does not consist in the physical action, but in the motive and purpose behind it. Two men may outwardly do the same thing; and yet the thing which they do may not be the same, because their motives are different. Thus, for example, two men may give an equal sum to charity; in the one case it is given out of love to God and man; in the other case it is given with the expectation of reaping some personal advantage, and is not a virtuous act. Two men may have shot a fellow man, and one of them be found to be a murderer because of the intention to kill, and the other not a murderer because the shooting was accidental. The

[11] Compare Augs. Conf. XVII, Jacobs', *Book of Concord*, p. 43, "Concerning free will they teach that man's will hath some liberty to work a civil righteousness and to choose such things as reason can reach unto; but that it hath no power to work the righteousness of God or spiritual righteousness without the Spirit of God, because the natural man receiveth not the things of the Spirit of God. 1 Cor. 2:14."

self-righteousness which afflicted the Pharisees of Christ's time and which afflicts many persons to-day, preventing them from feeling the need of a Savior, is due in large measure to a superficial conception of sin and of goodness as matters of external conduct only.

The causes of actual sins are found in the natural evil inclinations of the heart, in the allurements of the world, and in the temptations of the devil. Man's greatest danger lies in the original sin which infests his mind and heart, and which not only prompts him to many sins, but which also inclines him to lend a willing ear to the seductions of the world and the whisperings of Satan. Acts once performed tend toward repetition and the formation of habits. In this way actual sins often become habitual sins.

The following kinds of actual sin may be mentioned.[12]

Thought, Word and Deed. Sins may be classed as sins of thought, word and deed. It is in our thoughts that we sin most. It sometimes happens that men's outward life in word and deed is fair, while their mind is full of corrupt thoughts, desires and imaginations. It was so with the Pharisees, of whom Christ declared that they were whited sepulchers, beautiful without, but inwardly full of dead men's bones.

Against God, Self and the Neighbor. Sins may be classed as sins against God, against self and against the neighbor. The Ten Commandments naturally divide into two tables, of which the first guards against sins committed directly against God, and the second guards against sins committed directly against our fellow men. The latter kind are committed indirectly against

[12] Numerous other kinds or classes of sins are mentioned by the old dogmaticians. Thus Quenstedt (II, 65), in addition to the classes mentioned in the text, distinguishes between our own sins and the sins of others, sins which cry out for punishment and sins which do not, more or less grievous sins, secret and manifest sins, dead and living sins, remaining and remitted sins, venial and mortal sins. But we believe that the classifications which are practically useful are given in the text.

God. In the last analysis all sins are sins against Him, because it is His law that is transgressed. The Ten Commandments contain no prohibitions or commands with respect to self. But there was no need that God should enjoin on man to love himself, since man is only too ready to do that of his own accord. What he needs is to be warned against loving himself too much. For this reason he is commanded to love God above all, and to love his neighbor as he loves himself.

Commission and Omission. Sins may be classed as sins of commission and of omission. The former are those by which man transgresses a negative command of God, and does what has been forbidden. The latter consists of the failure to do what God has positively enjoined or commanded. In the minds of many persons sins of commission are practically the only kind there is; and because they have not been guilty of gross crimes they pride themselves on their own goodness. They would have a different opinion of themselves if they realized, as they should, that every failure to love God with all their heart and soul and mind and strength, and every failure to love their neighbor as themselves, constitutes a sin of omission and deserves punishment.

Voluntary and Involuntary. Sins may be classed as voluntary and involuntary. The latter class includes sins of ignorance, precipitancy and infirmity (Ps. 19:12, 13). By voluntary sins are meant those consciously and intentionally committed, with the full participation of the will. Such deliberate sins in the case of Christians cause a fall from grace, and necessitate repentance and conversion anew. Involuntary sins are those committed in ignorance, haste, thoughtlessness, stress of emotion, or weakness.

Against the Holy Ghost. There is a sin against the Holy Ghost (Matt. 12:31, 32). This is the unpardonable sin. But it is unpardonable, not because God does not desire to have those persons who have committed this sin repent and be forgiven, nor because Christ has not made sufficient sacrifice for them, but because the very nature of their sin precludes their repentance. They could and would be forgiven if they repented; but they cannot be forgiven because they never will repent. Their sin involves the willful rejection of what is known to be the truth, the deliberate choice of falsehood and evil because they are false and evil, and a bitter hostility to the Gospel, not as something believed to be false, but as something known to be the truth of God and hated for that reason. There must be and is in this sin something of a diabolical nature, something which makes those who commit it unsalvable even as the devils are unsalvable, because they no longer have a conscience to which the good may be made to appeal. They have deliberately put their consciences to death, and have chosen evil to be their good. The distress of those persons who tremble for their salvation, because they imagine that they have committed the sin against the Holy Ghost, is to be removed by pointing out to them the fact that if they had committed it they would not be anxious about their soul's salvation.

The distinction sometimes made between venial and mortal sins is unwise and apt to mislead. It is better to drop the distinction entirely. All sins are venial, if repented of; and all sins are mortal, if unrepented of. No sins are venial in the sense of being negligible or capable of being committed with impunity.

PART II

THE RECONCILIATION AND REDEMPTION BY
JESUS CHRIST

CHAPTER VIII

THE SAVING GRACE OR BENEVOLENCE OF GOD

Man's Need of Saving Grace. The sinful and lost state in which man finds himself by reason of his original and his actual sin is one from which he cannot by any possible means deliver himself. He is not only guilty and deserving of condemnation at the hands of a holy and just God; but he is spiritually helpless, unable to serve God by his own natural powers, and unable to do anything to free himself from the guilt or the bondage of sin. If he is to be saved at all, it must be by divine grace alone. This grace is offered to all men in Christ the Redeemer (Tit. 2:11. R. V.).

God's Purpose to Save Man. The divine plan of redemption was formed from all eternity (1 Pet. 1:20; Eph. 1:4). God's determination to save man was coeternal with His determination to create him. Indeed, the creation of man, in the face of God's foreknowledge that man would sin, cannot be understood apart from the eternal purpose to redeem him. The promise of redemption was given immediately after the fall, when God said that the seed of the woman should bruise the serpent's head (Gen. 3:15). The promise of a coming Savior was repeated many times during the period represented by Old Testament history. It was made to Abraham (Gen. 12:1, 3), Isaac (Gen. 26:2, 4), Jacob (Gen. 28:14), Judah (Gen. 49:10) and David (2 Sam. 7:16). The prophets, looking into the future, saw and proclaimed His coming (Deut. 18:18; Isa. 7:14; 9:2; Micah 5:2). He came in the fullness of time (Gal. 4:4, 5).

Between the time when God in Eden gave the first promise of redemption and the time when the Savior actually appeared on earth, many centuries passed away. The history of the earliest ages of that intervening period is largely enshrouded in darkness, though the first eleven chapters of Genesis give a brief outline history of those prehistoric days. For the knowledge of succeeding ages we are dependent on such records and traditions as have come down to us from pagan sources, and upon the record given in the Old Testament.

A Twofold Preparation. The statement of the apostle that God sent His Son in the fullness of time indicates that His coming was delayed until a certain preparation had been made for it. A study of the history of the world shows that this preparation was twofold: a preparation of the world for salvation, and a preparation of salvation for the world; and that this twofold preparation was brought about through God's providential dealings with the Gentiles and the Jews.

The heathen more and more lost the natural knowledge of God written originally in the heart, and worshiped the creature instead of the creator. Left to themselves without a supernatural revelation, they universally practiced idolatry. Many of them sank into barbarism and savagery; others rose to a high state of civilization. The intellectual culture of pagan antiquity prepared the way for the Gospel: negatively, by showing the limitations of the unaided human intellect, the inability of man to solve his moral and religious problems, and the need of a divine supernatural revelation; and positively, by providing a universal language of marvelous richness and flexibility, the Greek, and a universal empire, the Roman, and thus making possible the rapid spread of the Gospel. Without a world language and without a world empire which facilitated intercourse between all parts of the world, innumerable barriers of nationality, language, tribal feuds and barbarous isolation would have presented almost insurmountable obstacles to the spread of the Gospel.

There was also a preparation of salvation for the world. The Jews were chosen by God to be the people among whom the Savior should be born. By His supernatural revelation God preserved among them the knowledge and worship of the one true God, implanted and preserved faith in the coming redemption, and by the Law and the Promise, by rites, ceremonies and sacrifices, educated them to receive the coming Savior in repentance and faith, thus preparing a place and an environment in which the Savior could be recognized and received as the divinely sent Messiah.

God's Saving Love. Salvation is a revelation of the loving heart of the Triune God. The Father, moved with compassion, determined from all eternity to send His only Son into the world to redeem men. The Son, in the fullness of time, came into the world, taking upon Himself human nature and redeeming men by His holy life and innocent death. And the Holy Ghost applies Christ's redemption to the souls of men by bringing them through the means of grace to a state of repentance and faith, and thus to sonship with God. The consideration of the salvation which God has graciously provided for the children of men falls naturally, therefore, into three parts: The Benevolence of God toward our Fallen Race, The Redemption accomplished by Christ the Son of God, The Gracious Application of Redemption by the Holy Spirit.

THE BENEVOLENT WILL OF GOD

The Benevolent Will of God, or His eternal purpose to save men, is one will and not two wills. But it may very properly be regarded under two aspects: *First,* as a General benevolent will regarded without reference to men's attitude toward His grace, and simply as a will to save all. *Secondly,* as a Special benevolent will to save those who, He foresees, will accept His grace in Christ.

God's General Benevolent Will. The General benevolent will of God is the saving will of God considered only in its intent and purpose to save men by preparing the means of salvation and efficaciously offering salvation to all, without regard to the question whether they will accept or reject His grace. It may be defined, therefore, as that act of divine grace and mercy by which, out of pure love and compassion, and moved by a desire for the salvation of all men, God from all eternity determined to make adequate provision for the salvation of all by sending His Son to redeem them, by instituting the means of grace, and by earnestly seeking through the work of the Holy Spirit to bring them to true faith in Christ and to the enjoyment of eternal salvation in Him. This General benevolent will of God is sometimes called the Antecedent will, because it is regarded antecedently to any question concerning man's attitude toward the grace offered. It has the following eight characteristics.

(1) *Eternal.* The benevolent purpose of God to save men is eternal. It was first announced immediately after the fall in Eden; but it was not then first formed. Redemption is not an afterthought by which God purposed to repair as best He could the damage wrought by an unforeseen catastrophe. God was neither in unavoidable ignorance of the sin which man would commit, nor did He by an act of His own will hide from Himself the manner in which the man whom He was about to create would conduct himself. By His omniscient foreknowledge He was aware from all eternity that men would fall into sin; but from all eternity He determined to save them. The purpose to create man and the purpose to redeem him were coeternal in the mind of God. The believers were chosen in Christ Jesus before the foundation of the world (Eph. 1:4).

(2) *A Free Act of Grace.* The purpose of God to save men

is a free act of His divine grace. There was nothing in man to deserve such gracious treatment. On the contrary he had by his sin justly deserved punishment and eternal banishment from God's presence. He could not have complained of any injustice if such a fate had been permitted to come upon him without any effort on God's part to avert it; for it would have been exactly what he deserved. But the love of God is so vast, that it prompted Him to do all that lay within His almighty power to rescue man. He so loved the world that He gave His only begotten Son (John 3:16).

(3) *Universal and Impartial.* The purpose of God to save men is universal and impartial. His general benevolent will includes every individual of the human race. It is not a will to save an arbitrarily selected few to the exclusion of others, but a will to save all. He loves all men with an infinite love; He has sent His Son to make propitiation for all men; he offers salvation to all men in the Gospel; and the Holy Spirit seeks to bring all men to faith and salvation. The universality and impartiality of God's will to save is clearly taught in Scripture.[1] While there are passages which, if taken alone, might seem to teach a doctrine of predestination which arbitrarily limits the number of the saved, such passages must be interpreted in the light of the passages which plainly declare the universality of divine grace, and in consonance with the whole tenor of Scripture in its description of the attitude of the God of Love toward fallen men. God would have all men be saved and come to the knowledge of the truth (1 Tim. 2:4). He is not willing that

[1] Passages which seem to imply particularism and partiality do not do so when properly understood and interpreted. The hardening referred to in Matt. 13:14, John 12:40 and Exod. 7:3 is not the result of an arbitrary decree, but the result of an inevitable law by which the persistent sinner gradually becomes hardened in sin. The passage in Acts 13:48 declaring that "as many as were ordained to eternal life believed," a main reliance of the absolute predestinationists, is, as the context shows, a historical statement of fact, and not an explanation of the divine eternal decree. The principal passage, Rom. 9 and 10, has a historical and not a dogmatic purpose, and deals with the fact that Israel could and did lose salvation, because it would not walk in the way of righteousness through faith which God ordained.

any should perish, but that all should come to repentance (2 Pet. 3:9) and live. He so loved the *world* that He gave His only begotten Son that everyone who believes in Him should be saved (John 3:16). The universality and impartiality of God's saving grace are seen in the unlimited scope ascribed to the sacrifice for sin made by Christ; for He died for all (2 Cor. 5:14, 15), and His death is a propitiation for the sins of the whole world (1 John 2:2). They are also seen in the command to go forth into all the world and to offer salvation to all men. Salvation is bestowed on all who believe in Christ and are baptized (Mark 16:15, 16; Matt. 28:19, 20).

(4) *Sincere and Earnest.* The purpose of God to save all men is sincere and earnest. The Gospel is not simply an apparent or an inefficacious call to all men to believe in Christ and be saved. God actually offers salvation to all who hear the Gospel. And since the natural man is unable by his own powers to accept the salvation which is offered, the Holy Spirit, who is always with the Word, earnestly seeks to produce in the heart of everyone through the Gospel the will and the power to believe in Christ. If man is not brought to faith in Christ, it is the fault of his own willful and obstinate resistance, and not of any failure on God's part really to offer him the needful grace. The doctrine that God calls only the elect and calls these with irresistible grace, and that He does not really call the non-elect nor make it possible for them to be saved, though He pretends to call them in the Gospel,[2] charges God with an insincerity

---

[2] Calvin says (*Institutes,* Book III, Ch. 21, Sec. 5): "Eternal life is foreordained for some, and eternal damnation for others. Every man, therefore, being created for the one or the other of these ends, we say he is predestinated either to life or death." Calvin distinguishes (Book III, Ch. 24, Sec. 8) between the merely external call which God intends for the non-elect as "a savor of death and an occasion of heavier condemnation" and the special call through which "by the inward illumination of His Spirit He causes the Word preached to sink into the hearts of the elect." In the case of the sons of Eli (Book III, Ch. 24, Sec. 14) Calvin declares that "though the Lord was able to soften their hearts, yet they were left in their obstinacy because His immutable decree had predestinated them to destruction."

that is in utter conflict with all that we know of Him as a truthful God, as well as with the particular teachings of the Word concerning the call. God really and sincerely calls all; and His call is always efficacious, because the Gospel is always accompanied by the gracious power and working of the Holy Spirit in the human heart.

(5) *On Account of Christ's Merits.* The purpose of God to save men is a purpose to save them on account of the merits of Christ. The Gospel is the offer of salvation for the sake of what Christ has done and suffered (Luke 24:46, 47). The plan of God from eternity was a plan to save men through the redemption which Christ should accomplish. Without this redemption the justice of God would require men's condemnation. It was, therefore, God's purpose from eternity to send His Son to make atonement for human sin, and thus to make possible the granting of forgiveness and eternal life on account of His merits.

(6) *Those Who Believe.* The purpose of God is to save those who believe in Christ. The benevolence of God is general and universal in the sense that He desires the salvation of all, has made provision for the salvation of all, and works for the salvation of all through the Means of Grace. But it is not a benevolence which aims to save or which can save all men irrespective of their attitude toward Christ. While salvation is offered to all, it is actually possessed only by him who accepts it by faith. For it is only by faith that the merits of Christ are accepted and appropriated, and become ours individually. The benevolent will of God is not a will to save men by necessity or compulsion, nor by any magical or mechanical process. It is a will to save men *from* their sins (Matt. 1:21), that is, from the guilt and from the love of sin. It is not a will to save them *in* their sins, that is, while they still love and cling to their sins. Salvation is not merely a local transfer from a place called earth

to a place called heaven, but is a deliverance from the guilt and power of sin through faith, and the making out of man a new creature who is fitted for eternal life and eternal communion with God (Col. 1:12).

(7) *Ordinate and Conditioned.* This general benevolent will of God is therefore not an absolute will, but one which is ordinate and conditioned; so that the accomplishment of the benevolent purpose of God with regard to men is conditioned upon the acceptance of the grace which He offers through means ordained by Him (John 3:18). In spite of the universal benevolent will of God some men will still be lost. But it will be in spite of God's desire to save them, and not on account of any unwillingness on His part to save them.

(8) *Efficacious.* God's benevolent will is always efficacious; that is, it is adequate and sufficient for the accomplishment of His purpose. It does not in every case result in the actual salvation of the man; but that is not due to any lack of power or efficacy in God's will, but to the failure on man's part to accept His gracious offer.

God's Special Benevolent Will. The Special benevolent will of God is His will considered in connection with His foreknowledge of the treatment which men would accord to His grace. It is sometimes called the Consequent will, because it is consequent upon His foreknowledge of men's attitude.

(1) *Predestination or Election.* The Special benevolence of God takes the form of Predestination or Election; and these are the terms under which it is usually discussed. By Predestination or Election we mean the eternal decree of God to save those individual persons of whom He foresaw that they would enduringly believe in Christ. It differs from the General benevolence, in that the latter is the purpose of God to provide and offer salvation to all men on account of the merits of Christ, and to bestow it on all who will believe; while Predes-

tination is the purpose actually to bestow salvation on certain persons of whom He foreknows that they will believe. This foreknowledge is not the cause of their believing, nor is it to be confounded with foredetermination that they shall believe. The foreknowledge is logically consequent upon the fact that they will believe, and is the basis on which the decree to save these particular persons is made. From eternity God foresees who will and who will not accept His grace; and from eternity He decrees that the particular persons who, as He foreknows, will accept it shall have eternal salvation. This will is sometimes called the Particular will of God because it has reference to a particular class of persons, namely, to those who accept the grace of God in Christ; and it is also called the Consequent Will of God because it is consequent upon God's foreknowledge of those who will believe. The Special benevolent will of God has the following seven characteristics:

(a) *A Free Act of God's Grace.* Predestination or Election is a free act of God's grace. Faith is, indeed, the condition without which no election would have taken place. But faith does not constitute a merit on account of which God has elected some. It is merely the hand which accepts the gift proffered by divine grace. And if, therefore, some are elected and some are not, it is not because God sees a merit in the former which He misses in the latter. The only merits which come into account in God's decree of predestination are the merits of Christ the Savior. It is on account of these merits that God predestinates the elect to eternal life.

(b) *Eternal.* Predestination or Election is eternal. From all eternity God foresaw who would enduringly believe in Christ, and from all eternity He decreed that those particular persons should be saved. He chose them in Christ before the foundation of the world (Eph. 1:4), and saved them according to His own purpose and grace which was given to us in Christ before the world began (2 Tim. 1:9), choosing them from the beginning unto salvation (2 Thess. 2:13) and giving them an inheritance prepared for them from the foundation of the world (Matt. 25:34).

(c) *Not Absolute.* Predestination is not absolute, but ordinate and relative. God did not from eternity arbitrarily choose from among men certain ones and predestinate them unto eternal life, while He arbitrarily excluded others. Nor does He compel some to be saved, while He compels others to be lost. The decree of predestination is ordinate, that is, it is determined by a certain order which God has established and upon which salvation depends. God has not decreed that, no matter what they do, certain persons shall be saved. On the contrary, He has made His decree of predestination in accordance with the order which He has established and with His foreknowledge of the treatment which this order will receive among men.

(d) *In View of Faith.* Predestination or Election is in view of faith.[3] This does not make faith the cause of man's election. The cause is simply the unmerited grace of God in Christ. But the foreseen faith is the condition without which the decree of election for a particular person would not have taken place. In the last analysis predestination is simply the eternal justification of the sinner for Christ's sake. By it God from all eternity imputes to the believer the righteousness of Christ, just as by justification in time He imputes to the believer the righteousness of Christ. Just as He now justifies the sinner in view of his *seen* faith in Christ, without in this way making faith the cause of justification; so God from eternity predestinates or elects the sinner in view of his *foreseen* faith, without in this way mak-

---

[3] *Intuitu fidei.* Missouri rejects the doctrine that election is in view of faith; contends that such a doctrine leads to synergism; and lets the doctrines of the General Benevolence of God and of the Special Benevolence of God stand side by side unreconciled.

ing faith the cause of his election. In both cases the cause is the unmerited grace of God in Christ.

(e) *Categorical.* Predestination or Election is not conditional, but categorical and simple. The forming of the decree by God is, indeed, conditioned on His foreknowledge of man's faith. But the decree itself is categorical and unconditional. It has no "if" in it. It is not a decree, for example, that John Smith shall be saved if he believes; but it is a decree that John Smith shall be saved. God foreknows that John Smith will enduringly believe, and hence elects or predestinates him to salvation. In this foreknowledge God cannot be mistaken. If John Smith would fail to believe or fail to endure in the faith, God would foreknow it. But He foreknows that John Smith will believe and endure, and therefore predestinates him.

(f) *Particular.* Predestination or Election is particular. God has predestined to eternal life every individual person who will finally obtain it. Each predestinated person has been foreknown as an enduring believer, and each has individually been elected to eternal life.

(g) *Immutable.* Predestination or Election is immutable and irrevocable. No elect person will or can become reprobate. This is not because of any exercise of compulsion on God's part, or of any irresistible grace, but because God cannot err or be mistaken in His foreknowledge. If the decree of predestination had to be revoked by God in the case of any individual, it would mean that God had not correctly foreseen what that individual would do. But this supposes a contingency which can never occur. Election is based on a divine foreknowledge which cannot err, and on a divine love which cannot fail. The elect shall certainly be saved. They may, indeed, for a time fall from grace, but they will come to true faith again, or else God would not have foreknown that they would.

(2) *Reprobation.* The decree of predestination has refer-

ence only to the saved, and not to the lost. God has not predestinated anyone to eternal death. But all those who reject the
grace of God offered to them in the Gospel will become reprobate.

Reprobation is the eternal act of God by which, as a just and
holy God, He determined to leave to their well-deserved fate
all those persons who, He foresaw, would reject His offer of
grace and salvation in Christ. It is not His desire that any persons shall become reprobate; for He wills that all men shall
believe and be saved. Reprobation is, therefore, not to be regarded as a predestination to hell. There is a wide difference
between predestination and reprobation as acts of God. Predestination is the decree of grace by which God determined to
raise from their fallen and condemned state all those persons
of whom He foresaw that they would permit Him to save them
according to His plan of salvation. Reprobation is the eternal
determination of God to leave in their fallen and condemned
state all those persons of whom He foresaw that they would
refuse to permit him to save them according to the plan of salvation which He has ordained. He is not therefore the cause of
the condemnation of the reprobate, as He is the cause of the
salvation of the elect. The latter are saved by God's grace
alone; the reprobate are lost by their own fault alone. By their
sin the lost brought eternal destruction upon themselves; and
by their unbelief they refused to be saved from that destruction
by divine grace. Hence the blame of their eternal reprobation
rests wholly on themselves; while the credit for the salvation
of the elect belongs entirely to God.

(a) *Eternal*. Reprobation is eternal. The lost shall remain
forever in the state of condemnation from which they have
refused to be delivered, and shall suffer eternally all the punishment involved in that state.

(b) *Immutable*. Reprobation is immutable. From all eter-

nity God foresaw who would finally reject His grace, and repro-
bated those persons. He cannot be mistaken in His foreknowledge, or reverse His judgment.

(c) *Many.* The Reprobate are many. This is plainly taught
in Scripture (Matt. 2:16; 22:14). They may for a time be
among the truly believing, but as God foreknew their failure
to persevere, they were always included in the number of the
reprobate.

CHAPTER IX

THE PERSON OF CHRIST

THE redemption which was foretold in Eden immediately after the fall, and without which no salvation for men was possible, was accomplished in the fullness of time by Jesus Christ.

The Need and Purpose of Redemption. The need of redemption is grounded in the sinfulness of man and the righteousness of God. The purpose of redemption is to restore the fellowship or communion between God and man which was broken by sin.

It is true, God is love and takes no pleasure in punishing. But since He is just and holy, He cannot look with favor or complacency on personal beings whose nature is corrupt, and whose actions are a constant transgression of His commands. He cannot overlook or condone sin. And while He is a God of love, and desires to save men from their lost condition, He cannot do so in any manner which would conflict with His justice and holiness; for these are just as much attributes of His being as love. He would not be God, if He ceased to be just and holy; just as He would not be God, if He ceased to be loving and kind. When, therefore, He planned from eternity to save men, His plan of redemption comprised the satisfaction of His justice and holiness as well as of His love.

A Divine Redeemer Needed. For the accomplishment of redemption there was needed a person who combined in Himself both a divine and a human nature. Redemption had to

140

come from God in order to be valid for Him; and it had to be wrought out in organic connection with the human race in order to be valid for men. Hence, God from eternity planned to send His only Son into the world; and when the proper time was at hand, the Son of God became incarnate.

Since redemption could be accomplished only by a unique person who combined in Himself both a divine and a human nature, who passed through successive states of humiliation and exaltation, and who perfectly performed the functions of prophet, priest and king, it is customary to consider the work of redemption under the following three heads: The Person of Christ, The States of Christ, The Offices of Christ.

The Place of Christ in History. Christ is the center of human history. All the centuries that preceded His coming looked forward to Him, and all the times that have followed look back to Him. He is the meeting point of God and man, and the foundation and center of the Christian religion. The names which He bore are significant of His mission and work. Jesus was His personal name, and signifies that "He should save His people from their sins." Christ was His official title, the Greek equivalent of the Hebrew word Messiah, and signifies the Anointed One—the One who was divinely anointed and set apart for the work of redemption.

The Reason for the Incarnation. The ground of the incarnation is to be found in man's need of redemption, and not in any philosophic idea of God and man and their kinship. It is true, the Son of God could not have become man, if man were not made in the image of God. But the necessity of the incarnation cannot be deduced from the possibility of it. The Scriptures plainly describe the coming of Christ as a coming to redeem men, and nowhere give any indication that without the need of redemption He would nevertheless have become incarnate in order to bring a needed unity into the universe. Christ cannot be understood or explained from any other standpoint than from that of sin and the need of redemption.[1]

The God-man. Christ is God and man in one person, the God-man. This is the great outstanding fact with reference to the Person of Christ. Emphasis must be laid both on the unity of the person and on the duality of the natures. He is one person with two natures, a divine and a human. He is true God and He is true man; yet He is not two persons, but one. This marvelous personality of Christ raises many problems, and remains, after all the study expended upon it, a profound mystery.

The great basic facts are clear, however: Christ is the Son of God from all eternity; and He is also the Son of man born in time of the Virgin Mary. The statement of John that the Word was made flesh (John 1:14) describes the entrance of the eternal Son of God into vital unity with our race as a member of it. He who exists from eternity as God exists from the incarnation also as man.

The Virgin Birth. The immaculate conception of Christ by the Virgin Mary is fundamental to the true conception of the Person of Christ. This birth of a virgin has been strongly assailed. But it is plainly taught in the Gospels of Matthew (Matt. 1:20) and Luke (Luke 1:34, 35), and is demanded by the preëxistence of Christ which is asserted by John (John 1:1-3) and Paul (Rom. 8:3). Dogmatically the Virgin birth of our Lord is not a matter of indifference, as is asserted by some. Without it Christ would necessarily sink to the level of a mere human being, with perhaps an infusion of divinity in

[1] The notion that the Logos would have become incarnate even if man had not sinned was held by certain mystics of the Middle Ages and by Duns Scotus. In the period of the Reformation it was held by Osiander, the Socinians, and a number of Reformed theologians. The view has been advocated in modern times by Nitsch, Martensen, Liebner, Lange, Rothe, Ebrard, and others. It has been rejected by nearly all the orthodox teachers of the early Church, by Calvin and by the seventeenth century dogmaticians of the Lutheran Church. Augustine's statement holds good, *"Si homo non periisset, filius hominis non venisset."*

Him. He could not then be the Son of God incarnate; nor could His perfect freedom from original and actual sin be accounted for. Those who reject the Virgin birth are confronted with a greater difficulty than that which belief in the Virgin birth involves; for they are left without any way by which to account for the appearance of one human being and only one who is without sin, and who towers high above the rest of the race like a mountain peak above the surrounding plain. Christ in the midst of human history is utterly inexplicable except upon the Scriptural basis, that the Son of God became man, that He assumed human nature in the womb of the Virgin Mary by a miraculous conception, and that He had no father but God. A birth "after the common course of nature" with a human father would have precluded the possibility of sinless perfection. The theory of a natural evolution of the perfect man in Christ will not explain it; for in that case the perfect flower of humanity should have appeared at the end of human history and not in the middle of it; and Christ according to that theory appeared upon the scene thousands of years too soon.

The Uniqueness of Christ. The Jesus Christ whom the New Testament sets before us is an absolutely unique personality, who is God and man in one person. He is exhibited as a true human being with all the essential marks of humanity, and at the same time as the eternal Son of God who stands in a unique relation of absolute and perfect communion with the Father. There exist in Him a divine and a human side which are clearly distinguishable, yet which are intimately and indissolubly united in oneness of person. The Synoptics, beginning with the human side, follow the historical steps of His career on to the final revelation of His divine majesty and glory; and John, beginning with the divine side, exhibits the fullness of the Godhead dwelling in the humanity of Christ. In the former we have a historical progression which more and more reveals the divine in Him; in the latter we have the simultaneous presentation of the divine and the human.

The Two Natures. There are in Christ two natures, the divine and the human.[2] He is true God, and possesses the eternal divine nature of the Logos from God the Father; and He is also true man born of the Virgin Mary, and possesses a human nature since the incarnation. Both natures are true and entire. He is as completely God as is God the Father; and He is as completely man as we are. He is God incarnate, God become man. That He is true man is evident from every page of the Gospels; and that He is true God is equally evident from His life and works, from what He says of Himself, and from what His apostles declare of Him.[3]

One Person. Just what the incarnation involves will always remain a deep mystery to us in this world. The only approach to its understanding lies in making a clear distinction between person and nature, and conceiving of Christ as one divine person with two natures, a divine and a human. The unity of the person is the key to such understanding as is possible to us of the Christ who is set forth in the Holy Scriptures. He is true God and true man; but He is only one person, not two persons. There is not the least indication in Scripture that Jesus was conscious of a double personality. His consciousness embraced His temporal existence as a man and at the same time reached back to the farthest eternity. But it is the consciousness of a single person, and through it all runs the sense of the self-identity and unity of the *ego.* Because of this inner oneness Jesus, speaking to the hostile Jews, was able to say, "Before Abraham was, I am" (John 8:58).

As the Logos from eternity Christ was a divine person with a

---

[2] The Ebionites maintained that Christ had only a human nature; the Docetists maintained that He had only a divine nature.

[3] For the Scriptural proof, see Chap. II, The Trinity, under "The Deity of Christ."

divine nature; from the time of His incarnation He was a divine person with both a divine and a human nature. "The Word was made flesh" (John 1:14) ; God became man. The Logos, who from eternity existed as the second *hypostasis* of the Trinity with a divine nature, added to Himself at His incarnation a human nature. He did not add to Himself a human person, but only a human nature. He *became* man; He did not take possession of a man, nor enter into or inspire a man. He did not cease to be the Son of God, nor lose or lay aside His divine nature and attributes. But remaining God He also became man.

As the divine *ego* lay from eternity at the center of the divine nature of the Logos, so at the incarnation that same *ego* became also the center of the human nature which the Logos assumed. There was thus a common center of two circles of being, the one infinite and the other finite, but harmonious with one another and revolving, as it were, around the same center. The same person of the Logos who functioned from eternity through a divine intellect, divine sensibilities and a divine will, began with the incarnation to function also through a human intellect, human sensibilities and a human will, and through a human body. Or, to use a more accurate psychological terminology, the same person of the Logos, who from eternity thought and felt and willed in a divine manner, began with the incarnation to think and feel and will in a human manner also. This union of divine and human psychological activity by the one divine *ego* is a deep mystery. But that it is a fact is plain from the evidence of Scripture that Christ is true God and true man in one person. In thinking of the mystery we should bear in mind that even the activity of our own purely human *ego* in thinking, feeling and willing is a complete mystery which we cannot fathom.

The Divine Nature. Christ has a true divine nature. He is in

the substantial sense the Son of God. The Scriptural evidence
of this fact has been considered under the doctrine of the Trinity, and need not to be repeated here. He is "God of God, Light
of Light, Very God of Very God, Begotten, not made, being of
one Substance with the Father." In His divine nature He is the
Son of God, the Second Person of the Trinity, who is coeternal,
consubstantial and coequal with the Father and the Holy Ghost.
He is the Son of God, not by adoption, nor as one who worked
His way into divine sonship by His perfection, but He is divine
in the full and substantial sense of the term.

The Human Nature. Christ has a true human nature, with
body and soul. He is bone of our bone, and flesh of our flesh,
and was in all points tempted like as we are, yet without sin
(Heb. 4:15). The genuineness of His humanity appears on
every page of the record which the evangelists give of Him.
He was born (Luke 2:7), increased in wisdom and stature
(Luke 2:52), grew to manhood, associated with other men,
entered upon His public ministry, and gathered disciples around
Him. He had human attributes, wants and feelings. He hun-
gered (Matt. 4:2), thirsted (John 4:7), was weary (John 4:6),
slept (Matt. 8:24), prayed (Matt. 26:39), was tempted (Matt.
4:1), rejoiced (Luke 10:21), sorrowed (Matt. 26:38), suffered, died and was buried.

Characteristics of Christ's Human Nature. From the fact
that in Christ the divine and the human natures are united in
one person there follow certain conclusions with regard to the
human nature.

1. The human nature has no separate personality of its own,
but has as its personality the person of the Logos. The *ego* of
the Logos is the *ego* of the whole Christ, including the human
nature. There is one divine person functioning through both
natures.

Theology employs the term *anhypostasia* to denote the fact
that the human nature has no separate personality of its own,

and the term *enhypostasia* to denote the fact that there are in Christ not two persons, but one.

2. The human nature of Christ is true and entire. Christ is a true human being such as each of us is, except that He is without sin. The incarnation did not mean the assumption of a human body only; for humanity does not consist in the possession of body alone, but of soul and body. Hence Christ assumed both a body and a soul when He became incarnate. It was the error of Apollinarianism to maintain that Christ assumed only a human body, and that the Logos took the place of the spirit or mind.[4]

3. The human nature of Christ partook of the natural human weaknesses of mankind, such as weariness, pain, suffering and the like, not by necessity, but by free choice. The fact that Christ was God incarnate and not born after the common course of nature lifted Him above all those infirmities which exist in man as a consequence of sin. But for the sake of achieving that redemption for which He had come into the world, He voluntarily partook of the natural human weaknesses, and became in all things tempted or tried as we are.

4. There was in Christ no original sin. Since original sin is the result of our natural descent from Adam, and Christ's birth was miraculous in that He had no human father but only a human mother, He was born without that natural inherited corruption which belongs to all other men. Having God alone for His Father, He was born a sinless being. There were in Him no such evil tendencies and no such absence of the fear, love and trust toward God as mark all ordinary men from birth. Sin is a matter of the person, and consists in a deflection of the will. Since in person Christ was the Logos incarnate, He was from birth perfect in His relation to His heavenly Father, and utterly lacking in that sinful bias which afflicts all other men.

[4] Apollinaris was a trichotomist, and in that sense ascribed to Christ a human body and soul, but no *nous* or spirit. In the dichotomist sense this was equivalent to conceding to Christ a human body but not a human soul.

5. There was in Christ no actual sin. His life as a human being was free from every blemish and fault. He "did no sin, neither was guile found in His mouth" (1 Pet. 2:22). The record of His life given by the evangelists is the record of a perfect life—perfect in love to God and to man. In the midst of a world of sinful beings He towers as the one sinless human being in all history.

6. Christ could not sin. The explanation of this fact is found in His personality. Since sin is a personal matter and Christ is in His person the divine Logos, the question as to whether He could sin or not is really a question as to whether God can sin or not. The answer must, of course, be that God cannot sin, and that therefore Christ could not.

Immediately connected with this question is another, namely, whether Christ could really be tempted if He could not possibly fall. Could He really be tempted in all points like as we are, and not only be without sin but without the possibility of sinning? The answer must be found by carefully observing what is involved and what is not involved in temptation. In the use of the word in connection with men, who may fall and often do, temptation has in the minds of many persons acquired a connotation which does not necessarily belong to temptation as such. From the fact that men often yield to temptation it does not follow that there can be no temptation, unless there be the possibility of yielding to it. Temptation is literally a testing, to see whether the tested one will choose God's service or not. This does not necessarily imply the possibility of a failure to stand the test. Gold may be tested as well as dross. And gold can never fail to stand the test. Theoretically, that is, as long as we do not know that the metal in question is gold, there may be a possibility in our minds that it will fail when put to the proof. But actually there is no such possibility. The gold, just because it is gold, will stand the test and cannot possibly fail to do so. If we were in ignorance of the true nature of

Christ's person, we should suppose that He might have failed in the hour of temptation. But knowing, as we do, that He is the veritable Son of God, we know that He could not have sinned. Being pure gold, He could not fail to stand the test. He might be tempted by Satan in many ways; but it was not possible that he should fall, because He was the Son of God.

It needs to be borne in mind that this is the very kind of Savior we needed, and the only kind that could have delivered us. We needed one who could not sin, one who from His very nature was abundantly able to repel all the onslaughts of the evil one. The first Adam was one who when tempted was able to sin, and did. The second Adam was one who could not sin. And it is this very fact which forms the foundation of our salvation. We needed a champion from whom all the fiery darts of the wicked one would fall harmless to the ground. And such a one we have and could have only in Him who in His person is the Son of God, and, as such, was unable to sin.

7. The body of Jesus was in itself immortal. That He died was the result, not of any natural susceptibility to death, but of His own choice and volition. He assures us that His death was the laying down of His life by Himself, and not the taking it away by others (John 10:18).

8. Christ's body and soul possessed peculiar excellence. Being free from sin and from all its consequences, His body and soul were exempt from all those natural imperfections and blemishes which in one form or another affect the ordinary human being as a result of sin. His mind was perfect in its functioning, and His body was a faultless organ of the soul that dwelt within.

The Personal Union. The union of the divine and the human natures in Christ is a personal one, that is, the natures are united in and through the person. This union does not involve any commingling of the natures themselves, any more than the union of body and soul in one person in man involves a commingling of his physical and spiritual natures. Each nature remains genuinely what it is: the divine does not become human, and the human does not become divine. The human is not swallowed up in the divine, and each remains unchanged and unalloyed. There is, however, a *perichoresis* or permeation of the human nature by the divine, as heat permeates iron. But just as the heat remains heat, and the iron remains iron, so the divine nature remains divine, and the human nature remains human, even while the latter receives from the former through the personal union a communication of powers which human nature ordinarily does not possess.

In this personal union the bond that unites the natures is the person. The union is therefore a close and inseparable one. The natures are not joined in an external or mechanical manner, but in an intimate and vital way through the person. There is, therefore, no separation or distance between the natures. The union between them exceeds in closeness even the relation between the soul and body in man. In His death the soul and body of Jesus were temporarily separated; but the divine nature was not for a moment separated either from His soul or His body. The union is also a permanent one. In becoming incarnate the Logos became man for all time and for all eternity. To the farthest ages of eternity He will remain the incarnate Son of God. He will never cease to be God; but just as surely also He will never cease to be man.

In order to guard against possible errors, the old dogmaticians defined the personal union negatively: as not being a union of essence, so that the divine and human natures amalgamate; as not being natural, like the union of soul and body in one person, but supernatural and miraculous; as not being an accidental union, like that of two qualities in one substance, such as whiteness and sweetness in milk; nor like the union of a quality and a substance, such as a learned man; nor like two substances in juxtaposition, such as two boards nailed together;

and as not being merely a verbal or figurative union. While these negations seem at first glance to be purely formal and unnecessary, they actually guard against errors which have been more or less widely held, and still are held in some quarters. Thus there are those who maintain that the divinity of Jesus is not substantial, but is a divine quality added to His humanity. The Eutychians maintained a doctrine which practically meant a union of the divine and the human essence. The Nestorians stood for a doctrine which made the relation of the two natures practically one of juxtaposition. And the statement that Christ is the Son of God has frequently been regarded as merely a verbal or figurative expression.

In opposition to these and other false theories, it is to be maintained that the union of the two natures is true and real; that it is personal, that is, a union in one person; and that it is perpetual, Christ remaining the God-man forever.[5]

The Catechism and the Athanasian Creed. The nature of the personal union is expressed very simply and clearly in Luther's

[5] The Socinians or Unitarians assert that the existence of the two natures in one person is an impossibility. They regard Christ as only a man, though begotten in some supernatural way, instructed before the opening of His public ministry by God through a *raptus in coelum*, endowed with the power of miracles, and exalted to heaven as a reward for His obedience and as a pledge of our future life, made the regent over the believers, and made the object of religious adoration, not of necessity like God, but by permission.

The Arminians acknowledge that Christ is the God-man, but hold a Trinitarian subordinationism. Rationalism makes Christ merely a man, a natural product of His age, but an unapproachable example of wisdom and virtue. His supernatural origin and His ascension are myths, and He performed no miracles. He is not the Son of God in the metaphysical sense.

Kant regarded Christ as the abstract idea and the ideal of moral perfection. Salvation comes by faith in this moral ideal, not in the historic Christ.

Philosophic pantheism regards the significance of Christ as lying in the fact that He was the first one to recognize and express the absolute unity of human existence with the divine.

Dorner holds that the Logos only gradually imparted Himself to the man Jesus, and that this was the manner in which the union of God and man took place in Christ. But this would make of the incarnation, not the beginning, but the result of the earthly life of our Lord.

According to Ritschl the predicate of deity is only a value-judgment of Christ. How the person of Christ came to be is not an object of theological inquiry. What the tradition of the Church offers in this respect is unclear. The deity of Christ is only an expression of the fact that He fully reveals God according to the moral world-purpose.

explanation of the Second Article of the Apostles' Creed in his Small Catechism: "I believe that Jesus Christ, true God, begotten of the Father from all eternity, and also true man, born of the Virgin Mary, is my Lord." It is stated more fully in the Athanasian Creed, as follows: "Our Lord Jesus Christ, the Son of God, is God and man; God of the substance of the Father, begotten before the worlds; and man, of the substance of His mother, born in the world; perfect God, and perfect man, of a reasonable soul and human flesh subsisting. Equal to the Father as touching His Godhead, and inferior to the Father as touching His manhood; who although He be God and man, yet He is not two but one Christ; One, not by the conversion of the Godhead into flesh, but by taking manhood into God; One altogether, not by confusion of substance, but by unity of Person. For as the reasonable soul and flesh is one man; so God and man is one Christ."

The Creed of Chalcedon. It is stated still more comprehensively by the Symbol of Chalcedon: "We, then, following the Holy Fathers, all with one consent teach men to confess one and the same Son, our Lord Jesus Christ, the same perfect in Godhead and also perfect in manhood; truly God and truly man, of a reasonable soul and body; consubstantial with the Father according to the Godhead, and consubstantial with us according to the manhood; in all things like unto us, yet without sin; begotten before all ages of the Father according to the Godhead, and in these latter days for us and for our salvation born of the Virgin Mary, the mother of God according to the manhood; one and the same Christ, Son, Lord, Only-begotten, to be acknowledged in two natures, inconfusedly, unchangeably, indivisibly, inseparably; the distinction of natures being by no means taken away by the union, but rather the property of each nature being preserved and concurring in one Person and one Subsistence, not parted or divided into two persons, but one and the same Son and only-begotten God the Word, the Lord Jesus Christ; as the prophets from the beginning have declared concerning Him, and the Lord Jesus Christ Himself has taught us, and the Creed of the Fathers has handed down to us."

CHAPTER X

THE COMMUNION OF NATURES

Since the two natures of Christ are indivisibly and inseparably united in one person, it follows that there is between these two natures a peculiarly close and intimate relation. This is described under the term, The Communion of Natures.

In view of the fact that the union of the two natures is personal, all the powers and resources of the divine nature belong to the person of Christ, and may be employed through the human side of His being. For there is a communion of the natures in such a way that there is a communication of attributes and powers from the divine to the human. This does not imply that the natures are in any way confused or commingled. On the contrary, they remain distinct and unconfused. But the divine pervades, permeates, perfects and appropriates the human nature. As observed in the preceding chapter, heat may permeate a bar of iron and give to it attributes which it did not possess before, and yet the iron remains iron and the heat remains heat; and so, in a similar manner, the divine nature may and does permeate and give supernatural powers to the human, without on that account producing any commingling or confusion of the natures. This permeating, which is called a *perichoresis,* takes place through the person, because the person is the bond of union and the avenue of communication. In this communion the divine nature is active and communicating, and the human nature is passive and receptive. The divine nature is unchangeable and cannot receive anything from the human. But through the person it puts at the disposal of the human nature all the resources of divinity.

Personal Propositions. As a result of this intimate personal union and of this communion of the two natures in and through the person, there follows the correctness of certain so-called personal propositions. Thus, since Christ is both God and man in one person, it is correct to say, "The Man Christ Jesus is God," "God is man," "Man is God," "The Son of God is the Son of Man." In other words, the personal designations or names of Christ drawn from the divine and from the human nature may be predicated of each other. The statements given above do not signify that the terms God and man are identical in meaning, but that the same person who is God is also man.

The appropriateness and correctness of such personal propositions must be maintained in view of the oneness of Christ's person. A denial of these propositions would imply not simply that Christ has two natures, but that He is two persons. The propositions cannot, however, be made in the abstract, but only in the concrete. Thus we cannot say, "The divine nature is the human nature," or "deity is humanity"; for that would not be true. The two natures are not the same, but remain true, entire, distinct and unconfused. But in the concrete, that is, as the natures concretely exist in the God-man, the divine and the human designations of Christ are predicable of each other. God is man, and man is God; that is, in Christ. Thus even such a statement as this is correct, "Mary is the mother of God." This does not mean that Mary is the mother of the divine nature; but it does mean that she is the mother of the person, Jesus Christ, who is God at the same time that He also is man. She is the mother of the Son of God according to His human nature. She is not simply the mother of a nature, but of a person. This person, Jesus Christ, was according to His divine nature begotten of the Father before all worlds; but according to His human nature He was born in time of the Virgin Mary. "The Son of God is the Son of Mary" must be interpreted in this sense, and not in the Nestorian sense that the man who is united with the Son of God is the Son of Mary. For Christ is not a man united with God, but is God and man united in one person, God incarnate, God become man.

Communication of Attributes or Communicatio Idiomatum [1] follows as a further result of the communion of natures. This means that there is a communication of the *idiomata,* i.e. of the properties, attributes or peculiarities, from both natures of Christ to the person, and from one nature to the other through the person; and that an act of either nature is an act of the one person, and hence is participated in by the other nature. This does not involve any transfer or merging of the one nature as such in the other. But it means that all the attributes, whether of the divine or of the human nature, are attributes of the person; and that the acts of Christ are acts of the person, and not of either nature independently of the person.

The Communication of Attributes or *Communicatio Idiomatum* is considered under the following three *genera:* The Attributive Genus or the *Genus Idiomaticum,* The Majestic Genus or the *Genus Majestaticum,* The Official Genus or the *Genus Apotelesmaticum.*

(1) *The Genus Idiomaticum.* The Attributive Genus or *Genus Idiomaticum* is that form of the communication in which the attributes or peculiarities of either or of both natures of Christ are predicated of the whole person, whether the person

---

[1] While this doctrine in its abstract form has the appearance of a scholastic subtlety, it sets forth truths of fundamental importance in connection with the person and work of Christ. It was forced to the front by the difference between the Christology of the Lutheran Church and that of the Reformed. The latter was inclined to an undue separation of the natures of Christ. In opposition to the Calvinistic maxims, *"Finitum non est capax infiniti,"* and *"nulla natura in se recipit contradictoria,"* the Lutheran maxim is *"Humana natura in Christo est capax divinae."* The Christology of the Lutheran Church guards the unity of the person and the duality of the natures, and emphasizes the genuineness of the personal union by the doctrine of the *Communicatio Idiomatum.*

is designated or named from one nature or the other, or from both.

In order to understand more clearly what is meant by the Attributive Genus, let us take up the matter from the standpoint of the person. The person unites in Himself the two natures. The person is exactly the same whether called by one name or another. We may call Him Jesus, or Christ, or the Son of God, or the God-man; but in every case we mean exactly the same person. Of this person, who is the same whether designated by a divine or by a human name or by both, certain things may be asserted. These things which are asserted are derived either from the divine nature or from the human nature. Thus, omnipotence is a peculiarity of the divine nature, and hunger is a peculiarity of the human nature. But when either omnipotence or hunger is asserted of Christ it is asserted of Him as a person, no matter by what name He may be designated. Thus we say, "The Son of God is omnipotent," or we say, "The Son of Man is omnipotent." Thus also we say, "The Son of Man was hungry," or we say, "The Son of God was hungry." The language is correct and Scriptural. In other words, all the peculiarities of either or of both natures are peculiarities of the person, and may be predicated of Him under any name by which He is known.

The Attributive Genus or *Genus Idiomaticum* may be subdivided into three kinds: By Appropriation. By Communication. By Reciprocation.

(a) *By Appropriation.* In this case human peculiarities are asserted of the person named from the divine nature. Thus, "Ye killed the Prince of life (Acts 3:15) ; and "They crucified the Lord of glory" (1 Cor. 2:8). Being killed or crucified is distinctly a human peculiarity; but it is something predicated of the person designated by a divine name. The fact that the name of the person is here derived from the divine nature, while the peculiarity is derived from the human nature, does not in any way affect the correctness of the statement. For while Christ was crucified according to His human nature, it was the person who was crucified, and it is the person who is referred to and meant by the divine name which is used. The death of Jesus was not merely the death of His human nature, but the death of Christ the person. And since He is both God and man, a name derived from either nature is appropriate and correct as a designation of the person.

(b) *By Communication.* In this case the divine peculiarities are ascribed to the person named from the human nature. Thus, "What and if ye shall see the Son of Man ascend up where He was before" (John 6:62) and "No man hath ascended up to heaven but He that came down from heaven, even the Son of Man which is in heaven" (John 3:13). The preëxistence in heaven and the coming down from heaven spoken of in these passages are peculiarities derived from the divine nature; but they belong to the person, and the fact that the name "Son of Man" used to designate the person is derived from the human nature does not affect the truth and correctness of the statements made.

(c) *By Reciprocation.* In this case both divine and human peculiarities are predicated of the person designated from either or from both natures. Thus, "Whose are the fathers, and of whom as concerning the flesh Christ came, who is over all, blessed forever" (Rom. 9:15). Here it is asserted that the one person who is called Christ, a human name, was descended from the fathers—a human peculiarity; and yet He is over all, blessed forever—a divine peculiarity. Thus both divine and human peculiarities are predicated of Him in one sentence and under one name. But it is all appropriate and true, because Christ is at one and the same time God and man. Peculiarities of both natures are predicated of the person, because the person is one and unites the two natures in Himself.

(2) *The Genus Majestaticum.* The Majestic Genus or

Genus Majestaticum is that form of the communication in which the Son of God communicates His divine majesty to His assumed human nature. By the incarnation, the person of the Logos has become that of the human nature also. It follows therefore, since the two natures are united in one person, that the human nature has through the person been made partaker of the attributes of the divine nature, and hence of its glory and majesty.

The incarnation was a "taking of manhood into God," and this inevitably resulted in a communication from the divine nature to the human of attributes and powers which human nature otherwise could not possess, and which must be distinguished from that peculiar excellence of soul and body which belonged to Christ as a sinless man. The communion of natures in and through the person carries with it the permeation of the human by the divine, and thus a communication of divine attributes to the human nature. This communication is not mutual or reciprocal.[2] The human nature communicates nothing to the divine, because the latter is unchangeable and incapable of receiving anything from the human nature. The divine nature is the higher and active one, and the human is the lower or passive. The human nature has no excellencies to bestow upon the divine.

By reason of what is here called the *genus majestaticum* Christ possessed according to His human nature such divine and majestic powers as omnipotence, omniscience and the like. That He did not according to His human nature constantly exercise these divine powers, but ordinarily refrained from their use while on earth, will be considered under the head of the Humiliation.

The communication of divine powers to the human nature is

---

[2] The Reformed, who reject this doctrine, object that if there be a communication, it must be mutual; and that if there be a *genus majestaticum* or a communication from the divine to the human nature, there must also be a *genus tapeinoticon* or a communication from the human nature to the divine. But this would conflict with the immutability of the divine nature.

not a transfusion of the divine properties into the human nature so that no true human nature is left, nor is it a merging of the human nature into the divine. But it is such a communication of the divine to the human that the former inwardly penetrates, permeates and perfects the latter.

The divine attributes which thus come to be ascribed to the human nature are, of course, relative attributes; and not the immanent or absolute attributes of God, such as eternity, self-existence and the like, which are not communicable to a nature which is temporal in origin.

The doctrine of the *Genus Majestaticum* is Scriptural. Christ according to His human nature possesses divine majesty; for He says of Himself, "All things are delivered unto me of my Father" (Matt. 11:27) ; and the apostle declares that the Father "set Him down at His own right hand in heavenly places" (Eph. 1:20). He possesses omniscience; for we are told that in Him "are hid all the treasures of wisdom and knowledge" (Col. 2:3). He possesses omnipresence; for He says, "Lo, I am with you alway, even unto the end of the world" (Matt. 28:20) ; and again, "Where two or three are gathered together in my name, there am I in the midst of them" (Matt. 18:20). He possesses power to quicken (John 5:21), and power to judge (Matt. 16:27). On account of the personal union the whole Christ, including His human nature, is to be worshiped and adored [3] (John 5:23; Phil. 2:9-11; Acts 7:59).

(3) *Genus Apotelesmaticum*. The Official Genus or *Genus Apotelesmaticum* means that the acts of Christ and the influ-

---

[3] The Reformed maintain that Christ is to be worshiped only according to His divine nature. They reject the whole *genus majestaticum,* and deny that the properties of the divine nature have been truly and really communicated to the human nature through the personal union. Hence they hold that Christ is not omnipotent, omniscient and omnipresent according to His human nature; and, consequently, that it is impossible for Christ's body to be present wherever the Lord's Supper is celebrated. Some Lutheran theologians hold that the omnipresence of Christ's body is to be understood as meaning that His body is present wherever He determines that it shall be present.

ences proceeding from Him must be ascribed to the whole God-man, and not to the one or the other nature alone. The redemption is to be ascribed to both natures united in the one person. Christ through each nature performed that which was peculiar to that nature, but the other nature participated. The person suffered according to His human nature, but the divine nature participated in the sufferings, in that it willed them and supported the human nature under them.

Thus "The Son of God was manifested that He might destroy the works of the devil" (1 John 3:8). "The Son of man is come to seek and to save that which was lost" (Luke 19:10). "The blood of Jesus Christ His Son cleanseth us from all sin" (1 John 1:7). Both as the Son of God and as the Son of man, that is, as both in one person, Christ came to redeem men. The blood which He shed for our salvation was not simply the blood of the Son of man but the blood of the Son of God. Were this not so, there would be no salvation for us. For as through the divine nature alone Christ could not have offered a ransom for us, because He could not have died for us; so through His human nature alone He could not have offered a ransom for us, because in that case His sufferings and death would not have been sufficient. But through both natures together, united in one person, Christ as the God-man offered a ransom which is perfect and adequate.[4]

---

[4] The *Communicatio Idiomatum* as elaborated by the dogmaticians is somewhat heavy and cumbersome. But its virtue lies in the fact that it guards the genuine nature of the personal union. Since the validity of the atonement depends on the personal union, it is of fundamental importance to guard that union. The greatest weakness of the doctrine is the extreme logical abstractness with which it is usually treated. But it sets forth the work of redemption as a unified whole, performed according to the human nature, and validated and made adequate by the participation of the divine nature through the personal union. We are bound therefore to hold fast the truth maintained by this doctrine, whether we cling to the form in which the dogmaticians put it or seek to find simpler forms for it.

CHAPTER XI

THE STATES OF CHRIST

WE have seen that, by reason of the personal union, the divine nature of Christ communicated its majesty to the human nature. As soon, therefore, as the Son of God had become incarnate, He possessed according to His human nature the communicated divine majesty. How then are the lowly life and the sufferings and death of Jesus to be harmonized with the possession of divine powers and attributes? The answer is that Jesus lived on earth in a voluntary state of humiliation in which, while He possessed the divine attributes through the personal union, He voluntarily abstained from the full use of them, and humbled himself unto death, even the death of the cross. Only occasionally, as in His miracles, did He use the divine power which belonged to Him as man. Had He chosen to do so, He might have appeared among men in the full splendor of divine glory. But He did not do so. On the contrary, during His life on earth He refrained from the full use of His divine majesty, and used it fully only after His work of redemptive suffering had been completed. We therefore distinguish two States of Christ: The State of Humiliation, and The State of Exaltation.

THE HUMILIATION

The Humiliation is that state in which Christ, in order that He might redeem men by His sufferings and death, voluntarily, truly and really renounced, during His lifetime upon earth, the

162

full use of the divine majesty which He possessed according to His human nature through the personal union, as described in the *Genus Majestaticum.*

The term humiliation, like the term exaltation, is derived from the second chapter of Philippians, which is the *sedes doctrinae* or chief passage with respect to the doctrine of the humiliation and the exaltation. In the seventh verse of that chapter Christ Jesus is said to have *"emptied* Himself, taking the form of a servant, being made (or becoming) in the likeness of men."* Hence the state of humiliation is sometimes spoken of as an emptying of Himself, or a *kenosis,* which is the word employed in the Greek text.[1]

A study of the passage in Philippians reveals several fundamental facts which need to be borne in mind. In the first place, the person spoken of is not the Logos as such, that is, the Son of God before His incarnation or in the act of becoming incarnate, but the incarnate Son of God who is called Christ Jesus, and who is held up for us as an example. It is not the mind of the preëxistent Logos about to become incarnate, but the mind of the actually incarnate Son of God, Jesus Christ, which is to be in us. The emptying spoken of is, therefore, one that took place not before nor through the incarnation, but subsequent to it. The meaning is not that Christ as God emptied Himself in becoming man, but that after becoming man He emptied Himself. Since the divine nature is unchangeable and the laying aside of the attributes of God on the part of the Logos would mean the laying aside of Godhead itself, the emptying spoken of has reference, not to Christ according to His divine nature, but according to His human nature.

Having become man, Christ still existed as God, or, as the text puts it, still existed in the form of God. He might, therefore, during His earthly life have let the divine glory constantly

---

[1] Greek: κένωσις. Latin, *Exinanitio.*

be exhibited through the human nature. But this appearing before men on an equality with God He counted not a thing to be grasped. On the contrary, He had come into the world for a very different purpose, namely, to redeem men by a life of lowliness and suffering; and this redemption necessitated a temporary refraining from the full use of His divine majesty, so that He might suffer and die at the hands of His enemies. Therefore He emptied Himself, and instead of appearing among men in splendor as the Master and Lord, He took the form of a servant, and was made in the likeness of the rest of mankind, voluntarily assuming the natural weaknesses and limitations of ordinary men, and becoming like us in all things except sin. He emptied Himself by taking the form of a servant and by being found in fashion as a man. And while His glory could be seen (John 1:14) in His mighty works, He placed Himself by His state of humiliation in a condition of dependence on the Father (John 5:19; 7:16; 12:29; 8:28; 5:36; 8:29; 10:32), and limited His knowledge (Mark 13:32). In this sense the Father is greater than He (John 14:28). Only occasionally, as in His miracles, did He employ the divine majesty which He actually possessed from the moment of the incarnation. Ordinarily He refrained from its use, thus humbling or emptying Himself for our sakes, becoming obedient unto death, even the death of the cross. The passage, "Though He was rich, yet for your sakes He became poor" (2 Cor. 8:9) teaches no *kenosis* of the divine nature; on the contrary, the meaning is that Christ according to His human nature, though rich through the personal union, voluntarily became poor in order to make us rich. He humbled Himself that by His humiliation He might make us rich through the possession of salvation.

Characteristics of the Humiliation. In view of what has been said above, and of what is involved in the personal union which

we have previously considered, the following nine characteristics of the humiliation of Christ are to be noted.

(1) The humiliation was not a *kenosis* or emptying on the
part of the preëxistent *Logos,* but an emptying on the part of
the incarnate Christ. Having become man, the incarnate One
humbled Himself as a man, and became obedient unto death,
even the death of the cross.[2]

(2) The humiliation is not identical with the incarnation.
The Son of God condescended to become man. But that con-
descension is something entirely different from the humiliation of which we speak here. The humiliation is contrasted by
Paul in Philippians with the exaltation. The humiliation was
temporary. It came to an end with the exaltation. But the
incarnation is permanent. Christ has never ceased and never
will cease to be incarnate, though He has long since ceased to
be humiliated. The humiliation did not constitute the essence
of the incarnation, but was an accident of it. Humiliation and
incarnation must therefore be clearly distinguished. The beginning of the humiliation was, indeed, cotemporaneous with the
incarnation, in that the incarnation took place under humiliating forms in order that the incarnate one might be the Redeemer; but they are not the same thing. Christ is God incarnate even now as He sits at the right hand of the Father, but
He is in the state of exaltation, and no longer in that of
humiliation.

(3) The humiliation began cotemporaneously with the incarnation. At the very moment when Christ was conceived by the
Holy Ghost of the Virgin Mary, He humbled Himself in the

[2] In opposition to the doctrine set forth above, the so-called Kenoticists
teach a self-emptying of the preëxistent Logos at the incarnation. Thomasius
refers it to the relative attributes of the divine nature, or to the cosmical position
of the Son. Gess extends the *kenosis* to the immanent attributes also. Kahnis
regards it not as an emptying Himself of the possession of the divine person and
nature, but of their use.

mode which He chose of assuming human nature. His humiliation is found in the particular way in which the incarnation took place and the particular way in which He chose to live among men.

(4) The humiliation began with the conception and extended to the moment before the quickening of Christ in the sepulcher. It included His entire life on earth, together with His death and burial. It was a gradual descent to the lowest depths.

(5) It was a humiliation of Christ the person according to His human nature. It was not a humiliation simply of the human nature, but of the person. It was not a humiliation of the person according to the divine nature, because the divine nature can be neither humiliated nor exalted.

(6) It was a humiliation or emptying Himself of the use of powers and properties which He already actually possessed. By virtue of the *Genus Majestaticum* divine majesty and glory belonged to Christ according to His human nature; and it was His refraining from the constant and full use of this majesty and glory which constituted the humiliation. Possessed of all power in heaven and on earth, Jesus lived among men as if He also were only an ordinary man like them. When He was arrested in the Garden, He might have prevented His enemies from carrying out their purpose; He had the power to do so. But He refrained from the use of that power, in order that the Scriptures might be fulfilled, and that He might accomplish the purpose for which He had come into the world (Matt. 26:53, 54). It was a voluntary and real self-abnegation. It was a voluntary renunciation of the use of a majesty which He possessed.

(7) The humiliation was not a concealing of the use of the divine powers by the person according to His human nature, but an actual renunciation of their use. Christ did not as man

secretly exercise the divine power and majesty, while He appeared not to be using them. He actually refrained from their use, and lived in real though self-chosen weakness and lowliness.[3]

(8) The humiliation was not an uninterrupted non-use of the divine powers according to the human nature. For sometimes, as in His miracles, Christ used His divine powers for the furthering of the mission for which He had identified Himself with our race. It was a refraining *ordinarily* from the use of the divine majesty, but did not carry with it any inability to use that majesty when He chose to do so. His miracles were occasions on which the divine glory of Jesus shone, as it were, through the garment of humility in which He was clad and in which He ordinarily went about among men.

(9) The humiliation was a renunciation of the use of the divine majesty made out of regard for the accomplishment of the work for which He had come into the world; namely, the redemption of mankind. Had He constantly used His divine majesty, His sufferings and death in our behalf could not have taken place. But by humbling Himself, even unto the death of the cross, He redeemed us from sin and death.

Stages of the Humiliation. The stages of the humiliation, when viewed according to the order given in the Apostles' Creed, are, like the stages of the exaltation, five in number. Thus there is a balance established of five stages each. This is very convenient for the popular presentation of the subject in catechetical instruction. But it is found advisable in dogmatics to divide the humiliation into eight stages, as follows.

(1) *Manner of Conception.* The first stage of the humiliation consists in the manner of Christ's conception. This is de-

[3] A controversy broke out between the theologians of Tübingen and those of Giessen as to whether the man Christ Jesus governed all things as a king secretly, the former affirming and the latter denying that He did. The seventeenth-century dogmaticians follow the latter.

scribed by St. Luke's Gospel with exceeding delicacy (Luke 1:35). But it is still a fact that the manner involved a humiliation. This is expressed in the *Te Deum:* "When Thou tookest upon Thee to deliver man, Thou didst not abhor the womb of the Virgin."

(2) *Manner and Circumstances of Birth.* The second stage consists of the manner and circumstances of Christ's birth. He was born amid all the humiliating accompaniments of human birth; and in addition to that, He was born in a stable and cradled in a manger, because there was no room for Him in the inn. The great wide world paid no attention to His birth. Only the lowly shepherds and the wise men from the East sought Him out and worshiped Him.

(3) *The Circumcision.* The third stage consists in the circumcision. The humiliation is found not only in the physical operation, but also in the voluntary placing of Himself under the Law and assuming its obligation in man's place and stead, when in reality He Himself was the Giver of the Law. He took His place under the Law as if He were simply an ordinary Israelite.

(4) *Life in Nazareth.* The fourth stage is found in His early life in Nazareth. His home was in a humble and despised village, amid rough and uncouth neighbors, in a narrow and contracted environment, and in the deepest obscurity. He was despised by the more cultivated members of His race as a "Nazarene." Though Lord of all, He was subject to Joseph and Mary like an ordinary child of men, labored at the carpenter's bench, and subjected Himself to the hardships and limitations of the poor and the lowly.

(5) *Public Life.* The fifth stage is found in His public life and contact with men. His public ministry brought Him into contact with all sorts and conditions of men, the best of whom

were weak and sinful, and the worst of whom were quite depraved. Though divine and holy, He associated with them day by day as if He were simply one of them. He mingled with all kinds and classes of people, and dined with despised publicans and with self-righteous Pharisees. He was often hungry and thirsty, had no place to lay His head, like the lowliest among them, and endured bitter hostility and persecution at the hands of the ruling classes of the Jews.

(6) *Passion.* The sixth stage consisted of His passion. The sufferings which Jesus endured included the whole compass of His life, though they were greatly accentuated and reached their climax in His sufferings under Pontius Pilate. The nature of these sufferings is not appreciated as it should be, when the sufferings are regarded as consisting simply of those which He endured in His body. These were, indeed, exceedingly great. But the sufferings which lacerated His soul were even greater. Holy and perfect as He was, He was obliged by His voluntary humiliation for our sakes to associate with sinful men during all His earthly life, to be pained by their evil motives, words and actions, by the opposition of men to the truth, and by the spirit of hostility with which He was received by the ruling classes. His greatest sufferings came at the end of His life; in His agony in the Garden of Gethsemane, when He took upon Himself the world's sin and wrestled in prayer till the sweat like great drops of blood rolled to the ground; in His arrest by the officers of the High-priest as though He were a wicked criminal; in the defection of His disciples, the denial by Peter and the betrayal by Judas; in His delivery to Pontius Pilate; in the slanderous accusations of the Jews, the insults of Pilate and Herod, the rejection in favor of Barabbas, the scourging, the crown of thorns, the purple robe, the condemnation, and the long hours of agony in which He hung suspended from the

cross amid the mockery and derision of His foes. The extremity of His sufferings is indicated by His cry, "My God, My God, why hast Thou forsaken me?" (Matt. 28:46).

(7) *Death*. The seventh stage is found in His death. He who in His own person was the Lord of life humbled Himself unto death, even the cruel and shameful death of the cross, in order to redeem us. He who did no sin, and on whom death therefore had no hold, died because He voluntarily gave up His life for others. He had power to lay it down and power to take it again (John 10:18). His death separated His soul from His body, but it did not affect the personal union. The divine nature was not separated from the human, but remained united both with the soul and the body after death.

(8) *Burial*. The eighth stage is found in His burial. He was laid away in the grave as if His end was the common end of men, who die and are buried, and whose bodies decay in the grave. For three days it seemed to men as if He had utterly passed away. The very depths of humiliation were reached in His burial out of the sight of men. But with His burial His humiliation came to an end. All things that He had set out to accomplish by His voluntary humbling of Himself were now accomplished. The penalty for sin was paid, the atonement was made, the work of redemption was finished. There was no further humiliation. The body was not given over to decay, but rested in the tomb until the morning of the resurrection.

THE EXALTATION

The Exaltation is that state of Christ in which He laid aside the infirmities of the flesh, and according to His human nature assumed the full use of the divine majesty which belonged to it by virtue of the personal union. Like the humiliation, it took place according to the human nature, and not according to the divine. According to the latter He had not been humiliated, and could not be, because no increase or diminution can come to the divine nature; and hence there was no need or possibility of any exaltation according to the latter nature. It is immutable.

Its Stages. The exaltation began with the quickening of the body of Jesus on Easter morning. Its stages are the Descent into Hell, the Resurrection, the Ascension, and the Sitting at the Right Hand of the Father. The coming again to judgment, which is usually counted as a stage of the exaltation when an explanation of the Apostles' Creed is given, is not really an additional stage; for no glory or majesty will be added to Him at that time; on the contrary He will then simply exhibit publicly to all men the majesty which He is now exercising at the right hand of the Father. The exaltation was progressive. It reached its completeness in the Session at the Right Hand of the Father. Christ rose step by step until He had assumed the full and complete exercise of all His powers according to His human nature. His exaltation is permanent. He will never again be humiliated, but will remain exalted forever. When He comes again to earth, as He will at the end of the world, it will be in power and majesty as the judge of the world.

(1) *The Descent.* The first stage of the exaltation is the descent into hell or Hades.[4] It is expressed in the clause of the Apostles' Creed which reads "He descended into hell [Hades]." This clause is a late addition to the apostolic symbol, and is not found in it earlier than 390 A.D. By whom it was first added we do not know. Just what the author of the clause had in mind in framing it is not clear. The Reformed Church regards the descent as the last stage of the humiliation, maintaining that it refers to the anguish, pains and terrors which Christ endured on the cross and before, and by which He redeemed us from

[4] *Descensus ad inferna* or *ad inferos;* Greek, *Hades,* the place of the departed spirits, like the Hebrew *Sheol.* In many places in the Authorized Version of the English Bible "Hades" is translated "hell." In the Revised Version the Greek word "Hades" is used, and the translation "hell" is reserved for *gehenna.*

the anguish and torment of hell.[5] Or it identifies the descent into hell with the three days' stay of Christ in the place of the departed spirits,[6] thus finding the seat of the doctrine in Acts 2:27.

The statement of the Formula of Concord with regard to the *Descensus* is: "We simply believe that the entire person, God and man, after the burial, descended into hell and took from the devil all his might. We should not, however, trouble ourselves with sublime or acute thoughts as to how this occurred."[7] And it declares: "How this occurred we should reserve until the other world, where not only this point but also still others will be removed, which we here simply believe and cannot comprehend with our blind reason."[8]

It will be observed that this confessional statement is simply a general declaration that Christ won a complete and full victory over Satan for us. It does not specify what Scripture passage lies at the basis of the doctrine of the descent, nor give any details concerning it as the first stage of the exaltation.

The old dogmaticians, however, find the seat of the doctrine in 1 Peter 3:18, 19, "Being put to death in the flesh but made alive in the spirit; in which also He went and preached to the spirits in prison." Accordingly, they regard the descent as the first stage of the exaltation, and as having taken place immediately after the quickening in the tomb, and just before the resurrection. Christ is said to have descended into hell in order "to triumph over the demons (Rev. 1:18; Col. 2:15), and to convince condemned men that they were justly confined in the eternal prison (1 Pet. 3:19). The preaching of Christ was

[5] Heidelberg Catechism, Question 44. Comp. Calvin's Institutes, Book II, Chap. XVI, 8 seq.
[6] Larger Westminster Catechism, Question 50: "Christ's humiliation after His death consisted in His being buried and continuing in the state of the dead and under the power of death until the third day, which hath been otherwise expressed in these words, He descended into hell."
[7] Jacobs' *Book of Concord*, p. 643.
[8] *Ibid.*, 522.

not evangelical . . . but legal, accusatory, terrible, and that too both verbal, by which He convinced them that they had merited eternal punishments, and real, by which He struck frightful terror into them."[9]

In connection with this statement of Hollazius it is to be borne in mind that the doctrine that Christ after His burial descended into hell in order to manifest Himself to the devils and to damned souls as a conqueror,[10] and to triumph over them, is not a confessional doctrine of the Lutheran Church, but an endeavor of the dogmaticians to explain a statement of the Apostles' Creed of which no one knows what its author meant, and of which the Formula of Concord says that we will do well not to inquire curiously.

If 1 Peter 3:18, 19 be taken as the *sedes doctrinae,* the main question to be determined is, what was the nature of the proclamation which Christ made. *Kerussein* means in the New Testament to proclaim something; generally, but not exclusively, to preach the Gospel. Here it must mean simply to proclaim, since there will be no preaching of the Gospel in the other world. What, then, was proclaimed or announced? No definite answer to this question can be given, since the Scriptures do not enlighten us on this point. But it seems reasonable to infer that the announcement was simply the announcement of completed redemption. By such an announcement the dealings of God with Old Testament believers and unbelievers would be completely vindicated. The godly would see that they had not believed in vain; and the unbelievers would see that they had no one but their own unbelieving selves to blame for the wretched state in which they found themselves.

(2) *The Resurrection.* The second stage of the exaltation is the resurrection. The resurrection is the act by which Christ according to His human nature came forth alive from the tomb

---

[9] Hollazius, 778. [10] Quenstedt, III, 373.

in which He had lain dead and buried. It is the crowning event of redemptive history, and a fact with which Christianity stands or falls.

The resurrection was a fulfillment of Old Testament prophecies and of Christ's own. According to Jewish reckoning, which counted a part of a day as a day, Jesus rose on the third day. The first day ended and the second began on Friday evening at six o'clock, and the third day began on Saturday evening at six o'clock. Thus Jesus rose on the third day "according to the Scriptures."

The risen Jesus appeared repeatedly to His disciples, and gave them "infallible proofs" (Acts 1:3) that He was alive from the dead. The following appearances during forty days following Easter are recorded. The women who went to the grave early on Easter morning did not see the risen Lord, but found the grave empty and heard the message of the angel, "He is risen" (Mark 16:5, 6). Mary saw Him in the garden, and mistook Him for the gardener, but was convinced when He called her by name (John 20:15, 16). He was seen by Simon Peter (Luke 24:34), though under what circumstances we are not told. He appeared to the two disciples on the way to Emmaus, and conversed with them (Luke 24:13 seq.). Twice He appeared to the Twelve as they were gathered together, once when Thomas was absent and once when he was present (John 20:19 seq.). Again He appeared to some of the disciples as they were fishing on the sea of Tiberias (John 21:1 seq.). Paul informs us that He was seen by more than five hundred brethren at once, after that by James, and then by all the apostles (1 Cor. 15:5 seq.). He was seen and was accompanied by the disciples to Mount Olivet, where before their eyes He ascended into heaven (Acts 1:9). After His ascension He appeared to Paul and spoke to him on the way to Damascus (Acts 9:3-5; 22:7, 8).

The disciples at first were very skeptical. They regarded the report of the women who returned from the grave on Easter morning "as idle tales, and they believed them not" (Luke 24:11). Thomas declared that unless he should see in Christ's hands the print of the nails and put his finger into them, and thrust his hand into the spear wound in His side, he would not believe (John 20:25). The general effect of the crucifixion on the disciples had been utterly disheartening, and they were on the point of losing faith in Him as the Messiah. The assertion of the chief priests and elders of the Jews that the disciples had stolen the body in order to deceive men into believing that He had risen (Matt. 28:11 seq.) was an evident lie, because the disciples had forgotten His promise to rise again, and nothing was farther from their thoughts than the perpetration of such a fraud. And even if they had cherished such a purpose, it would have been impossible to carry it out because of the presence of the Roman guard before the tomb.

The strongest proof of the resurrection is found in the complete change which took place in the minds and hearts of the disciples. The transformation wrought in them by the evidence of the resurrection and by the presence of the Holy Spirit whom Christ sent upon them was nothing short of marvelous. They were absolutely convinced of the reality of Christ's resurrection, and their confidence in Him as the Son of God and the Savior of men was thenceforth unshakable. They went forth everywhere boldly preaching the Gospel of the crucified and risen Jesus, and showed themselves ready to suffer and die in His cause. The same confidence and devotion are manifest in Paul. Nothing but the actual appearance of Christ to Paul on the way to Damascus, and that apostle's absolute conviction that Jesus was risen from the dead and is the Son of God, can account for his transformation from a bitter persecutor of the Christians into an ardent and indefatigable advocate of the

Gospel. The reality of the resurrection formed the basis of the preaching of all the apostles, and of the Church in its entirety.[11]

The resurrection is ascribed to the activity of the Father and the Holy Spirit, as well as to that of the Son Himself. Christ is said to have been raised up from the dead by the Father (Col. 2:12; Acts 2:24) and by the glory of the Father (Rom. 6:4), by the Holy Spirit (Rom. 8:11), and by His own act (John 10:18; 2:19). The explanation lies, of course, in the fact that the Father, the Son and the Holy Ghost are one Triune God.

The body with which Christ rose and appeared to His disciples was not a seeming body temporarily assumed, but a real body which had flesh and bones (Luke 24:34), and which was the same body which was crucified. It was recognized by the disciples, and had the marks of the nails and the spear (John 20:27). But it had undergone a great change, so that it was also a new or different body. It had new powers and properties. During the forty days after Easter when Jesus appeared to His disciples, His body was manifestly no longer hampered by the limitations of the body in its natural state. He was able to pass through closed doors and to appear and disappear at will in widely separated places. With the completion of the exaltation through the ascension and the session at the right hand of the Father, the body of Christ evidently underwent a still further spiritualization; for it has become the prototype of our own resurrection bodies (Phil. 3:21), which as Paul tells us shall no longer be psychical but spiritual (1 Cor. 15:44 seq.). It appears that temporarily for the disciples' sake Christ remained between His resurrection and His ascension in only a partially glorified state (John 20:17), but that He entered upon His completely glorified state when He ascended and sat on the right hand of the Father.

[11] Comp. 1 Cor. 15:17; Acts 1:22; 2:32; 3:15; 10:41; 1 Cor. 15:5-8.

The resurrection holds a central place in the Christian religion. It proves Jesus to be the Son of God and the Savior of men, and guarantees our own resurrection from the dead on the last day. Because of this central place which it holds, the resurrection has been the favorite point of attack by the enemies of the Gospel. Thus the chief priests and elders disseminated the slander that the disciples had stolen the Lord's body from the grave. In modern times the effort has been made to explain away the resurrection by means of various theories. The principal ones of these are the swoon theory and the vision theory. The former asserts that Christ did not die on the cross but merely swooned, and afterwards revived and rejoined His disciples. But the theory is utterly discredited in the face of the clear facts of Christ's crucifixion and death, and of the certainty that the complete change in the disciples, after they were assured of the resurrection, could not have been produced by the appearance among them of a crucified man who had been resuscitated from a swoon and who would necessarily be a weak and pitiable object to look upon.

The Vision Theory maintains that the disciples, by brooding over Christ's death and His promised resurrection, became the victims of hallucinations, in which they imagined that they saw Him risen from the dead. The conditions necessary for such hallucinations, however, were not present. There was no glowing faith in the promised resurrection which would incline them to imagine that it had taken place. There was no lapse of sufficient time for such supposed brooding to produce hallucinations. It is utterly unlikely, if not impossible, that an identical hallucination should exist on the part of so many different individuals, or that five hundred brethren should simultaneously have the same visual delusion; or that such hallucinations, if they existed, should all cease among all the disciples at the end of forty days.

The resurrection guarantees that Jesus is the Son of God, as He claimed to be; for God would not have raised an impostor from the dead. It guarantees the actuality and sufficiency of the redemption, because He who paid the ransom for us is proved by the resurrection to be God as well as man and to have paid the price of redemption in full. It guarantees the certainty of our own resurrection from the dead, because as Christ rose, so we also shall rise in Him. It guaranteed the coming of the Holy Spirit who was poured out on the disciples on the day of Pentecost, and who equipped them for the preaching of the Gospel in all the world. Without the resurrection the disciples could not have persuaded men to believe on Christ; for without it they would have had nothing to proclaim but that a good man had been put to death on the cross of Calvary. But the resurrection was the crowning and irrefutable proof that Jesus is the Son of God and the Savior of men.

(3) *The Ascension.* The third stage of the exaltation is the ascension. The ascension of Christ is the act of the risen Savior by which forty days after His resurrection He visibly ascended into heaven from Mount Olivet before the eyes of the disciples, a cloud receiving Him out of their sight (Acts 1:9). The ascension is the counterpart of His coming down from heaven. Having completed the redemption for which He had come to earth, He returned to His heavenly home. He ascended far above all heavens (Eph. 4:10). This ascension is not to be understood as a removal from earth to some other part of the physical universe, but the transition of Christ into another relationship to the visible world. It was an ascension to the abode and presence of the Father in heaven. Where that heaven is and what is its exact nature we cannot in this world know. Christ left the world and its entire mode of existence for a new and heavenly mode in the holy place of the Father's immediate presence.

It was an ascension of Christ according to His human nature, and hence an absence from the world in the local sense. But he is nevertheless always present with His disciples according to His promise (Matt. 28:20). He is present according to His human nature wherever He wills to be. The ascension was the complete laying aside of the form of a servant, and the full entrance upon a state of transcendence on the part of His human nature, so that now as man and as God He is over all, blessed forever. His human nature is now completely glorified, exalted above all human limitations, and exercising fully all the attributes received from the divine nature through the personal union. Though removed from His disciples as regards His former mode of presence, He is with them always and is present in a special sacramental manner in the Holy Supper. The ascension was at once a triumphal act after completed redemption, and a going to prepare a place for them that believe in Him (John 14:2, 3).

(4) *The Session.* The fourth stage of the exaltation is the session. The session of Christ at the right hand of the Father is the act of Christ by which according to His human nature He assumed the full use of the divine majesty and power which belonged to it by reason of the personal union. This session is the last stage in the exaltation, and means that Christ now, both as man and as the second person of the Trinity, participates in the omnipotent government of the world. The ascended Lord sits at the right hand of the Father (Mark 16:19; 1 Pet. 3:22). The phrase "right hand of God" is a figurative expression for God's power. God, being a Spirit, has neither a right nor a left hand. But the term right hand of God is used anthropomorphically to denote His might and majesty (Exod. 15:6; Ps. 89:13). We read in Scripture of the right hand of power (Matt. 26:64), the right hand of majesty (Heb. 1:3), the right hand of the throne of majesty (Heb. 8:1), and the right hand

of the throne of God (Heb. 12:2). Christ now according to His human nature participates in God's rule and dominion over all things in heaven and earth. He no longer exercises full sway simply according to His divine nature, as He did during the period of His humiliation, but He now exercises that full sway also according to His human nature. He rules as the God-man over all things in a mediatorial reign designed to further the kingdom which He founded by His redemptive work on earth. By sending forth the Holy Spirit to work in the hearts of men, He calls, enlightens, gathers, sanctifies and preserves the believers unto life eternal. In this majesty He will come as the God-man to judge the living and the dead. When the judgment is past, the mediatorial reign will be over, and Christ will deliver up the kingdom to God, even the Father; and God shall be all in all (1 Cor. 15:24-28).

CHAPTER XII

THE PROPHETICAL OFFICE OF CHRIST

CHRIST came into the world to be the Mediator between God and men. His work is therefore called a mediatorial work. It embraces a threefold activity or a threefold office. The work performed in these three offices is one that cannot be separated into three concrete parts, because the activity of Christ as a mediator is a unit. But the three offices can be separated in thought. For the work which Christ has done and does includes the announcement of God's gracious purpose with regard to men, the accomplishment of redemption, and the establishment, increase and guidance of the Church. The mediatorial work of Christ is, therefore, usually treated under three heads: The Prophetical Office, the Priestly or Sacerdotal Office, and the Kingly or Regal Office. This nomenclature is based on the language of Scripture, which both in the Old and in the New Testament speaks of the Savior as Prophet, Priest, and King.[1] The historical progression of Christ's work as described by the evangelists begins with His work as prophet in His public ministry, continues with His work as priest in His sufferings and death, and concludes with His ascension and His sovereignty as king at the right hand of the Father.

The Scriptures date Christ's entrance upon His mediatorial work from His baptism, which, with the accompanying mani-

[1] Old Testament: *Prophet*. Deut. 18:15-18; Isa. 40. *Priest*. Ps. 110; Zech. 3:8; 6:9 seq.; Ezek. 40. *King*. Ps. 2; 45; 72; 110; 2 Sam. 7; Mic. 2:13; 5:2. New Testament: *Prophet*. Matt 13:57; Luke 13:33; 24:49; Acts 3:22; 7:37. *Priest*. Heb. 4:14; 2:17; 5:1-5; 7:26-28; Matt. 20:28; John 17:19. *King*. Matt. 27:11 25:31-34; Luke 19:12 seq.; John 18:33-36; Rev. 17:14; 19:16.

181

festation, was a setting apart of Jesus for His office. He now became known and acknowledged as the Son of God, and gathered the disciples around Him. The temptation was a testing in which He approved Himself for the office, and from which He came forth without sin.

As Mediator (1 Tim. 2:5) the function of Christ is the reconciliation of God and man, hence the doing of all that was necessary to bring that reconciliation about. It is a work which could be performed only by one who is God and man in one person.

Definition. The Prophetical Office is that work by which Christ during His sojourn on earth fully and completely revealed to men the saving will of God, and by which after His ascension to heaven He makes that will known through the administration of the Means of Grace and the operation of the Holy Spirit in men's hearts.

The office of a prophet is not simply nor chiefly that of predicting future events, but of proclaiming God's will to men. The chief task of the Old Testament prophets was to call men to repentance by the earnest preaching of the Law, and to faith by the proclamation of the coming redemption. They did, indeed, sometimes predict future events. But such predictions were incidents in their work and not the chief purpose.

The Great Prophet. Christ is the greatest of all the prophets. The Old Testament prophets were types of Him. The revelation of God's will which they made was only partial and incomplete. The revelation which Christ made is complete and perfect. For "God, having of old time spoken unto the fathers in the prophets by divers portions and in divers manners, hath at the end of these days spoken unto us in His Son, whom He appointed heir of all things" (Heb. 1:1). Coming from the bosom of the Father, Christ was able to reveal God's will with a fullness of which the Old Testament prophets were incapable

(John 1:18). Hence He spoke with authority (Matt. 7:28, 29), and not as the scribes, and was recognized as a teacher come from God (John 3:2). The Old Testament prophets said, "Thus saith the Lord"; but Jesus said, "I say unto you." The miracles which attested the prophetical calling of the Old Testament prophets were miracles either directly commanded by God or performed by Him in answer to prayer. But the miracles which attested the prophetical calling of Christ were wrought by His own power.

The Revelation by Christ Final. The revelation given by Christ is final. Beyond that which He has revealed our knowledge of God in this world will not go. No additional revelation will be given. Even the Holy Spirit, whom Christ sent to guide the apostles into all truth, did not come to bring any new revelation, but to make clear that which Christ had already brought.[2] (John 16:13, 14). The entire will and purpose of God are revealed in Christ. They are made known by what He taught and proclaimed, and also by what He did. He was Himself in His own person the revelation of God to men (John 14:9). For if we know the unfathomable love of God from the declaration of Jesus that "God so loved the world that He gave His only begotten Son, that whosoever believeth on Him should not perish but have everlasting life" (John 3:16), we know it even more vividly from Christ's life of love among men and from His sacrificial death upon the cross.

Law and Gospel. The substance of Christ's preaching was the Word of God, the Law and the Gospel. In His teaching of the Law, He separated the permanent moral elements from the forensic and ceremonial elements with which they were intertwined in the Old Testament, emphasized the fundamental

---

[2] There is on the part of the apostles a growing appreciation of the full meaning and scope of the Gospel. The freedom of the Christians from the Mosaic law and the universality of the Gospel were not completely realized by them at first. But they were led by the Holy Spirit into a full appreciation of the meaning and scope of the Gospel. Cf. e.g. Peter and Cornelius, Acts 10.

meaning of the Law as a command to love God above all and our neighbor as ourselves, set forth clearly its spiritual character, and freed it from the false and purely external interpretation which it had received at the hands of the scribes and Pharisees. The fullest and completest example of His teaching of the Law is found in the Sermon on the Mount, as given by St. Matthew. He came to be the Mediator between God and man. But in so doing He came not to destroy the Law but to fulfill it (Matt. 5:17). He lived a life of perfect love to God and man, thereby not only fulfilling the Law for us and in our place, but giving us an example of the manner and the spirit in which we as His disciples should seek to fulfill it (1 Pet. 2:21; Phil. 2:5).

The chief work of Christ as a prophet was to proclaim the Gospel—to announce the coming of the kingdom of God. It is a kingdom which came with Him, its founder and king. It is a kingdom into which all are invited and urged to enter, but into which they can enter only by undergoing a change of mind (Matt. 3:2), by becoming converted (Matt. 18:3), by being born again (John 3:3). Unless there is a complete inner change of attitude on the part of the natural man toward sin and God, he cannot become or remain a member of the kingdom.

Christ Himself is the founder and center of the kingdom, in whom men must believe as the Savior. He is the way, the truth and the life, and no one cometh unto the Father but by Him (John 14:6). He is the Good Shepherd who gives His life for the sheep (John 10:11); the bread of life on whom the members of the kingdom must feed (John 6:35); the vine in which they must be branches (John 15:1 seq.); and the one in whom alone they must find peace and rest (Matt. 11:28).

The Prophetical Office Still Exercised. The prophetical office of Christ did not cease with His ministry on earth, but is carried on in the labors of His servants who proclaim His Word for Him and in His stead (2 Cor. 5:20). He will continue to exercise that office through the Church and its ministry until the end of this mediatorial era of the world. While on earth He exercised this office *immediately* and in His own person. Since His ascension He exercises it *mediately* through the preaching of the Word and the administration of the sacraments. He has commanded His Church to make disciples of all the nations, and has given her the Means of Grace for the accomplishment of this purpose; and He sends the Holy Spirit to accompany the Word and the sacraments with His constant operation. Ministers are, therefore, prophets prophesying in Christ's stead. They are ambassadors for Christ, as though God did beseech men by them. They pray men in Christ's stead to be reconciled to God (2 Cor. 5:20). It is through them that Christ continues His work as prophet. This makes the Gospel ministry at once the most exalted and the most responsible office in the world.

CHAPTER XIII

THE PRIESTLY OFFICE OF CHRIST

IN the accomplishment of our redemption Christ is our great High Priest, who, as the Mediator between God and man, has satisfied in full for us all the demands of the divine law, and intercedes for us. The priests of the Old Testament, and espeically the high priests, were types of Christ in His priestly office; they offered sacrifices to God, and interceded for the people.

The priestly work of Christ naturally falls into two parts, namely, Satisfaction and Intercession. The word "satisfaction" is a theological and not a Biblical term. But the work which is designated as a satisfaction is amply set forth in those passages of Holy Scripture which speak of the vicariousness of Christ's sufferings, of the ransom which He paid, of the redemption which He accomplished, and of the reconciliation which He effected. It is called a satisfaction, because through that which Jesus has done and suffered He has satisfied for us all the demands of divine justice.

Definition. The Priestly office of Christ may be defined as that mediatorial activity or work by which, through His active obedience, He fulfilled for us and in our stead all the holy requirements of the divine moral law; by which, through His passive obedience, He bore the full penalty of our sins; and by which, also, He is and will continue forever to be our Intercessor with God. By His twofold obedience He satisfied in full all the demands of divine justice for us; and His complete satis-

186

faction of the divine law is imputed to all those who believe in Him.

The Need of Priestly Mediation. That there is need of priestly mediation between God and man is a persuasion of the natural moral consciousness, and finds expression in the sacrifices of the heathen, whose priests offered animals and even human beings for the purpose of propitiating their deities. Among the Israelites the ceremonial law gave divine sanction to the natural religious conviction by the appointment of a priesthood and the offering of stated sacrifices for sin. These sacrifices of animals by God's command were not in themselves an actual atonement for human sins; but they were types and figures of the real atonement which God Himself would effect through His Son Jesus Christ; and they were accepted by God in the meantime in view of the atonement which He would make (Rom. 3:25). Christianity, therefore, brings the fulfillment of that which was foreshadowed in the ceremonial law of Israel. Christ is the true High Priest, and at the same time He is the true and real sacrifice for sin.

Christ Our Priest. That Christ's work is that of a priest is abundantly attested in the Gospels, in the Acts and in the Epistles. John the Baptist declares that Jesus is "the Lamb of God that taketh away the sin of the world" (John 1:29). Christ Himself tells us that His death is a voluntary act of love (John 10:11, 15, 17), that it is a ransom for many (Matt. 20:28; Mark 10:45), and that it is the founding of a new covenant in His blood (Mark 14:22-24; Matt. 26:26; Luke 22:19). The extreme agony in the Garden of Gethsemane and the cry of forsakenness on the cross can be adequately explained only on the assumption that the sinless One was bearing the world's guilt and punishment.

The book of Acts sets forth Christ as the Messiah and Savior in spite of His sufferings and death (Acts 2:36; 3:14 seq.;

4:10 seq.). The Epistles, on the other hand, represent Him as the Messiah because of His sufferings and death. The cross is the center of the Apostolic Gospel (1 Cor. 5:7; 1:23). Christ's death is the founding of the new covenant (1 Cor. 10:16; 11:24-26). It is a voluntary act of sacrifice (Eph. 5:2; 1 Pet. 2:24) by which God and men are reconciled (2 Cor. 5:14-19; Eph. 2:16; Rom. 5:10; Col. 1:20). This reconciliation means the change of the old relation of enmity between God and man into a new relation of fellowship and love—a change which takes place because our sins have been imputed to Christ and His righteousness is imputed to us (2 Cor. 3:21; Gal. 3:13; Rom. 3:25). We have been redeemed by the precious blood of Christ as of a lamb without blemish and without spot (Pet. 1:19).

In the Epistle to the Hebrews the work of Christ's priesthood is compared with that of the Old Testament. Christ is the great High Priest (Heb. 2:17; 5:6) who becomes incarnate in order to function in this high office (Heb. 2:9-10), and He entered once for all into the Holy Place (Heb. 9:12), and offered Himself once for all (Heb. 10:10) as an adequate sacrifice (Heb. 1:3; 9:12), and thus secured forgiveness for us (Heb 1:3; 9:26).

According to Both Natures. In His priestly office Christ functions according to both natures, the divine and the human. In accordance with the *Genus Apotelesmaticum,* as we have seen, all His official acts are ascribed to the *person* of Christ. While, therefore, the sufferings were endured by Him according to His human nature, the divine nature participated in them because of the personal union, by willing and permitting the sufferings and by supporting the human nature under them. The priestly work of Christ is, therefore, not a work of Christ according to His human nature alone, but a work of the person, and hence according to both natures. It is not as God nor as man that Christ is our great High Priest; but it is as the God-man, as God and man in one person, that He stands between God and men and offers sacrifice and intercession in order to effect a reconciliation between them.

Since the priestly office of Christ comprises a work already accomplished, namely satisfaction or atonement, and a work which is still being performed, namely, intercession, the further consideration of the subject naturally falls into two parts, Satisfaction or Atonement, and Intercession.

Atonement. By atonement we mean the work of Christ by which He satisfied for us all the demands of divine justice.[1] Such an atonement was absolutely essential for the salvation of men.

Divine justice demands of men that they shall be perfectly righteous by complete obedience in thought and word and deed to the requirements of the moral law; and it also requires that they shall be punished for every sin of commission and of omission. Hence man in his natural state of sin lacks the righteousness which he should have before God, and deserves punishment for his transgressions. And however much God in His love desired to save man, it was not possible for Him to do so unless satisfaction was made to the divine law. For God is a holy, just and truthful God. As a holy God He hates sin, and cannot overlook or ignore the transgressions of His law. As a just God He must punish sin, and cannot give the reward of obedience for disobedience. And as a truthful God He must fulfill the threats which He has made against transgressors.

---

[1] Men's consciences enforce the eternal law of righteousness. Sin involves guilt and demands punishment; and there can, according to the demands of righteousness, be no forgiveness without expiation. The essence of punishment is retribution. The wrong must be balanced by a corresponding penalty. Retribution is a fundamental law of the universe, and the necessity of retribution from the standpoint of righteousness and equity springs unbidden to the mind. This is especially noticeable in our reactions when some particularly atrocious crime has been committed. In the retribution we see an expiating punishment, though the expiation may not seem sufficient in every case.

Consequently, if man was to be forgiven and saved, some way had to be found by which forgiveness could be bestowed without doing violence to God's holiness, justice and truth. In other words God had to be in a position to forgive men in love without at the same time ceasing to be holy, just and truthful. Hence satisfaction had to be made to the divine justice, and the sin of men had to be atoned for. The guilt and punishment of sin had to be borne for men, and a merit had to be acquired on account of which they could be rewarded.

The God-man Atones. This satisfaction of the divine justice was a work which no mere man could accomplish. For every man "born after the common course of nature" is born with original sin and becomes guilty of actual transgressions as soon as he is old enough to perform voluntary acts. No mere man, therefore, could save himself; still less could he save his fellow men. All that a mere man is able to deserve at the hands of God is wrath and condemnation.

What man was thus unable to do for himself, God undertook to do for him. From all eternity He determined to send His only Son into the world to become the Redeemer. Immediately after the fall in Eden and throughout Old Testament history the coming of the Savior was promised. And then "in the fulness of time God sent forth His Son, made of a woman, made under the law, to redeem them that are under the law" (Gal. 4:4, 5). Thus the Son of God became man, in order that He might fulfill for us all the holy demands of the law, and might bear for us all the penalty which we have deserved by our sins.

Christ the God-man performed the work of satisfaction or atonement. Being true God and true man in one person He was able to do and bear all things necessary for our salvation. His atonement is full and ample, and includes the whole race. For "He is the propitiation for our sins, and not for ours only, but for the sins of the whole world" (1 John 2:2). The satisfaction which He has made includes all the sins of all men, and not simply, as Rome maintains, the sins committed before baptism.

It was necessary that Christ should be both God and man in one person. If He had been man only, He would have been sinful like the rest of mankind, and would have needed to be redeemed Himself. And even if He had been a sinless man, yet only a man, He could not have paid a ransom sufficient for our deliverance from guilt, nor have acquired any merit to bestow upon us. Such merit as He might have acquired He would then have needed for His own standing before God. On the other hand, if He had been God only, He could not have put Himself in our place under the law, nor could He have suffered and died for us. But as true God and man in one person Christ was able to atone and did atone for the sins of the whole world. Being true man He did all that the law commanded, and endured all that it required as the penalty of human sin; and being true God as well as man, that which He has done and suffered has infinite value to save, and is full atonement for the sins of the whole world.

Active and Passive Obedience. Christ's work of satisfaction or atonement has both an active and a passive side. These are called His Active and His Passive Obedience. They can be distinguished in thought, but they cannot be separated in the life of our Lord. Through all His life He was perfectly obedient to His heavenly Father's will in all that He thought and said and did, while at the same time through all His life and especially at the end of His days He endured the sufferings which the human race deserved by its sins. The active and passive obedience existed simultaneously and concurrently in His life. At the same time that He passively endured He was also actively obedient. Nevertheless it is useful to consider His atonement as consisting of both an active and a passive obedience, because

it enables us more fully and satisfactorily to view the work
which He has accomplished for us as our Priest.

By His Active obedience Christ, who in His own person was
not under the Law, but was the Giver of it, placed Himself
under the Law and fulfilled all its demands in our stead by
living a life of unfailing and perfect love to God and man. His
was an absolutely sinless life. He "did no sin, neither was
guile found in His mouth" (1 Pet. 2:22). The entire record of
His life given in the Gospels is one of spotless perfection. By
this active obedience to God's law which was rendered for
men and in men's stead, He has acquired for them a positive
righteousness before God, which becomes theirs by faith.

By His Passive obedience Christ, who Himself did no sin
and was perfectly holy, bore the full penalty for the sins of
men by the sufferings which He endured throughout His entire
life and especially by His sufferings in the Garden of Gethsemane, before the Sanhedrin, under Pontius Pilate, and on the
cross of Calvary. He was obedient unto death, even the death
of the cross. By this passive obedience He has borne in our
stead the wrath of God against sin. And His payment of the
penalty of sin is counted as our payment, if we believe in Him.

Thus by His twofold obedience rendered for man and in
man's stead, Christ has made to the divine justice a satisfaction
which is full, complete and adequate; and has removed the
barrier which otherwise would have prevented God's love from
extending forgiveness and eternal life to men. And now that
Christ has made the atonement, God's justice as well as His
love prompts Him to forgive the believer. For, as the apostle
declares, "If we confess our sins, God is faithful and *just* to
forgive us our sins, and to cleanse us from all unrighteousness
(1 John 1:9).

Christ's Merits Imputed. By His active and passive obedience Christ has acquired merit. This merit, as we shall con-

sider fully under the head of justification, is imputed or credited to us by faith. This means that all that Christ has done and suffered is counted as belonging to the believers, and is regarded as having been done and suffered by them. Hence, in Christ believers have fulfilled the law and have borne the penalty for their sins, and are counted righteous for His sake. Through Christ they have forgiveness of sins, peace with God, and eternal life. By His passive obedience Christ has freed them from the guilt of sin; and by His active obedience He has provided them with a positive righteousness. By His passive obedience He has rescued them from hell; and by His active obedience He has acquired for them entrance into heaven.

The Sufficiency of the Atonement. The atonement which Christ has made is full and complete. His sufferings and death are the equivalent of the sufferings and death of all. The Scriptures do not countenance the theory that His atonement was really inadequate, but that God graciously accepted it as complete payment for us.[2] The death of Christ is an actual propitiation for the sins of the whole world. It has been asked how Christ in the space of one lifetime could suffer as much as all the children of men would suffer in an eternity of punishment for sin? To this it is to be replied not that Christ suffered exactly as much as all the members of the human race would have suffered if punished for their sins, but that the sufferings of Christ have a value equal to or greater than those which men deserved to suffer. The sufferings of Christ were not, indeed, eternal, but were comprised within the period of His lifetime on earth; but their value and weight must be judged, not by the length of time during which they lasted, but by their intensity on the one hand and by the person of the sufferer on the other.

The intensity of Christ's sufferings is and must be beyond the

[2] This is the so-called Acceptilation theory.

power of our comprehension. For how can we understand or even adequately conceive of the sufferings endured by a perfectly pure and spotless person, and a divine person at that, in His contact with the sin and vileness of men? How can we in any adequate measure gauge the agony which filled His soul in the Garden of Gethsemane when the burden of the world's guilt threatened almost to overwhelm Him, and when He prayed that if it were possible the bitter cup might pass from Him? How can we fathom the anguish of the Son of God, who had always beheld His Father's face turned toward Him in loving favor, when on the cross for the time being His Father's face was averted from Him because He was counted guilty in our stead, and when the vials of wrath were poured out on His innocent head? The agony in the garden and the cry of for-sakenness on the cross enable us partially, yet after all imperfectly, to appreciate the intensity of His sufferings.

The fact that He who thus suffered was not merely a holy man but was in deed and in truth the Son of God makes it clear that His sufferings and death are the equivalent and more than the equivalent of the sufferings and death of all, and that He is, as the Scriptures declare, the propitiation for our sins, and not for ours only, but for the sins of the whole world. The divine nature which was united with the human nature in one divine personality gave to Christ's sufferings and death infinite value.

Scriptural Declarations. The work which Christ accomplished as our Priest is represented in Scripture as a vicarious atonement, a redemption, a voluntary act of sacrifice, a propitiation or expiation, and a reconciliation.

His work was vicarious. It was done in our place and stead.[3] He was our substitute. He took our place under the law and

---

[3] See especially the Greek prepositions ἀντὶ and ὑπέρ, Acts 20:28; 2 Cor. 5:15, 21; Rom. 5:6; 1 Pet. 3:18; Comp. Isa. 53:5; 1 Pet. 2:24.

assumed its obligations and penalties in our place. His work was a redemption, that is, a deliverance effected by the payment of a ransom; and the price paid was His own life.[4] It was a voluntary act of sacrifice[5] by which He gave Himself as an offering for us. It was a propitiation or expiation for the sins of men.[6] And it was a reconciliation by which the old relation of enmity was changed into a new relation of friendship through the imputation of our sins to Christ and the imputation of His righteousness to us.[7] It removed the obstacle which prevented God from viewing the world with favor.

The atoning work of Christ has power to save, and it results in the forgiveness of the sinner who trusts in Christ. On account of it God does not impute our trespasses to us.[8] But the benefits of the atonement do not become ours until we are willing to be reconciled to God; that is, until we accept by faith the redemption which has been provided.[9]

Objections. The Scriptural theory of the atonement [10] as a

---

[4] Rom. 3:24; 1 Cor. 1:30; Eph 1:7; Col. 1:14; Heb. 9:12; Matt. 20:28; Mark 10:45; 1 Tim. 2:6; Gal. 3:13; 4:5; Luke 24:21; Tit. 2:14; 1 Pet. 1:18.

[5] Eph. 5:2; 1 Pet. 1:24; Matt. 20:28; John 10:17, 18.

[6] Heb. 2:17; 1 John 2:2; 4:10; Rom. 3:25.

[7] 2 Cor. 5:21; 5:19; Rom. 5:10, 11; 2 Cor. 5:18; Col. 1:20; Eph. 2:16; Gal. 3:13. The atonement has not made a change in God Himself; for His attitude toward sin and righteousness is always the same. But in making a change in man's relation to the law, it has brought about a change in God's attitude toward man; it has enabled Him to regard the believer with favor for Christ's sake, because through Christ all the demands of the law have been satisfied.

[8] John 1:29; 1 Pet. 1:19; 1 John 1:7; 2 Cor. 5:19; Col. 1:14; Rom. 3:24.

[9] See 2 Cor. 5:20, together with the many passages which speak of the necessity of faith for salvation.

[10] While the Church from the beginning held fast the idea of atonement as the essence of Christ's work, it did not for centuries get beyond the notion that the ransom paid by Christ was paid to the devil. This theory survived in parts of Christendom to the time of Luther. The clarifying of the doctrine was due to Anselm's "Cur Deus Homo?" in which he refutes the theory of a ransom paid to the devil, and grounds the atonement on the necessity of making satisfaction to the honor of God, which is offended by sin. He emphasizes the passive to the neglect of the active obedience of Christ. The restitution of what has been taken away is not sufficient satisfaction for sin. The sinner must give back more than he took, something of infinite value, "something which is more than all that is not God." Man could not make this satisfaction. In order that

vicarious satisfaction has frequently been attacked. The doctrine that without the shedding of blood there is no remission of sins (Heb. 9:22) has been objected to by many on the ground that such a blood atonement is offensive to man's finer feelings; that the punishment of one person for others is not morally permissible; and that the entire Christian theory of the atonement represents God as a hard and cruel God, while in reality He is a God of love. To these objections it may be replied that the vicarious atonement is the clear teaching of Holy Scripture, and therefore to be accepted on its authority; that God's justice cannot be set aside even by His own love, and that its demands must be met; that the world in which we live is full of the vicarious sufferings of the innocent for the guilty; and that to represent the atonement as an expiation offered from the outside in response to a cruel demand on God's part is a travesty of the Christian doctrine of the atonement. The teaching of Scripture plainly is, that God Himself in the person of His only Son met for man the demands of His own justice, in order that He might carry out His loving purpose of saving men. For God was in Christ, *reconciling the world unto Himself* (2 Cor. 5:19).

False Theories. Various theories of the atonement have from time to time been propounded as a substitute for the Scriptural doctrine set forth in these pages. The best known of these

---

God might do it, it was necessary for Him to become man. The death of the God-man is of infinite value. Christ's merit consists in this sacrifice which gave more than was demanded; and it is imputed to men in the forgiveness of sins.

There are some serious weaknesses in Anselm's theory. There is first the notion that God planned to save a certain number of men to make up for the fallen angels, a notion which fails to do justice to the comprehensive love of God. Secondly, his conception of sin as an offense against the honor of God is unsatisfactory when contrasted with the deeper view that sin is an offense against God's holiness. The exclusion of the active obedience of Christ is a further defect. But there is much in his theory to commend it, notably the idea of guilt and satisfaction and the consolation of consciences through Christ's death. It is marked throughout by great moral earnestness. Because of its essential soundness, Anselm's theory became the basis for the Church's doctrine of the atonement.

erroneous theories are the Governmental or Rectoral theory,
The Moral Influence theory, and the Ritschlian theory. These
theories, which are set forth in modified forms by different
authors, are essentially as follows.

The Governmental theory holds that God has the right by
reason of His absolute sovereignty to relax at will the demands
of the law, and freely to forgive men without any expiation
or sacrifice for sin. But in order that this grace of God may
not encourage sinners to imagine that they may sin with impunity, Christ is made to suffer as a warning that sin shall not
escape.

The Moral Influence theory holds that the death of Christ
was not a satisfaction or expiation for sin, but merely a transcendent display of divine love for sinners; and that the purpose of this display of divine love in the crucifixion of Christ
is to melt men's hearts, so that they may be moved to forsake
their sins.

The partial truth in these two theories lies in the fact that the
death of Jesus actually is a warning that sin shall not go unpun-
ished, and that the surpassing love of God displayed in Christ's
death on the cross ought to move men to hate and forsake their
sins. But these are by no means the only things involved in
the death of Christ. The full and essential truth with regard
to Christ's death is that by His death He actually atoned for
and expiated our sins; that His death was vicarious; and that it
was an actual redemption and reconciliation. The burden of
the apostolic preaching was not simply that Christ's death is a
warning against sin, nor simply that it is a transcendent display
of God's love, but that Christ was crucified for our offenses,
and was raised again for our justification.

The Ritschlian theory holds that there is no wrath of God
against the sinner, from which the sinner needs deliverance.
All that is needed is that the feeling of guilt and of distrust

of God on the part of man should be removed through Christ, and that man should be assured that God is not angry with him. Not God, but only man, needed reconciliation.[11] The conflict of this theory with the plain declarations of Scripture concerning the wrath of God against sin is evident.

The Intercession. The second part of Christ's priestly work, and one which is still being performed, is His Intercession (Heb. 7:25). As a true High Priest He intercedes for us.

The Intercession is that work of the exalted Christ by which, on the ground of His merits, He constantly intercedes with God for all men, and especially for the elect, that they may have the benefit of all the blessings which He has secured for them by His sufferings and death, and may receive all things needful for their temporal and spiritual welfare. It is distinguished into General intercession, in which Christ prays for all men, that His saving merit may be applied to them; and Special intercession, in which He prays for the regenerate, that they may be preserved and sanctified in the true faith.

This intercession of Christ for us must not be understood to imply that the Father does not desire to forgive us, and must be placated by the constant pleading of the Son. We are assured by Christ that the Father Himself loves us (John 16:26, 27). And the apostle asks, "He that spared not His own Son, but delivered Him up for us all, how shall He not with Him also freely give us all things" (Rom. 8:32). It was the Father who so loved the world that He gave His only begotten Son to save it.

At the same time, however, the intercession of Christ is an actual intercession; not figurative, but real. It is perpetual, and will endure throughout eternity. Now and through all the ages to come Christ points and will continue to point to His work of atonement for us as an all-sufficient ground and reason why

[11] Comp. Orr: *The Ritschlian Theology,* p. 149.

those who believe in Him shall be forgiven and saved, and shall continue through all eternity to enjoy the blessedness of heaven.

While He was on earth Jesus offered intercessory prayer for the disciples (John 17) and for others (Luke 23:34); and these prayers are a type of the intercessory prayers which He now offers at the right hand of the Father.

CHAPTER XIV

THE KINGLY OFFICE OF CHRIST

THE kingly office of Christ is that activity of the exalted Christ by which, sitting at the Right Hand of the Father, He rules both according to His divine and His human nature over all things in heaven and earth for the extension of His kingdom and the salvation of men.

As the Second Person of the Trinity Christ exercised divine power and dominion over all things from eternity. At and through the incarnation this divine majesty, as explained in the *Genus Majestaticum,* was communicated to the human nature. But during His state of humiliation, as we have seen, Christ voluntarily renounced its full use according to His human nature, and ordinarily lived among men as though He were simply a man like other men, only using His divine power occasionally for the furtherance of His mission and work. But with His exaltation to the right hand of the Father, Christ assumed according to His human nature the full use of the divine power and majesty, and now as the God-man rules over all things in heaven and earth for the purpose of applying the redemption which He has accomplished. He is the Mediatorial King, seeking by His Spirit, through whom He is ever present and active, to bring the lost children of men into the fellowship of His kingdom, and using His omnipotent power to develop His kingdom of grace into the kingdom of glory.

A Threefold Kingdom. It is usual to consider the Kingdom of Christ as a threefold one: The Kingdom of Power, The Kingdom of Grace, and The Kingdom of Glory.

The Kingdom of Power. The Kingdom of Power is that by virtue of which Christ upholds and governs the universe with all that it contains, visible and invisible. All power is His in heaven and in earth, over all flesh and over the angels (Matt. 28:18; Eph. 1:20-23). He upholds all things by the word of His power, and is to be worshiped and adored by all (Heb. 1:3; Phil. 2:11). The material world, the angels, the devils, and men all belong to His kingdom of power.

The Kingdom of Grace. The Kingdom of Grace is that spiritual kingdom in which He rules by His grace in the hearts and lives of the believers. It is composed of all those who from the heart believe in Him as Savior and Lord. It is the kingdom in which, through the operation of the Holy Spirit and the use of the Means of Grace, He gathers, enlightens, sanctifies and preserves the Church on earth (John 17:17; Eph. 5:26). It is a kingdom which is in this world but not of it (John 18:36; 17:16), which exists in men's hearts, and is "righteousness, peace and joy in the Holy Ghost" (Rom. 14:17), and in which Christ operates, not by any display of external power and magnificence, but by divine persuasion on men's minds and hearts. Its membership on earth is identical with that of the true Church on earth, which is the fellowship of true believers. It is a kingdom which in one sense is already here (Luke 17:20, 21; Col. 1:13) and in another sense is still to come (Luke 11:2; 2 Pet. 1:11). Its borders are meant to be extended till it includes all the children of men, because He died for all and desires to save all. It recognizes no distinctions of person, sex, class, rank, color or nationality (Gal. 3:28). The means which He uses for its enlargement are the Word and the sacraments, and the instruments which He employs are men. At the end of the world this kingdom will merge into the kingdom of glory. And the believers, as a royal priesthood and as those who have been made kings and priests unto God, shall reign with Christ forever (1 Pet. 2:9; Rev. 1:6; 22:5).

The Kingdom of Glory. The Kingdom of Glory is that in which Christ rules over the Church Triumphant in heaven, and over the good angels. It began with His ascension, and reaches its completion and consummation at His second coming.

Those who in the kingdom of grace have been faithful to the end shall triumph and reign with Him. The entrance of men into the kingdom of glory is through the kingdom of grace. Those who by faith in Christ have become and remain members of Christ's spiritual kingdom on earth become and remain members of that spiritual kingdom in heaven.

Duration of Christ's Kingship. The kingship of Christ shall last during the entire mediatorial era, that is, during all that time in which Christ applies to men through the Gospel the blessings of the redemption which He has accomplished, and assigns to them their eternal destiny. With the second coming of Christ and the final judgment the mediatorial era will come to an end. God's efforts to save men will then have exhausted all the resources of divine grace, and the fate of men, good and bad, will be fixed forever. Then, as St. Paul tells us, Christ, having reigned till He has put all enemies under His feet, will deliver up the kingdom to God even the Father, that God may be all in all (1 Cor. 15:24-28). This does not mean that the Son from that time on will have no part in the dominion of the world. On the contrary the Son, as the second person of the Holy Trinity, shall continue to reign to all eternity, even as He has reigned from all eternity. But the dominion which He is now exercising as the God-man during the mediatorial era for the purpose of establishing, extending and perfecting His Church will come to an end when that era is concluded. Then the Triune God shall rule and be all in all.

PART III

THE WORK OF THE HOLY SPIRIT

CHAPTER XV

GRACE AND FAITH

IT is the work of the Holy Spirit to apply the redemption of Christ to the souls of men by bringing them to a state of faith in which they accept and possess the salvation provided for them. His work is as necessary *in us* as Christ's work is necessary *for us*. For while Christ has redeemed us, the benefits of His work become ours only when through the gracious operation of the Holy Spirit faith has been produced in our hearts.

The work of the Holy Spirit may be considered under two main heads, or from two main viewpoints. First, from the standpoint of the State of Grace to which the Holy Spirit brings men, and in which through faith they are justified and viewed with favor by God for Christ's sake. Secondly, from the standpoint of the Order of Salvation, or of the logically successive steps by which the Holy Spirit accomplishes His gracious purposes in men.

Under the head of the State of Grace we shall consider, 1. Grace itself. 2. Faith, by which grace or salvation is appropriated by man. 3. Justification, which results from the appropriation of grace. When this has been done, we shall take up the study of the Order of Salvation.

GRACE

Grace is the unmerited good will of God toward the sinner. It is the foundation of the whole work of redemption (Eph. 1:6, 7), and was manifested in the advent and work of the Son of God (John 1:14; Rom. 5:20, 21; Eph. 2:7; Tit. 2:11).

It is also the active principle in the appropriation of salvation; for by grace alone do we obtain faith and become children of God and possess righteousness and salvation (Acts 15:11; Rom. 3:24; 4:16; Tit. 3:7). Thus the state of the believer is a state of grace (Rom. 5:2; 1 Pet. 2:10), a state which stands in contrast and opposition to sin and the corrupt nature of man (Rom. 5:15, 20; Eph. 3:5, 6), as well as to all ideas of merit or worthiness on man's part (Rom. 4:4, 16; 11:6).

The grace operative in the application of redemption is the grace of the Holy Spirit, who is the New Testament gift promised by Christ (John 7:39; 14:26; 16:7; Acts 1:5). He carries on the work of Christ (John 18:26; 16:13-15), and hence is called the Spirit of Christ, and is given and sent by Him (Rom. 8:11; John 20:22; Acts 2:33). He makes the objective salvation wrought out by Christ the subjective possession of men (Rom. 8:2; Acts 19:2 seq.; 1 Cor. 12:3), creates in them a new spiritual life, and restores to them the spiritual powers lost by the fall.[1]

[1] The doctrine of grace is closely connected with that of the free will. The Greek Church regards grace as meant to assist human freedom, and not to create a new spiritual life. Pelagius taught that we can live a holy life by the mere power of our own determination to do so, without the aid of the supernatural grace of the Holy Spirit. Augustine conceived of grace as a new creative principle, but taught an absolute predestination and the irresistibility of grace, thus doing violence to the universality of God's grace on the one hand and to the moral nature of man on the other. Semi-pelagianism regarded grace as the power which assists man's natural powers. The scholastics taught that grace is a superadded gift, which simply completes man's nature. Protestantism returned to the doctrine of Augustine. But while Calvin carried out Augustine's doctrine to its logical consequences, Lutheranism rejected his doctrine of absolute predestination and of irresistible grace. According to the Lutheran conception man can by his natural powers resist the grace of God, but he can and does accept that grace only by means of powers which grace itself bestows upon him. Roman Catholicism regards grace as being infused into the soul and producing an ability to do good, so that, as a consequence, justification is regarded as a making righteous, and not as a declaring righteous.

The old dogmaticians, following the example of Augustine, distinguished the following kinds of grace: *Prevenient* grace, which offers the benevolence of God and the merit of Christ through the Word, removes the natural incapacity, and invites, excites, impels and urges to repentance; *Preparing* grace, which restrains the natural resistance, imbues the mind with the letter of the Gospel and bruises the will through the law, so that it is more and more disposed to

FAITH

We must believe in Christ, if we would be saved; and it is the work of the Holy Spirit to produce faith in us.

Grace Must Be Accepted. The redemption accomplished by Christ is for all men. His obedience to the law and His death on the cross have made salvation a possibility for all. In His name forgiveness of sins and everlasting salvation are to be preached to every human being (Luke 24:47; Acts 2:38; 5:31; 10:43; 13:38; 26:18). Salvation is offered to all as the free gift of God's grace, bestowed for Christ's sake, without any merit on man's part. By His Holy life and innocent death Christ has acquired merit and righteousness for all. And all that God asks of men is that they believe in Christ as their Savior, so that His merit and righteousness may be counted as theirs. Salvation is through faith alone. It is, therefore, of great importance that we should know what is meant by saving faith.

Scriptural Conception of Faith. The Scriptural conception of faith is fundamentally that of trust in God as the God of salvation, though the term is used at places in other than this fundamental sense. Faith is a conviction of things not seen, a certainty concerning invisible realities (Heb. 11:1), a confidence in spite of appearances to the contrary, a hoping against hope (Rom. 4:18), and an antithesis to sight (2 Cor. 5:9). It

accept salvation by faith; *Operating* grace, which confers the power of believing and kindles justifying faith (regeneration, justification, mystical union); *Coöperating* grace, which concurs with the justified man in the promotion of sanctification and good works; *Conserving* grace, by which faith and holiness are conserved and confirmed.

Quenstedt distinguishes between *assisting* grace and *indwelling* grace. The former works on man from the outside, and includes incipient, preparing, exciting, operating and perfecting grace. The latter is the grace which dwells in the believer, and which coöperates with him in his sanctification.

The activity of the Holy Spirit is described by the later dogmaticians as constituting four offices: the elenchtical, to awaken a knowledge of sin; the didactic, to give a knowledge of the way of salvation; the pedagogical, to convert the sinner; the paracletic, to console and strengthen the converted.

is a seeing in Christ the absolute revelation of God (John 14:9). It is a believing that God is (James 2:19), a believing of His word (Acts 27:25; Rom. 4:3), a believing that Jesus is the Christ (John 8:24; 1 John 5:1).

Even in the Old Testament faith is the essential factor in religion. It is not simply faith in God's omnipotence, holiness and the like, but faith in Jehovah as the God of salvation, on the basis of His promises. Abraham was an example of this faith (Gen. 15:6), Israel had it (Exod. 14:31) and Nineveh exhibited it (Jonah 3:5). It lay at the basis of the obedience demanded by the Law (Exod. 20:2).

In the New Testament faith is central, and is demanded at the very beginning of Christ's ministry (Mark 1:15). It is specifically faith in Christ (John 3:16; 6:40; 8:24; Matt. 18:6). It was possessed by the disciples (John 2:11), by the thief on the cross (Luke 23:40 seq.), and by the woman that was a sinner (Luke 7:36 seq.). It has the central place in the Synoptics as well as in the Gospel of John and the Epistles. In the Sermon on the Mount, Christ does not set forth the fulfillment of the law as a substitute for faith, but describes the conduct which should characterize those who have faith. The Sermon is addressed to His disciples, whose very relationship to Him implied that they believed in Him, and who would be called on to endure persecution for His sake (Matt. 5:11). Individuals who sought help found it according to the measure of their faith (Mark 8:10, 13; 9:22, 29; 15:28; Mark 5:34).

The emphasis on faith in John's Gospel is very evident. It was written that men might believe that Jesus is the Christ (John 20:31). Faith in God and in Christ belong together (John 14:1; 6:45; 10:38; 17:3, 8), and such faith means receiving Christ (John 1:12) and His witness (John 3:11, 32). It is coming to Him (John 5:40; 6:35), following Him and obeying His voice (John 10:3). It is the being united with Him in personal fellowship (John 6:51). It is being in Him (John 15:4). To believe in Him is true obedience to God (1 John 3:23); and the lack of this faith condemns (John 3:36).

According to St. Paul faith is obedience (Rom. 1:5), and is wrought by God (Eph. 2:8; Col. 2:12) through the Word (Rom. 10:14). It is a matter of the heart (Rom. 10:9). It is faith in Christ (Acts 20:21; 1 Tim. 3:13), the faith of Christ (Gal. 2:16, 20), faith in His blood (Rom. 3:25), faith in the Crucified One (1 Cor. 1:22, 23; 2:2) and in Him who was crucified and rose again (Rom. 4:25; 10:9). It is confidence in Christ (Rom. 4:20, 21), and makes of the believer one who is in Christ (Rom. 8:1) and in whom Christ is (Gal. 2:20; Col. 1:27).

Much that is called faith by men is not faith in the sense in which the Holy Scriptures use the term. Saving faith is not a mere belief that the Gospel is true, nor a mere intellectual acceptance of certain doctrines concerning Christ. It is not, as the Roman Catholic Church maintains, simply a belief of all that the Church teaches. It is something vastly more fundamental. It involves an entirely new attitude toward God and the things of God.[2]

Definition. Saving faith may be defined in either of two ways: as an attitude toward Christ the Savior, or as an attitude toward the gracious promise of salvation which God has given to us in Christ. When defined in the former way, Faith is the confident reliance of the soul on Christ for salvation. When defined in the latter way, Faith is the confident reliance of the

---

[2] Augustine's distinction between *credere Deum, credere Deo* and *credere in Deum* illustrates the difference between mere belief and faith. Saving faith is *credere in Christum.* It is an act of the will and not simply an act of the intellect. It is confidence in Christ—the reliance of the soul on Christ for salvation.

soul upon the promise of God to forgive us all our sins and to grant us eternal salvation on account of the merit and righteousness of Christ.

From both these definitions it appears that the essential factor in faith is confidence—confidence in Christ, or confidence in the promise of God given to us in Christ. The dogmaticians of the seventeenth century described faith as consisting of three factors, namely, knowledge, assent and confidence, on the ground that man must first know about the grace of God in Christ Jesus and then assent to God's gracious promise before he can have confidence in it. The argument used is sound; for the apostle asks, "How shall they believe in him of whom they have not heard" (Rom. 10:14). But knowledge and assent may more properly be regarded as steps leading up to faith than as parts or elements of faith itself, for in the last analysis faith is confidence. If we say, I believe in that man, or, I believe in that bank, we mean that we have confidence in them. It is true, we should not likely have confidence if we did not know something and assent to something that breeds confidence in us. But the faith or confidence is in its essence distinct from the knowledge and assent that precede.

Knowledge. Knowledge, as a presupposition of saving faith, means not simply such intellectual or historical acquaintance with the facts and truths of the Gospel as the natural man by his own power can obtain from Holy Scripture or from the preaching of the Word, but is the inner spiritual knowledge and understanding of God's grace in Christ which comes from the illumination of the Holy Spirit through the Word. Unless this inner spiritual knowledge is wrought in man, faith will not follow. For "the natural man receiveth not the things of the Spirit of God; they are foolishness unto him; neither can he know them, because they are spiritually discerned" (1 Cor. 2:14).

Assent. Assent, as a presupposition of saving faith, is not simply an intellectual assent to the truth of the Gospel such as might be given by the natural man by virtue of his own powers, but is that certain conviction of the heart concerning the truth of the Gospel and concerning its significance for his own soul which is wrought by the Holy Spirit. A distinction has been made between General Assent and Special Assent. The former means simply the intellectual approval of the Gospel as true. The latter means the assent to the promise of the Gospel as one meant for and applied to the individual himself. The latter leads directly to faith. If assent does not go beyond what is called general assent, it results in mere belief.

Confidence. Confidence, as the very essence of faith, is the act of the will by which we confidently rely on Christ as our personal Savior. It is distinctly an act of the will—an act of grasping and holding fast to Christ; or an act of complete surrender of self to Christ to have Him save us from sin and destruction. Faith means trusting in Christ as our own personal Savior. It is relying on Him or on His merit and righteousness as the sure ground of our salvation. It is the firm personal assurance that in Christ and for Christ's sake salvation is really and actually ours. When the soul has this faith, this trust or confidence in Christ, it says, "Christ loved *me,* and gave Himeslf for *me; I* am saved in Him."

The Cause of Faith. It is the Holy Spirit who produces saving faith in the heart. No one can produce it in himself (1 Cor. 12:3). On account of original sin man is not only born without trust or confidence in God, but cannot by his own powers understand or appreciate the message of the Gospel or appropriate it by faith (1 Cor. 2:14; 1:23). The faith which he needs for salvation must be wrought in him by the gracious operation of the Holy Spirit through the Word. The process by which man is brought to faith will be considered more fully in a later chapter, when we treat of the various steps in the Order of Salvation. Here we simply purpose to emphasize the fact that no man can believe by his own power, and that faith is the result of the working of the Holy Spirit. The principal Efficient Cause of faith is God. Since, however, the Holy Spirit does not produce faith in a magical or a mechanical manner, but through the Word and the Sacraments, these latter are called the Instrumental Cause.

The Value of Faith. The value of faith, or its justifying power, lies not in the faith itself but in that which it apprehends and holds fast, namely, Christ and His merits. Faith has no merit in itself; the merit lies in what it apprehends. The beggar who sits by the wayside and holds out his hand for alms receives alms, not as a reward for the merit of holding out his hand, but as an act of grace and benevolence on the part of the passer-by. The empty hand has no financial value in itself; it has such value only when it grasps the gift. The value lies in the gift, and not in the hand; but the hand is the organ or instrument through which the gift becomes his. Faith is not a merit on account of which God forgives the sinner and rewards him with salvation. It is simply the organ through which salvation is accepted. The justifying power of faith lies altogether in the merit and righteousness of Christ which it apprehends. It is not the faith itself, but the content of faith, that saves. The ground of our salvation is the meritorious work of Christ.

By Grace through Faith. The statements of Scripture and of theology that we are saved *by* faith must not be understood to mean that faith is the cause of salvation. It is divine grace alone that saves us. But faith accepts what grace freely bestows. Faith, therefore, is not the cause or the ground of salvation, but the organ through which we appropriate it. The classic formulation of this fact is found in the statement that we are saved *propter Christum per fidem, et non propter fidem per Christum;*

that is, on account of Christ through faith, and not on account of faith through Christ. Divine grace offers salvation on account of Christ, and faith accepts what is offered. God promises to forgive freely for Christ's sake; and faith believes and relies on that promise.

There are three things to be noted with regard to the salvation which is appropriated by faith. It is promised by God; it is promised gratuitously; and it is promised on the basis of the merits and righteousness of Christ. All, therefore, that is expected of the sinner, and all that he can do to obtain salvation, is to accept it by faith as a free gift bestowed for Christ's sake. If salvation is not obtained by men as a free gift, it will not be obtained by them at all. For salvation is not at all through works, but by or through faith alone.

Penitence or Contrition. The existence of saving faith in the heart presupposes the existence of penitence or contrition. This contrition, which is produced by the Holy Spirit through the law, is a frame of mind in which the sinner recognizes his sins, acknowledges and confesses them, genuinely laments them, is determined to hate and forsake them, and earnestly desires forgiveness. The sorrow involved in contrition is not simply sorrow for the consequences of sin, but for the sin itself. Judas, who betrayed Christ, was sorry for the consequences of his sin; but Peter, who denied Christ, was sorry for the sin itself. Unless this condition of contrition or penitence exists in the heart, there can be no true saving faith. If a man who is impenitent professes to have faith, he either deceives himself or is trying to deceive others. True faith always includes penitence, and cannot exist without it.

It must be borne in mind that the soul which does not lament its sinfulness and does not desire forgiveness will not, in the very nature of the case, seek or accept forgiveness. And furthermore it is to be remembered, that the impenitent man has

no promise of forgiveness in which to place his faith. He has
no promise given to him. Nowhere in all the pages of Holy
Scripture is a promise of forgiveness held out to any persons
but the penitent and contrite. And since a man cannot possibly
believe a promise which has not been made, nor accept a gift
which has not been offered, the impenitent man cannot possibly
have saving faith. Before he can have it, he must first genuinely
acknowledge and lament his sins, and earnestly desire deliverance from them; for only then will he have a promise in which
to place his trust.

Twofold Effect of Faith. The effect of faith is twofold,
namely, justification and sanctification. Through faith the believer is justified before God; and through faith he also becomes
gradually and increasingly sanctified in heart and life. Justification and sanctification must not be confused. Justification
means that through faith the merit and righteousness of Christ
are imputed to the believer, and that he is counted righteous for
Christ's sake. Sanctification, on the other hand, means that
faith is active as a vital principle in the heart and life of the
believer, and that because of its presence the believer becomes
more and more holy. Justification is instantaneous and complete; the believer is at once and fully forgiven all his sins.
But sanctification is gradual and incomplete in this world, and
will become perfect only in the world to come.

Twofold Power or Activity of Faith. The twofold effect of
faith corresponds to a twofold activity of faith. For saving
faith is at once a receptive and an operative power. As a receptive power it receives grace and forgiveness from God. As an
operative power it worketh by love. Every faith that is true and
real has this twofold activity. It has, so to say, two hands, with
one of which it reaches out and accepts God's grace, and with
the other of which it reaches out in the performance of works
of love. Being a living active thing, it is at once a saving and

a renewing power. By its receptive power it results in the justification of the sinner; by its operative power it results in his sanctification. For, being not a mere intellectual assent to certain truths, but a new attitude of heart consisting of firm trust in Christ as the Savior, faith implies that a great moral change or transformation has taken place in man. He has become a new creature in Christ. He not only stands in a new outward relation to God through justification, but his heart has undergone such a change that he now loves God and seeks to do His will. Faith is an appreciation of God's love to us. Where this appreciation exists we shall inevitably love Him in return. Hence faith produces love, and works by it. The very existence of faith in the heart implies a new and right disposition toward God and an honest endeavor to do His will. A so-called faith which does not result in a new life of love to God and man is a dead faith, and cannot save. It is not really a faith at all, but a mere belief. Saving faith results in a life in which love is the active principle.

Faith and Good Works. Good works are, therefore, the natural and inevitable result of true faith. The believer has become a new kind of man, and hence he leads a new kind of life. Loving God because God first loved him, he exhibits that love in his life as a Christian. Faith produces good works as surely as a good tree produces good fruit, or a good spring sends forth good water. Having been made by divine grace into a good man, that is, one in whose heart love has been enthroned as the guiding principle of action, he not only leads a good life, but he cannot help but lead it. As Christ Himself declares, "a good tree cannot bring forth evil fruit, neither can a corrupt tree bring forth good fruit" (Matt. 7:18). Where faith is present as a living power in the heart, its presence will become manifest in the life. Luther, in a notable passage, says of it, "Faith is a living, active, busy, mighty thing, so that it is impossible for one who has faith not to do good incessantly. He does not ask whether good works are to be done, but before the question can be asked, he has already done them, and is always busy." [a]

These good works have nothing to do with justification before God, but are the evidence and proof that we have faith and are justified or saved persons.

Degrees of Faith. There are degrees of faith. Some persons possess a much stronger faith than others. It is not, however, by the strength or weakness of our faith that we are saved, but simply by apprehending and holding fast to Christ. Both the strong and the weak faith apprehend Him and His merits, and hence even a weak faith saves. A weak hand may hold as great a treasure as a powerful one. But a strong faith is eminently desirable, and should be prayed and striven for. The weak hand can much more easily be robbed of the treasure which it holds than a strong one. The weak faith cannot give to its possessor the same degree of comfort and peace which a strong faith gives. And it is the man of strong faith, and not the one of weak faith, who is able to accomplish great things for the kingdom of God.

Certainty of Salvation. Faith gives the certainty of salvation. He who relies on Christ may and should do so with the absolute assurance that salvation is his. The Roman Catholic condemnation of this teaching and its claim that no one can be sure of salvation except by a special revelation, is due to its erroneous conception of faith and its office. Conceiving of faith as an intellectual assent to the Church's teaching, and basing man's salvation, in part at least, on works, it has no basis for certainty. As long as salvation is made to depend in any measure at all on man's own goodness and works, so long

[a] Preface to the Epistle to the Romans. Comp. Jacobs' *Book of Concord,* p. 583.

doubt as to salvation is bound to remain. But when salvation is conceived of as the free gift of God's grace for Christ's sake, the believer is and should be certain of his salvation. His certainty must not be based, however, on his own feelings, for they are not constant, but on the sure promise of God. Since our salvation is not at all dependent on what we are able to do, but solely on what Christ has done for us and on the promise of a faithful God to forgive and save us for Christ's sake, faith gives certainty. For what Christ has done for us is complete and perfect, and is ample provision of merit and righteousness for us. And what God, who is absolutely reliable and truthful, has promised for Christ's sake, He will most certainly perform.

If salvation had to be secured through the law or on account of our own good works, we could have no certainty of salvation. For the law demands a perfection which we cannot possibly attain. We do not and cannot always and everywhere love God above all and our neighbor as ourselves, as the law requires. But since salvation is offered freely, as an unmerited gift, to all who accept it, we have certainty through faith.

The Joy of Faith. The Christian's faith in Christ gives him the right to rejoice in the salvation which is his, and to be filled with inward peace. The apostle frequently calls on the Christians to rejoice. But believers do not always use this right which they possess, and do not always have in their hearts the depth of joy that ought to flow from faith. This may be because their faith is still weak, or because Satan assails them with doubts, or because they are strongly tried by the stress of this earthly life. If such seasons of uncertainty come, we should cling all the more firmly to God's gracious promise; and the certainty and joy will return. The Christian should be the happiest of men. He has the right to be. He should pray for the constant growth and increase of his faith, so that he may possess fully the peace and happiness which are his right as a believer and a child of

God. It is a mistake, however, to base the assurance of salvation on the degree of happiness experienced. Physical and mental conditions often induce a doubting and desponding spirit, which must not be mistaken for loss of faith and salvation. The assurance of salvation rests not on our feelings of joy, but on the immovable rock of Christ's merit and righteousness.

Knowing that We Have Faith. Closely akin to the question of certainty and joy is the question whether we can know that we have faith. To this the reply is, that the believer may know that he has saving faith from the testimony of the Holy Spirit; for the Spirit bears witness with our spirit that we are the children of God (Rom. 8:16). This witness is sometimes called a sealing (Eph. 1:13; 2 Cor. 1:22). If we are thus assured by the testimony of the Holy Spirit that we are God's children, then we also know that we have saving faith.

In one place the apostle exhorts us to examine ourselves whether we be in the faith (2 Cor. 13:5). Such self-examination means inquiry into our spiritual condition, whether there is real penitence for sin, real personal trust in Christ our Savior, and real love for God. Such a self-examination is likely to reveal great spiritual poverty. But if there be a hunger and thirst after righteousness and a looking to Jesus for forgiveness, faith is present.

It is unfortunately quite easy for this self-examination to become morbid in some persons, and to resolve itself into an inquiry as to whether we believe that we do believe. If such a situation should confront us, we need to remember that we are justified, not by believing that we do believe, but by believing on Christ; that is, by looking to Christ and relying on Him for salvation. Assurance that we have faith must not be put into the place of faith itself. We are not justified on account of possessing faith, but on account of Christ. We are saved, not by the confidence that we have faith, but by the confidence that Christ is our Savior. When we ask, "Am I saved?" we should not look within to see whether we believe in Christ, but we should look to Christ and say, "There is my righteousness and my salvation." We are saved by confidently relying on Christ, and not by believing that we are relying on Him. Faith is strongest when it is so absorbed in looking to Christ and leaning on Him that it forgets self.

Faith as a State. In its inception faith is an act of the will by which the sinner relies upon Christ for salvation. But that which begins as an act continues as a state. The believer is in a state of faith—a state in which he continues holding fast to Christ as his personal Savior. A faith which did not become a habit or state would speedily fail to justify, because it would fail any longer to exist. This habit or state of faith is extremely important. If we were believers only when by a conscious act we clung to Christ, then we should be lost if we were to die while our mind was occupied with labor or business, or while we were asleep. But faith becomes the constant attitude of the believer; and hence he not only has justification as soon as he believes, but he constantly continues to have it, because he is in a state of faith, or, as it is often expressed, in a state of grace.

Loss and Restoration of Faith. Faith can be lost. There is no inamissibility of grace, such as the Calvinists maintain on the basis of their doctrine of an arbitrary election. The loss is not necessarily the loss of what only seemed to be faith, yet actually was not. That faith may be lost is evident from clear statements of Scripture to that effect (Gal. 5:4; 1 Tim. 1:19, 20; Rev. 2:5; Luke 8:13), from parables and figures used in describing the loss of faith, like the dead branch in the vine and the salt which has lost its savor; and from the explicit warning, "Let him that thinketh he standeth take heed lest he fall" (1 Cor. 10:12). On the other hand, faith which has been lost by reason of a great fall into sin may be restored, as is seen notably in the case of David and of Peter.

Necessity of Faith. Faith is essential to salvation. We are saved by faith alone, without works (Eph. 2:8, 9; Rom. 3:28). Without faith there is no salvation for anyone. The plain teaching of God's Word is that salvation can be obtained only through faith in Christ (Acts 12:4; John 14:6; Mark 16:16; Heb. 11:6; John 3;16, 18; Heb. 2:3). This is God's way of salvation for men. It has been the only way since the fall. Man cannot save himself; and if he is to be saved at all, it must be by divine grace on account of Christ's merit and righteousness which faith apprehends. The saints of the Old Testament were saved through faith. In their case it was faith in a Redeemer who was yet to come; in our case it is faith in a Redeemer who has come.

As regards those who have had no opportunity to come to faith, because they had no opportunity to hear the Gospel, we quote the following from Luther: "If God were to save anyone without faith, He would act contrary to His own Word . . . that is impossible. . . . But it is quite a different question whether God could give men faith in death or after death, and thus save them through faith. Who would doubt that He could do that? But that He does do it, who can prove?" [4]

Theological Distinctions with Regard to Faith. There are a number of theological distinctions which have been made with regard to faith, whose meaning it will be well to note.

Human faith is mere historical belief or an intellectual mastery of the catechism or dogmatics. Divine faith is saving faith, wrought in us by God's grace.

Direct faith is the faith of infants, without ability to examine self or to recognize faith as present. Discursive faith is the faith of an adult, who is able to reflect upon and analyze his faith.

[4] De Wette, *Luthers Briefe*, II, 455.

Explicit faith is a faith which involves a definite knowledge of what is believed. Implicit faith is a faith in which the belief of what is known involves the acceptance of unknown particulars. This implicit faith was stretched by the scholastics to mean that a man's subjection to the authority of the Church implied his acceptance of all the Church's teachings, even though he had no knowledge of what those teachings are.

Subjective faith is the faith with which one believes. Objective faith is the faith which is believed, that is, the doctrines which are accepted and held.

The Roman Catholic distinction between Crude faith and faith Energized by Love [5] is untenable. The so-called crude faith is not a faith at all in the true sense, but only a belief of the Church's teachings. Saving faith is never crude, but always worketh by love. Love is not something added to faith in order to energize it and make it effective, but is something which inevitably flows from faith itself, if the faith be real and true.

General faith means the belief of God's Word in general, and has as its object the entire revealed will of God. It believes all that God says. Special faith means justifying or saving faith, which has as its special object the grace of God promised on account of the merits of Christ, or Christ the Savior Himself. General faith accepts as true all that God declares in His Word. Special faith confidently relies on Christ as Savior. If the general faith were destroyed, no special faith in the particular promises of the Gospel would be possible.

[5] *Fides informis,* and *Fides formata caritate.*

CHAPTER XVI

JUSTIFICATION

THE immediate result of faith is justification. The believer is justified by or through faith. This does not mean that the believer has been made personally righteous or holy, but that he has been pronounced or declared righteous for Christ's sake. *A Forensic Term.* The word justification is used by St. Paul in a forensic sense, and that is the sense in which the word is used here. It means a judicial act of acquittal. It is the judgment of God upon the believer with respect to the divine law, and means that the man is pronounced "not guilty" but "righteous" for Christ's sake. It is not something which takes place within man, but is an external judicial act of God. In it God pronounces the sinner free from guilt and possessed of perfect righteousness on account of the merit acquired for him by Christ in whom he believes. It has no reference to any moral quality in man, and produces no inner change in him. It is the establishment of a new relation between him and God, in which he who deserves only wrath and condemnation is regarded and treated by God as one who in Christ has paid the full penalty of the law and has met all its requirements, and who is now regarded and treated as if he had never sinned at all.[1]

Definition. Justification is that act of God by which, for the sake of the active and passive obedience of Christ rendered in

[1] The Apology does not discriminate clearly between justification and regeneration, and says that "to be justified means that, out of unjust men, just men be made or be born again; it means also that they should be pronounced or accounted just." Jacobs' *Book of Conc.*, 95, 72. This confusion is removed by the Formula of Concord, which restricts the meaning of justification to the forensic act.

man's stead, He graciously and freely forgives the sinner who believes in Christ as his personal Savior all his sins, and regards and treats him as a righteous person. The sinner thus acquires a new standing before God as one with whom God is no longer angry but with whom for Christ's sake He is well pleased. He is regarded and treated by God as one who in Christ has paid the full penalty of sin and has met in full all the holy requirements of the divine law.

By Faith. Justification is by or through faith (Rom. 5:1; 4:5). For by faith we apprehend and cling to Christ, and thus appropriate his merit and righteousness. Those who believe are regarded by God as having in Christ met all the demands of divine justice. When God looks upon them He no longer sees their own guilt and unrighteousness, but the righteousness of Christ which they have put on by faith.

This is God's plan of salvation for men. They are to be saved by faith in Christ. He sent His only begotten Son into the world, "that whosoever believeth on Him should not perish but have everlasting life" (John 3:16). The message which the disciples were commanded to proclaim in all the world was, "He that believeth and is baptized shall be saved" (Mark 16:16). And to every soul which inquires, "What must I do to be saved?" the answer is that of Paul to the Philippian jailor, "Believe on the Lord Jesus Christ, and thou shalt be saved" (Acts 16:31).

The Cause of Justification. The *efficient* cause of justification is the grace of God; for without any merit or worthiness on our part, God out of pure grace justifies us for Christ's sake. The *meritorious* cause of justification is the satisfaction which Christ has made by His active and passive obedience. Faith is not to be regarded as a cause of justification. And the statement that we are justified by faith means that we are justified by the merit and righteousness of Christ which faith apprehends and appropriates. Justification by faith means justification in view of faith, but not on account of faith. It is the condition without which the justification does not take place. The relation between grace as the cause of justification and faith as the condition is brought out by Paul when he declares that we are saved by grace through faith (Eph.2:8).

By Imputation. Justification takes place because of the imputation of Christ's righteousness to the believing sinner. The word impute, like the word justify, is Biblical, and not simply theological. It means to count as belonging to, to charge with, or to credit with. In the case of a debt, it means to charge with; in the case of grace, to credit with. In justification, a righteousness which man has not himself acquired, and which does not, therefore, belong to him in that sense, is imputed or credited to him; namely, the righteousness of Christ. Possessed of this imputed righteousness, the believer is viewed and treated by God as a righteous person.

Necessity of Imputation. The necessity of the imputation of Christ's righteousness for salvation is found in the sanctity of God's law and the inexorableness of His justice. The sinner cannot possibly meet the holy demands of God's law, or deliver himself from the condemnation which he has deserved by his transgressions. The only way in which he can possibly obtain a righteousness which will enable him to stand before God is by the imputation of the perfect righteousness which Christ has acquired for him. Unless that righteousness is counted as belonging to him, the sinner is lost.

Faith Imputed. The statement that faith is counted or imputed for righteousness (Rom. 4:3; James 2:23), contains a figure of speech, in which the container is put for the thing contained. In reality it is the merit of Christ which is imputed. Our sins were imputed to Christ, and He was counted a sinner for our sakes; and now His righteousness is imputed to us as believers in Him, and we are counted righteous for His sake. Those who were spiritually poor and loaded down with a great debt of sin are made rich by the transfer of Christ's great wealth of righteousness to their account.

Two Sides of Imputation. The imputation of Christ's righteousness has two sides, corresponding to the passive and active obedience of Christ. By the imputation of His sufferings and death we are pronounced free from the penalty of sin; by the imputation of His holy life and of His complete fulfillment of the law we are provided with a perfect righteousness. There is thus a positive and a negative side to imputation, which may be logically distinguished, but which are not separated in the act of justification.

By Faith Alone. Justification takes place by or through faith alone, solely on account of the merit and righteousness of Christ, and entirely without any merit or worthiness on our part. It is purely an act of grace on God's part for Christ's sake. It is true, the heart which believes in Christ, and thus appreciates God's love, will love God in return and strive to please Him. Good works will always follow upon true faith. But the justification is a result of the faith, and not a result of the works. The only works that have power to justify are the works of Christ. It is his righteousness put on by faith, and that alone, which will enable us to stand before God on the day of judgment.

Good Works. By good works we understand those acts of the believer by which, out of faith as the vital principle and love as the active principle, he does what God commands. These good works have nothing to do with our justification. It is Christ's merit and not ours that justifies. A saving faith is, indeed, always accompanied by a right disposition and by corresponding good works; but this right disposition and these good works are in no sense the ground or reason for our salvation. It is only after a man believes and is justified that he possesses the inner disposition from which all good works spring. The love which lies at the root of every work which is entitled to be called good is a love which springs up in the heart as a result of faith, and never without faith. Since the believer is justified the very moment that he believes, he does good works, not in order to be saved, but because he already is saved by faith. They are the evidence of His gratitude for the salvation which he has freely received. He does them because God wills them, and not for the purpose of obtaining any merit before God on account of them. Justification is not at all on account of these works, but solely on account of Christ's merits apprehended by faith. We are justified by faith alone without works.[2] This does not mean that faith can continue to exist without works, but that faith alone, independently of and apart from the works, and solely because it apprehends Christ, justifies and saves.

Good works, therefore, have nothing to do with our justification before God. They are the evidence or proof that we have faith and are justified persons. The believer's best works are after all imperfect, and if he were judged according to what he deserves by them, they would only cause him to be lost. Though they are called good works, their goodness is still very defective. Loving God as a result of his faith in Christ, the believer seeks to please Him and to do His will. But his works are not good in the sense of being a complete and perfect fulfillment of the law. If they are called good, it is because they proceed from a heart that has good intentions, and not because they are completely the kind of works which they ought to be. Indeed, we may say that the good works of the Christian are

[2] In his translation of Rom. 3:28, Luther added the word "alone" after the word faith. He has been criticized for so doing. The word "alone," however, simply accentuated and did not alter the sense of the verse. Erasmus defended the translation. And it is justifiable in view of the only alternative, namely, justification by works, which Paul expressly repudiates.

called good by courtesy. God accepts the will for the deed, as a loving Father who is dealing with weak and imperfect children. The attempts of the little child to be helpful in the home are regarded by the father and the mother with delight, not because the attempts are actually successful or the results really good, but because they see and appreciate the motive behind the act. So the believer's works, imperfect as they are, please God and are accepted by Him.

In our justification before God nothing has any weight but the merit and righteousness of Christ made ours by faith. The most sanctified believer on earth will enter heaven at last, not because he has been good, but because Christ "has redeemed him with His holy and precious blood, and with His innocent sufferings and death."

Justification Instantaneous. The justification of the sinner is instantaneous, and takes place as soon as he believes. When God looks on the believer, He no longer sees his sin and unrighteousness, but He sees the righteousness of Christ put on the believer by faith. God therefore at once justifies the believer, and counts him righteous for Christ's sake. The believer, according to Paul's phrase, is "in Christ." The phrase is significant, and implies that God cannot see the believer without looking through Christ, and hence sees him clothed and protected round about by Christ's righteousness.

Justification Complete. The justification of the sinner for Christ's sake is full and complete, including the guilt both of his original sin and of his actual sins, of the sins committed before baptism and after baptism. God never forgives a man only a portion of his sins; on the contrary, He either forgives them all or forgives none. Forgiveness is a personal matter. God forgives the sinner. Strictly speaking He does not forgive the sins, but forgives the sinner his sins. He can never look with favor upon sin, but he does look with favor upon the

penitent and believing sinner. Hence, either the sinner is forgiven and reconciled with God, or else he is unforgiven and
unreconciled. Either he has been received as a child of God,
or he has not been so received. There is no such thing as a
partial forgiveness, a partial reconciliation, a partial sonship.
The believer could not be regarded with favor and counted
righteous if a single sin remained unforgiven. But God forgives them all to him who believes. He casts them all behind
His back (Isa. 38:17), and no longer sees them. In those cases
in which men say or think that God has forgiven them all their
sins but this one or that one, they either rest under a most
unfortunate delusion which robs them of the inward peace
which they might otherwise have, or else the sin which they
fear is not forgiven is one of which they have not sincerely
repented, and which they are still shielding and cherishing.
Genuine contrition and faith are followed by free and complete
forgiveness.

In justification all sins, no matter how heinous, are forgiven
to the penitent believer. The Prodigal Son went, apparently, to
the extreme limit of sin; yet when he repented and came back,
he was received and forgiven. Peter committed a most grievous
sin against His Lord when he denied Him; but when he sought
forgiveness he found it. Even Judas Iscariot, who betrayed the
Lord for thirty pieces of silver, might have been forgiven if he
had repented. But he did not repent, "and went and hanged
himself."

The Same for All Believers. Justification is the same for all
believers. When two persons are pronounced perfectly righteous for Christ's sake, one of them cannot be counted more
righteous than the other. Both are forgiven all their sins, and
both have Christ's righteousness imputed to them. There is,
indeed, a difference in the sanctification of believers. Some have

made much more progress in grace than others, and are more sanctified. But sanctification is an entirely different thing from justification. While believers are not all equally sanctified, they are all equally justified through faith. This does not mean that the believer may safely neglect his growth in holiness of heart and life; for without the continued hatred of sin and the constant striving after holiness, faith cannot endure. But it does mean that his justification is not based on his own holiness, and that he is perfectly justified so long as he remains a true believer in Christ.

Justification and Sanctification. The terms justification and sanctification must be carefully distinguished. Justification means being pronounced righteous on account of the imputed righteousness of Christ. Sanctification means growth in personal righteousness or holiness on the part of the already justified believer. Justification is an outward judicial act of God; sanctification is an internal condition in man. Justification is instantaneous, perfect and complete; sanctification is progressive, imperfect and incomplete.

Always by Faith. The doctrine of justification by faith, as already observed in the previous chapter, is not a new method of salvation promulgated in the New Testament. Ever since the fall in Eden, there has been only one way of salvation for men, and that is by faith: either, as in Old Testament times, by faith in a Savior who was yet to come; or, as in New Testament times, by faith in a Savior who has come. It is a great mistake to suppose that salvation was through the law in the Old Testament dispensation, and is through the Gospel in the New Testament dispensation. The law was not given in order to enable men to be saved by it, but in order to convince them of their need of salvation, and to turn their eyes to the Savior for help. The doctrine of justification by faith is, however, taught more clearly in the New Testament than in the Old, and is set forth more emphatically as the Way, in opposition to ways devised by men.

In the Old Testament. At the very beginning of human history, when man fell into sin, the promise of redemption was given in the declaration of God that the seed of the woman should bruise the serpent's head (Gen. 3:15) By faith in this word of promise the relationship between man and God which had been broken by sin was restored. Abel was counted righteous because he brought his offering in faith (Heb. 11:4). Noah by faith "became heir of the righteousness which is by faith" (Heb. 11:7). All the Old Testament saints were pleasing to God through faith (Heb. 11). The relation between faith and righteousness is seen especially in the case of Abraham. He is preëminently the Old Testament man of faith. His whole life was one of faith in God's promises. We are told that "he believed in the Lord; and He counted it to him for righteousness" (Gen. 15:6). His faith was not simply the belief of the promise that he should have numerous descendants, or faith in the omnipotence of God, but it was specifically faith in God's promise of salvation. Hence Paul regards Abraham's faith as essentially identical with New Testament faith (Rom. 4).

This fundamental importance of faith in Old Testament times was not affected by the dispensation of the law (Gal. 3:17). Obedience to the law was not to be a means of salvation, but an evidence of faith in Jehovah, the God of salvation. Only when the law was fulfilled in love and hence as a result of faith, was it pleasing to God (Deut. 6:5). This relationship between faith and the fulfillment of the law is not always clearly brought out in the Old Testament, but it is there (Ps. 106; 12; 24). Faith is set forth by the prophets as the condition of salvation (Isa. 7:9; 28:16). The people of Nineveh were spared because they believed God (Jonah 3:5). And Habakkuk declares in the passage quoted by St. Paul, that "the just shall live by his faith" (Hab. 2:4; Rom. 1:17; Gal. 3:11).

In the New Testament. In the New Testament the necessity of faith as the only right attitude toward the revelation of divine grace in Jesus Christ, and as the condition of salvation is very clear. When John the Baptist came preaching in the wilderness and baptizing, he called on men to repent, that is to undergo a change of mind,[3] if they would obtain remission of sins (Mark 1:4). So also when Jesus began to preach He called on men, as a condition of entrance into the kingdom, that they should undergo a change of mind (Matt. 4:17), and should be born again (John 3:3), both of which terms denote a new attitude of contrition and faith. He demanded faith of those who sought his help by miracles (Matt. 9:22, 29). Forgiveness of sins was imparted to the woman that was a sinner, because she believed (Matt. 7:50). Those who believe in Him, He declares, have eternal life (John 3:14-16), while those who do not believe are still under God's wrath (John 3:36). The saved have washed their robes, and made them white in the blood of the Lamb (Rev. 7:14).

The significance of faith for justification is clearly brought out by Paul. Through Christ all that believe in Him are justified (Acts 13:39). The law cannot justify, and we obtain forgiveness through faith in Christ (Rom. 3:20, 26). In opposition to the Judaizing teachers among the Galatians who insisted on the observance of the law for salvation, Paul maintains that we are not justified by the works of the law but through faith in Jesus Christ (Gal. 2:16). Justification by faith stands in antithesis to salvation by works. The latter kind of salvation is impossible. Salvation is by grace through faith, and not of works (Eph. 2:8, 9). And grace saves because it is the grace

---

[3] The Greek word μετάνοια, which is translated here and elsewhere in the New Testament as repentance, means literally a change of mind.

revealed in the redemption through Christ from the curse of the law (Gal. 3:13). It makes us the children of God by faith in Christ Jesus (Gal. 3:26). And faith is not only receptive but operative and results in a new life in Christ (Gal. 2:20).

In his Epistle to the Romans Paul's theme is the righteousness of faith (Rom. 1:17). It is a righteousness of God, that is, a righteousness which God provides, and which becomes ours by faith in the Gospel which proclaims it. It is based on the propitiation which Christ has made (Rom. 3:21-26). It has to do primarily, not with the personal righteousness or holiness of men, but with their deliverance from guilt and condemnation. God justifies the believer, that is, He counts him and looks upon him as a righteous person for Christ's sake. Justification is by faith alone and not by works (Rom. 3:28). It is not conditioned upon the observance of the law, but only upon the faith which accepts the grace of God (Rom. 4:9, 16). This justification is a forgiveness of sins (Rom. 4:5-7) and gives peace with God through Christ (Rom. 5:1), and saves from condemnation (Rom. 8:1). Just as our sins were imputed to Christ while He Himself remained sinless, so His righteousness is imputed to us though we ourselves are still sinful (2 Cor. 5:21). Paul's own righteousness amounts to nothing, but he clings to the righteousness of God which is by faith (Phil. 3:8, 9). It is not of works, but by faith, and is a gift of God (Eph. 2:8). Faith gives boldness and access with confidence (Eph. 3:12).

The Epistle of James, while apparently in contradiction to Paul's teaching (Jas. 2:14, 21, 24, 25) is not really so. It is of earlier origin than Paul's writings, and is not directed against the Pauline teaching, but against a dead orthodoxy and a purely intellectual faith. James does not have the same forensic conception of justification as Paul, but means by the term an estimate of men concerning those who profess to have faith.

He labors to show the necessity of proving the possession of faith by the conduct. He quotes the Scripture which declares that Abraham's faith was imputed to him for righteousness; but he is particularly concerned to call attention to Abraham's obedient conduct as an example for Christians to follow. Those to whom righteousness is imputed by faith are bound afterwards to exhibit personal righteousness in their lives. As Paul emphasized justification by faith alone in opposition to those who sought to establish a doctrine of justification by works, so James emphasized the insufficiency of a purely intellectual or historical faith against those who acted as if such a dead faith were sufficient for salvation. The Epistle of James does not contradict the writings of Paul. In his own way Paul says the same things as James.[4]

Attacks. The doctrine of justification by faith has been attacked on the ground that it is inimical to morality. The doctrine may indeed, be abused, as it evidently was by some persons in St. Paul's day (Rom. 6:1). But the attacks are due to a misconstruction of the doctrine, as though the faith which justifies were merely assent to certain truths concerning Christ, and not a vital relation of spiritual union with Him. The opponents of the doctrine emphasize the subjective behavior of the believer rather than the objective salvation accomplished by Christ. But while seeming to rescue the doctrine from the danger of a dead faith, they lose the doctrine of salvation by grace alone.[5]

---

[4] Comp. e.g. Rom. 6.

[5] While the doctrine of justification by faith remained the possession of individual believers here and there, it gradually disappeared from the public teaching and theology of the early Church, and was replaced by a doctrine of justification by works.

The Fathers taught the Pauline doctrine, but not with sufficient discrimination. Confusion was wrought by errors which crept in, such as the distinction between sins committed before baptism, which were removed by the administration of the sacrament, and sins after baptism, for which satisfaction was supposed to be made; and the doctrine of a higher morality by obedience to the so-called evangelical counsels. Justification came to be regarded as a moral process, in which man's own actions and merit have much weight. The Scholastics regarded faith as an intellectual act which became meritorious when love was added to it. Justification was regarded, not as a forensic act, but as an infusion of righteousness. It was therefore never complete or certain. Justification was regarded as an act of transmutation out of a condition of sin into one of righteousness, by which man is enabled to do works which entitle him to salvation. Thus the doctrine of salvation was wedded to the doctrine of human merit. By his attitude toward prevenient grace man acquires a *meritum de congruo*, and as a reward he receives indwelling grace; and this in turn enables him to acquire the *meritum de condigno* which is rewarded with salvation. The *meritum de congruo* is a good work performed by the free will of man before grace is bestowed; the *meritum de condigno* is a good work performed after the infusion of grace. By the *meritum de congruo* grace or justification is merited; by the *meritum de condigno* grace and justification are increased, and salvation is received as a reward.

The Reformation gave to the doctrine of justification by faith the place which belongs to it. Its task was to rescue this truth which, while never wholly lost, had been buried under a mass of churchly tradition, and to impress it indelibly upon the consciousness of the Church by giving it clear and definite formulation.

The doctrine was regarded both by Luther and Melanchthon as the chief article of faith, and as the very heart of the Gospel. It is "the chiefest point of all the Gospel" (Augs. Conf., *Book of Conc.*, 65, 52). "Of this article nothing can be yielded or surrendered, though heaven and earth and all things should sink to ruin. . . . And upon this article all things depend, which against the pope, the devil and the whole world we teach and practice. Therefore we must be sure concerning this doctrine, and not doubt; for otherwise all is lost, and the pope and the devil and all things against us gain the victory and suit." (Schm. Art., *Ibid.*, 312, 5).

Luther's appreciation of the great truth of justification by faith grew rapidly from 1517 on, and by 1520 his convictions were firmly established. In opposition to the Roman doctrine that justification is an infusion of righteousness, he taught that it is nothing else than the forgiveness of sins. To apprehend Christ by faith and to have him in our hearts is righteousness. "Faith apprehends Christ and has Him present and holds Him enclosed, like the ring the gem; and whoever is found with this faith apprehending Christ in the heart, him God counts righteous." Erl. Ed. Com. Gal. I, 195. "Hence there is only this one way of avoiding condemnation, namely, to believe and say with certain confidence, 'Thou, Christ, art my sinful and cursed one, or rather, I am Thy sin, Thy curse, Thy death, Thy wrath of God, Thy hell; Thou on the other hand art my righteousness, blessing, life, favor of God, heaven." *Ibid.*, II, 37. "With faith thou art able to say, "I am Christ, that is, Christ's righteousness, victory, life, etc. are mine; and again Christ may say, 'I am that sinner, that is, his sins, death, etc. are mine, because he adheres to me and I to him, for we are joined through faith in one flesh and bone.'" *Ibid.*, I, 247. "We do not acquire that divine righteousness except through gratuitous imputation." *Ibid.*, I, 16. Melanchthon's statements are similar, but are set forth in a more didactic manner. See Augs. Conf. IV. Apol. Art. IV. Loci (ed. Kolde), p. 164 seq.

The Roman Catholic doctrine found its definite formulation in the Decrees and Canons of the Council of Trent "If any one says that the sinner is justified by faith alone, etc., let him be anathema." Sess. V. I, Canon 9. "If any one saith that man is truly absolved from his sins and justified because he assuredly believes himself absolved and justified, etc., let him be anathema." Canon 14.

CHAPTER XVII

THE CALL

The Order of Salvation. The great moral and spiritual change which the Holy Spirit, through the Means of Grace, brings about in the heart and life of man may be regarded as taking place in various steps or stages following one another in a certain logical order. This order is called the Order of Salvation. It is customary to consider the work of the Holy Spirit under the heads which this order furnishes. It includes the whole work of the Holy Spirit in the bringing of man to faith and to the functioning of his faith in his life.

A partial order of salvation is given by Luther in his explanation of the Third Article of the Creed, when he says, "I believe that I cannot by my own reason or strength believe in Jesus Christ my Lord, or come to Him; but the Holy Ghost has *called* me by the Gospel, *enlightened* me by His gifts, and *sanctified and preserved* me in the true faith." But for the purpose of dogmatics this order is incomplete, and needs to be enlarged.

The Order of Salvation is as follows: The Call; Illumination, Awakening and Persuasion; The Inner Transformation (i.e. Contrition and Faith); Conversion, Regeneration, and Repentance or Change of Mind; Justification; Mystical Union; and Sanctification.[1] (See chart on page 237.)

This order of salvation is not to be regarded as a chronological but only as a logical one. It is the order in which the

---

[1] With some modifications this is the usual order employed.

235

various steps most naturally occur to the mind in considering the many-sided work of the Holy Spirit. Many steps or stages overlap or occur concurrently. The one does not always stop where the other begins, and some of the stages represent processes which continue from the first moment of the Call to the end of the believer's life on earth. Some of the terms employed have been used in the confessions and the theology of the Church in several senses. But for the sake of clarity of thought it is important to assign to every term a very definite and circumscribed meaning.

Definition of the Call. The Call is that activity of the Holy Spirit by which through the Gospel He makes known to the sinner the saving grace of God in Christ, and both invites and enables Him to believe in Christ and be saved.

The Call comes first in the order of salvation, because it is the form in which God makes known to men His saving will. In its essence the Gospel is a call to come and partake of the good things which God has provided. God is constantly calling men away from sin to Himself. The entire history of salvation as recorded in the Scriptures is a continuous call to men. When Jesus began His public ministry He called men to His discipleship and kingdom. He came to call sinners to repentance (Matt. 9:13) and invited the weary and heavy laden to come to Him for rest (Matt. 11:28). He set forth the call and its nature in the parables of The Great Supper and The Marriage Feast of the King's Son, and pointed out that many are called but few chosen (Matt. 22:14).

In the Epistles we find that the Christians are those who are called (Rom. 1:6; 1 Cor. 1:2) according to God's purpose (Rom. 8:28 seq.) into the grace of Christ (Gal. 1:6), and into fellowship with Him (1 Cor. 1:9). The call is earnestly urged upon men (Luke 14:23). It may be rejected, however (Acts 13:46; Rom. 10:16-21), and rejection excludes from salvation

THE ORDER OF SALVATION

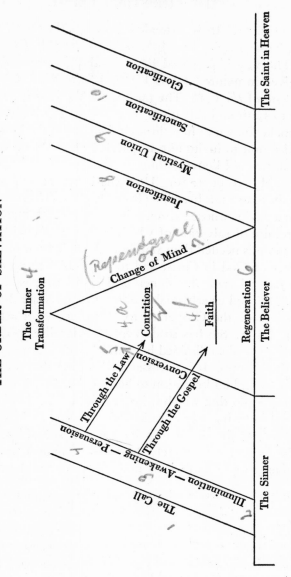

(Luke 14:24). It is extended to all (Matt. 28:19; Mark 16:15; Luke 24:47) and gradually reaches all (Rom. 11:30-32). The way is prepared for it by the general revelation of God given in nature [2] (Acts 14:17; 17:27; Rom. 1:19; 2:15).

Purpose of the Call. The purpose of the Call is to bring the sinner to faith and salvation. It is therefore necessary first of all to make known to him through the Gospel the grace of God in Christ, and to invite him to partake of it. Without the call the sinner would know nothing of that grace, and hence could not possibly accept it: for "How shall they believe in Him of whom they have not heard?" (Rom. 10:14). The sinner cannot trust in a Savior whose existence is unknown to him, nor believe in a promise of salvation of which he has no knowledge.

But more is needed than simply to make known to the sinner the grace of God in Christ and to invite him to partake of it. In his natural state the sinner is dead in trespasses and sins (Eph. 2:1), and utterly unable either to appreciate the spiritual significance of the Gospel or to accept it by an act of faith (1 Cor. 2:14). Sin has so darkened his intellect, so perverted his feelings, and so disabled his will, that these cannot function in spiritual things. It is necessary, therefore, that the call shall not only extend an invitation to believe, but that it shall enable the sinner to do that which it invites him to do. Hence the call is defined in such a way as to include not only an invitation but an enabling of the sinner to believe in Christ and be saved.

If the Gospel were merely the word of man it could do no more than simply extend an invitation. It could not bestow

---

[2] This preparation for the call has been described since Quenstedt's time as "the general and pedagogical or indirect call by which God more obscurely and from afar invites sinners who are out of the Church to inquire with regard to the true worship of God and the assembly in which it flourishes, and leads them to the gate of the Church." But the real Call is the special or direct call through the Gospel. It is this call with which we are dealing in this chapter.

A distinction has also sometimes been made between the ordinary call which comes through the Gospel, and the extraordinary call which came immediately in the case of Abraham and Paul or mediately through a miracle in the case of the Magi.

power to accept it. But the Gospel is the Word of God and is always accompanied by the power and working of the Holy Spirit, and hence it is able by reason of His presence and operation to bestow the power which the sinner needs in order to believe. The dead young man at the gates of Nain was unable either to hear or to rise, and yet he both heard and rose at the invitation and command of Jesus, because His Word brought to the dead man the power to hear and obey. So the man who is spiritually dead and cannot by his own powers hear or rise from his sins is by the very call which comes to him in the Gospel enabled to hear and rise, because the Gospel is always accompanied by the power of the Holy Spirit.

Through the Gospel. The call is through the Gospel, and not through the law. Being essentially an invitation to partake of the good things which God's grace has provided, it cannot, strictly speaking, be conceived of as coming through the law. The latter does not give an invitation to partake of grace, but brings a threat of wrath and punishment. There is, indeed, a work which the law must do; for it is our schoolmaster to bring us to Christ (Gal. 3:24). Unless the sinner is convinced through the preaching of the law that he is a lost and condemned sinner and in dire need of divine grace, he will not desire nor accept the grace which the Gospel offers. But the call itself, being an invitation to accept the proffered grace of God, is given through the Gospel and not through the law. By the law is the knowledge of sin; by the Gospel is the knowledge of grace.[3]

Serious and Earnest. The Call is serious and earnest. It is not a call which only seems to be directed to all, while in reality it is directed to only a few who have been arbitrarily

[3] The distinction sometimes made between an indirect call which comes through the conscience and a direct call which comes through the Gospel is calculated to lead to confusion. For the conscience of the natural man knows only of God's law, and knows nothing of God's grace in Christ. A real call, an actual invitation to partake of the salvation which has been prepared, can come only through the Gospel.

elected to salvation.[4] It is God's earnest desire to save all
(1 Tim. 3:4); the satisfaction which Christ has rendered has
been made for all (1 John 2:2); the call to preach the Gospel
to all the nations includes all men (Mark 16:15); and the
message itself is addressed to all (Acts 17:30). To say that
God pretends to call all but in reality calls only some, and
that the Word is intended to produce saving effects only in a
chosen few, is to accuse God of an insincerity which is utterly
in conflict with His nature as a truthful God.[5]

Sufficient and Efficacious. The call has in it, through the
accompanying grace of the Holy Spirit, all the power that is
needed to bring men to faith and salvation. Hence it is sufficient and efficacious. If it fails to bring men to faith, the fault
lies not in any lack of efficacy in the call, but in the willful
resistance of some men to divine grace. Thus Christ said to
Jerusalem, "How often would I have gathered thee . . . and
ye would not" (Luke 13:24). The call is an invitation, not a
compulsion. Men may reject the invitation if they will. In
spite of the fact that the call brings with it the power to accept,
some men refuse to use that power and prefer to remain in
their sins. Divine grace is powerful and efficacious, but not
irresistible.[6] And many do resist to their eternal destruction.

Universal. The call is universal. Its universality is a necessary conclusion from the universality of the divine will to save;
from the universal human need of salvation; and from the
command to preach the Gospel to all men. But the universality

[4] In opposition to the Calvinistic doctrine of absolute predestination and the
consequent doctrine that God does not really call the non-elect.
[5] The distinction of the Calvinists between an internal and an external call,
of which the former only is efficacious, is to be rejected. There is indeed an
external preaching of the Word which comes to all who are within reach of
its sound, and an internal application of the truths and principles of the Gospel
to the heart and conscience by the Holy Spirit. But it is exceedingly important
to remember that one does not occur without the other, and that the preaching
of the Gospel is never a dead sound without spiritual power, but is always
accompanied by the inner working of the Holy Spirit.
[6] The Calvinists teach that grace is irresistible in the case of the elect.

of the call does not mean that the call actually comes to every individual of the human race. There are large areas of the world to which the Gospel has not penetrated, and whose inhabitants know nothing of the redemption accomplished by Christ. And there are even in Christian lands many persons who know little if any more about the Gospel than the heathen do. The universality of the call is a universality of purpose and intention. It is meant and intended for all, and in this sense includes all nations and tribes, and all the individuals in them. It excludes none, and makes no distinction of race, color, sex or rank. The moral and the immoral, the rich and the poor, the high and the low—all need the grace which God offers, and all are invited to partake of it.[7] The call is meant for all, and in this sense it is unquestionably universal. The decree of a king may be none the less universal, even though many of his remoter subjects never hear of it. It is God's will that the Gospel shall actually reach every individual. He has laid upon the Church the obligation to make the call universal in the actual sense. She is to go into all the world and preach the Gospel to every creature. But only to the extent to which the Church performs her evangelistic duty will the call reach every individual of the race.

Why some nations and individuals are favored above others by the possession of the Gospel is a question which we cannot answer. But the fact that we are favored with the Gospel should be an incentive to do our utmost to bring the call to all men everywhere.

[7] Some of the old dogmaticians maintained the actual universality of the call on the basis of its supposed universality in Adam and Noah, and in the apostles' preaching of the Gospel. But the apostles did not actually present their message to every individual, nor penetrate to all parts of the whole world. And while the descendants of Adam and Noah failed by reason of sin to receive the call given through their ancestor, that does not alter the fact that many of those descendants actually lived and died in utter ignorance of God's gracious plan of redemption. To say that a man has actually received the call, when he has in fact never heard a word of the Gospel, is not a correct statement of the case.

CHAPTER XVIII

ILLUMINATION, AWAKENING AND PERSUASION

THE second step or stage in the Order of Salvation is usually called simply Illumination or Enlightenment. It is a term which has sometimes been employed in a sense so wide as to include the entire work of the Holy Spirit in bringing men to a state of grace. The later dogmaticians, however, employed it in a narrower and definitely restricted sense to designate the second step in the order of salvation. It is not altogether satisfactory, however, as a designation for the specific activity of the Holy Spirit which it is meant to describe. For under the head of illumination much more is included in dogmatics than is indicated by the etymological meaning of the word. To illumine means to give light. The use of the term here would indicate, according to its etymology, that the work of the Holy Spirit which is treated at this point has to do simply with giving light to the intellect. But the work of the Holy Spirit which is to be described here as the second stage in the order of salvation has a much wider scope. It is not confined to making the sinner see things which he did not see before. Its aim is to lead the sinner to contrition and faith, and thus to make a believer or a Christian out of him. And for the accomplishment of this purpose the sinner not only needs to have his intellect enlightened, but to have his feelings moved and his will persuaded. An enlightenment which ends with the intellect, and results simply in giving knowledge concerning spiritual things, does not bring about the results which God intends.

Since, therefore, the work of the Holy Spirit at this point in

242

the order of salvation has to do with the whole man, intellect, feelings and will, and, indeed, aims ultimately at reaching and persuading the will through the intellect and the feelings, the heading of this chapter is made to read: Illumination, Awakening and Persuasion, instead of simply Illumination. The additional words are used for the sake of clarity, and in order to guard from the start against any notion that we are here dealing with a work of the Holy Spirit which is confined to the intellect alone.

Definition. Illumination, Awakening and Persuasion are that activity of the Holy Spirit by which, through the Law and the Gospel, He causes the sinner to recognize his sinful and lost state, and the grace of God which desires to save him from it; awakens him to a lively sense of his need of salvation; and persuades him to repent of sin and to believe in Christ as his Savior. It is an activity of the Holy Spirit which deals with intellect, feelings and will.

Illumination, Awakening and Persuasion follow logically upon the call as the second step in the order of salvation; for through the Word, by which the call comes, the Holy Spirit seeks to produce in the sinner a knowledge of sin and grace; to awaken him to a realization of his perilous state; and to persuade him to repent and believe.

The Need. The need of Illumination, Awakening and Persuasion is plain from the teachings of Scripture concerning the state of the natural man. He lacks spiritual discernment; and hence the things of the Spirit are foolishness unto him, and he cannot receive them (1 Cor. 2:14). He walks in the vanity of his mind, and his understanding is darkened because of the ignorance that is in him (Eph. 4:17, 18). His natural mind is enmity against God (Rom. 8:7); and he is unwilling and unable to trust in Christ for salvation (Eph. 4:17, 18). His heart is hardened (Eph. 4:18 R.V.). The call discussed in the previous chapter would be ineffective, if it were not accompanied by the activity of the Holy Spirit in enlightening, awakening and persuading the sinner through the Law on the one hand, so that the sinner sees and laments his sins and desires forgiveness, and through the Gospel on the other hand, so that he sees and appreciates the grace of God in Christ and believes in Him as his Savior.

The Work Described in Scripture. This activity of the Holy Spirit in enlightening, awakening and persuading the sinner is described in the Scriptures. Light has come into the world (John 3:19) and shines in the darkness (John 1:5), to give light to those that sit in darkness (Luke 1:79), to open their eyes and to turn them from darkness to light (Acts 26:18), so that they may behold the beauty and glory of God's grace in Christ in a way in which they could not behold it without the illuminating operation of the Holy Spirit (Eph. 1:17, 18). Men are told to awake from sleep and to arise from the dead (Eph. 5:14; 1 Cor. 15:3), and to awake to righteousness (1 Cor. 15:34). They are to be persuaded by the thought of God's wrath against sin (2 Cor. 5:11) and by the message of His grace in Christ to repent and believe (2 Cor. 5:20).

The activity of the Holy Spirit, as already indicated, is not simply one by which He enlightens the intellect, but by which also He influences the feelings and the will. The sinner must be enlightened with regard to his lost condition, must be awakened to a sense of his peril, and must be stirred to action, so that he may turn his back upon sin and his face toward Christ his Savior.

Through Means. The means which the Holy Spirit employs to enlighten, awaken and persuade the sinner is the Word of God. His work is not magical or mechanical, but is done in accordance with the personal nature of man and the ethical character of the process. It is an illumination, awakening and

persuasion by means of the *truth,* by a process adapted to the
psychological nature of man. It is not by the mere act of hearing or reading the Word, but by the influence of the truth
conveyed by that Word that the sinner is enlightened, awakened and persuaded. And the measure of the effect produced
is in proportion to the measure in which, by the gracious working of the Holy Spirit, the truth is brought home to the sinner's
mind and heart.

Forms of the Word. By the Word of God through which the
Holy Spirit illumines, awakens and persuades the sinner is
meant the truth of God as comprehended in the Law and the
Gospel, in whatever form it may be presented to the mind. It
may be the Word as read in the Scriptures, or as heard from
the pulpit. It may also be the Word which as a passage of
Scripture is stored in the mind and is meditated upon. Or it
may be a truth whose exact form in the Scriptures has escaped
the memory, but whose essence is retained by the mind, and
which by its power gradually shapes the thinking, feeling and
willing of the man. The Word employed by the Holy Spirit
is the truth (John 17:17)—the divinely revealed truth concerning sin and the wrath of God against it, and the truth concerning God's grace in Christ Jesus and His readiness to save every
soul that flees to the Savior for refuge. The mode of the Holy
Spirit's working is an ethical one, and is aimed at the production of an inner revolution or transformation in the sinner by
which he is brought to contrition and faith. In the production
of this inner transformation the Holy Spirit is the cause, and
the Word is the means.

Law and Gospel. The Word of God through which the Holy
Spirit works consists of Law and Gospel. Through the Law the
Holy Spirit produces in the mind of the sinner a recognition
of his sinful and lost condition, fear of God's wrath and punishment, and a desire to be forgiven. Through the Gospel He

produces in the mind of the sinner a knowledge and appreciation of God's unspeakable grace and mercy in Christ, stirs up a desire to partake of it, and persuades the sinner to accept by faith the forgiveness and salvation which are offered. In other words, the aim of the Holy Spirit is to produce contrition through the Law, and faith through the Gospel. The use of the Law is elenchtico-pedagogical, to effect a knowledge and renunciation of sin, and a desire for salvation. The use of the Gospel is consolatory, to bring to the troubled heart of the penitent sinner the assurance of God's grace in Christ and to persuade him to accept it by faith.

Gradual. The work of the Holy Spirit is carried on through the continued pressing home of the truth upon the heart. It is a gradual process. In some cases it takes longer than in others. But in every case the effect is produced through the influence of the divine truth upon the mind. In those cases in which the Holy Spirit seems to have brought men suddenly and almost instantaneously to a state of contrition and faith, it will usually be found upon investigation that the climax was preceded by a longer or shorter period in which the truth was struggling with the mind of the sinner, and in which gradually the sinfulness of sin and the need of saving grace was dawning upon him and preparing the way for the act of repentance and faith.

Illumination increases constantly up to the moment of the sinner's conversion. It requires, however, that the divine grace shall be appropriated step by step, otherwise the process will be arrested. Illumination does not stop with conversion. Through all his life, even to the end, the believer continues to be more and more enlightened by the Holy Spirit through the Word, that he may grow in grace and in the knowledge of the Lord, and may increase day by day in holiness of heart and life.

The claims of the mystics to a direct and immediate illumination apart from the Word as the result of a passive attitude of

receptivity toward God is unsound and unscriptural. The necessary presupposition of illumination is serious occupation with
the Word. That Word is to be earnestly preached, diligently
read and heard, and prayerfully pondered.

Illumination Sometimes Arrested. Illumination does not always lead to contrition and faith. It is sometimes arrested by
the willful resistance of men before its purpose has been accomplished. Since the process is ethical and not compulsory, it is
possible for the sinner at any point in it to frustrate the Holy
Spirit's purpose by hardening his heart against the truth and
deliberately choosing the service of sin. A notable instance of
this kind is found in Felix the governor, who, when Paul
reasoned of righteouness, temperance and judgment to come,
trembled and answered, "Go thy way for this time; when I have
a convenient season I will call for thee." Felix hardened his
heart against the working of divine grace within him; and in
all probability the convenient season never came, and he died
unconverted.[1]

[1] The immediate effect of the calling and illuminating Word was designated
by the Confessions and the old dogmaticians as "the first beginnings of faith
and conversion." Later, on the basis of Eph. 5:14, "Awake, thou that sleepest,"
it was designated as an awakening. The Pietists and Wesley and Whitefield
emphasized the awakening as a particular state. Martensen (*Christian Dogmatics,* p. 384-5) says: "Awakening is a state which precedes regeneration;—
it is the spirit seeking its home, in answer to the effectual call of grace; but
it is not yet the permanent indwelling of grace within the soul. The awakened
man is as yet only roused by grace, he is not actually endowed with grace; he is
still only one of the called, not of the chosen. There is still wanting the deciding resolve on his part. Awakening as such is only a state of religious distress
. . . the critical and jeopardous point in the progress of man's conversion."

CHAPTER XIX

THE INNER TRANSFORMATION

A Radical Change. By the inner transformation referred to in this chapter is meant that radical inner change or revolution which takes place in the sinner when he is brought to a state of contrition and faith. The change is so radical and fundamental that he may truthfully be said to have become a new man. Thus Paul declares, "If any man be in Christ, he is a new creature; old things are passed away; behold all things are become new" (2 Cor. 5:17). Instead of the old impenitence and love of sin there are now a humble acknowledgment and confession of his sins, sincere sorrow for them, and a hating and forsaking of them. Instead of ignorance of God and of His grace, and indifference or opposition to His offer of mercy and forgiveness to the penitent, there are now a sincere appreciation of God's love, a glad acceptance of the forgiveness offered in Christ, and a thankful loving heart which prompts to obedience and service.

Produced by the Holy Spirit. This inner transformation is one which man cannot produce in himself, but which must be produced by the operation of the Holy Spirit. The natural man is not only under the deserved wrath of God, but is spiritually dead (Eph. 2:1), and thus not only unwilling but utterly unable by his own powers to take the right attitude toward God and His grace. He is not, as Pelagianism maintains, morally in an indifferent state, so that he is quite free to choose either good or evil. Nor is he one who has been merely weakened, and who, as Semi-pelagianism maintains, only needs the assisting grace of God to establish the right relation between himself and God. Nor can he by his own natural powers complete the inner transformation after the Holy Spirit has begun it, as the Synergists maintain. He is by nature altogether helpless in his sins; and it is not by any powers of his own but altogether by divine grace that he must be brought to a state of contrition and faith, and thus be inwardly transformed.

Possibility. The possibility of this inner transformation is found in the fact that the effect of sin, destructive as it is, has not been to destroy the essence of man, but to introduce a wrong moral quality, which is not necessarily irremovable. If it were irremovable and man could not be inwardly transformed by divine grace, man would be unsalvable, like the devil. But even in those who have fallen to the lowest depth there is still a conciousness of God and of their own sinfulness, and a conscience which reproves them for wrong,[1] so that there is a possibility of their conversion by divine grace.

Essential Factors. The essential factors of the inner transformation are contrition and faith. Where these are found, there the inner transformation has taken place, and the man has become a Christian. Where these are not found, there man is still in his natural state of sin and unbelief. What is meant by contrition and faith has already been considered in Chapter XV, and need not be repeated here.

He who has undergone this inner transformation, that is, he who has been brought to contrition and faith, possesses salvation. But he possesses it, not because the inner transformation makes of him one who deserves it or because the contrition and faith which constitute the essence of the transformation are a merit on account of which salvation is bestowed. Contrition is necessary for salvation, but it is in no sense a meritorious action

---

[1] The one exception is found in those persons who have committed the sin against the Holy Ghost, and whose conscience no longer functions.

by which the sinner deserves forgiveness. All the tears which a penitent sinner can shed will not wash away the stain of a single sin. So also faith is not a merit on account of which the believer is accepted with God. Salvation is altogether and only on account of the merits of Christ. The contrite man is the only kind of man to whom salvation for Christ's sake is offered; and the believing man is the only one who accepts it. Contrition and faith are thus a condition of salvation, but not a meritorious cause.

A Scriptural Requirement. The inner transformation, whose essential factors are contrition and faith, is recognized and referred to throughout the New Testament as a basic fact of Christianity. Reconciliation with God and entrance into His kingdom are conditioned on the possession of faith. Without it man cannot share in the benefits of Christ's redemption. But the possession of this faith involves the fact of an inner transformation. And so, in addition to those passages which lay down faith as the condition of entrance into the kingdom, there are passages which express the same thing in a different way, and demand an inner transformation as a condition of entrance.

The necessity of an inner transformation for entrance into the kingdom of God is plainly stated by Christ Himself in three forms. For there are in the New Testament three words by which this inner transformation is designated. They are Repentance or Change of Mind, Conversion, and Regeneration. These three words all refer to the same inner transformation; but each of them describes it from a different point of view. Repentance or Change of Mind describes it from the psychological standpoint; for the word *metanoia* (μετάνοια), imperfectly translated by the English word repentance, means literally a change of mind. Conversion describes the inner transformation from the standpoint of direction, and views the believer as one who has been converted or turned around, and is now facing and moving in an opposite direction. Regeneration describes the inner transformation from the standpoint of life, and views the believer as one who has been made spiritually alive by divine grace, and thus has been born again.

Christ Himself uses all three of these terms in laying down the fundamental condition for entrance into His kingdom. At the beginning of His public ministry He said, "Repent for the kingdom of heaven is at hand" [2] (Matt. 4:17). Later in His ministry He said, "Except ye be converted and become as little children, ye shall not enter into the kingdom of heaven" (Matt. 18:3). And to Nicodemus He said, "Except a man be born again, He cannot see the kingdom of God" (John 3:3). In making these declarations Christ did not lay down three different conditions of entrance into His kingdom, but one condition stated in different terms and from different points of view. He simply emphasized the necessity of a certain fundamental change or transformation in man as a requirement for entrance into the kingdom which He was founding. But He used three different words which emphasize three different aspects of the same inner transformation. What He means in all three cases is, that before any man can expect to enter into the kingdom of God he must first undergo a spiritual transformation which consists in coming to a state of contrition and faith.

The man who has undergone this inner transformation is a repentant man, a converted man, a regenerate man. But he is not three different kinds of man. He is simply a man who has been brought by divine grace to contrition and faith, and who may therefore be described as repentant, converted, or regenerate. He is a new man, a Christian, a believer. And that which makes him such is his new inner state of contrition and faith.

[2] Literally, "Undergo a change of mind, for the kingdom of heaven is at hand."

Use of the Three Terms. The three terms, Change of Mind (Repentance), Conversion and Regeneration are used in the Scriptures sometimes in a wider and sometimes in a narrower sense, and in places interchangeably. In the widest sense they are employed to designate the entire work of God in man, including justification and sanctification. In the narrower sense they refer to the production of the inner change or transformation wrought in man when he is brought from a state of unbelief to one of faith.

In the Book of Concord the theological meaning of the terms is not yet definitely fixed. Regeneration is sometimes used in a sense which includes justification and sanctification or renovation. Sometimes it is used to denote only the remission of sins, or adoption as God's children. Justification and regeneration are even used as synonymous terms; and justification by faith is declared to be in fact a regeneration, inasmuch as the sinner by his justification through faith becomes a child of God instead of a child of wrath, and is thus transferred from a state of death to one of life.[3]

Gradually, in the further development of dogmatics, the three terms Repentance, Conversion and Regeneration obtained a definite theological meaning which sharply distinguished them from justification and sanctification; and they became three designations for the internal change or transformation which takes place in the man who is brought by divine grace through illumination to a state of faith. In the treatment of these topics, the emphasis is usually placed upon conversion and regeneration. But repentance, in the Scriptural sense of a change of mind, deserves to be placed in the same class with conversion and regeneration as an illuminating description of the inner transformation which takes place in man when he becomes a believer in Christ.

[3] Form. Conc. Sol. Decl. III, 19 seq.

CHAPTER XX

CONVERSION

CONVERSION describes the spiritual transformation in man from the standpoint of direction. The man who has been brought to contrition and faith has been converted or turned around, and faces in an opposite direction. He has been converted or turned from sin to God.

The term conversion, as stated in the last chapter, has been used by the confessions and some of the dogmaticians in a wide sense in which it includes the Holy Spirit's entire work of sanctification in man.[1] But it is used here in the narrow sense, to designate a step or stage in the order of salvation, and as one of the three words, conversion, regeneration and repentance, used to designate the inner transformation which takes place when the sinner becomes a believer.

In the Scriptures. Conversion is described in the Scriptures as a work of divine grace, and again as an act of man. The divine character of the process is exhibited in the Old Testament by the fact that God promises to give a new heart (Jer. 24:7; Ezek. 11:19; 36:28), and that the Psalmist prays Him to give one (Ps. 51:10). In the New Testament the divine character of the process is emphasized by the fact that it is described as the production of a new life or new birth (John 3:3; 1 Pet. 1:23), and as an awakening from a state of death (Eph.

---

[1] The dogmatical terminology is not yet as sharply defined in the confessions and in the writings of the earlier dogmaticians, as it is later. Thus the Apology identifies repentance and conversion (183, 14), conversion and renovation (184, 46) conversion and regeneration (186, 58).

253

2:5; Col. 2:13). The new state of the converted man is expressly ascribed to the work of divine grace (1 Cor. 4:7; 15:10). It is God who has begun the good work in man (Phil. 1:6), and works in him both to will and to do of God's good pleasure (Phil. 2:13). The contrition and faith which are the essential factors of conversion are produced by God (Acts 5:31; 11:18; 2 Tim. 2:25; Eph. 1:19; 2:10).

At the same time contrition and faith are demanded of men as an act on their part. They are called upon not to harden their hearts (Heb. 4:7), to obey the Gospel (1 Pet. 4:17), and to turn again (Acts 3:19).

Conversion is thus at once a work of God and man's own act of turning about. The explanation lies in the fact that man is a personal being, whose spiritual powers are restored by divine grace, and whose unwilling mind is made willing by the operation of the Holy Spirit, so that he can and does repent and believe. For the Word which comes to man is accompanied by a divine power which draws him (John 6:44), causes his heart to burn within him (Luke 24:32), pricks him in the heart (Acts 2:37), and opens it (Acts 16:14), so that he is able to receive the Word. In spite of all this drawing, however, man may nevertheless reject the proffered grace (Matt. 23:37).

Definition. Since the sinner is sometimes said to be converted and sometimes said to convert or turn himself, a distinction is made between *transitive* and *intransitive* conversion. The former regards the act or process from the standpoint of God's activity in man. In this sense conversion may be defined as that act of the Holy Spirit by which through the divine law He produces in the heart of the sinner contrition for his sins, and through the Gospel produces in him faith in Christ as his personal Savior, so that he is justified and saved. In this sense man is said to be converted.

Intransitive conversion looks on the act or process from the standpoint of man's act of contrition and faith. While the result is to be ascribed to working of the Holy Spirit and not to man's own powers, it is man who repents and believes, and not the Holy Spirit. Hence in turning away from his sins to Christ, the sinner is said to convert or turn himself (Acts 3:19; Joel 2:12; Luke 22:32, R. V.). In this sense conversion may be defined as that act of the sinner by which, drawn, persuaded and enabled by the Holy Spirit, he turns away from his sins in true contrition and turns to Jesus Christ his Savior in true faith.[2]

Essential Factors. Contrition and Faith are the marks or essential factors of conversion. They are produced by the Holy Spirit through the Law and the Gospel respectively. Through the Law is the knowledge of sin; through the Gospel is the knowledge of grace.

The Law was given to convince men of sin. This is its function in conversion. Through the preaching of the law man

[2] The distinction between transitive and intransitive conversion made by Baier and Hollazius suggests an interesting relation between conversion, regeneration and repentance. Expressed in modern terms, the distinction means that conversion has an objective and a subjective side. Objectively considered, it is the act of God by which He converts man and brings him to a state of contrition and faith. Regarded in this aspect it is essentially equivalent to regeneration which is the act by which God makes the man spiritually alive. In conversion God turns man by bringing him to contrition and faith; in regeneration He makes man spiritually alive by bringing him to contrition and faith.

Subjectively considered, conversion is the act by which man converts himself or turns from sin to God, and from impenitence and unbelief to contrition and faith. In this sense conversion is essentially equivalent to repentance, which is the act by which man cuts loose from sin and trusts in Christ. When in conversion man turns about in a new direction, his mind has been changed, in other words he repents.

In general it may therefore be said that regeneration emphasizes the divine activity in the inner transformation, in that the Holy Spirit makes man spiritually alive. Repentance emphasizes the subjective side of the inner transformation, in that the sinner through the operation of divine grace changes his mind and trusts in Christ. Conversion emphasizes both the divine and the human side of the inner transformation—the divine, in that God converts the sinner, and the human, in that the sinner turns from sin to God.

learns to know his sin and helplessness and the wrath of God against him on account of sin. When this fact is pressed home upon his consciousness, there ensue distress of conscience and deep humility before God. He feels his unworthiness, and is filled with sorrow, shame and confusion, and with a detestation of the sins which he once loved. He ceases to excuse or extenuate them, acknowledges them as transgressions of the law of a good and holy God, and longs for mercy and forgiveness. This is contrition, the negative side of conversion.

The Gospel is given to console troubled consciences. If the Gospel did not console and lift up, those who have been brought to contrition would be driven to despair. But the Gospel proclaims God's grace in Christ, and announces to the contrite sinner the free forgiveness of all his sins for Christ's sake, if he will only accept it. When this blessed truth is realized by his troubled soul, the man reaches out by faith and takes hold of Christ as his Savior. Thus faith is the second or positive side of conversion.

Contrition and faith belong together in conversion. And they belong together through all the earthly life of the Christian. For there is a daily repentance or conversion of the Christian—a daily contrite acknowledgment of weakness and sin, and a daily trusting in Christ for the washing away of guilt.

A Work of the Holy Spirit. Conversion is to be ascribed entirely to the work of the Holy Spirit through the Word. While it is true that God is not far from every one of us, and that even in his natural state man is not wholly outside the influence of the Spirit of God, yet conversion is never accomplished through the ordinary and natural influence of God on the mind, but only by the operation of the Holy Spirit through the supernaturally revealed truth. Man in his natural state and by his natural powers cannot possibly convert himself. The Scriptures declare that the natural man is in a state of spiritual death

(Eph. 2:1). He cannot, therefore, by his natural powers respond to any spiritual appeal even when he hears the Gospel. For he cannot even understand the Gospel until he has been spiritually enlightened and enabled to do so by the Holy Spirit (1 Cor. 2:14). He can see and appreciate and accept the grace of God in Christ Jesus only through the activity of the Holy Spirit within him. It is the Holy Spirit who makes the spiritually blind man see, and the spiritually unable and unwilling man able and willing. The Holy Ghost both enables and persuades the sinner to repent and believe. The process is ethical and not mechanical or magical. Man is not converted or turned about like an inanimate or unreasoning object. Conversion is essentially a process in which the Holy Spirit makes the unwilling willing. The will itself is converted, and yet in such a way that man's nature as a self-determining being is not interfered with or destroyed.

Since conversion begins with a sinner who is both unwilling and unable to believe, and ends with the same sinner both willing and able to believe, and actually doing so, it is clear that the transformation is one which must be ascribed entirely to the working of the Holy Spirit, and not to any natural powers of man. Hence, looking at the process as a whole the Formula of Concord,[2] quoting Luther, declares that in conversion the human will is purely passive. Only God can and does make the unwilling willing; and all the credit of conversion goes to Him, and none of it to man.

On the other hand, when the process of conversion is looked at in detail, it is evident that as the process proceeds there is a certain activity on the part of man. If the process is to be completed and is to end in actual conversion, the new powers which the Holy Spirit gradually gives to the sinner must be used in that conflict between the flesh and the spirit which ensues pre-

[2] 499, 18; 569, 89.

vious to the actual decision against sin and for God.[4] But this activity on man's part is produced by the Holy Spirit, and is exercised through new powers given by Him, and not at all through powers which are native or natural to man.

Hence, we reject the Pelagian position which holds that man can by his own natural powers convert himself; also, the Semi-pelagian position which holds that man can begin the process but that the Holy Spirit must complete it; and thirdly, the Synergistic position which holds that the Holy Ghost must begin the work of conversion but that then man is able by his own powers to complete it. The fact is that, from beginning to end, conversion is due to the agency and activity of the Holy Spirit, and not at all to any natural powers of man. There is, indeed, a certain activity of man in the process, since it is an ethical one; but that activity is produced by the Holy Spirit and is exercised by means of powers which the Holy Spirit has bestowed, and not by means of any which are native or natural to man. Hence the entire work of conversion is to be ascribed to the Holy Spirit.

Gradual or Instantaneous? Regarded as a process culminating in contrition and faith, conversion is gradual. On the other hand, regarded as a transition from a state of unbelief to one of faith, it is instantaneous, inasmuch as there is a moment when the man ceases to be an unbeliever and has become a believer.

It is not, however, possible in every case for a man to point to the very moment when he was converted from unbelief to faith. Sometimes the transition is so gradual that he cannot

[4] Chemnitz, I, 199. "Conversion or renovation is not such a change as is straightway completed and perfected in all its parts in one moment; but it has its beginning, its progressions through which in much weakness it is perfected. It is not therefore to be thought that with a secure and idle will I shall wait until renovation or conversion according to the grades described has been completed by the operation of the Holy Spirit without any movement of mine. Nor, indeed, is it possible with mathematical exactness to show where the liberated will begins to act."

recall the exact time when faith actually came into being within him. A sudden and violent conversion is by no means essential in every case, nor is it to be regarded as the normal type. In the case of those persons who were baptized as infants and trained up from childhood in the Christian religion, it is quite generally impossible for them to point to a time when their conversion took place. They cannot remember a time when they were not in a converted state, that is, when they were not sorry for their sins and believing in Christ as their Savior. The important question for every man is not whether he can recall when he was converted, but whether he is now in a converted state.

Grace Efficacious, but not Irresistible. The grace of the Holy Spirit in conversion is efficacious; that is, there is brought to bear on every man who hears the call and comes under the illuminating influence of the Holy Ghost a power sufficient to convert him, if he does not frustrate it by his own willful and persistent resistance. There is a natural resistance to divine grace on the part of every man. But there is also a willful and persistent resistance after the Holy Spirit has brought spiritual light and insight to the soul. Man cannot, indeed, by his own natural powers do otherwise than willfully resist. It is therefore necessary that he shall receive from the Holy Spirit the power which he needs to cease his willful resistance to the work of grace. This power is given through the Word with which the Holy Spirit operates. But it is a power which the sinner must use. If he refuses to do so and persists in obstinately resisting the workings and promptings of grace, he remains unconverted. For the grace of the Holy Spirit, though most powerful and efficacious, is not irresistible.

If, then, the sinner is converted, it is entirely due to the grace of God. He does not and cannot by any natural powers of his own produce conversion or in any way assist in it. When he is brought to faith it is entirely by the working of the Holy Spirit in him. But if, on the other hand, the sinner is not converted, his failure to come to faith and salvation is due only to his own obstinate resistance to divine grace. He is in the same class with the inhabitants of Jerusalem of whom Christ said, "Ye would not" (Matt. 23:37).

CHAPTER XXI

REGENERATION

THE term regeneration is used in this chapter to designate the same inner transformation which is designated in the preceding chapter by the word conversion. The man who has been brought by the Holy Spirit to a condition of contrition and faith has been regenerated, just as also he has been converted. The two words, conversion and regeneration, are used to denote two aspects of the same thing. In conversion the inner transformation is described as a turning about; in regeneration it is described as the impartation of a new life. The regenerate man is one who has been born again.

The term regeneration is used in the confessions of our Church in a number of senses. Thus in the Apology it is used as the equivalent of justification,[1] and in the Formula of Concord it is made to include the renewal or sanctification which follows.[2] But it is used in this chapter in that definite theological sense in which it refers to the inner change in the adult from unbelief to conscious faith, and is practically equivalent to conversion. It is a stage or step in the order of salvation, and is a regeneration wrought by the Word. It deals with that conscious inner change from a state of impenitence and unbelief to one of penitence and faith which takes place and can take place only in one who has reached a certain degree of mental development. We are not dealing in this chapter with the regeneration which is wrought in baptism (John 3:5; Tit. 3:5), but with the regeneration which, according to the Scriptures, is wrought through the Word (1 Pet. 1:23; Jas. 1:19).

[1] 95, 72; 96, 78.   [2] 572, 19.

261

A New Man. Regeneration, like conversion and repentance or change of mind, is a Scriptural term describing what has taken place in the man who has been brought to faith in Christ. He has become a new man; he has been born again. This does not mean that he has been in any way changed in his essence as a man, but that he has been made over with respect to his spiritual state and powers. He has not received a new *ego.* But that side of him, namely the spiritual, which hitherto was dead, has been made alive. He is a new *kind* of man. He is a new man in the sense that his attitude, mind, direction, disposition and aspirations have been totally changed. The change is not a substantial one in the technical sense, but an accidental one. But it is a real and fundamental change. Qualitatively he is an entirely different kind of person. He is now spiritual and no longer carnal in mind.

Faith is the beginning of a new life in Christ. He who has faith is one who has been made spiritually alive. He has been inwardly transformed by divine grace. He has become a child of God by faith in Christ Jesus (Gal. 3:26). He has been brought out of the kingdom of darkness into the kingdom of God's dear Son (Col. 1:13). He is now a child of God instead of a child of sin. He has received a new birth, and is a new man, a new creature (2 Cor. 5:17), who henceforth will walk in newness of life (Rom. 6:4), and serve in newness of spirit (Rom. 7:6). The natural man is in a condition of spiritual death, and is dead in trespasses and sins; but in being brought to faith he has been made alive.

Definition. Regeneration may be defined, therefore, as the act of God by which He makes the sinner spiritually alive; or, as the act of God by which He imparts a new, spiritual life to the sinner. The vital principle of this new life is faith. Wherever faith is present, there the new life is also present. Wherever faith is wanting, the new life also is wanting.

Since, however, we do not really know what life is, and have never seen or touched either physical or spiritual life, but only recognize their presence by their phenomena, it is of much more practical benefit and more truly enlightening to define regeneration in a concrete way by defining a regenerate man. What, then, is meant by a regenerate man? When has a man been made spiritually alive? The answer is, that a regenerate man is one who has been brought by the Holy Ghost to true faith in Christ, and thus has been born again as a child of God. A regenerate man is a believer, and a believer is a regenerate man. It follows, therefore, that regeneration may also be defined as the act by which the Holy Ghost makes a man a believer. A state of faith is a state of regeneration.

It will be remembered that, as we have stated above, we are speaking here of regeneration through the Word, and in the sense in which regeneration is practically identical with conversion. The Holy Spirit has worked in the sinner's heart through the Word until the sinner has come to faith, and thus has become spiritually alive. He now exhibits the phenomena of spiritual life, and responds to his spiritual environment. He now understands the spiritual significance of the Gospel, recognizes the sinfulness of sin, laments its guilt and power, appreciates the grace of God in Christ, and trusts in his Savior for forgiveness and salvation. The outward evidence that he is spiritually alive is furnished by the fact that his faith at once begins to work by love.

The Work of God. Regeneration is solely the work of God, and not at all the work of man himself. No dead man can make himself alive. God alone can do that. When the young man at Nain was carried to the grave he could not possibly have given life to himself. But he received life through the power of God. So the spiritually dead man cannot possibly give life to himself; but he can be made alive by the Holy Spirit through the Word.

Relation to Illumination and Sanctification. Regeneration is closely related to illumination which precedes, and to sanctification or renewal which follows. But it must be carefully distinguished from both. Illumination leads to regeneration, and regeneration leads to sanctification. Since there is a moment when the man ceases to be an unbeliever and becomes a believer, regeneration is, strictly speaking, an instantaneous act, while illumination which precedes and sanctification which follows are processes which continue throughout the believer's life on earth.

Relation to Justification. Regeneration is closely related to justification. The regenerate man is a justified man, and the justified man is a regenerate man. But the terms regeneration and justification are not synonymous. They are, indeed, used synonymously by the Apology, as already stated; but the Formula of Concord points out and corrects this confusion of terms.[3] As the various theological terms gradually became more sharply defined, regeneration and justification were made to stand for two very different things. Justification means that God counts the believing sinner righteous for Christ's sake; regeneration means that God makes the sinner a believer, and thus gives him a new, spiritual life.

Lost and Regained. Can regeneration be lost and regained? If the conception of regeneration is that which we have outlined here, and it consists of contrition and faith, then certainly regeneration can be lost; and it can also be regained if there be a return to true contrition and faith. The notion held by some persons that regeneration can never be lost is due either to a Calvinistic idea of the inamissibility of grace, or to a confusion of regeneration with the covenant which God makes in baptism and to which He is always faithful, no matter what man does.

[3] 501, 8; 572, 19.

CHAPTER XXII

REPENTANCE OR CHANGE OF MIND

THE inner spiritual transformation regarded from the subjective side involves a change of mind [1] or repentance, which includes an acknowledgment of sin, sorrow for it, a turning away from it, and a turning to Christ in faith, with a determination henceforth to live for God alone.

The English word "repentance" is used in the English version of the Scripture and in theology in two senses which must be carefully distinguished from each other, in order to avoid confusion of thought. In the narrow sense it means contrition or penitence. In the wide sense, as a change of mind, it means contrition *and faith,* [2] and is practically synonymous with conversion and regeneration, though describing the inner transformation from a different point of view.

In discussing the subject of repentance in this chapter, it is to be understood from the outset that we are using the term here in the wide sense as including contrition and faith, and not in the narrow sense as including only contrition or penitence. The wide sense is the one in which, with a few exceptions, it is used in the New Testament.

Metanoia. The Greek word *metanoia,* of which repentance has become the English rendering, means literally a change of mind. This is a meaning which is quite inadequately rendered by the English word repentance; for repentance has come to

---

[1] Greek, μετάνοια.
[2] The Form. Conc., p. 590, calls attention to the use of the word in two senses.

mean in many cases simply an experience of inner pain or sorrow. The translation of the Vulgate is even more unsatisfactory, since it renders *metanoia* as "doing penance." [3] The delight with which Luther learned that to repent in the Scriptural sense means to undergo a change of mind, instead of to do penance, is well known. The discovery changed his whole outlook upon religion, and was a prime factor in bringing on the Reformation.

Apparently the translators who produced the Authorized Version of the English Bible as well as those who produced the Revised Version were not able to find a satisfactory English equivalent for *metanoia*, and used the word repentance for lack of a better one. It is certainly a great pity that in English we do not possess a word which without any extended explanation expresses what is meant by the New Testament term in the original. But we must take matters as they are, and make the best of the situation. This means that it is incumbent upon us constantly to remember that repentance in its principal use in the New Testament and in theology means not simply penitence or contrition, but a change of mind. This is important not only for pastors but for the laymen also; otherwise the word repentance is apt to be understood merely in the narrow sense of regret or sorrow for sin.

Repentance or a change of mind is a basic condition of entrance into the kingdom of God (Matt. 3:2, 8; 4:17). Christ came to call sinners to repentance (Matt. 9:13), and there is joy in heaven over one sinner that repenteth (Luke 15:7). The substance of the message to be proclaimed by the apostles was a call to repentance, so that man might participate in the benefits of salvation (Luke 24:47; Acts 2:38; 3:19; 11:18; 17:30; 26:20). It is a repentance to which God seeks to lead men not only by admonition (Rom. 2:4; 2 Tim. 2:25; Rev. 2:5, 16;

[3] *Poenitentiam agere.*

3:3), but also by judgments (Rev. 9:20, 21; 16:9); and it is a repentance unto salvation not to be regretted (2 Cor. 7:10. R.V.). It is the intransitive side of conversion.

Definition. Repentance is that act of the Holy Spirit by which through the Law and the Gospel He works a change of mind in the sinner, so that he comes to contrition for his sins and to faith in the Lord Jesus Christ as his personal Savior. This change of mind affects the intellect, the emotions and the will.

Since contrition and faith have been considered in previous chapters and call for no further treatment at this point, it remains for us to consider the psychological side of the inner transformation, which is emphasized by the Biblical term repentance. It is a change of mind; not, however, a substantial but a qualitative change. The repentant man does not actually have his old mental powers and faculties taken away and an entirely new set put into their place. But the mind itself in all the phases of its activities undergoes a thorough qualitative change. The repentant man has a new mind in the sense of having a mind which functions in new spiritual activities. He thinks and feels and wills, indeed, by means of the same essential human powers and activities by which he thought and felt and willed before. But he is able to exercise and does exercise these essential activities in new ways. Using a psychological phraseology which belongs to the past but which is still extremely useful from the practical standpoint, the man has the same intellect, feelings and will as he had before he came to faith, but these function in a way and in a sphere which are new.

Change in the Intellect. First, as regards the intellect. Substantially the believer has the same intellect as before. If he had a trained mind, he still has it; if he had an untrained one, he still has it. What he knew or was ignorant of so far as earthly knowledge is concerned, he still knows or is ignorant of. But his intellect now functions in a sphere in which it previously did not and could not function, namely, the spiritual. As a natural man he was spiritually blind. He could not see, perceive or understand spiritual things; they were foolishness unto him. The condemnation under which he rested as a consequence of his sins, and the grace of God which would save him from the destruction which he had deserved, were hidden from his eyes. He did not see the things that belonged to his peace. He could see many other things clearly enough, and may even have displayed great powers of intellect. In respect to sin and grace, however, he was blind. But now, having been brought to repentance by the Holy Spirit, a great light dawns upon him, and he exclaims, "Once I was blind, but now I see." He sees his own sin and helplessness, and he sees the saving arm of God outstretched to save him. He perceives facts and truths which had never penetrated his mind before. He also sees in a new light many things which he had seen before, because he now sees them in a new perspective. The things which once seemed of greatest importance to him have now faded into comparative insignificance; and things which appeared to him of no consequence before now assume a place of primary importance. Once he regarded the Gospel as foolishness, but now he sees that it is the wisdom of God. The blind spot before his mental eyes which prevented him from seeing the things of God is removed. He sees as he never saw before.

Change in the Feelings. As regards his sensibilities there is a change equally great. In his natural state he was unmoved by the thought of his sinfulness and guilt, and went on his way in indifference or false security. The wrath of God against sin did not trouble him, and the Gospel of salvation through Christ left him unmoved. He was callous to the threats and the promises of God. He loved sin, self and the world, and he disliked and really hated God and the things of God. But with the change of mind wrought by the Holy Spirit in him, his feelings have been reversed, as it were. He now hates what he formerly loved, and loves what he formerly hated. He is filled with shame and confusion and sorrow at the thought of his sin and former ingratitude to God, and detests the sins which once he loved; and, on the other hand, he regards with deep appreciation and gratitude the divine grace and mercy which have rescued him from the pit of destruction, given him a new vision of time and eternity, and endowed him with the ability, though coupled with much remaining natural weakness, to love God and walk in His ways.

Change in the Will. As regards his will, there is a great change in that also. His will had formerly functioned in antagonism to God's. By reason of the natural limitation which clung to it as a result of original sin, he was unable as well as unwilling to obey the command to repent. Bound with the shackles of sin, his will, though able to function in the purely moral or civil sphere, was unable to function in the spiritual sphere. He could not love God nor do His will. But now, having been brought to contrition and faith, he finds his will freed from its spiritual paralysis and functioning in the spiritual realm. He is now by an act of the will clinging firmly to Christ his Savior, and, by virtue of the power which comes to him from Christ through faith, he is beginning to will and to do, imperfectly indeed, but none the less truly, the will of God. He has relegated self to the background; and he shuns sin and follows after righteousness. The will of God has now become the norm of his life.

Change of Mind Necessary. The repentant man has thus undergone a radical change of mind, which is evident in his intellect, his feelings and his will. A new spiritual quality has permeated his soul, and given him a new insight, a new love, and a new direction of the will. In the literal sense, of course, he has the same mind and the same mental faculties as before. But he has undergone an inner revolution. He now has a spiritual instead of a carnal mind. The carnal mind had been enmity against God; the spiritual mind is loving trust and confidence in Him.

This repentance or change of mind is necessary for salvation. For only by repentance, that is, by contrition and faith, is the salvation which God has prepared made personally ours. It is this necessity of repentance, this requirement of a radical change of mind, that marks Christianity as an ethical religion.

The preaching of repentance varies, of course, according to the persons to whom the Word is proclaimed. The preaching of repentance to those who are merely nominal Christians or to sincere Christians or to benighted heathen will require variety of method. But in every case the emphasis must be upon the necessity of a changed mind, an attitude of contrition and faith, as a *sine qua non* of salvation.

Private Confession and Absolution. The demand of Rome that all sins must be confessed to the priest in the confessional, that absolution must be obtained from him, and that all sins must be enumerated if pardon is to be secured is, of course, to be rejected. But private confession and absolution may be retained for the benefit of those who desire privately to confess their sins and to receive the absolution, and especially for those who labor under some peculiar distress of conscience. Enumeration of all sins is, however, unnecessary and impossible.[4] Along with Rome's confessional, its doctrine of satisfaction for the temporal punishment of sins is to be rejected also. When the sinner has repented and has been forgiven for Christ's sake, no

---

[4] The statement of the Augsburg Confession on this point is (Art. XI), "Concerning confession they teach that private absolution be retained in the churches, though enumeration of all offences is not necessary. For this is impossible according to the Psalm, 'Who can understand his errors!' " Ps. 19:12.

punishment of any kind any longer hangs over him. He is not asked to do penance.[5]

In concluding this chapter, we recall that repentance, conversion and regeneration are three separate Biblical and theological terms which refer to one and the same inner transformation wrought by the Holy Spirit through the Word. The essence of that transformation is that the sinner is brought to contrition and faith. The three words all refer to the same inner state, but each describes it in a different way. The term conversion emphasizes the fact that the sinner has been turned about and faces in a new direction; the term regeneration, that he has been made spiritually alive in Christ; and the term repentance, that he has undergone a change of mind, and has an entirely new attitude toward God and the things of God.

[5] According to Roman Catholic teaching, the Sacrament of Penance consists of three parts. *First,* attrition and contrition, the first being sorrow for sin on account of its eternal punishment, and the latter being sorrow for sin on God's account. *Secondly,* confession to the priest, who decides concerning the gravity of the sin and the necessary expiation, and who alone can impart the needed sacramental pardon. *Thirdly,* satisfaction by works, through which the sinner endures the temporal punishments of sin in order to receive judicial absolution from the eternal punishments. "If any one denieth, that for the entire and perfect remission of sins there are required three acts in the penitent, which are as it were the matter of the Sacrament of Penance, to wit, contrition, confession and satisfaction, which are called the three parts of penance; or saith that there are two parts only of penance, to wit, the terrors with which the conscience is smitten upon being convinced of sin, and the faith, generated by the Gospel or by the absolution, whereby one believes that his sins are forgiven him through Christ: Let him be anathema." *Council of Trent,* Sess. XIV, Can. 4. In this way the doing of penance by command of the Church replaced true repentance of the heart, and the relation of man to the Church took the place of his relation to God.

CHAPTER XXIII

THE MYSTICAL UNION

THERE is a mystical union of God and the believer, which is taught in the Scriptures and experienced by the Christian, but which is difficult to describe. Chronologically its beginning coincides with regeneration and justification; logically it follows upon them, and forms the next stage in the order of salvation. It is not to be interpreted simply as an activity of God in us, but possesses the nature of a personal fellowship (1 John 1:3). God lives in the believer, and the believer in God. It is the starting point and living source of that progressive sanctification which begins in the justified man and continues to the end of his earthly life.[1]

The Scriptures teach not only that by faith man is justified and forgiven, but that Christ dwells in him, and through Christ

[1] This doctrine is not contained in the Augsburg Confession or in the Apology; and the Formula of Concord barely touches it. It was developed by the later dogmaticians, Calovius, Quenstedt, Koenig and Hollazius, to guard against the pantheistic conceptions of the mystics, and at the same time to do justice to the partial truth contained in the false doctrines of Schwenkfeld, Weigel and Osiander. The Formula of Concord does not develop the idea of the mystical union, but has this to say: "For although in the elect, who are justified by Christ and reconciled with God, God the Father, Son and Holy Ghost, who is eternal and essential righteousness, dwells by faith (for all Christians are temples of God the Father, Son and Holy Ghost, who also impels them to do right); yet this indwelling of God is not the righteousness of faith of which Paul treats and which he calls the righteousness of God; but it follows the preceding righteousness of faith, which is nothing else than the forgiveness of sins and the gracious acceptance of the poor sinner alone for the sake of Christ's obedience and merit" (579, 54). It rejects the teaching "that not God Himself but only the gifts of God dwell in the believer" (581, 65). The mystical union is defined by Hollazius as "the spiritual union of the Triune God with the justified man, by which He dwells in him as in a consecrated temple with a special presence, and that a substantial one, and operates in him by a gracious influx" (p. 932).

272

the Holy Trinity. St. Paul declares of the Christians that they
are in Christ (Rom. 8:1) and again that Christ is in them
(Gal. 2:20). They live in fellowship or communion with God
(1 John 1:3). Not only does the Holy Spirit dwell and work
within them, so that they have the earnest of the Spirit in their
hearts (1 Cor. 1:22), the witness of the Spirit that they are
God's children (Rom. 8:16) and the sealing with the Spirit of
promise (Eph. 1:13), but the Father and the Son also come
to the believers and take their abode in them (John 14:23).
Christ is in the believers (Col. 1:27) and they in him (Rom.
8:1). As many as have been baptized into Him have put on
Christ (Gal. 3:27) and are in the Lord (Rom. 16:11) and are
made nigh because they are in Him (Eph. 2:13) and are free
from condemnation (Rom. 8:1). They are members of His
body, of His flesh and of His bones (Eph. 5:30), members of
Christ (1 Cor. 6:15) and partakers of the divine nature (2 Pet.
1:4). Christ lives in them (Gal. 2:20) and dwells in their
hearts by faith (Eph. 3:17), is in them (Rom. 8:10), and is to
be formed in them (Gal. 4:19). The believers are members of
His body (Rom. 12:4, 5); they are united with Him as the
branch with the vine (John 15:5), and their life is His life
flowing through them.

A Mystery. This union, as its name indicates, is a mystery.
It is experienced by the believer, but cannot adequately be put
into words. The fullness of the experience is proportioned to
the degree of faith and sanctification. The union is established
when the sinner comes to faith and is justified, and grows more
close, intimate and strength-giving as his sanctification increases. The spiritual life which he leads has its source and
vitality in Christ. Believers live in Christ, and He in them, and
His life flows into and through them. Without Him they can
do nothing (John 15:5).

The source of all spiritual life is in God through Christ. By faith the believer is reunited with God from whom he was separated and cut off by sin. Thus he who was spiritually dead is now made spiritually alive. As the severed branch which is grafted back into the tree lives again because of its new union with the tree, so the believer lives again because of his union with God through Christ. The branch grows and puts forth leaves and fruit; but it does so only because and as long as it is vitally united with the tree from which its life comes. The believer lives and bears fruit in holy living; but he does so only because and as long as he is united with God by faith. Through this mystical union life comes to him from God. Only by virtue of this union does he live spiritually. What this union meant to Paul he tells us when he says, "Nevertheless I live, yet not I, but Christ liveth in me; and the life which I now live in the flesh, I live by faith of the Son of God who loved me and gave Himself for me" (Gal. 2:20).

The indwelling of God in the believer must not be understood in the pantheistic sense, as though the person of the believer were absorbed by Christ. On the contrary it is a close personal union in which the believer rests in Christ and draws strength from Him. Nor must the union be understood in such a way as to make man divine. The personality of man is not changed in any way, but it is united in a mystical and indescribable yet real and comforting way with Christ, or with God in Christ, so that Christ lives in him and he in Christ. The mystery of this union finds its explanation in the faith which grasps Christ and makes Him its very own, and in the love which flows from that faith and binds the soul and Christ together in the most intimate and loving fellowship.[2]

---

[2] Luther has many mystical elements in his writings. He says in his commentary on Galatians, 2:20: "Christ therefore, joined and united unto me and abiding in me, liveth this life in me which I now live. Yes, Christ Himself is this life which now I live. Wherefore Christ and I in this behalf are both one. . . . So Christ, living and abiding in me, taketh away and swalloweth up all evils which vex and afflict me. . . . Because Christ liveth in me, therefore

Though the mystical union cannot be fully described because it is a mystery, it is nevertheless not to be regarded as a figure of speech, but as a reality. It is not to be understood as denoting merely that harmony has been established between man's will and God's, or that there simply exists a union of God and man in love, such as might exist between two human persons. Nor is it to be understood as denoting merely that the believer receives special and peculiar gifts from the Holy Spirit. It is a real indwelling of God in man, a real union between them, which the old dogmaticians described as a union of substance with substance, but which they took care to guard against the notion that the divine and human substances are confused or amalgamated.

St. Paul, in speaking to the Athenians, refers to the natural union between man and God as the source of life (Acts 17:28). But the mystical union is carefully to be distinguished from the natural one spoken of by the apostle. It is a spiritual union. It is, of course, also to be distinguished from the personal union of God and man in Christ, and from the pantheistic notion that man is swallowed up in God.[3]

---

look what grace, righteousness, life, peace and salvation is in me; it is His, and yet notwithstanding the same is mine also by that inseparable union and conjunction which is through faith; by the which I and Christ are made as it were one spirit. . . . Thou art so entirely and nearly joined unto Christ, that He and thou are made as it were one person; so that thou mayest boldly say, I am now one with Christ, that is to say, Christ's righteousness, victory and life are mine. And again Christ may say, I am that sinner, that is, his sins and death are mine, because he is united and joined unto me and I unto him. For by faith we are so joined together that we are become one flesh and one bone (Eph. 5:31), we are members of the body of Christ, flesh of His flesh and bone of His bone; so that this faith doth couple Christ and me more near together than the husband is coupled with the wife."—Engl. Transl. Publ. by S. S. Miles, 1840.

[3] The Reformed deny the doctrine of the mystical union. Ritschl regarded the doctrine as worthless and unsound, and called it "apocryphal."

CHAPTER XXIV

SANCTIFICATION

Meaning. The word sanctification is sometimes used in a wide sense to denote the entire work of the Holy Spirit as given in the Order of Salvation. It is thus used as the heading of the Third Article of the Creed in Luther's Small Catechism to designate the whole work of the Holy Spirit beginning with the Call, while in the body of that article it is used in the narrow sense to designate a particular part of that work. In the other confessions of our Church the words sanctification and renewal are sometimes used to cover both regeneration and renewal, and even justification. It is important to remember, however, that the word sanctification has acquired a definite and restricted meaning, and now refers to the progressive growth in holiness which follows in the life of the believer after his justification by faith alone.

In this chapter, therefore, the word sanctification is used in the narrow sense in which it refers to the last stage of the Order of Salvation. The words renovation and renewal may be used as its synonyms, because they also, while originally used in a more comprehensive sense, have acquired the same definite and restricted meaning as sanctification.

Definition. Sanctification is that work of the Holy Spirit by which the believer, coöperating with God through powers divinely bestowed in regeneration, grows in personal holiness by more and more overcoming sin in his heart and life and by cultivating and exercising the Christian graces and virtues. Faith

276

worketh by love, and the new life of the believer is a life lived
in love to God and his fellow men. Having had his will set
free in regeneration, the believer now coöperates with the grace
of God, so that as a result he lives a new life of holiness and
does good works. This new life of the Christian, while accompanied by much weakness and failure, exhibits a constantly
nearer approach to the likeness of Christ, until in the next world
the believer is perfectly transformed and glorified.

Sanctification and Justification. Sanctification deals with the
increase of personal righteousness or holiness. But this righteousness must be carefully distinguished from that with which
we deal in justification. The righteousness with which justification has to do is not the believer's personal righteousness at all,
but the righteousness of Christ which is imputed to him. The
righteousness of sanctification, on the other hand, is the personal righteousness or holiness of the believer. For the sake of
avoiding confusion it is better to speak of this personal righteousness of the believer as his holiness. This personal holiness of the believer has nothing at all to do with his justification, but comes into existence only after justification has taken
place. No man is capable of acquiring any holiness at all until
he has first become regenerated and justified by grace; for only
after he has faith and has been justified is he able to love God
and do His will. This personal holiness always remains imperfect; and, because of its imperfection, it would, if taken into
account in justification, only help to condemn us. The only
righteousness that counts in justification is the righteousness
of Jesus Christ made ours by faith.

Sanctification and Regeneration. Sanctification needs also to
be carefully distinguished from regeneration. Regeneration is
the act by which the Holy Spirit makes man a believer, while
sanctification is the gradual process by which the believer becomes more and more renewed in heart and life. Regeneration

is an instantaneous act; sanctification is a gradual process. Regeneration is the creation of a new spiritual life; sanctification is the growth, development and fruitage of that new spiritual life. Sanctification is the natural and normal sequence of regeneration. For in that inner transformation which we call regeneration or conversion the old sinful nature is cast out of the controlling center of the man, and a new principle, that of love to God and man, takes its place. The faith established in the heart by divine grace in regeneration is ready to work by love; and being a living, active thing, it begins to work at once, and with its working sanctification begins. In regeneration, the sinner has become a new man; and in sanctification he continues more and more to think and feel and act as a new man.

Sanctification and Faith. The possibility of sanctification is conditioned on the possession of faith. And therefore it is the believers and not the unbelievers who are admonished to be holy. The admonition addressed to the unbelievers is to repent; the admonition addressed to the believers is to approve themselves as God's children by leading holy lives. Paul magnifies the grace of God in his Epistle to the Romans, but he makes it very clear that the Christian must not and will not live in sin (Rom. 6). The true believer lives in the Spirit, hence he should walk in the Spirit (Gal. 5:25). He is created in Christ Jesus unto good works (Eph. 2:10), and he loves God because God first loved him (1 John 4:19). This love of God is accompanied by love to his fellow men (1 John 4:20, 21).

Sin not Eradicated. By regeneration the sinner has undergone a radical and fundamental change in the very center of his being. He has been brought into harmony with God; he loves God and wills what God wills. Sin has been cast out from the citadel, and faith and love have been installed in its place. But sin has not been eradicated from his nature. It remains in the believer alongside the new nature wrought by grace. Though cast out of the citadel, it lingers in the surrounding regions, ready at the first opportunity to retake the citadel and regain the control. The new principle of love, though enthroned in the center of the believer's being, is by no means at once in control of all his acts. In his inner self, in his *ego,* the believer wills to serve God only. But sin is strongly intrenched in his nature, and the gradual reduction of all the territory of our being under the new law of love entails a lifelong conflict, in which the believer makes headway, but in which he never achieves a victory so complete as to drive sin over the border. Every inch of ground is contested. And the triumph of the new principle of love in all the thoughts, words and actions of the believer is a slow and arduous process of driving sin ever farther and farther toward the circumference of his being. If the sinner be regarded as a dark circle of sinfulness, then the regenerate man is one in whom the center has been made light, and in whom by a gradual process of sanctification the light is to drive out the darkness through the whole area of the circle. Psychologically speaking, the regenerate man is a new man in his pure *ego,* and in sanctification he is to become new throughout all the area of his psychological *Me.* The nature of the conflict involved in this process of sanctification and the pain experienced by the Christian in his failure to live up to his ideals are strikingly depicted by St. Paul in the seventh chapter of his Epistle to the Romans.

In seeking to bring the new principle of love into complete control of his life the believer meets with temptations from within and without. He has made in his conversion the great and fundamental act of decision for God; but day by day he is called upon to make innumerable subordinate decisions in his effort to carry out what has now become the main purpose of his life. The degree and stress of the struggle required of him in seeking to bring every thought, purpose and act into subjection to the law of Christ depends on his natural disposition and his environment. Some persons are exposed to great temptations in one direction, and others in another. But for every Christian, growth in personal holiness means earnest prayer and ceaseless struggles to overcome the evil tendencies of the heart, the temptations of the world, and the delusions of the devil. The degree of growth in sanctification depends upon the extent to which love to God and man is made the sole guiding principle in thought, word and deed, but also on the nature of the obstacles to be overcome. Slower progress in sanctification in many cases is due to the greater difficulties presented by a bad heredity and environment.

Two Sides. The sanctification of the believer has two sides, a negative and a positive, which the apostle describes as a putting off of the old man and a putting on of the new (Eph. 4:22, 24). Negatively it consists in subduing and overcoming the old sinful inclinations and habits; and positively, in acquiring and practicing Christlike modes and habits of thinking, speaking and acting. This putting off of the old man and putting on of the new man is called a renewal of the believer in the moral image of God which was lost by the fall (Eph. 4:24; Col. 3:10).

There is a remnant of sin in the believer which prevents him from achieving the perfect holiness which he desires (Rom. 7:14-25). The flesh lusteth against the spirit and the spirit against the flesh, and there is a conflict and contradiction within him (Gal. 5:17). He must therefore be dead unto sin and alive unto righteousness (1 Pet. 2:24), and must be more and more transformed by the renewing of his mind (Rom. 12:2). He must deny himself and take up his cross and follow Jesus (Matt. 16:24), be willing to forsake all that he has if necessary for Christ's sake (Luke 14:33), crucify the flesh with its affections and lusts (Gal. 5:24), and mortify his members which are upon earth (Col. 3:5). He must not love the world nor the things of the world (1 John 2:15-17) and must be strong in the Lord to resist the devil and all his assaults (Eph. 6:10). On the other hand he must be renewed in knowledge after the image of him that created him (Col. 3:10), put on the new man (Eph. 4:24) and put on the Lord Jesus Christ (Rom. 13:14). He is to grow up into Christ (Eph. 4:15), walk in him and be rooted and built up in Him (Col. 2:6, 7). He is to follow after holiness (Heb. 4:12), cultivate Christian virtues (Col. 3:12; Phil. 4:8), abound in the work of the Lord (1 Cor. 15:58), do everything in His name (Col. 3:17, 23), and hope for the consummation at the second coming of Christ (I Pet. 1:13).

The essence of this new life of the Christian is love. Without love the seemingly good action is vain and worthless in God's eyes (1 Cor. 13). This love is love to God (1 John 4:19), to his fellow believers (1 John 4:11), to his fellow men in general (2 Pet. 1:5-7), and to his enemies (Matt. 5:44). It is the antithesis of selfishness (1 Cor. 13:5), and constitutes the real fulfillment of God's law (Rom. 13:10).

Psychological Effect. The psychological effect of sanctification is apparent in the intellect, the emotions and the will. The intellect acquires a constantly keener discrimination between right and wrong, and a fuller appreciation of God's mercy in Christ. The emotions are more powerfully stirred against evil and sin, and more fully enlisted in the cause of truth and righteousness. And the will, already conformed in its main life purpose with the will of God, becomes ever more conformed to God's will in its individual acts and its newly formed habits. Sanctification is a continuous transformation into a greater likeness to the ideal set before us (Rom. 12:2), and an increasing possession of the mind of Christ (Phil. 2:5).

The Vital and the Active Principle. The *vital* principle of the new life of the believer is faith. By the production of faith in his heart he has been made spiritually alive. The life he leads is a life of faith. The *active* principle of the new life of the believer is love. Faith worketh by love. He who believes that all his sins are freely forgiven for Christ's sake is of necessity one who is grateful to God for His mercy and loves Him in return. This love becomes the true motive of the believer's acts. Only what is done out of love to God is in reality a doing of His will and a part of the process of sanctification or renewal.

The Work of the Holy Ghost. The sanctification of the believer is the work of the Holy Spirit. He who has begun the good work in us also continues it (Phil. 1:6). It is God who sanctifies us, and He does it through the truth, which is His Word (John 17:17). As the branch bears fruit only through its union with the vine, so the believer grows in holiness only through the spiritual life and strength which come to him from God (John 15:4, 5).

The Coöperation of the Believer. Sanctification involves the coöperation of the believer with the grace of God. This coöperation is now possible, because in regeneration and conversion the will has been made free in the spiritual sphere. The believer has been made willing and able to love and serve God. This coöperation is accompanied with much human weakness and imperfection, and what the believer succeeds in accomplishing is far from a perfect fulfillment of God's holy law. But it is still an effort in the right direction; and since its motive is love to God it is, in a measure at least, a doing of His will.

The coöperation which takes place between the believer and God is not to be regarded as the coöperation of two equals toward a certain end, but as the feeble coöperation of man with the mighty grace of God (1 Cor. 15:10). Paul realized thoroughly his own weakness; but he leaned on the grace of God, which was mighty in his weakness (2 Cor. 12:9). The impulses, the motives and the strength which are needed for a right life do and must come from God. The believer never ceases to need a strength greater than human to enable him to fight the good fight of faith and to endure to the end. And hence, whatever the degree of holiness to which he attains or whatever the greatness of the labors which he performs in Christ's cause, he must ascribe all his growth and accomplishment to the grace of God, and not to his own strength. It is by God's grace that the believer is what he is and does what he does (1 Cor. 15:10).

Perfection. The gradual transformation of the believer's character and life into conformity with God's will and with the example of Christ will never reach perfection in this world. The conflict between the flesh and the spirit continues to the end of life on earth. When we are exhorted to be perfect as our Father in heaven is perfect (Matt. 5:48), perfection is set before us as an ideal to be striven for, and not as a goal attainable in this world. The command of Christ to offer daily in the Lord's Prayer the petition for the forgiveness of our trespasses shows that in this world the believer will always be in need of forgiveness. John, a Christian of the highest type, assures us that "if we say that we have no sin, we deceive ourselves and the truth is not in us (1 John 1:8). The advocates of perfectionism either lower the standard of the divine law by making it demand only what the Christian can actually render, or else they do not count involuntary transgressions and shortcomings as sins.[1]

The Means of Grace. The growth and development of the spiritual life are dependent on the faithful use of the means of grace. The believer is to be sanctified through the truth. As the Holy Spirit uses the Word for the sinner's conversion and

---

[1] To the latter class belonged John Wesley. See his *Plain Account of Christian Perfection.*

regeneration, so He also uses it for his progressive renewal and sanctification. What the believer has learned from God's Word to see, he must learn to perceive with ever-increasing clearness; what he has learned to feel, he must learn to feel ever more profoundly; what he has learned to will, he must learn to will with increasing strength and determination. Through the continued hearing and study of the Word his perception of sin and righteousness must become more clear and discriminating, his hatred of sin and his love of righteousness must become more intense; and his determination to serve God alone must become more firm and steadfast. He must grow in grace (2 Pet. 3:18), and in the doing of God's will. And he can do this only in the proportion in which the Holy Spirit through the Word makes increasingly known to him the riches of grace in Christ Jesus, and thus strengthens his faith and increases his love and devotion.

In this growth in sanctification the sacraments, or the visible Word, as well as the Word itself, have an important place. The remembrance of baptism with its solemn covenant of grace, and the participation in the Lord's Supper with its assurance of forgiveness pledged by the body and blood of Christ, confirm the faith wrought by the Word, deepen the believer's appreciation of God's grace, and strengthen his love and devotion to God.

Neglect of the Word and Sacraments cuts men off from the means intended for the promotion of the spiritual growth, inevitably leads to a lowering of their spiritual vitality, and eventually results in a loss of their faith itself. The faithful use of the means of Grace leads, on the other hand, through the activity of the Holy Spirit in man, to an increase of faith and love and an ever closer approach to the Christian ideal.

Good Works. The question of good works is inseparably connected with that of sanctification. Good works are the outward fruitage and evidence of the inward sanctification and renewal. They are the external manifestations of the inner attitude and disposition. When the tree is good, the fruit will be good also; and when the tree is corrupt, the fruit will be corrupt also (Matt. 7:17). The believer does good works. Indeed, if he is a true believer, he cannot help but do them. Having been made by regeneration into the right kind of man, he naturally and inevitably leads the right kind of life.

Good works do not make a good man, but a good man does good works. Hence in seeking to undo the damage done by Satan in Eden, God does not undertake to place a new patch upon an old garment, or to have external works of apparent obedience to his law performed by men who have no love for him. On the contrary, He undertakes by His plan of redemption to make man into a new creature, knowing that when man once has been made what he ought to be, he will do what he ought to do.

The Fruit of Faith. Good works are the fruit of faith. In coming to faith through the work of the Holy Spirit the believer has undergone an inner transformation which has given him an entirely new attitude toward God and the things of God. His faith is essentially an appreciation of God's love and mercy, and a willing consent to let God work His saving will in him. Such an attitude is necessarily one of gratitude and love to God, and its natural and inevitable consequence is an effort to do God's will. The result is seen in good works.

The Nature of Good Works. The Roman Catholic conception of good works differs radically from the Protestant conception. For the Roman Catholic a good work consists of a work of supererogation. For him good works do not consist of those things which are done in accordance with God's will, but of those things which are done over and above the demands of the divine law, as a voluntary additional service. These supererogatory works are supposed to be done by obeying the so-called evangelical counsels, especially by living a monastic life of celibacy, poverty and obedience.[2] These works are regarded as earning merit; and the saints are supposed to have acquired more merit than they need for themselves. These supererogatory merits of the saints are regarded as being in the keeping of the pope, and may be dispensed to the faithful, thus releasing them from certain penances or from certain torments in purgatory.

For the Protestant supererogatory merits do not exist. No man can do as much as God's law requires, and still less can any man do more than it demands. A good work in the Protestant and Scriptural sense is a work done in compliance with God's will and command, and out of love for Him and our neighbor. The Christian's best works are imperfect, and they are not really good in the sense in which Christ's works are good. But they are done out of a sincere desire to do God's will. And though much imperfection clings to them, they are accepted by God and please Him, because they are the sincere though feeble efforts of His children to do His will. Works which look good outwardly, but do not have behind them the proper motive of love to God, are not really good. Two men may seem to do the same thing, and yet it is not the same, if they act from different motives.

Good Works Do Not Justify. Good works are the result of faith; and justification also is the result of faith. Since both

---

[2] Matt. 19:21, for example, is supposed to be an evangelical counsel of perfection. If the young man had obeyed the counsel and given away all his goods to the poor, he would have acquired supererogatory merit. It was something over and above what the law of God demanded. But such an interpretation of the passage is wrong. The command to give away his possessions was not a counsel which he might accept or leave, but a command on obedience to which his salvation hinged. His wealth stood between him and his acceptance of Christ as his Savior. The command has general application, not as an "evangelical counsel," but as a necessity, and must be obeyed by everyone who would have salvation, if his wealth stands between him and Christ.

result from faith, one cannot be the cause of the other. The believer is justified by faith alone, and not at all by any good works. He does not do good works for the purpose of acquiring merit or of deserving salvation. He does them out of love and gratitude to God, because God has saved Him out of grace. The lack of good works shows the absence of faith, and the presence of good works shows the presence of faith. But it is the faith alone that justifies. The believer must and will do good works. But he will never depend on them for salvation, but only on the merit and righteousness of Christ.

The Believer and the Law. The believer is no longer under the law but under grace. The Law is not abrogated. Representing as it does the holy and unchangeable nature and will of God it cannot be altered or annulled. But the believer has been freed by Christ from the demands of the law. His salvation is decided, not on the basis of the law, but on the basis of grace. The law no longer has anything to say to him, because all its demands have been met for the believer by Christ. So far as his salvation is concerned he is free from the law. But he is not free from the law in the sense that he is at liberty to live in antagonism to its commands. He who deliberately lives and acts in opposition to God's law shows that he lacks penitence, and hence that he lacks faith. And although the believer is not under obligation to fulfill the law in order to be saved, he sincerely desires to fulfill it. With the new disposition which accompanies faith the law has been taken into his heart, and he does freely, voluntarily and gladly what the law commands. He does good works because he desires to do them: not under the outward constraint of a demand, but from the inward constraint of love. Because his heart has been changed, he wills what God wills and obeys the law of his own accord. As he grows in knowledge and grace, the doing of God's will becomes more and more a delight. He finds God's service to be the most joyful freedom, because in doing God's will he finds himself doing the very things which he takes pleasure in doing. He experiences the truth of the Scriptural statements, that God's commandments are not grievous (John 5:3), and that Christ's yoke is easy and His burden light (Matt. 11:30).

Reward of Good Works. There is a reward of good works. The believers shall be rewarded in heaven for the persecutions which they faithfully endured for righteousness' sake (Matt. 5:11, 12). Their reward shall be great for loving their enemies, doing good, and lending without hoping for a return (Luke 6:35). They shall in no wise lose their reward even for the giving of a cup of cold water in the name of a disciple (Matt. 10:42). But it will be a reward of grace and not of merit; a reward, *not for* the deeds, but *according* to the deeds. The believers shall be told by Christ to inherit eternal life, because they possess a faith which caused them to do good deeds and to minister to His needy brethren (Matt. 25:34 seq.).

CHAPTER XXV

THE MEANS OF GRACE

IN accomplishing His work of regeneration and sanctification in man, the Holy Spirit employs the Word of God and the Sacraments. These are called the Means of Grace, because they are the means through which God's grace is brought to men, and through which the Holy Ghost works His saving effects.

Means Adapted to Purpose. The Means of Grace are adapted to the nature and purpose of the Holy Spirit's work. In the last analysis, His work is that of drawing and persuading men to believe and to continue to believe. In the broad sense of the term the *Word* is the means of persuasion. In saying this we include the Sacraments along with the Word proper. For essentially the Sacraments are the Word also; God speaks to us in them. Not only is the Word the principal part of the sacraments, but the sacraments themselves as a whole, including the sacramental action and the words connected with it, are meant to convey the very same essential truth as is conveyed by the Word proper. And it is through the *truth* set forth in Word and Sacrament, that the Holy Spirit draws and persuades men to believe and be saved.

Definition. The Means of Grace are those divinely ordained means through which the Holy Spirit graciously offers to men the salvation acquired by Christ, and through which He produces, confirms and preserves in them true faith in Christ their Savior.[1]

[1] The Means of Grace include only the Word and the sacraments. Prayer is not a means of grace in the sense in which the Lutheran Church employs the latter term. Prayer is not a vehicle which God employs to make known and

Ethical Means. Through the Means of Grace the Holy Spirit aims to reach men's minds and hearts; for without reaching their minds and hearts He cannot convert and sanctify men. They cannot be dealt with as inanimate objects or as brutes. They are personal beings; and in dealing with them, God does so in conformity with the ethical relation which personality establishes between them and Him. The transformation needed in the natural man cannot be brought about by a sovereign fiat or by any process which would do violence to man's self-consciousness and self-determination. When in the beginning God determined to make man in His own image, i.e. to make him a person, that determination necessarily carried with it the determination to respect the personality of the man whom he was about to create. By the very act of creating man a person, God restricted Himself, freely indeed, but none the less truly, to methods of dealing with man which conform to the nature of a personal being. Force and compulsion have here no place. What man is compelled or forced to do against his will is not really his own act. That only is his own act which he does of his own will. And if he is unwilling to do what he ought, the one way of prevailing upon him to do it is by persuasion. The inability of the human will in spiritual things makes it necessary also for the Holy Spirit to give to man the needed power to will as he ought. Hence the work of the Holy Spirit through the Means of Grace is a work by which He both enables and persuades man to believe and be saved.

Persuasion through the Truth. How does the Holy Spirit seek to persuade men? How does He seek to remove from their minds the natural enmity against God and to prevail on them

convey His grace to men. It is an activity on man's part, by which he seeks grace from God. That grace is, indeed, given in answer to prayer. But it is conveyed by means of the Word and the sacraments. Prayer is subjective; the Means of Grace are objective. Prayer might be described as a means *to* grace, but not as a means *of* grace.

voluntarily to turn their faces toward Him in loving trust and friendship? The answer is, Through the truth (John 17:7). The truth must make men free (John 8:32). The truth must convert them from the error of their way to God. If this result cannot be accomplished through the truth, there exists no other means by which to move and persuade a personal being to do what he ought.

The truth to which reference is made here is in its essence the promise of salvation for Christ's sake to all who believe. That truth is brought to men through the Word of God, both in its literal sense as the audible Word and in the Sacraments as the "visible Word." For Word and Sacraments are the divinely ordained means through which the truth of God's saving grace is brought to men. Eliminate these means, and the truth has no way of access to their minds and hearts. As men are constituted in this world, we know of no way by which ideas can be conveyed from one mind to another except through the use of signs. Ideas are put into signs, and are translated back into ideas by him who perceives them. To this method of conveying truth by signs God adapts himself in dealing with men. And the signs which He uses to convey the divine ideas or divine truth to men are the Word of God and the Sacraments.

Signs. It is well known that the Sacraments are frequently called signs. This is done not only by the Reformed Churches, which do not regard the Sacraments as conveying any grace, but also by the Lutheran Confessions. But when Lutherans call the Sacraments signs, the appellation means more than when the Reformed do so. For the Lutherans the Sacraments are signs in the same sense in which the Word of God is a sign. Both are signs, not simply in the sense of being emblems of divine grace, but in the sense that they are means through which divine truth is communicated to men and divine grace brought to them.

It is to be borne in mind that the Sacraments have essentially the same purpose as the Word. Both are meant to make known to men in a clear and intelligible way what is in the mind and heart of God with respect to men. God loves men with an everlasting love, and desires their salvation. This is the great truth of the Christian religion. And the Word and Sacraments are signs through which that great truth is brought home to men's minds and hearts.

The Word as a Sign. The Word is an audible sign that strikes upon the ear. It is a sign meant to convey an idea. If the word is in an unknown language, the hearer gets no meaning from it. But if it is in a language familiar to him, the word has a definite meaning. This meaning is something which has been arbitrarily connected with the sound. The words "horse," "Pferd," "equus," and "hippos" all have a different sound. They are different words. But they all mean the very same thing to the hearer, if he understands the languages to which they belong. When he hears the word, he translates the sound into the idea of a well-known quadruped. The words in themselves are purely arbitrary sounds. But they are significant because of the meaning attached to them. It is so with all words. They are audible signs to which certain meanings are attached by the hearer's mind, and through which certain ideas are conveyed from one mind to the other. Thus a purely spiritual thing like a concept or idea is communicated from one mind to another by means of a purely physical thing, an audible sound.

When we say, therefore, that the Word of God is a sign, we mean that it is a means through which God communicates truths or ideas from His mind to ours. Without the intervention of signs for conveying ideas, it is impossible for us to conceive how the wondrous truth of God concerning the redemption of Christ could be made known and become the power of God unto salvation to them that believe. Constituted as we are in this world, intellectual communication from one mind to another is bound to signs.

The Sacraments as Signs. The Sacraments are signs in the same sense as the Word, and are meant to convey in essence the same divine truth. They are not meant to add anything to the truth of the Gospel, and do not do so. They agree with the Word in purpose, but differ in method. They are simply meant to communicate by different signs, visible ones, the same divine saving truth. They are visible signs added to the audible one, not for the sake of adding new truth, but for the purpose of communicating the same truth in a different manner, and of giving added force to the promise contained in the audible Word. The Gospel is essentially a promise of God to sinful men, a promise of free salvation in Christ and for His sake. This promise is given in the Word. That Word ought to be a sufficient guarantee to men, because it is the Word of a truthful and loving God, who will not and cannot lie or deceive. But in His mercy God has given the Sacraments as additional and visible signs to confirm the Word. They are given, not because of any need on God's part, but because of the weakness of men and of their need of reiterated assurance of God's love and mercy.

The oral promise of a wealthy and truthful man to give us on a certain date a hundred thousand dollars ought to be enough to give us faith and certainty that the gift will be bestowed. But if to the audible promise there is added the visible promise in the form of a promissory note for one hundred thousand dollars, written to our order and duly signed and delivered to us, the certainty is confirmed. The purpose of the note is to give absolute certainty. Essentially of this nature is the purpose of the Sacraments. They give expression to the very same divine saving promise as the Word. But they confirm and strengthen our faith in the promise, because that promise is given to us in a visible as well as an audible form. And the Sacraments have been added to the Word for that express purpose in view of our natural human weakness and tendency to doubt. The news of absolutely free forgiveness for Christ's sake proclaimed by the Gospel is bound at times to seem to the sinner to be too good to be true. And he asks, "Can it really be true that God will freely and fully forgive me all my sins, guilty and unworthy as I am?" The Word says, Yes. He believes the Word, but tremblingly. There is added the Sacrament with its visible promise, and his faith is confirmed. For in Baptism God has made with us a covenant of grace, and has promised us forgiveness and divine Sonship for Christ's sake by a definite visible act. And in the Lord's Supper, as often as it is administered, the same promise of free forgiveness given in the Word is brought home in a visible form which strengthens and confirms the faith; for Christ's body which was given and His blood which was shed for us are given to the communicant along with the bread and wine as a pledge which seals the gracious promise of forgiveness.

Word and Sacraments. It has been customary to call the Word the audible Word and the Sacraments the visible Word. The distinction is worth retaining, even though writing and printing make the Word visible in some sense also, as well as audible. In general the distinction is useful and helpful. Both the Word and the Sacraments bring the truth of divine grace to the human mind and heart, the Word audibly (and visibly), and the Sacraments visibly.

In the Word the grace of God is brought to men through the audible (and written or printed) sign; in the Sacraments it is brought to men through a sacred action instituted by God. It is the same Holy Spirit who is active in both, and it is essentially the same promise offered in both. Their purpose and effect is the same.[2] The Sacraments are intended for the same purpose as the Word, namely to bring to men and to apply to their souls the salvation which God has prepared in Christ. As the essence of the Word is the gracious promise of God to forgive the sinner freely for Christ's sake, so the essence of the Sacraments is the same gracious promise. This real essence of Word and Sacraments needs to be borne in mind, if the relation between them is to be understood. Both make known and bring to bear on men the grace of God in Christ. The purpose of both is to produce and confirm faith. And the Sacraments are added to the Word, not because the Word in itself is insufficient, but in order that the same truth which the Word brings may be brought under different forms and with added power. The substance both of Word and Sacraments is found in the statement that "God so loved the world, that He gave His only begotten Son, that whosoever believeth on Him should not perish but have everlasting life" (John 3:16).

The Means of Grace Necessary. The necessity of the Means of Grace is thus evident. Take them away, and we know of no means through which God's thoughts can be communicated from His mind to ours. Language, which is the communication of minds with one another through signs, is the one avenue of approach by one person to another; it is the one means of persuading another. Hence if men neglect the Word and the Sacraments, they close up the only avenue of approach to themselves. And if the Church fails to send the Word and Sacraments to heathen lands, it deprives the heathen of the only

---

[2] "The effect of the Word and of the rite is the same, as it has been well said by Augustine that a sacrament is 'a visible word,' because the rite is received by the eyes, and is, as it were, a picture of the Word, signifying the same thing as the Word. Wherefore the effect of both is the same." *Apology,* Art. XIII, Ch. VII, p. 214, 5.

means known to us through which the Holy Spirit can work in them that ethical transformation whose essence is faith in Christ.[2]

That God might in some way, purely spiritual, communicate His truth to men's minds may be acknowledged, since He doubtless has some way of communicating with angels, who are pure spirits, and doubtless has some way of communicating with the sainted dead before the resurrection of their bodies. But in this world God chooses to convey His truth to men by those very means which men use in communicating with one another. He uses signs which represent conceptions and thoughts, and brings them home to men's minds by means of those very signs to which men are bound in this world in their communications with one another. Whether He could bring His truth home directly to men's minds without the use of the Means of Grace is not here the question. The fact is that He uses those means, and that we not only have no assurance that if they are neglected He will communicate His truth to any man directly, but we are told that without the Means of Grace the Holy Spirit will not produce His saving effects in the heart. We are bound to the Word and the Sacraments. God's gracious will is recorded in His Word and set forth in the Sacraments, and apart from them there is no saving knowledge of the truth and no saving work of the Holy Spirit.

[2] The necessity of the Means of Grace is repeatedly emphasized by the Lutheran Confessions. Augs. Conf. Art. V. "For the obtaining of this faith, the ministry of teaching the Gospel and administering the Sacraments was instituted. . . . They condemn the Anabaptists and others, who imagine that the Holy Spirit is given to men without the outward word." Schm. Art., Part II. Art. VII, p. 333, 10, "Therefore in regard to this we ought and must constantly maintain that God does not wish to deal with us otherwise than through the spoken Word and the Sacraments, and that whatever without the Word and Sacraments is extolled as spirit is the devil himself." Form. Conc. 562, 50, "And by this means, and in no other way, namely, through His holy Word, when it is heard as preached or is read, and the holy Sacraments when they are used according to the Word, God desires to call men to eternal salvation, to draw them to Himself, and to convert, regenerate and sanctify them."

The Efficacy of the Means of Grace. Through the Word and Sacraments as the outward means the Holy Spirit produces an inward effect upon the heart. This effect of the Holy Spirit's work is not dependent on the worthiness of those who administer the Means of Grace, nor is it in itself prevented by their unworthiness. But since the preaching of the Word is meant to enlighten and persuade, the work of the Holy Spirit may be hampered and hindered by the inefficiency or slovenliness of those appointed to preach. The failure rightly to divide the Word of truth undoubtedly results in many instances in the loss of souls. On the other hand, the saving effect of the Word and Sacraments is not dependent on the wisdom, learning or skill of the minister, but on the gracious operation of the Holy Spirit. Without His work in the heart, the most able preacher of the Gospel would not succeed in converting a single soul.

The efficacy of the Means of Grace lies in the inner power with which the Holy Spirit presses the truth conveyed by them upon the minds and hearts of men. This power is always present and operative. The Word is God's Word and the Sacraments are His Sacraments; and hence the Holy Spirit is always present in them and operative through them.[*] The Lutheran Church lays great emphasis upon the Means of Grace and their efficacy. But it needs to be carefully borne in mind that this efficacy is not a magical one, and that the Word and Sacraments produce the effect intended only in the proportion in which the truth conveyed by them is made clear and pressed home upon the mind and heart. In the Means of Grace God adapts Himself to the nature of the being with whom He deals, and works

[*] This position is maintained in opposition to the Reformed Church, which conceives of the Holy Spirit's work as taking place, not so much through, as alongside of the Means of Grace. In the Reformed view, the Means of Grace are in themselves empty and powerless, and become efficacious only through the addition of the inner Word through which the Holy Spirit works; and this is supposed to be added only in the case of the elect. An extreme in the Reformed direction is represented by the Quakers, who reject the Means of Grace entirely, and depend on a direct inner light.

along psychological lines. He seeks to enlighten the intellect, move the feelings and persuade the will. And if the truth of God, as Scripture and experience prove, has a power all its own to convert and to sanctify, this power is to be sought, not in any magical activity of God through Word and Sacraments, but in the power of the living truth made clear through human agency to the intelligence, and made powerful and efficacious by the omnipotent personality of God back of the Word. The Word and Sacraments possess divine efficacy because through them God Himself speaks to the mind and heart of the sinner.

The power of a word depends not only on the truth contained in it, but on the personality of the speaker. The greatest being in all the universe, the infinite God Himself, speaks with divine power of enlightenment and persuasion in Word and Sacraments. This fact gives to them a corresponding efficacy. The greatest possible power is brought to bear on the souls of men. But in some cases even this infinite power is brought to bear in vain, and men refuse to repent and believe. It must in such cases be evident, that when God has brought all His enlightening and persuading power to bear upon men, and they willfully resist His gracious working, there is no other power in the universe by which they as personal beings can be saved. Where divine persuasion has failed, no greater is available.

Saving Effect Conditioned on Faith. The saving effect of the Means of Grace is conditioned on the production of faith in those on whom they are brought to bear. Without faith neither the Word nor the Sacraments will save. The Gospel, set forth in Word and Sacraments, is the power of God unto salvation to everyone that believeth. But without faith there is no salvation. The Word and Sacraments do not work *ex opere operato,* that is, through the mere act of preaching the Word or of administering the Sacraments. Conversion is an ethical transformation which consists essentially of the production of faith in man. If this faith is not produced, Word and Sacraments fail to save.[5]

The Church and the Means of Grace. According to God's ordinance the Means of Grace are administered through the human agency of the Church for the production of faith in the hearts of men. Unless the Word is clearly and purely preached and the sacraments are rightly administered by the Church, the gracious purposes of God cannot be accomplished. The implications of this fact will be considered later under the head of the Church and the Ministry.

[5] This necessity of subjective faith in the promise contained in the Word and the Sacraments is maintained by the Lutheran Church in opposition to the Romish doctrine of an *opus operatum;* and the necessity of the objective Means of Grace is maintained against all manner of "enthusiasts" who regard them as unnecessary. Thus the Augsburg Conf., Art. XIII, says: "Wherefore they condemn those who teach that the Sacraments justify *ex opere operato,* and do not teach that faith, which believes the remission of sins, is requisite in the use of the Sacraments." The Schm. Articles, p. 332, 3, declare: "We must firmly hold that God grants His Spirit or grace to no one except through or with the preceding outward Word. Thereby we are protected against enthusiasts."

CHAPTER XXVI

THE WORD OF GOD AS THE MEANS OF GRACE

THE term Word of God is used in a number of senses. *First,* it is used to denote the Holy Scriptures of the Old and New Testaments. In this sense the Bible is the Word of God. *Secondly,* it is used to denote all the truth divinely revealed, whether it comes to us in the words of Holy Scripture or paraphrased in the words of men. *Thirdly,* it is used to designate specifically the truth concerning God's grace in Christ, whether brought to us through the written or spoken Word or through the Sacraments. *Fourthly,* it is used to designate the truth concerning God's grace in Christ when it is brought to us through the spoken or written Word. In this last sense, namely, the Word as the Means of Grace, we purpose to treat the subject in this chapter.

The Means of Grace. When we speak of the Word of God as the Means of Grace we mean by it the truth of God concerning human sin and divine saving grace. This truth of God is contained in what is called the Law and the Gospel. The Law is employed by the Holy Spirit to bring the sinner to contrition; and the Gospel is employed by Him to bring the sinner to faith and sanctification. It is through the truth that men are sanctified; that is, it is through the truth that the Holy Spirit produces His gracious effects in their hearts and lives.[1]

---

[1] "We must distinguish between the Word of God as it is *materially* expressed and exhibited in written characters, points, letters and syllables adhering to paper and parchment . . . or even in sound and external words formed in the air . . . and *formally* considered as the divine conception and sense which is expressed in the written letters and syllables and in the words

300

Its Efficacy. The Word of God is not simply informing and directive, but is a power. It is the power of God unto salvation to everyone that believeth (Rom. 1:16). In whatever form it comes to us it possesses divine power and efficacy. It is God speaking to men, and therefore it possesses a supernatural power not possessed by any merely human word, however eloquent. It is "quick and powerful," searching out the innermost recesses of the soul (Heb. 4:12). It has a power to convert, regenerate and sanctify which is utterly foreign to the mere words of men. It does not simply point out externally the way of salvation, but presses the truth so forcibly upon men that they are convinced, persuaded and turned from sin to God. Its power is not simply that of the words of an eloquent and convincing speaker who sways men by his logic or eloquence, but it is a supernatural power based on the fact that it is the Word of God and not the word of man. It possesses this supernatural power of conviction and persuasion because it is always accompanied by the presence and working of the Holy Spirit. He is always in and with the Word, and does not first need to unite Himself with it in order to make it efficacious. And because of this inseparable connection of the Holy Spirit with the Word, it is always efficacious; that is, it always possesses the power to accomplish the result at which the Holy Spirit aims. That His aim is not always actually accomplished in the case of the sinner, is not due to any lack of efficacy in the Word or to any absence of the Holy Spirit's power and operation, but to the obstinate resistance of some men to divine grace.

The efficacy of the Word is not to be conceived of as magical or as exercised *ex opere operato.* It is a real word with the

---

of the preached Gospel. In the former sense it is called the Word of God only figuratively; in the latter, however, validly and strictly it is the Word of God, the wisdom of God, the mind of God, the counsel of God. We ascribe not to the former but to the latter divine power and efficacy." Quenstedt, I, 169.

purpose of a real word. It is meant to be understood, taken to heart, and acted upon. And unless this is done, it produces no effect. The mere sound of the words without any appreciation of their meaning on the part of the hearer, or the mere reading of the Word without a comprehension of its sense and application will not accomplish any result (Acts 8:30, 31). The Word is the divine truth addressed to the intellect of man, in order to stir his feelings and to move his will to action. And while it is true, that man does not by nature have the power to understand or feel or will as he should, that power is given through the Word itself; for the Holy Spirit uses it to give understanding, to move the feelings, and to enable and persuade the will. Because of its supernatural power the Word always produces its effect when it is not willfully resisted. But it is not irresistible. Its efficacy rests on the intimate union of the Holy Spirit with it. It has a supernatural power of persuasion, because the Holy Spirit persuades through it. It is a persuading Word which has all the power of God behind it, and which therefore not only points out the way on which men should travel, but enables and persuades them to travel on it. The Word has power to make the spiritually dead hear, to enable them to obey, and to make them spiritually alive.[2]

Fundamental. The Word is of fundamental importance, and the progress of God's kingdom is bound up with it. This was true under the Old Testament dispensation, when God spoke through the prophets; and it is true under the New Testament dispensation, when He speaks by His Son Jesus Christ. Faith cometh by hearing and hearing by the Word of God (Rom.

[2] From the eighteenth century the view became more and more prevalent that the power of the Word was only a logical and moral power, which aroused in us simply in a natural way certain thoughts and feelings. But while the Word or truth of God in its operations is adapted to the psychological constitution of man, its power is not confined to the natural persuasive power of truth as such, but is derived from the Holy Spirit, who by supernatural and divine power converts and regenerates.

10:17). The Word must be heeded, if there is to be escape from perdition (Heb. 2:3).

The proclamation of the Word has been entrusted to the Church. She has been commissioned to preach the Gospel in all the world and to all men. Preaching is the most important thing she has to do. It was the first activity in which she engaged (Acts 2:14). The efficiency of the Word was not limited to the preaching of the apostles, nor destroyed if the Word was proclaimed by the unworthy (Phil. 1:5-18). But it must be the preaching of the true and not of a false Gospel (Gal. 1:8; 1 John 4:1). It is a preaching of the cross of Christ (1 Cor. 1:18) and of Christ crucified (1 Cor. 1:23), and is a call to repentance and faith (Acts 2:38; 17:30; 20:21). Those who proclaim it are ambassadors for Christ (2 Cor. 5:20) and through them Christ Himself preaches peace to men (Eph. 2:17). True preaching is in the words which the Holy Ghost teaches (1 Cor. 2:37), and it begets men anew as children of God (Jas. 1:18; 1 Pet. 1:23).

Since the preacher is an instrument in the hands of the Holy Ghost to save men, he is in duty bound to preach the Word with all the clearness, force and persuasiveness of which he is capable, even while he realizes that the results are not to be ascribed to him but to the Holy Spirit's working. The preacher cannot convert or sanctify men; the Holy Ghost must do that. But the preacher must be careful that he does not by carelessness and inefficiency in his preaching hamper and hinder the work of the Holy Spirit, and thus be to blame for the loss of souls. He must study to be a workman that needeth not to be ashamed, rightly dividing the word of truth (2 Tim. 2:15).

So far as the plan of God is made known to us in His revelation, the salvation of men is completely dependent on the preaching of the Gospel. The measure, therefore, in which the Church lives up to the command of Christ to preach the Gospel to every creature is the measure of men's opportunity for salvation. For how shall they believe in Him of whom they have not heard? and how shall they hear without a preacher? and how shall they preach except they be sent? (Rom. 10:14, 15).

Law and Gospel. The Word of God as a means of Grace consists, when regarded as to its essential nature, of two factors, namely, Law and Gospel. Both of them reveal the will of God to men, and both of them are essential for the accomplishment of the Holy Spirit's work. The Law makes known the will of God as a demand upon men with regard to the character and conduct which should mark them. The Gospel, on the other hand, makes known the will of God as a desire and purpose to save them from their sins. The Law comes with commands and prohibitions; the Gospel comes with the promise of gratuitous forgiveness and salvation for Christ's sake.

Different but Not Contradictory. Law and Gospel stand in the greatest possible contrast with each other; but they are not contradictory, and both have an essential function in the work of conversion and sanctification. It is the work of the Law to prepare the way for the Gospel. Unless through the Law man is brought to the knowledge, confession and hatred of his sins and a desire to be rescued from them, the Gospel will make no appeal to him. The Law without the Gospel would drive men to an attempted work-righteousness or to despair. And the Gospel without the Law would fail to find contrite hearts willing and glad to receive it, and could only leave them in impenitence and presumption.

Importance of Clear Distinction. To distinguish clearly between law and Gospel is a matter of the utmost importance.[a]

---

[a] Law and Gospel are terms which are employed in wider and narrower senses. Thus Law is used to describe the revelation of God given in the Pentateuch (Luke 24:44) and in the Old Testament (Ps. 1:2). But in the strict sense in which the word is used above it refers to the demands of God with regard to man's character and conduct. So Gospel is used to describe all the teaching and preaching of Christ and His apostles, and of the minister of the Gospel. But in the strict sense in which the word is used above, it refers to the promise of grace for Christ's sake.

The Law commands or forbids us to be or to do something; the Gospel tells us to receive something freely and graciously offered by God. The Law commands, reproves and threatens; the Gospel offers salvation, encourages and consoles. The Law exhibits human sinfulness; the Gospel exhibits divine grace. The Law shows the disease from which mankind suffers; the Gospel shows and offers the remedy. Unless this fundamental distinction between Law and Gospel is appreciated, there will result on the part of the preacher not only confusion of mind but ineffectiveness in the administration of the Word as the Means of Grace. For the word of truth must be rightly divided: Law and Gospel must be proclaimed in proper measure and at the proper times. The impenitent or defiant sinner needs the Law; but when through the Law he has been brought to a state of contrition, he needs the Gospel.[4]

In the Old and New Testaments. Both Law and Gospel are found in the Old Testament and in the New. But the Law preponderates in the former and the Gospel in the latter. The promises of coming redemption and the types and shadows of things to come which are found in the Old Testament are not Law but Gospel. So on the other hand the commands and directions for right living which are found in the New Testament are not Gospel but Law. But it still remains true that the Old Testament is essentially the revelation of the Law and the New Testament essentially the revelation of the Gospel. For "the law was given by Moses, but grace and truth came by Jesus Christ" (John 1:17).

Moral, Ceremonial and Forensic Law. When examined as to the nature of the commands contained in the Old Testament law given to the Israelites, the law is seen to be of three kinds.

---

[4] Romanism makes of the Gospel a new law. Modernism, by eliminating from the Gospel its fundamental features, such as the deity of Christ, the vicarious atonement, the resurrection and the like, also turns the Gospel into a new law, and teaches men to be saved, not by divine grace in Christ, but by practicing the precepts of Christ and living after His example.

We distinguish these as the Moral Law, the Ceremonial Law, and the Civil or Forensic Law. This distinction is one which the Israelite did not make, and which is not mentioned in the Old Testament. For the Israelite the law of God was of one piece. Whether the commands involved fundamental moral principles, or concerned merely some outward regulations of worship or of civil conduct, they were all equally binding on him as a member of God's chosen people. There was no reason, therefore, why he should distinguish the three kinds of law. But while there was no reason for him to do so, there is much reason for the Christian to make the distinction. For the Moral Law, containing as it does, abiding fundamental moral principles, is binding on us, while the ceremonial and forensic laws are not. The ceremonial law has been abrogated and abolished by the coming of Christ and the introduction of the New Testament dispensation; and the forensic law, which was the civil and political law for the Israelitish or Jewish state, is abolished because there is no longer such a state in existence, and even the Jews cannot be governed by it. Christians as citizens are bound by the laws of the government under which they live, and not by those which prevailed in the theocracy of Moses' time or in the Israelitish or Jewish kingdoms. The ceremonial and forensic laws were thus temporary in character, and have no binding power on the Christian.[5] The moral law, on the other hand, is universal and permanent. It expresses the nature and will of God, and can never be changed or abolished. Right character and conduct will always in this world and the next be such as conforms to the moral law.

The Revelation of the Moral Law. The moral law was writ-

---

[5] The abrogation of the ceremonial law is clearly indicated in the New Testament Scriptures. See such passages as Col. 2:16-20; Gal. 2:4, 5, 14; 4:9 seq.; 5:1, 2, 7; Acts 15:1, 10; Heb. 7:12; 9:9; Jas. 2:12. Old Testament precepts which are expressly sanctioned and enjoined in the New Testament belong to the moral law.

ten in man's heart at creation. He knew without any external law what was morally right and wrong. Something of this original law still remains in the mind or heart of the natural man. The heathen give evidence, as Paul tells us, that the law is written in their hearts by the fact that to some extent they observe its requirements, and are accused by their own consciences for wrong-doing (Rom. 2:14, 15). But much that was originally written in the heart has become erased as a consequence of sin, and the natural knowledge of the moral law has become much obscured. Thus the obligation of the first commandment to worship is still appreciated by the heathen, but the obligation to worship none but the true God is not. The portions of the law which still remain in the human heart are not sufficient for the purpose of convicting men of the total sinfulness and corruption of the human heart, and of its need of saving grace. The deep meaning of the law as a demand to love God with all our heart and mind and soul and strength is unknown to the heathen.

The moral law was revealed by God anew and in an external manner through Moses in the giving of the Ten Commandments or Decalogue. These commandments contain specific applications of the fundamental moral principle of love to God and man (Deut. 6:4; Matt. 22:37-40). They naturally divide into two parts or tables, the first of which embraces our duty to God, and the second our duty to our fellow men. The duty to love ourselves, though implied in the obligation to love our neighbor as ourselves, is not specifically mentioned, probably because man can be depended on to love himself without a command, and needs rather to be commanded not to love himself too much.

While the Ten Commandments contain the moral law, there is in the Third Commandment a ceremonial as well as a moral element. The ceremonial element is found in the setting apart of the seventh day of the week as the sabbath or day of rest. The moral element is found in the duty to observe a day for common worship, and for physical rest as grounded in God's order of creation. The sabbath therefore is abolished (Col. 2:15; Rom. 14:5; Gal. 4:10), but the obligation to observe Sunday, the day set apart by the Christian Church for the preaching and hearing of the Word of God, remains.[6]

Meaning of the Moral Law. The substance of the moral law is given by Christ in the double commandment of love (Matt. 22:37-40). The Decalogue points out some of the ways in which that love is to be exhibited. Some of the commandments of the Decalogue are stated in the form of a positive injunction, and others in the form of a prohibition. But in every

---

[6] By some of our theologians, as for example by Gerhard (ed. by Frank, Vol. III, pp. 59 seq.) it is held that the commandment requires the observance of one day out of seven.

The confessional position as given in the Augsburg Confession and the Large Catechism is as follows: The Augsburg Conf. (Art. XXVIII) says: "They that think that the observance of the Lord's Day was appointed by the authority of the Church, instead of the Sabbath, as necessary, are greatly deceived. The Scripture, which teacheth that all the Mosaical ceremonies can be omitted after the Gospel is revealed, has abrogated the Sabbath. And yet, because it was requisite to appoint a certain day, that the people might know when they ought to come together, it appears that the (Christian) Church did for that purpose appoint the Lord's Day; which for this cause also seemed to have been pleasing, that men might have an example of Christian liberty, and might know that the observance neither of the Sabbath nor of another day was of necessity."

"The Large Catechism (*Book of Conc.,* 402, 82 seq.) says: "This commandment, therefore, according to its gross sense, does not pertain to us Christians; for it is altogether an external matter, like the other ordinances of the Old Testament, which were bound to particular customs, times, persons and places, and all of which have now been made free through Christ.

"We keep the festal days . . . first of all for bodily causes and necessities, which nature teaches and requires. . . . Secondly and most especially, that on such day of rest (since otherwise it cannot be accomplished) time and opportunity be taken to attend divine service, so that we meet to hear and treat of God's Word, and afterwards to praise God in singing and prayer.

"But this, I say, is not so limited to any time, as with the Jews, that it must be just on this or that day; for in itself no one day is better than another, and this should indeed occur daily; but since the mass of the people cannot give such attendance, there must be at least one day in the week set part. But since from of old Sunday (the Lord's Day) has been appointed for this purpose, we should also continue the same, that everything be done in harmonious order, and no one by unnecessary innovation create disorder."

commandment there is a positive and a negative element. There is something to be done as well as something not to be done out of love to God and our neighbor. All the commandments enjoin or prohibit a disposition or state of mind, as well as words and actions. This is emphasized in the Decalogue itself, in the ninth and tenth commandments, which deal with sin in the heart. The profound meaning of the moral law is brought out by the Savior in His Sermon on the Mount, in which He lays emphasis upon the right state of heart as well as upon right outward actions. Only that is truly moral which is done out of love to God above all, and love to our neighbor as ourselves. What appear as good and even noble actions are not morally good in God's sight unless they spring from love (1 Cor. 13).

Nature of the Law's Demands. Since the moral law is the expression of the will and nature of a holy and just God, its demands are strict and inexorable (Gal. 3:10). They cannot be lowered to meet the wish or weakness of men. They are comprehensive and include every thought and word and deed. And since the moral law is a unit and the Ten Commandments are simply ten ways in which the fundamental moral principle of love is to be applied, the breaking of one commandment involves the breaking of the whole law (James 2:10). The man who leaps over a single board of a fence which marks off forbidden territory is on the wrong side of the whole fence. This is why he who offends in one point is guilty of all. He who would keep the law of God must love God with all his heart and mind and soul, and his neighbor as himself, always and everywhere, and without a single failure.

Uses of the Law. The Law has three uses, the Political, the Elenchtico-pedagogical, and the Didactic. By the Political use is meant the use of the law as a curb to hold in check wicked men, and to protect society against their aggressions. By the

Elenchtico-pedagogical use is meant its use to convict men of sin and thus indirectly to lead them to Christ (Gal. 3:24).[7] This use of the Law refers primarily to the unconverted. But there is an elenchtical-pedagogical use of the Law even for the regenerate, inasmuch as the Christian's life should be a daily repentance, and the law enables him to see his daily shortcomings and his need of Christ more and more clearly. The Didactic use of the law is its use as a guide for the Christian mind and conduct. Because the believer has been regenerated, his will has been brought into harmony with God's and he desires to walk in God's ways. But he needs the law to show him what those ways are. The desire to do right is not engendered in the Christian by the law, but by grace. The law, however, is the guidepost pointing out the right way. The believer says, I desire to do God's will and to walk in the right way; the law says, This is the right way which you seek.

The Moral Law not Abrogated. While the Christian has nothing to do with the law so far as obtaining salvation is concerned, and through Christ is free from it in the sense that he need not fulfill it in order to be saved, the moral law is not abrogated for him. It still stands as the expression of the divine will of righteousness, and as the norm with which the Christian compares his mind and conduct. He grows in sanctification just in the proportion in which he walks in accordance with that law. He is, however, no longer under the law but under grace. So far as his salvation is concerned the law has nothing to say to him any longer. All the demands which it makes of us have been fully and completely met by the active and passive obedience of Christ; and by faith His obedience becomes ours. There is, therefore, no demand which the law makes that we have not already fully met in Christ. But the believer, having been

---

[7] By some dogmaticians the elenchtical and pedagogical uses of the Law are made separate classifications. But they can be most conveniently considered together.

regenerated, has a desire to do God's will of his own accord. Out of gratitude and love for the salvation freely received, his fundamental aim in life is to do God's will. The law therefore has become, as it were, a part of himself, and he obeys the law of God, not because of any outward demand, but because the love of Christ constrains him.[8]

The Gospel is the antithesis of the Law. While the law demands and threatens, the Gospel offers and consoles. It is through the Gospel that salvation comes, and not through the law. By the law is the knowledge of sin (Rom. 3:20); by the Gospel is the knowledge of grace. It is the Gospel and not the law that is the power of God unto salvation (Rom. 1:16). Though the way is prepared for the Gospel through the law, it is through the Gospel that men are saved. For salvation is by faith, and it is through the Gospel with its gracious offer of forgiveness for Christ's sake that the Holy Spirit works faith in the heart. Clearness on this relation between the law and the Gospel is essential, if there is to be clearness and not confusion with regard to justification. We are justified by grace alone through faith, and not at all through the works of the law.

The Gospel is the promise of the gratuitous forgiveness of sins for Christ's sake to everyone that believes in Him. Unless

---

[8] The two extremes conflicting with the view set forth above are nomism and antinomianism. Nomism is a legalism which seeks to maintain the Old Testament external relation to the law, in opposition to the liberty wherewith Christ has set us free (Gal. 5:1). It divides the law into a multitude of detailed prescriptions and regulations, and imagines that obedience to these makes a good man. The typical Old Testament nomists were the Pharisees. The Roman Catholic Church is nomistic, and makes of the Gospel a new law. Pietism also is nomistic when it makes the truly Christian life consist of obedience to a multitude of regulations and prohibitions instead of the free development of a life in Christ. Antinomianism, on the other hand, denies the necessity and universal obligation of the law. Apparently Paul had to deal with antinomians in his day (Rom. 6:1). The theory was held by the Gnostics. In the days of the Reformation, John Agricola maintained that the law is abolished for the Christian, and belongs only in the courthouse and not in the pulpit. Repentance, he said, is not to be produced by the law, but by the Gospel, especially through the sufferings and death of Christ. He was answered by Luther, and recalled his statements in 1540.

this is the essence of the preaching, it is not a preaching of the Gospel, but of something else.[8] When the apostles were commanded to preach the Gospel in all the world, they understood this to mean, as their preaching plainly shows, that they were to proclaim forgiveness and salvation through faith alone in Christ as the Redeemer and Savior.

[8] When the Modernist speaks of the Gospel of Christ, he understands by the term something quite different from the real Gospel. What he means by the Gospel is a proclamation of justification by a right life and good works, while the real Gospel is a proclamation of justification by faith alone.

CHAPTER XXVII

THE WRITTEN WORD OR THE HOLY SCRIPTURES

THE truth which God has supernaturally revealed to men has been recorded by inspired men in the Holy Scriptures. These Holy Scriptures consist of the Canonical Books of the Old and New Testaments. They possess primarily the character of a record of the divine revelation. The revelation, which was given historically in connection with God's dealings with the human race, existed before the written record of it was made. Thus, for example, God made Himself known to Abraham as the God of salvation long before the record of His dealings with Abraham was written by Moses. So also the Gospel of the crucified and risen Savior was known and widely preached before the New Testament books were written. But if the revelation which God made was to be preserved in its purity, a divinely inspired record of it was indispensable. This inspired record is given to us in the sixty-six books of the Bible.

Authority of Scripture. The Holy Scriptures, consisting of the canonical books of the Old and New Testaments, are the sole and exclusive authority in all matters of Christian doctrine and life. They are the supreme and absolute norm of Christian teaching. The Church is to set forth no other doctrines than those which are contained in the Bible, and must reject all doctrines which conflict with it.[1] The Apocryphal books, though useful for

[1] We have, however, another rule, namely that the Word of God should frame articles of faith; otherwise no one, not even an angel." Schm. Art. 315, 15.
"We believe, teach and confess that the only rule and standard according to which all dogmas and teachers alike should be esteemed and judged are noth-

313

reading, are not a part of the Holy Scriptures, and have no canonical authority.[2] Traditions,[3] creeds, confessions and other writings or opinions of men are by no means to be regarded as possessing equal authority with the Bible. If traditions and ecclesiastical customs and practices are not in conflict with the teachings of Scripture, they may be retained; but their retention is not necessary.[4]

Inspiration. The Lutheran Confessions are content to assert the divine inspiration and the supreme authority of the Holy Scriptures, without setting forth any theory of inspiration, and without attempting to explain its nature. But the seventeenth-century dogmaticians of the Church, on the other hand, impelled

---

ing else than the prophetic and apostolic Scriptures of the Old and New Testaments. . . . Other writings of ancient or modern teachers, whatever reputation they may have, should not be regarded as of equal authority with the Holy Scriptures, but should altogether be subordinated to them, and should not be received other or further than as witnesses, in what manner and at what places since the times of the apostles the doctrine of the prophets and apostles was preserved." Form. Conc. 491:1, 2.

[2] The Roman Catholic Church makes the Vulgate the authoritative text of the Bible, includes the Apocrypha as canonical, and makes tradition equally authoritative with the Holy Scriptures. "If any one receive not, as sacred and canonical, the said books entire [including the Apocrypha] with all their hearts, as they have been used to be read in the Catholic Church, and as they are contained in the old Latin Vulgate edition; and knowingly and deliberately contemn the traditions aforesaid let him be anathema." Canons and Decrees of the Council of Trent, Session IV.

[3] The necessity of tradition is maintained by the Roman Catholic Church on the basis of the claim that the Bible is not sufficiently complete and clear, and that it has obtained authority only through the tradition of the Church, which selected the books which are of divine origin. The refutation of this claim is found in the fact that the Canon of Scripture was not formed on the basis of a tradition handed down from the apostles, but on the basis of the inner content and authority of the various writings. In order to defend certain tenets which the Reformers showed to be based on later than apostolic tradition, such as auricular confession, the veneration of the saints, and the seven sacraments, the conception of traditions was enlarged to include "divine traditions" received from Christ, "apostolic traditions" received from the apostles, and "ecclesiastical traditions" resulting from ecclesiastical customs and practices. Thus it became unnecessary to vindicate traditions; and the authority of the Church was sufficient for them. In this way the Church was made of equal authority with Christ and His apostles.

[4] The Reformed Church takes a more negative attitude toward traditions, and is inclined to abolish everything that is not commanded in Scripture.

by a laudable desire to maintain the supreme authority of the Bible, formulated a very definite theory of inspiration. They regarded revelation and inspiration as identical, and conceived of revelation, not as an historical manifestation of God to men, but as the communication to men of the doctrines necessary for salvation.[5] The sacred writers were regarded as mere amanuenses who wrote down what God dictated. Consequently in their view no human element entered into the writing of the sacred books.[6] God alone is the author of the Holy Scriptures, and immediately communicated to the prophets and apostles the conceptions of all that is contained in the Sacred Scriptures, dictating all the words without exception to their pens.[7] The differences in style characterizing the various writers were explained by the statement that the Holy Spirit accommodated Himself to each individual writer, and dictated in the style peculiar to him. Hence it followed that the Holy Scriptures in the original text are to be regarded as completely free from all errors of any kind, and that "the style of the New Testament is free from every stain of barbarisms or solecisms." [8] On the basis of their theory of inspiration the dogmaticians ascribed to the Holy Scriptures the attributes of Authority, Perspicuity, Perfection or Sufficiency, and Efficacy.

The theory of inspiration described above was the outgrowth of a sincere conviction that the Bible is truly the Word of God, and of the need which the dogmaticians felt for a theory which would give them an infallible court of appeal with regard to

[5] Hence in the use of proof texts, the historical and progressive character of revelation was overlooked.

[6] The Biblical writers were amanuenses "to whom the very words were dictated to the pen, and who contributed nothing beyond the external writing or the making of the letters." Quen. I, 73.

[7] Holl., 83, 85.

[8] Quen., I, 82. Quenstedt regards the supposition that the Scriptures contain barbarisms as "no small blasphemy." I, 84. Some Reformed theologians, the Formula Consensus Helveticus of 1675 and even Gerhard declared that the Hebrew vowel points were inspired.

all the teachings of the Church. But it is evident that the theory which they propounded rests on an *a priori* basis, and not on a study either of the nature and purpose of the separate Scriptural documents or of the nature and purpose of Scripture as a whole. The relation of dictator and amanuenses does not properly represent the relation between the Holy Spirit and the writers of the Biblical books. And while the dogmaticians were right in their claim that the Holy Scriptures are divinely inspired, the facts in the case do not fit into their theory of inspiration. There is a human as well as a divine factor to be taken into account in considering the writing of the Holy Scriptures.

Scriptural Teaching Concerning Inspiration. In seeking to arrive at a theory of inspiration it is necessary not only to take into account the nature of the Bible as a collection of writings which give a record of revelation, but to examine what it has to say concerning the matter of its own inspiration.

It is clear that the New Testament vouches for the divine authority of the Old Testament. It quotes from the Old Testament and recognizes its canonical contents as extending from Genesis to Second Chronicles, which according to the Hebrew arrangement forms the closing book (Luke 11:50, 51).

The inspiration of the New Testament is grounded on the promise of Christ to send the Holy Spirit upon the apostles to guide them into all truth (John 14:26; 15:26 seq.) and on the fulfillment of that promise on the day of Pentecost (Acts 2). As soon as the apostles had received the gift of the Holy Spirit they began to understand clearly the significance of Christ's death and resurrection, and to preach the Gospel of salvation through Christ the Redeemer. In their preaching and teaching they were constantly under the guidance of the Holy Spirit, and were conscious of this fact (1 Cor. 2:13). Whether they taught the Gospel orally or in writing, this divine guidance remained theirs; and what they said was equally authoritative whether taught by word or by epistle (2 Thess. 2:15). Paul enjoins that his Epistle to the Thessalonians shall be read to all the brethren, thus implying that all are to respect and heed it as much as if it were an oral message of the apostle (1 Thess. 5:27). He distinguishes between what he says and what the Lord says, but he asserts that even in expressing his personal opinion he has the Spirit of the Lord (1 Cor. 7:10, 12, 40). He emphasizes the fact that what he writes are the commandments of the Lord (1 Cor. 14:37), and that what he preached is in truth the Word of God (1 Thess. 2:13). So certainly is that which he has preached the very truth of God, that if even an angel from heaven should preach any other Gospel, he should be accursed (Gal. 1:8).

While all the writers of the New Testament books were inspired, it is evident that their writings bear the marks of the personal characteristics of the authors, and that there is a human as well as a divine factor to be found in them. They were written by men, even though by inspired men. Inspiration did not make all the holy writers alike in their mental constitution, their types of thought, and their peculiar ways of expressing themselves. Each wrote in the style that was natural to him, and the personal characteristics are sometimes very marked, as for example in John and Paul. We can see in the writings of the latter, especially in his polemical epistles, that he seems to strain every power of his soul to the utmost in order to give clear and emphatic utterance to the truth. The Holy Spirit took the human faculties of the authors of the Biblical books into His service, exalted their powers, and through them gave to men the infallible truth of God. Inspiration did not make of the holy writers mere machines in the hands of God. But leaving them their personality, it furnished them with a true knowledge of what they should write, and so controlled and directed them in the writing itself, that they wrote only what was true, and were effectively guarded against any possibility of error in the communication of the divine will to men.

This inspiration permitted the apostle Paul to include in his epistles matters of a purely personal nature, such as the request to Timothy to bring his cloak from Troas (2 Tim. 4:13) and his personal advice to Timothy concerning his health (1 Tim. 5:23). His inspiration had to do with matters of religion and the communication of the divine revelation; and he was none the less an inspired man even though he was forgetful enough to leave his cloak at Troas and concerned enough about Timothy's health to give him dietetic advice, which may or may not be regarded as good advice by modern medical authorities. The inspired nature of what he wrote is not affected by such purely personal statements, nor by his admission that he is not quite certain as to how many persons he personally baptized at Corinth (1 Cor. 1:16). These things belong to the human side of the Scriptures. Paul was eminently human; but he was nevertheless an inspired man. His inspiration, however, was an inspiration in matters of religion; and its purpose was to give us an infallible knowledge of the revealed will of God.

Apparent discrepancies in the Scriptures, such as the substitution of the name of Jeremiah for that of Zechariah (Matt. 27:9), of "Abraham" instead of "Jacob" (Acts 7:16) and of twenty-three thousand instead of twenty-four thousand (1 Cor. 10:8), do not affect the substance or the purpose of the inspired record of revelation. The same is to be said of the matter of healing one or two blind men at Jericho (Mat. 20:30-34; Mark 10:46-52). The quite evident difference in the mode of presenting the Gospel history on the part of the Synoptics and of John is not a discrepancy, but a difference in the starting point. The Synoptics begin with Jesus the man and lead up to His divinity. John, on the other hand, begins with the deity of Christ, and pictures the Son of God as incarnate and dwelling among men.

Definition of Inspiration. The inspiration of the Holy Scriptures may be defined as that activity of the Holy Spirit by which He put into the minds and hearts of chosen men what to write, and directed them in the writing itself, so that they produced a correct and inerrant record of God's revelation of Himself to men. The individuality of the writers was not destroyed, and their personal characteristics are often quite marked. But at the same time they wrote as they were moved by the Holy Ghost (1 Pet. 1:20), and their writings are the Word of God. Thus the Bible is the inspired and inerrant record of all that God has supernaturally revealed to men concerning Himself and the way of salvation (2 Tim. 3:16, 17).

Inspiration applies only to the original text and not to translations, and is in the right sense of the term verbal. For while the dictation theory, according to which the writers of the Biblical Books merely wrote down what God dictated and became mere amanuenses in God's hands, is untenable, yet since the words exactly express the ideas which the Holy Spirit meant to have expressed, the words themselves must be regarded as inspired words, and the exact shades of meaning in the original words are often a matter of the utmost importance in deciding questions of doctrine and life. They are inspired words because they are the words of inspired men.[9]

The Bible and Science. It must be borne in mind that the Bible is a religious book, and not a textbook on science. The holy writers were inspired with a supernatural knowledge of God and of His will; and on these subjects their words are final and infallible. On scientific matters they neither knew nor

[9] In 1 Cor. 2:13 Paul expressly claims for himself a verbal inspiration, "Which things also we speak, not in the words which man's wisdom teacheth, but which the Holy Ghost teacheth."

professed to know more than other men of their day.[10] To criticize the Bible from the standpoint of modern science, as though it pretended to be an infallible treatise on scientific subjects, is to misconceive its spirit and purpose. The conflict supposed by some persons to exist between the Bible and science does not exist, because they operate in different spheres. The objections made by many to the miracles recorded in the Bible rest on arbitrary presuppositions.

Proofs of Inspiration. External proofs that the Scriptures are of divine origin are not required for the believer. His faith precedes all questions of inspiration. He has been brought to faith by the divine power and operation in and through the Word. Because he does God's will, he knows that the doctrine is of God (John 7:17). The proof of the divine character of the Scriptures is needed, not for him, but for those who are still outside the Church and for those within it whose faith is not established. The only absolute and inescapable proof of the divine character of the Holy Scriptures is found in the witness of the Holy Spirit to the heart of the believer and in the experience of the Christian. This proof, of course, is not available for those who are still unbelieving.

All other proofs of the divine character and authority of the Holy Scriptures are in the very nature of the case what are called probable proofs. These are not coercive and may be rejected by the unbeliever. They are external proofs or evidences of the divinity of the Scriptures which are calculated to incline him to yield to the gracious influence of the Holy Spirit, so that he may be brought to faith, and thus gain from experience that certitude which the believer alone can have. Such external proofs may be found in the following facts. The Bible makes known facts and truths which remained hidden from

---

[10] The Bible does not teach the Ptolemaic system of astronomy, even though Joshua evidently held some such view. Josh. 10:12.

those who have not possessed the Holy Scriptures, and which no man could have discovered or known apart from a supernatural revelation. It contains predictions of events which no man by his own natural powers could have foreseen, and which have already in part been fulfilled to the very letter. It contains moral teachings which are incalculably more exalted than any found in the writings of the greatest philosophers. And it has given and still gives evidence of a spiritual power of transforming the hearts and lives of men, such as belongs to no other book in the world. But in the last analysis even the Christian's certainty does not rest upon these external proofs, but upon the evidence of Christian experience.

For Our Learning. The Scriptures were "written for our learning, that we through patience and comfort of the Scriptures might have hope" (Rom. 15:4). They are meant to be "a lamp unto our feet and a light unto our path" (Ps. 119:105). Because of the progressive character of revelation and of the nature of Scripture as a record of that revelation, some books of the Bible are of greater value to us than others. This does not mean that they are not all inspired, but that some books contain larger and more potent measures of distinctly religious truth.[11] In this sense the Gospels and such an epistle as Romans with its fundamental treatment of sin and grace, are vastly more valuable to us than such a book, for example, as Esther or Ecclesiastes. This does not imply that the latter books have no value. It is with the books of the Bible as with the members of the body. Each is important in its place as a part of the

[11] Luther estimated the value of the books according to the measure in which they set forth Christ: *"ob sie Christum treiben."* He therefore assigned a higher value to the Gospel according to John than to the other three, because "it is the one tender, right chief Gospel." His opinion of James was not high. Compared with St. Paul's epistles, he declared that "it is quite a strawy epistle, inasmuch as it is not written in an evangelical style." *Preface to the New Testament, 1522.* He had some doubts about Hebrews and Revelation. But none of his strictures found their way into the Lutheran Confessions, and they were not echoed by the dogmaticians.

whole organism, though some are more directly essential than others.

The Scriptures are meant to give us a true and saving knowledge of God and to equip the Church with all that she needs for her mission on earth. Their one great and all-embracing purpose is to testify of Christ (John 5:39). He is their very center and theme. They set forth Christ, and all that in any wise concerns His nature, life and work, infallibly and inerrantly. They are the product of divine inspiration; not of such an inspiration as belongs to geniuses in general or to religious geniuses in particular, but a genuine inspiration by the Holy Ghost by virtue of which the record which the holy writers have given us is an inerrant record of the revelation of God to man. Hence, the Bible is the sole and absolutely authoritative rule of faith and life. Before it all human authority must bow and give way. Whoever despises its teaching despises the way of life. Whoever teaches contrary to it is accursed (Gal. 1:8, 9). Whoever adds to or subtracts from it shall be stricken from the Book of Life (Rev. 22:18, 19). As the Formula of Concord declares, It "is the only rule and standard according to which all dogmas and teachers should be esteemed and judged."

CHAPTER XXVIII

THE SACRAMENTS

THE Sacraments, like the Word, are Means of Grace, and serve the same purpose of making known and conveying divine grace to men. God has but one gracious will with respect to men, namely, to persuade them to believe the precious promises which He has given in Christ, and to save them. But the Sacraments differ from the Word in their method. Whereas in the Word we have the promise alone, in the Sacrament we have the promise accompanied by a significant action. The Sacrament thus becomes the visible Word. The Word enters the ear in order to move the heart, while the Sacrament strikes the eye in order to move the heart. Through both Word and Sacrament the Holy Spirit works to produce and sustain faith.[1]

The specific purpose of the Sacrament is to confirm and seal the promise given in the Word. In the Word there is the oral promise of God; in the Sacrament the promise is repeated and attested by a sacramental action, in order to add still greater assurance of its truth. There is in it also an individualizing of the promise of grace, inasmuch as the individual receives the Sacrament, and thus the promise contained in it must be meant for him. The promise in the Word is universal, and hence includes the individual also. But there is a peculiar force and comfort in the direct individual application of the Sacrament. There is no escape from the fact that whatever grace is offered in the Sacrament is offered to the individual to whom the Sacrament is administered. It is a special mercy of God out of con-

[1] Apology, 214, 5.

323

sideration for our human weakness, that He has instituted the Sacraments in addition to the Word.

The Name. The term Sacrament is not Biblical but ecclesiastical and theological. At first the word [2] was used in the Ancient Church to designate any sacred rite, ceremony or custom. Tertullian first applied it to Baptism. The precise meaning to be attached to the term has been a matter of much difference of opinion. The Protestant definition of what constitutes a sacrament differs so much from that of the Roman Catholic Church, that the former includes only two while the latter includes seven sacraments. It is true, the Apology speaks of Absolution as a sacrament. But the term soon came to be applied in the Lutheran Church only to Baptism and the Lord's Supper, as two rites of the Church which had certain characteristics not possessed by any others.

The Marks of a Sacrament. As the Lutheran Church defines a Sacrament, three marks or characteristics are necessary to entitle a rite or ceremony to be called by that name. It must have been instituted by divine command; it must make use of an earthly element in its administration; and it must offer and convey a heavenly gift. Viewed in the light of these requirements, only Baptism and the Lord's Supper are entitled to be classed as Sacraments.[3] The other rites or ceremonies of the Church are not sacraments or Means of Grace.

Definition. A Sacrament may be defined, therefore, as a sacred action appointed and commanded by Christ, in which,

---

[2] The word sacrament comes from the Latin *sacramentum,* which meant originally any sacred thing; also specifically the pledge deposited by parties at law with one another. The oath of allegiance was a *sacramentum. Sacramentum* was used in the Vulgate to translate the Greek work *mysterion.*

[3] The Roman Catholic Church's definition of a sacrament is wider, and does not insist on the three marks mentioned. Hence she has seven rites which she calls sacraments, namely, Baptism, the Lord's Supper or Mass, Absolution or Penance, Ordination, Confirmation, Marriage, and Extreme Unction. The Council of Trent anathematizes those who say that seven is not the exact number (Sess. VII, Can. 1). But it will be seen that all of these seven except the first two lack one or more of the three marks mentioned above.

through the use of a visible earthly element or elements in connection with the divine Word, an invisible spiritual or heavenly gift is offered to men, and is actually communicated to the believer.

The sacraments are signs, and are so called in the Confessions. But by this is not meant that they are simply signs or symbols in the Reformed sense of the term. They are visible signs in the same sense in which the Word is an audible sign. They are not mere symbolical acts which picture or typify the divine grace in a visible manner, but they are means or vehicles through which grace is actually offered and conveyed. They become such vehicles of grace because of the Word and promise which are connected with the visible action. Without the Word of God the earthly elements employed would remain nothing but earthly elements, which might symbolize divine grace but could bestow none. But when the Word is added to the outward action, the Sacrament exists as a divine means of producing and sustaining faith, and of bestowing forgiveness and salvation on the believer.[4] It is the divine Word and promise that give validity and value to the sacrament.

Efficacy. A Sacrament is an objective act of God conveying a definite promise of grace. Like the Word, its efficacy is dependent on God alone, and not on human factors. It possesses divine power because it is employed by the Holy Spirit as a Means of Grace. Its efficacy is not dependent, therefore, on the moral character of the administrant, or on his intention,[5] or on the validity of his call as a minister, or even on the faith of the recipient. For just as the Word has divine efficacy and power, even though it is rejected in unbelief, so also the Sacra-

[4] This relation of the Word to the action and elements is thus described by Augustine: *"Accedit verbum ad elementum et fit sacramentum."* The Word comes to the element and it becomes a sacrament. Cf. *Schm. Art.* 330, 1. *Large Catech.* 468, 18.
[5] The Roman Catholic Church makes the validity of the sacrament depend on the right intention of the administrant.

ment has divine efficacy and power even though the recipient does not receive it in faith. The unbelief of men cannot make the promise of God of none effect. A medicine may be an efficacious remedy, even though it be not applied.

Effect of the Sacraments. A distinction must be made between the innate power and efficacy of the sacraments, and the actual effect produced upon the recipients. The good effect is dependent on faith. The sacraments do not produce the effect which God desires and intends through the mere outward performance of the act.[6] Just as the promise contained in the Word must be received in faith if its purpose is to be accomplished, so the promise contained in the Sacraments must be received in faith, if the beneficent results intended are to be obtained. In the sacraments, as in the Word, forgiveness and salvation are conditioned on faith.

Administration of the Sacraments. The Sacrament exists only during its actual administration. It is an action accompanied by the Word, and thus exists only during the action with its accompanying Word. The actual Sacrament of Baptism exists when the water is applied in the name of the Father and of the Son and of the Holy Ghost, and the actual Sacrament of the Lord's Supper exists when the elements are distributed to the communicants with the accompanying words of Christ. Before and after the administration the water is simply water, and the bread and wine are simply bread and wine. In the subsequent handling of the elements, however, proper decorum should be observed.

The validity of the Sacrament depends, of course, upon its proper administration. Care must be exercised that it be administered in exact compliance with Christ's appointment and command. Nothing else may be substituted in the place of the ele-

---

[6] They do not work *ex opere operato,* as Rome maintains. The Council of Trent (Session VII, Can. 8) anathematizes those who deny that grace is conferred through the act performed or who declare that faith is necessary.

ments, and no other words may be substituted for the words of institution. The use of the elements appointed and of the words which Christ has connected with them constitutes the Sacrament.

Main and Subordinate Purposes. The chief purpose of the sacraments is to offer and convey divine grace. They are means through which the Holy Spirit seeks to accomplish His gracious work in our hearts. There are, however, other and subordinate purposes which are subserved by them. But these subordinate purposes must never be permitted to replace or obscure the chief purpose. While fundamentally they are the means through which the Holy Spirit comes to us with divine grace and power, they may properly be regarded also as marks of Church membership, as exhibiting the unity in the faith, as stimulation to a new life of faith and love, and in the case of the Lord's Supper as a memorial of Christ's Passion. Together with the Word, the Sacraments are also the marks by which the presence of the Church may be known.

Necessity. Since the Sacraments are Means of Grace, that is, means through which the Holy Spirit produces and sustains faith, they are necessary to salvation. But this necessity is to be described as ordinate and not as absolute. God has bound us to them as the means; but it does not follow that He has absolutely bound Himself to them. The sacraments are necessary because God has commanded them. "It is not the lack but the contempt of the sacrament that condemns." [7] There are cases in which, as in that of the thief on the cross, the reception of the sacraments on the part of one who has come to faith is impossible. The thief on the cross was saved without the Sacraments, because he had no opportunity to receive them. On the basis of Scriptural statements (John 3:5; Tit. 3:5; 1 Pet. 3:21),

[7] Augustine, *Ag. the Donatists*, Bk. IV, 32. Nicene and Post-Nic. Fathers, Vol. IV, p. 461.

the necessity of Baptism is to be regarded as of a higher order than that of the Lord's Supper. It is the Sacrament of adoption into divine sonship, or of introduction into Christ's kingdom, while the Lord's Supper is meant for the strengthening of the faith of those who already belong to His kingdom. But while a more fundamental necessity belongs to Baptism, it does not follow that the Lord's Supper may be safely neglected.

Old Testament Types. Circumcision and the Passover were the Old Testament types of the New Testament Sacraments. Circumcision was the rite of initiation into membership in God's Old Testament kingdom, and the Passover was a memorial of God's rescuing mercy. Both of them were types and figures of things to come, and foreshadowed the Sacraments of Baptism and the Lord's Supper.[8]

[8] To regard Circumcision and the Passover as Old Testament sacraments and as conveying the same grace as the New Testament sacraments, only in a less full and perfect manner, is an undue exaltation of those Old Testament rites, which rests on an ignoring of the progressive character of revelation and of the difference between the Old and New Testament dispensations.

CHAPTER XXIX

BAPTISM

WHEN Jesus was about to ascend into heaven, He commissioned His disciples to evangelize the world, and commanded them to employ two means in doing so, namely, baptism and the Word. They were to make disciples of all the nations, by baptizing them into the name of the Father and of the Son and of the Holy Ghost, and by teaching them to observe all things whatsoever He had commanded them (Matt. 28:19, 20). They were to evangelize the world, not by baptism alone nor by the Word alone, but by both. Thus baptism and the Word are the appointed means for making men into Christ's disciples or Christians. This appointment of the use of the two means for the evangelizing of the world is important for the understanding of the purpose and effect of baptism.

Definition. Baptism is a sacred and divinely appointed action in which, with the application of water in the name of the Father and of the Son and of the Holy Ghost, the sinner is received into a gracious covenant relation with God, and obtains, if he believes, the forgiveness of his sins and everlasting salvation.

Baptism is the sacrament of initiation or entrance into Christ's kingdom. It is baptism into the name of the Triune God, and thus is reception into the divine family. It is adoption as God's children. It is the offering to the baptized person all the benefits of Christ's redemption, and the actual bestowal of them if he believes.

329

A Sacrament. Baptism possesses the three marks or characteristics which the Lutheran Church requires in any rite or ceremony which is to be classed as a sacrament. It has been instituted by Christ's command; there is employed in it an earthly element; and there is bestowed in and through it a heavenly gift. The divine command was given by our Lord just before His ascension into heaven (Matt. 28:19, 20). The earthly element which is used in it is water. And the heavenly gift which is bestowed in and through it is the forgiveness of sins and everlasting salvation (Mark 16:16).[1]

Old Testament Type. Circumcision was the Old Testament type of baptism. It was not a sacrament in the sense in which baptism is. But it was a type of baptism, in that it was the rite of initiation into the Old Testament kingdom of God. New Testament baptism is of larger significance than circumcision, because it is a Means of Grace through which the Holy Spirit operates to produce His saving effects in men.

Baptism of John. The baptism administered by John the Baptist was not identical in its nature with Christian baptism. It was a baptism unto repentance, and its purpose was to symbolize the inner cleansing that was to take place in the sinner by repentance.[2] It was a preparation for the kingdom of God which was now at hand (Matt. 3:11; Luke 3:16), but not admission into it, nor accompanied by the special working of the Holy Spirit. When Paul found in Ephesus men who had

---

[1] The heavenly gift was variously described by the later dogmaticians as the Holy Trinity, the Holy Spirit, and the Blood of Christ. They supposed that there must be in baptism something which corresponds to the Body and Blood of Christ in the Lord's Supper. But this supposition is unnecessary, and is impossible to establish. It is better to follow the older dogmaticians, who declare that the purpose of baptism, as of the Word, is to impart evangelical grace. In his Small Catechism Luther asks, "What gifts or benefits does baptism convey?" And he replies, that "it works forgiveness of sins, delivers from death and the devil, and confers everlasting salvation on all who believe, as the word and promise of God declare."

[2] The old dogmaticians were inclined, but we believe without sufficient reason, to identify the nature of John's baptism, and of the baptism by the disciples before Christ's ascension, with Christian baptism.

been baptized by John, he did not count John's baptism sufficient, but preached to them of Christ, and baptized them with Christian baptism (Acts 19:2-5). What is here said of John's baptism applies also to that administered by the disciples of Jesus before His resurrection and ascension.

The Divine Command. The virtue of baptism as a sacrament is found in the fact that its administration has been commanded by Christ, and that it carries with it His promise of salvation to all who are baptized and believe. The command to baptize is accompanied by the command to teach. If the baptism comes first, as in the case of infants, the teaching must follow. If the teaching comes first, as in the case of adults, and faith is produced, baptism must follow.

Water and the Word. Baptism requires the use of water in connection with the Word. Water is to be applied "in the name of the Father and of the Son and of the Holy Ghost." It is the Word added to the element that constitutes the sacrament. The use of the water without the words which Christ has commanded us to use, or with any other words, would not be Christian baptism. For, as Luther declares, "Without the Word of God the water is simply water and no baptism; but with the Word of God it is a baptism, that is, a gracious water of life." [3]

The Water. The earthly element used in baptism is water. There are no specifications as to the kind of water to be used, whether salt or fresh, running or still, hot or cold, from fountain or cistern. Water is at once the most easily obtainable of all elements, and at the same time it is the most appropriate symbol of that cleansing from sin which comes to the believer in baptism. But baptism is not to be regarded as a mere symbol. On the contrary, it is a Means of Grace and not only symbolizes spiritual cleansing, but offers and bestows it.

Modes of Baptism. There are three modes by which baptism

[3] *Small Catechism.*

may be administered; namely, by immersion, by pouring, or by sprinkling. Each of these modes is valid. The essential thing in baptism is the application of water in the name of the Father and of the Son and of the Holy Ghost. The quantity of water used does not matter. It is not the water which produces the gracious effect, but the water used in connection with God's Word. God's Word and promise are as efficacious when used in connection with little water as with much. Christ did not specify any particular mode to be used. The word "baptize" does not necessarily mean immerse, but means to apply water or to wash. The word employed to designate Christian baptism is not a new word which Christ coined for the purpose, but one which was in common use, and whose meaning in its ordinary use can therefore be determined. It is employed in several places in the New Testament in the sense of washing. Thus in St. Mark's Gospel we are told, that when the Pharisees come from market "except they (baptize) wash they eat not" (Mark 7:4),[4] and the preceding verse shows that by washing was meant the washing of the hands. In the Gospel according to St. Luke the Pharisee is said to have marveled that Christ sat down to eat without first baptizing or washing, as the invariable custom of the Pharisees was (Luke 11:38). In his first Epistle to the Corinthians St. Paul declares that the Israelites in passing through the sea were all baptized unto Moses in the cloud and in the sea (1 Cor. 10:1, 2), thus using the word baptize to refer to the sprinkling of the Israelites by the spray which blew down on them from the walls of water on either side. The references to baptism by the Holy Ghost agree much better with the idea of pouring than of immersion.

The passages which speak of burial with Christ by baptism

[4] Westcott and Hort prefer the reading ῾ραντίσωνται, but Nestle gives βαπτίσωνται.

(Rom. 6:4; Col. 2:12) seem to refer to immersion. And it is possible that much of the baptizing in the early Church was by that mode. The symbolical meaning attached to that form would commend it. But there is no good reason for supposing that it was the only mode. In the case of a number of baptisms recorded in the New Testament immersion seems to have been quite impracticable. When the three thousand were baptized on the day of Pentecost, there was no stream nearer than the Jordan that was deep enough for immersion. The Philippian jailor was evidently baptized in the prison (Acts 16:33), and Cornelius seems to have been baptized in his own house (Acts 10:46-48). The fact that Jesus came up out of the water after His baptism by John may quite as easily mean that He stood in the stream while John poured water on His head, as that He was immersed.

"*The Teaching of the Twelve Apostles,*" dating from the first half of the second century, shows that at that period the validity of baptism by either immersion or pouring was recognized.[5] As the Gospel spread to colder climes, baptism by pouring or sprinkling naturally commended itself as more feasible and convenient. In the case of the sick, baptism would in most cases be impossible, if it had to be performed by immersion.

In the Lutheran Church the mode now universally employed is by pouring or sprinkling, because it is most convenient and is practicable under all circumstances. While baptism by immersion is, of course, recognized as valid baptism, a request for baptism by immersion should not be granted by a Lutheran minister, because he would thereby appear to sanction the notion that baptism by immersion is a little better than by

[5] Section VII. "And touching baptism thus baptize: having first declared all these things, baptize in the name of the Father and of the Son and of the Holy Spirit, in living water. But if thou have not living water, baptize in other water; and if thou canst not in cold, then in warm. But if thou have neither, pour on the head water thrice in the name of the Father, Son and Holy Spirit."

pouring or sprinkling, and he would probably arouse doubts in the minds of some persons as to whether their baptism by the latter mode was altogether satisfactory.[6]

Adults and Children. The command of Christ is to make disciples of all the nations by baptizing and teaching them. Since nations comprise adults and children, it is a fair inference that both are included in His command.

That adults are to be baptized is not disputed by any who acknowledge the need of baptism at all. And since the benefit of baptism is connected with faith (Mark 16:16) and the apostles baptized only those adults who professed faith, it is necessary that the baptism of adults should be preceded by adequate instruction in the Word and a profession of faith in Christ on their part. The sincerity of the faith professed is something which others, of course, cannot determine. If the profession of faith be untrue, the baptism is nevertheless a valid baptism, but the benefits of the sacrament do not belong to the baptized person until he comes to true repentance and faith. Baptism does not produce its effects *ex opere operato.* As in the case of the Word, so in that of baptism, the grace offered must be accepted by faith if it is to be personally possessed.

The Anabaptists of the Reformation times and the Baptists and others of to-day deny that infants should be baptized. Since the benefit to be imparted is conditioned on faith, and this faith is interpreted by them to mean only the conscious faith of the adult, the child, they hold, is not to be baptized, because he does not and cannot believe; and he must first be allowed to grow up to years of discretion, and then be converted, before

---

[6] Those who insist upon immersion as the only proper mode of baptism do not agree among themselves as to the method in which immersion is to be administered. Some are satisfied with one immersion, others insist on immersing the person three times. Some maintain that the person must be dipped backward, and others that he must be dipped forward. Some insist that baptism must take place in running water even in the dead of winter, and others are satisfied to immerse in a pool placed for the purpose in the church building.

he can be permitted to receive this sacrament. The teaching referred to in Christ's final command must, they maintain, precede the baptism. But the assertion is wanting in proof.[7]

Reasons for Infant Baptism. The following reasons may be adduced for the right and necessity of infant baptism:

1. Children form a large and important part of the nations whom Christ commanded his disciples to baptize and teach. There is no nation without children. The fact that they are not expressly mentioned in the command is no argument for their exclusion.

2. Baptism is a covenant of grace in which God offers to the baptized person all the benefits of Christ's redemption. Children are by nature sinful and need this grace of God; for they are born with original sin and a natural inclination to evil. The fact that children die proves that they have inherited original sin (Rom. 5:12). And while they have not as infants committed any conscious transgressions, the seeds of sin are in them, and grow into actual deeds of wrong as soon as the children become old enough to act.

3. Christ has commanded that little children be brought to Him (Luke 18:16); and we obey this command when we bring them to Him in Holy Baptism and afterwards, as they grow up, teach them to observe all things whatsoever He has commanded.

4. Christ declares of little children that "of such is the kingdom of God," and that "whosoever shall not receive the kingdom of God as a little child, he shall not enter therein (Matt. 18:16, 17; Matt. 18:3). If, as these words imply, adults must first become as little children before they can be baptized and fully enter the kingdom of God, then certainly children must

---

[7] Before the publication of the Revised Version of the New Testament it was a favorite popular argument of Baptists, that Christ commands us first to teach and then to baptize (in Matt. 28:19, 20). But the Revised Version shows that in the command of Christ the baptizing is mentioned before the teaching.

not be denied that sacrament by which they are to be made His children and members of His kingdom.

5. The apostle expressly declares that the promise of grace and of the Holy Ghost is given to the children as well as to the adults (Acts 2:38, 39). Children therefore must not be excluded from that sacrament in which grace and the Holy Ghost are given.

6. Circumcision, which was the Old Testament type of baptism, was administered on the eighth day. By this rite infants were admitted into the number of God's Old Testament people. By analogy we conclude that if it was God's will to receive infants into a covenant relation with Himself under the old dispensation, it must be His will to receive them by this initiatory sacrament into His New Testament covenant of grace.

7. The New Testament record shows that the apostles baptized the households or families of converted persons (Acts 16:15, 33; 1 Cor. 1:16). It is too much to assume that there were no children in any of these households.

The Heavenly Gift. The purpose of baptism is to bestow divine grace. The grace which man needs is the forgiveness of sins and eternal salvation. This is in essence the heavenly gift bestowed in baptism, though, while offered to all, it is actually given only to him that believes. Christ Himself tells us that the bestowal of this gift is the purpose of the sacrament, and that it is given only to the believer. For He says, "He that believeth and is baptized shall be saved; but he that disbelieveth shall be condemned" (Mark 16:16. R.V.).

The purpose of baptism, as of the Word, is to offer to men and to bestow upon the believer the benefits of Christ's redemption. It is a baptism into Christ's death (Rom. 6:3) and thus into a participation in all the benefits acquired by that death. It is a covenant relation into which God enters with the baptized person, and in which God assures the baptized person that all the blessings of redemption have been acquired for him and actually belong to him if he accepts them by faith. To the believer, therefore, baptism brings the remission of sins and everlasting life on the basis of Christ's merit and righteousness. It is thus a washing away of sin (Acts 22:16) and a washing of regeneration and renewal by the Holy Ghost (Tit. 3:5).

Faith Necessary. The salvation offered in baptism is conditioned on faith. Even without faith the baptism is a valid baptism if properly administered, and offers the grace of God to the baptized person individually. The covenant, so far as God is concerned, stands sure. But the unbelieving person fails to accept the grace and salvation which are offered, and consequently does not possess them. He has been adopted in baptism as a child of God; but so long as he remains in a condition of impenitence and unbelief he is a disinherited child. The offer of all the benefits of Christ's redemption made to him in baptism remains always open to him. But their possession depends on his repenting and believing.

Baptism Permanent. Baptism establishes a permanent covenant, and therefore is never to be repeated. Man's unfaithfulness cannot make the promise of God of none effect (Rom. 3:3). Once administered, baptism holds good for all time. If the baptized person does not believe, or if he has believed and afterwards has fallen away into wickedness and unbelief, he needs to repent and believe. But his baptism with its gracious promise stands. He needs not to be rebaptized. He is a son who has strayed off into the far country. But when he comes back in true repentance, his heavenly Father stands ready to receive him. He is then reinstated in the privileges of sonship, but he needs not to be readopted.

In those cases in which a person is in doubt as to whether he was baptized in infancy or not, and asks for baptism, careful inquiry should be made to discover, if possible, whether the person ever actually was baptized or not. In case the matter remains in doubt, it is proper to baptize the person. But this baptism should not be conditional; that is, the minister should not say, "If thou hast not been baptized before, I now baptize thee, etc." He should proceed to baptize the person in the same way as he would in the case of one of whom he knew for a certainty that he had never been baptized.

Administration. The administration of baptism must be in accordance with Christ's institution. The essential thing is the application of water to a person in the name of the Father and of the Son and of the Holy Ghost. In the case of an adult, a profession of faith in Christ as his Savior must be required. In the case of a child, sponsors should present the child for baptism, and should promise to instruct and train him in the Christian religion. The sponsors ought themselves to be baptized Christians, and, wherever possible, members of the Lutheran Church. If they are not Christians themselves, they cannot be fit to undertake the task of instructing and training the baptized child as he grows up. Baptism would still be a baptism, if administered without sponsors; but it would be a wrong against the child to baptize him without having someone obligated to give him the instruction in the Word which he will so soon need.

Lay Baptism. Ordinarily baptism is to be performed by the ordained minister. But in emergencies, when there is imminent danger that the child might die before a minister could be secured, baptism may be administered by any Christian man or woman. Care must be exercised in such cases that the baptism be properly administered. The fact that the child was thus baptized should afterwards be made known to the minister, and if possible a public announcement should be made, and those immediately concerned as well as the whole congregation should be assured that the baptism is perfectly valid. It should be entered in the record along with the baptisms performed by the minister.[8]

Exorcism, the sign of the cross and other ceremonies which have often formed a part of the formulas used for baptism are *adiaphora,* and are now usually omitted.

Validity. The validity of baptism does not depend on the intention or character of the administrant, or on his doctrinal position, or on the formula used, or on the faith of the baptized person. It is a real baptism if water is applied to a person in the name of the Father and of the Son and of the Holy Ghost. Its validity depends only on the command and promise of God. In the last analysis it is an act of God, and not an act of man, even though administered through human beings.

Effect. According to the statements of Scripture baptism is a means of being born again of water and of the Spirit (John

[8] It is important as a matter of Christian order, and adds solemnity to the act, to use a proper formula in the administration of baptism, whether infant or adult. Such formulas have come down to us from the early days of the Church. There are two historic formulas for infant baptism. In one of them the questions are asked of the sponsors; in the other they are asked of the child. The latter is practically identical with the formula for adult baptism, with the one modification, that the child answers through the sponsors instead of in person. In this formula the child is made to declare that it believes all that is in the Apostles' Creed. From the doctrinal and from the psychological standpoint this declaration is not true. According to the teaching of Scripture the child is born with original sin, that is, "without the fear of God and without trust in him." It is born without faith, and it has not yet been baptized. How then can it have any faith to confess? On the other hand the supposition that an infant believes all the statements of the Apostles' Creed, when it does not yet understand a single word, is absurd. The infant cannot possibly have the explicit faith which it is made to declare that it has. The formula employed in infant baptism ought to be in harmony with the doctrine of the Church and with the capacity of the infant. Hoefling (*Das Sakrament der Taufe,* II, 230 seq.) undertakes to vindicate this formula on the basis of its long use by the Church, and of the statement that the child's faith referred to is an anticipated faith. But a wrong formula does not become right because it is hoary with age, or because it is made to mean what it very clearly does not say. Besides, who knows that the particular child, now being baptized, will actually believe later on? If no formula that fitted the Lutheran doctrine had come down to us, it would be incumbent on us to frame one that did fit.

3:5), and a washing of regeneration by the Holy Ghost (Tit. 3:5). Being a sacrament and Means of Grace, its purpose is to offer and to bestow upon men divine saving grace.[9] There are but the two ordinary means of regeneration, namely, the Word (1 Pet. 1:23) and baptism (John 3:5). Since infants cannot be influenced by the Word, "they are regenerated, cleansed from the contagion of original sin, and made partakers of eternal life through baptism."[10] The Augsburg Confession declares that "by baptism the grace of God is offered, and that children are to be baptized, who by baptism, being offered to God, are received into God's favor."[11]

Baptism is enjoined upon all, infants and adults. "To infants baptism is primarily the ordinary means of regeneration and purification from sin; secondarily, it is the seal of righteousness and the confirmation of faith; to adult believers it serves principally as a seal and testimony of the grace of God, sonship and eternal life, but in a less principal sense it increases renovation and the gifts of the Holy Spirit. Infants by baptism receive the first fruits of the Spirit and of faith; adults, who through the Word have received the first fruits of faith and of the Holy Spirit, procure an increase of these gifts by baptism."[12]

Baptism is a divinely instituted form, rite or ceremony through which as a means of grace man is received into a new and blessed relation or covenant with God. It gives to the baptized person the right to call God his Father and to call Christ his Savior. It is the offer of all the blessings of Christ's redemption to the baptized individual. He is adopted as God's child,

---

[9] Holl., 1095. "The primary design of baptism is the offering, application, conferring and sealing of evangelical grace." Large Catechism, IV, 24: "The power, work, fruit and end of baptism is to save men. . . . But to be saved, we know is nothing else than to be delivered from the tyranny of sin, death and the devil, to be transferred into the kingdom of Christ, and to dwell with Him forever."

[10] Gerh. IX, 236.   [11] Art. IX.   [12] Gerh., IX, 169.

and is offered all the blessings of divine sonship. And all these privileges and blessings are actually his if he has the right filial attitude toward God, namely, if he has faith.

In the case of the adult the right filial attitude consists of *conscious* contrition and faith. If he has this, all the blessings of sonship are his. If on the other hand, he does not have the filial attitude, that is, if he does not believe, the blessings of sonship are not his in spite of the fact that he has been formally and solemnly adopted as God's child. Even though he disbelieves, however, the relation or covenant entered into is permanent on God's part; the adoption stands. And it need not be repeated if the unbelieving person subsequently repents and believes.

In the case of the child the same reception or adoption into sonship with God takes place in baptism. No *conscious* filial attitude or *conscious* faith toward God is required or can be required in his case. He is too young for that. But while in the case of the infant the conscious filial attitude must come later through the Word and cannot be present in infancy, that cannot and does not hinder him from being received in baptism and adopted as God's child. A man who desired to adopt both an infant and an adult as his sons would insist that the adult should signify his willingness to become his son and promise to behave as a son ought. But he would not make the same demand of an infant, because the infant is not yet old enough to express any willingness or to promise any proper behavior. The man would, however, nevertheless adopt the infant also, confident that with proper training in the home the conscious filial attitude would follow in due time. He would not insist on waiting with the adoption until the child is old enough to speak for itself. He wants the child as his, the child does not resist, and its very helplessness and need are an appeal to him to adopt it and give it proper care and a home. There is much in this analogy that fits the case of the baptism of an adult and that of a child.[13]

As pointed out by the old dogmaticians, it is to be maintained on the basis of Titus 3:5 that in baptism regeneration and faith are produced in infants. "Baptism is the washing of regeneration; but regeneration cannot take place without faith." [14] The exact nature of this faith is something which we cannot understand. But "it is not to be supposed that the actual benefit of regeneration, or the production of faith in infants, is to be deferred to years of discretion, and that they meanwhile are in no way received into grace." [15]

The opposition to the doctrine that in baptism the Holy Spirit works faith in the infant is largely due to the supposition that the faith of infants must in all respects be like that of adults; that is, that it must be a conscious faith based on knowledge and assent.[16] But this supposition is not warranted. That the child has capacity for faith and that Christ ascribes faith to children is clear from the Scriptures (Matt. 18:6). That the infant does not willfully reject the grace offered in baptism in clear also. That the infant may have an unconscious faith in

[13] Comp. Augustine (Ag. the Donatists, Nic. and Post-Nic. Fathers, Vol. IV, p. 461): "As therefore in Abraham the justification of faith came first, and circumcision was added afterwards as the seal of faith; so in Cornelius the spiritual sanctification came first in the gift of the Holy Spirit, and the sacrament of regeneration was added afterwards in the laver of baptism. And as in Isaac, who was circumcised on the eighth day after his birth, the seal of this righteousness was given first, and afterwards, as he imitated the faith of his father, the righteousness itself followed as he grew up, of which the seal had been given before when he was an infant; so in infants who are baptized, the sacrament of regeneration is given first, and if they maintain a Christian piety, conversion also in the heart will follow, of which the mysterious sign had gone before in the outward body."

[14] Gerh., IX, 275: "We are not solicitous about the mode of this faith, but we simply acquiesce in the fact that infants really believe."

[15] Baier, 690.

[16] Quenstedt, IV, 147, ascribed to baptized infants a faith which includes "spiritual knowledge, assent and confidence or the apprehension and application of Christ's merits." But it is evident that while infants may have faith, that faith cannot like the faith of adults be preceded by actual knowledge and assent.

God just as it has an unconscious faith or trust in its mother cannot be successfully disputed. Luther desired that children should be brought to baptism "in the hope that they may believe"; and Chemnitz desired that they should be brought to baptism so that the Holy Spirit might work *faith suitable to the child.*

In the case of the adult, his opposition and antagonism to God must first be broken down, and he must be brought to a state of conscious contrition and faith before he is willing to accept the blessings of divine sonship. But the infant offers no such willful resistance to God's grace, and when he is baptized the Holy Spirit can and does apply to him the benefits of Christ's redemption. If he dies before he is old enough to come to conscious faith, he is saved; for his baptism has made him a child of God and an heir of heaven.

The statement made earlier in this chapter, that baptism does not work *ex opere operato* means, indeed, that the mere administration of baptism does not in itself save the baptized person, but that faith on his part is required. But the statement is not meant to limit the power of the Holy Spirit who comes to the child in holy baptism. It is simply meant to exclude the notion that the minister or the priest by the outward act or work produces a saving effect.

It is true, the infant cannot know or assent to any truth, either religious or secular. Hence it cannot have a conscious, discursive faith like that of adults. But in its essence faith means not willfully resisting God's grace and permitting Him to apply Christ's saving merits. And faith in this sense certainly can be and is wrought in the child by the Holy Spirit in baptism.

It is a mistake, however, to endeavor to read the whole complex process of adult regeneration or conversion through the Word into the regeneration of the infant in baptism. It should be borne in mind that the purpose of God comprises the use both of the Word and of baptism for completeness—baptism receiving us into His gracious covenant as His children, and the Word producing in us conscious faith or the conscious filial attitude. Baptism establishes a new relationship of Fatherhood and sonship between God and man. Faith or the filial attitude is required in this relation, if its blessings are actually to be possessed and enjoyed. But certainly no demand is made or will be made of the child for the kind of faith or the kind of filial attitude which can be expected only in those who have reached the age of discretion.

Necessity of Baptism. Baptism is necessary for salvation, as passages previously cited show. But this necessity is ordinate and not absolute. God has ordained baptism as a means of grace, and has connected a certain benefit with it. Men cannot expect to possess and will not obtain this benefit if they despise the means with which God has connected it. But where baptism is desired and yet is unattainable, we believe that God will not count the absence of baptism against such a person. God has bound us to the Means; but that does not imply that He has bound Himself to them in such a way that He cannot possibly save without them. As previously observed, the thief on the cross was saved without baptism.

The Fate of Unbaptized Children. If children die unbaptized, it is not because they have despised baptism; for they are not old enough to despise it. There is, therefore, no reason to suppose that unbaptized children are necessarily lost.[17] This belief must not be permitted to impair our obedience to Christ's command and our insistence on the prompt baptism of infants. We do not have the same definite and comforting assurance based

---

[17] The statement of the Augsburg Confession, Art. IX, "They condemn the Anabaptists who allow not the baptism of children and affirm that children are saved without baptism," must be interpreted historically. The statement is aimed at the Anabaptist theory that children ought not to be baptized, and that this sacrament is not meant for them.

on Scripture concerning the unbaptized children as we have concerning those who have been baptized. The parents of the unbaptized child hope that it is saved. The parents of the baptized child are sure that it is saved. A distinction has sometimes been drawn between the unbaptized children of Christian parents and those of other parents, so that the former are to be assured that their child who died unbaptized is saved, while the latter are to be left in doubt. But there is no valid reason for this distinction.

Secondary Purposes of Baptism. The primary purpose of baptism is to be a Means of Grace, and to bestow forgiveness of sin and salvation on all who believe. It establishes a gracious covenant with the individual, in which all the blessings of Christ's redemption are his on the sole condition that he accepts them by faith. But this sacrament also serves several secondary purposes. It is a mark of the profession of Christianity, an admission into membership in the Church, and a constant reminder of the obligation to be a true child of God and to walk in newness of life.

Confirmation. The rite of Confirmation is not divinely enjoined, and is no sacrament. But it is a useful custom of the Church. It is not to be regarded as a completion or a ratification of baptism. It has direct reference to the catechetical instruction which has preceded it. The command of Christ is to baptize and teach. Confirmation is the Church's public testimony that the persons to be confirmed have been properly instructed in the Word of God, and are now fitted for intelligent and earnest participation in all the privileges of Church membership. Unless there has been adequate instruction or catechization, confirmation is a mere pretense; for it then certifies that these persons have been properly instructed in the truths of the Christian religion, when in fact they have not. The Church might do without confirmation, though it is a useful ceremony and ought to be retained; but the Church cannot do without adequate instruction or catechization. Teaching is a fundamental part of her work. She is to baptize and teach.

On the part of the catechuman confirmation involves a personal confession of faith and a promise of faithfulness to Christ. The obligations which he assumes are not new. They already rest upon him by virtue of his baptism. He is bound by his baptismal covenant. But having reached the age at which he is able to speak for himself, he voluntarily expresses his readiness to meet the obligations which have been resting on him ever since his baptism.

It is a mistake to speak of confirmation as if it signified admission into the Church. We become members of the Church through baptism, and not through confirmation. It is proper, however, to say, that confirmation admits us to *communicant* membership in the Church. Those who are confirmed are thereby adjudged fit to take part in the Lord's Supper, as well as to stand as sponsors in Holy Baptism.

CHAPTER XXX

THE LORD'S SUPPER

THE Lord's Supper was instituted by Christ on the night in which He was betrayed, while He sat with His disciples in the upper room after eating the Passover with them. The earthly elements which He used were provided in the Passover Supper, and the institution which He founded was the New Testament sacrament which would replace that Old Testament rite. The command of Christ was that they should do this in remembrance of Him. As often as we eat of this bread and drink of this cup we "show the Lord's death till he comes" (1 Cor. 11:26). It contains in itself a summary of Christ's redemptive work, and is therefore most appropriate as a memorial of His Passion. But the Lord's Supper is much more than a mere memorial. If it were only that, Matthew and Mark would not have omitted the words, "This do in remembrance of me." It is a sacrament, and conveys grace to men. Like the Word and baptism it is a Means of Grace through which the Holy Spirit not only makes known to men the grace of God, but works in their hearts.

Names. This sacrament is known by a number of different names. It is called the Lord's Supper, because it was instituted by the Lord, and was first partaken of at the time when the Passover supper had just been eaten. It is called the Lord's Table, because in this sacrament the Lord provides food and drink for our souls. It is called the Sacrament of the Altar, because it is usually administered at the altar. It is called the Communion, because there is a communion of the bread and

347

wine with the body and blood of Christ (1 Cor. 10:16), and a communion of believers with Christ and with one another. It is called the Eucharist, because the administration of this sacrament is attended with the giving of thanks. It is also called the Mass,[1] and this term is applied to it in the Augsburg Confession and the Apology. But the use of this term was later abandoned by the Protestants, because the Roman Catholic doctrine of a sacrifice became so closely associated with the name.

Definition. The Lord's Supper is a sacrament and Means of Grace, in which God communicates to us along with the bread and the wine the true body and blood of our Lord Jesus Christ, as a pledge of the forgiveness of sins acquired for us by His death on the cross; and in which He bestows actual forgiveness on all who believe.

The Divine Command. The divine command of Christ instituting this sacrament is recorded by Matthew (26:26-28), Mark (14:22-25), Luke (22:19-20) and Paul (1 Cor. 11:23-25). There are minor variations in these records, but there is essential harmony as to those things which constitute the nature of the sacrament. The records in Matthew and Mark, on the one hand, and those in Luke and First Corinthians, on the other, are quite similar. Luther in his Small Catechism gives an excellent composite statement of the essential points in all four records, and this form is generally employed for the consecration in the administration of the sacrament.

Earthly and Heavenly Elements. In baptism there is an earthly element, and there is a heavenly gift. But in the Lord's Supper there are both earthly and heavenly elements and a heavenly gift. The earthly elements are bread and wine; the heavenly elements are the body and blood of Christ; and the

---

[1] From the ancient custom of dismissing the catechumens just before the communion with the words, *Ite, missa est.*

heavenly gift is the forgiveness of sins. Frequently the body and blood of Christ have been regarded as the heavenly gift. But it is better to regard them as the heavenly elements, corresponding to the earthly elements of bread and wine, and to regard the heavenly gift as the forgiveness of sins. For the gift which God desires to bestow through each of the Means of Grace is, in the last analysis, the forgiveness of sins; and the body and blood of Christ are the pledge of that forgiveness.

The bread and wine are received in the Lord's Supper in the natural physical way of receiving food. The body and blood of Christ, though received along with the bread and wine, are not received in this natural physical way, but in a supernatural way which we cannot describe, and which we call sacramental. There is a mystery in this sacramental eating of the body and blood of Christ, which we cannot fathom. But we are not on that account to reject the plain teaching of Scripture that in the Lord's Supper we receive Christ's body and blood.

The Sacramental Union. There is a sacramental union between the bread and the wine, on the one hand, and the body and blood of Christ, on the other, a communion, as Paul calls it (1 Cor. 10:16), of the earthly and the heavenly elements, by virtue of which the communicant when he receives the bread receives also the body of Christ, and when he receives the wine receives also the blood of Christ. This presence of Christ's body and blood and its communication to the communicant along with the bread and the wine are usually described by the use of the three prepositions, in, with and under. Thus we are said to receive the body and blood of Christ in, with and under the bread and the wine. But these prepositions are not entirely adequate for the expression of what is meant. When the communicant receives the bread he receives also Christ's body, and when he receives the wine he receives also Christ's blood. In the English language the statement that we receive the body and blood of Christ *along with* the bread and the wine comes nearer than any or all of the three prepositions mentioned above to a setting forth of the Lutheran doctrine.[2]

The presence of Christ's body and blood in the Lord's Supper is a real and substantial presence, and not merely a potential one. Christ is present not simply in the sense that the benefits of His redemption are present. On the contrary He is present in such a real way that when the communicant receives the bread and the wine, he receives also the body and blood of Christ. When Paul declares that those who eat and drink unworthily are guilty of the body and blood of the Lord (1 Cor. 11:27-29), he thereby shows that all the communicants, and not simply the believers, receive Christ's body and blood.

The Real Presence. The real presence of Christ's body and blood in the Lord's Supper is maintained on the basis of the words of institution and of Paul's comment on unworthy communicants. In his controversies with those who denied the real presence, Luther's appeal was always to the words of institution. Christ says, This is my body, and This is my blood; and His words must not be explained away. If the doctrine of the real presence is rejected on the ground that it cannot be understood, the same reason could be adduced for the rejection of the doctrines of the Trinity, the Incarnation and the like.

The Reformed Churches reject the real presence, and interpret the words of institution as figurative: finding the figure of speech either in the word *is,* which is supposed to mean represents; or in the word *this,* which is supposed to mean a symbolical bread; or in the word *body,* which is supposed to be used in a figurative spiritual sense. But the Lutheran Church

---

[2] The German word *unter* has a meaning in this connection which is wanting in the English word under. Thus, *Einer unter vielen* is one among, not under, many. To receive *einen Diamanten unter vielen andern Steinen* is to receive a diamond among or along with many other stones. Hence in the Catechism and elsewhere the translation of the German word *unter* by the English word under does not do justice to its meaning.

adheres to the literal sense of the words, and maintains that
Christ really and truly gives us His body and blood in the Holy
Supper. It was a new ordinance that Christ was instituting, and
it was altogether unlikely that he would set it forth in figurative language without explaining its literal meaning elsewhere.
It was His last will and testament, and thus it follows that He
would be anxious to set it forth as unmistakably as possible. It
was meant to replace the Old Testament Passover, and if it
were purely symbolical it would be less satisfactory as a symbol
of Christ's sacrificial death than the Paschal lamb. The
Lutheran Church teaches and believes that the glorified Christ is
abundantly able to be present with His body and blood wherever the Lord's Supper is celebrated, and is able in a real though
to us incomprehensible way to give them along with the bread
and the wine as a pledge of forgiveness.

Doctrines Compared. To the Zwinglians the Lord's Supper
is purely symbolical, and its significance is that of a memorial.
We are to do this in remembrance of the Lord. To the Calvinists, indeed, the Lord's Supper means more than to the
Zwinglians; but denying, as they do, the *Genus Majestaticum*
and believing that Christ's body is locally confined to heaven,
they regard the real presence as an impossibility, and hold that
by faith the believer ascends, as it were, to heaven and spiritually partakes of Christ's body and blood.

The doctrine of the Roman Catholic Church is that of transubstantiation. It holds that by the act of consecration the
bread is turned into the body of Christ, and the wine is turned
into the blood of Christ. The accidents of bread and wine
remain, but the substance is that of Christ's body and blood.
The bread looks and tastes like bread, but is the body of Christ
and no longer bread. The wine looks and tastes like wine, but
is the blood of Christ and no longer wine. In the administration of this sacrament in the Roman Church the laity receive

only the bread, and the priest alone drinks the wine. Since
the wine is regarded as having been turned into the very blood
of Christ, not a single drop of it dare be spilled. The theory
is that the blood is included in the body—the theory of con-
comitance. Hence it is regarded as sufficient for the laity to
receive the communion in one kind, because the blood is
received with the body. Because of this doctrine of transubstantiation the hosts or wafers left over after the communion
are regarded as the veritable body of our Lord, and are worshiped in the ceremony of the elevation of the host.

The Lutheran, Reformed and Roman Catholic doctrines of
the Lord's Supper may be illustrated and compared by means of
a diagram, as follows:

Reformed	*Lutheran*	*Roman Catholic*
Bread-Body	Bread-Body	Bread-Body
Wine-Blood	Wine-Blood	Wine-Blood

From the standpoint of the Reformed doctrine, the communicant receives nothing but bread and wine. From the standpoint
of the Roman Catholic doctrine, he receives nothing but the
body and blood of Christ. From the standpoint of the Lutheran
doctrine, he receives the bread and the wine and also the body
and blood of Christ. For the Reformed Church bread and wine
merely symbolize Christ's body and blood. For the Roman
Catholic Church the accidents of bread and wine remain, but
the substance is only the body and blood of Christ. For the
Lutheran Church the bread remains bread and the wine remains
wine, but the communicant receives with them, in an incomprehensible but real manner, the body and blood of Christ.

Misconceptions of the Lutheran Doctrine. The reception of
Christ's body and blood is not to be conceived as a Capernaitic
eating and drinking. The body and blood are not masticated
and swallowed as are the bread and the wine. The natural

physical part of the process of eating and drinking is confined to the bread and the wine. They pass into the stomach like any other food. But the purpose of Christ when He comes to us through the bread and the wine is to come into our heart. He uses the physical as a vehicle for the spiritual. That belongs to the very nature of a Means of Grace. The Word enters into our physical ear, and Christ enters with it. But He does so, not in order that He may remain anywhere in our physical organism, but that He may enter and abide in our heart. In the Lord's Supper the bread and the wine enter into the mouth, and Christ's body and blood are received with them. But Christ comes to us in this way, not in order that He may remain anywhere in our physical organism, but that He may enter and abide in our hearts.[3] The eating and drinking of the body and blood of Christ are sacramental and spiritual;[4] not spiritual in the Calvinistic sense, but in that spiritual sense in which all the fundamental relations between Christ and us are spiritual. It is a coming of Christ with all His blessings of redemption, of which the giving of His own body and blood in the Sacrament is a pledge; and it is a reception and appropriation of those blessings through faith.

The Lutheran Church does not teach the doctrine of consubstantiation, though she has frequently been accused of teaching it. This doctrine means that the bread and the wine are combined with the body and blood of Christ into a third substance. Nor does the Lutheran Church teach the doctrine of impanation or of subpanation, that is, that the body and blood are locally included or inclosed in the bread and wine, or are located under them. Her teaching is that the body and blood of Christ are not locally but sacramentally connected with the bread and the wine; and that only during the actual reception

---

[3] Comp. Krauth, *Conservative Reformation*, p. 462 seq.
[4] *Form. Conc.*, 620, 105.

by the communicant are the body and blood present. Before and after the actual administration the bread and the wine are only bread and wine.

The Earthly Elements. The earthly elements used are bread and wine. The bread may be baked of wheat or any other flour; it may be leavened or unleavened; and may be baked in small portions or in loaves. The essential thing is that it be real bread. The Lord used unleavened bread, because it was the Feast of the Passover, when that kind alone dared be used by the Jews. The Lutheran Church generally uses unleavened bread in the form of wafers, which usually have a cross or a crucifix imprinted on them. The Reformed Church regards the actual breaking of the bread as an essential part of the administration; the Lutheran Church does not. The latter uses wafers because they are the most convenient form in which the bread can be prepared.

The wine which the Lord used was real wine, that is, fermented juice of the grape. And this is what should be employed in the administration of the Lord's Supper. It may be red or white wine; but it must be made of grapes, since Christ speaks of it as the fruit of the vine (Matt. 26:29; Mark 14:25; Luke 22:18).

The use of individual communion cups for sanitary reasons is becoming quite common. Does their use in any way affect the validity of the Sacrament? If the bread need not be broken, but may be placed upon the altar in individual portions or wafers, then by parity of reasoning the wine need not be administered in a large common cup or goblet, but may be placed on the altar in individual communion cups. The essence of the Sacrament, so far as its administration is concerned, is the use of bread and wine with the words of Christ according to His institution.

The Heavenly Gift. The heavenly gift bestowed in the

Lord's Supper should not be confused or identified with the
heavenly or celestial elements. The latter, as already pointed
out, consist of the body and blood of Christ. But the heavenly
gift is the forgiveness of sins. This is plainly indicated in the
words of Christ, assuring us that His body and His blood,
given to us in the Sacrament, "were given and shed for us for
the remission of sins." [5] Like the other Means of Grace, the
purpose of the Lord's Supper is to bestow forgiveness and salvation. The gift is offered to all in this sacrament with the body
and blood of Christ as a pledge; but it is actually received and
possessed only by those who accept it in faith. The heavenly
elements, namely, the body and blood of Christ, are received
by all the communicants, whether believers or unbelievers; but
the heavenly gift is received only by the believers.

The Lord's Supper is a sacrament and not a sacrifice. In it
God offers something to us, and not we to Him. Our gratitude
to Him for His goodness is a sacrifice of thanksgiving which
should attend our participation in the sacrament. But it is not
a part of the sacrament as such. The doctrine of the Roman
Church that in the Mass the priest offers an unbloody sacrifice
of Christ for the sins of men has no warrant in Scripture.

Administration. The administration of the Lord's Supper
includes three factors; namely, the consecration by the use of
the words of institution; the distribution of the bread and wine
with the utterance of the words of Christ, that this is His body
which was given for us and His blood which was shed for us
for the remission of sins; and the reception by the communicants.

The Reformed Church holds that the bread and wine should
be placed in the hand of the communicant. The Lutheran

[5] Compare what Luther says in his Small Catechism concerning the benefits
derived from such eating and drinking: "They are pointed out in these words,
'given and shed for you for the remission of sins'; namely, through these words
the remission of sins, life and salvation are granted unto us in the sacrament."

Church regards the placing them in the hand or the mouth as an *adiaphoron*. But it is well for the sake of order to adhere to one method. The one usually followed in the Lutheran Church is that of placing them in the mouth. The use of the individual communion cups has, however, resulted in many churches in offering the wine to the hand of the communicant.

The Lord's Supper is to be administered by the regularly called and ordained minister of the Gospel. No exception to this is made in the case of the Lord's Supper, as is done in that of baptism by a layman in case of emergency.[6] The necessity of the Lord's Supper for salvation is not to be regarded as of the same order as that of baptism.

Who Admitted. The Lord's Supper is the sacrament for adult Christians. Children who have not yet reached the age of discretion are not to be admitted. Only those who are able to examine themselves, as the apostle exhorts (1 Cor. 11:28), are to be permitted to partake of this sacrament. Hence, also, the Lord's Supper should not be administered to idiots or insane people, or to persons who have become unconscious. No general invitation should be extended by the pastor to all those who believe in the Lord to come to His table. Only those who believe the Lutheran doctrine of the real presence should be admitted, in view of Paul's words on not discerning the Lord's body (1 Cor. 11:29). Furthermore, admission to the Lord's Supper is an acknowledgment of unity in the faith; and this does not exist in the case of those who reject the Lutheran doctrine. And still further, before the Lutheran Church invites her own members to come to the Lord's Table she expects them to

---

[6] This is the position of the great majority of our theologians. On the other hand, Cotta remarks upon a statement of Gerhard's, "In a case of such necessity, where death seems immediately impending, if a pastor cannot be procured, and the dying person earnestly desires to enjoy the sacrament, many of our theologians maintain that the Holy Eucharist can be administered even by a layman. Let it suffice that I mention, among these, John Gallus and Tilemann Hesshuss." Gerh. X, 21. Quoted by Schmid, p. 594.

attend the service of confession and absolution, and thus to prepare themselves to come worthily. When she makes such a demand of her own members, she must not invite all others indiscriminately to come and partake of the sacrament.

Whether the minister should administer communion to himself has been a much discussed question. It has not been finally answered, and may be regarded as an *adiaphoron*. The general sentiment of Lutheran theologians from Luther himself on down is against the practice.

The custom of holding services of confession and absolution before the administration of the Lord's Supper has been referred to above. It is a valuable custom, and helps to add due solemnity to participation in the sacrament. In order to come to the Lord's Table and to profit by the communion, it is of fundamental importance that the communicant shall come with a contrite and believing heart. The service of confession and absolution is therefore a practical arrangement of great value. At the same time it must be remembered, that the service of confession and absolution is not an integral part of the sacrament as such, and that unavoidable absence from it need not absolutely hinder anyone from coming to the Lord's Table, if he has privately prepared himself for it and can come with contrite and believing heart.

People sometimes remain away from the Lord's Supper because, they say, they are not good enough to come. If this means that they are deliberately living in sin and are unwilling to repent, they are right in remaining away. But if what they mean is that they are deeply conscious of their sin and unworthiness, they should be urged to remember that that is the very kind of persons for whose benefit the Lord's Supper has been instituted. They are the very ones who need and desire the grace that is offered; and they should come.

The Lord's Supper, like baptism, individualizes the grace of

God. As each communicant individually receives the bread and along with it the body of Christ, and as each communicant individually receives the wine and along with it the blood of Christ, so to each communicant individually is spoken the comforting assurance that the body of Christ was *given for him* and the blood of Christ was *shed for him* for the remission of sins.

When Administered. The early Church administered the communion on every Lord's Day. And the chief service of the Lord's Day is one of which the Communion Service is an integral part. It is not customary now, however, to administer the communion so frequently. Often it is administered four times a year; often, also, it is administered six times a year, at the beginning of each special season of the Church Year. The neglect of the Lord's Supper is a prevalent sin.[7] Many come to the Lord's Table once a year—to keep up their church membership. Where the spiritual state is what it ought to be, the Christian will be glad to come to the Lord's Supper whenever it is administered, in order that he may have the comfort which it brings with its individual promise of grace and forgiveness to him.

[7] See Luther's Preface to the Small Catechism on this point.

CHAPTER XXXI

THE CHURCH [1]

THE Church, according to the Augsburg Confession,[2] "is the congregation of saints or assembly of true believers, in which the Gospel is rightly taught and the Sacraments are rightly administered." This confessional statement at once describes the persons who constitute the Church, and the place where the Church is found. It is composed of those persons who are true believers in Christ, who are united with Him and with one another by faith, and who are the Body of which He is the Head. And they are found on earth wherever the Gospel is rightly taught and the Sacraments are rightly administered; that is, they are banded together in congregations or assemblies around the Means of Grace. Wherever the Word of God is preached, there are some persons who are true believers (Isa. 55:11; Matt. 18:20).

Definition. Accordingly, the Church in the true and proper sense is to be defined as the communion of saints or the fellowship of true believers. This is in essence not only the definition given by the Augsburg Confession, but also by the Apostles' Creed. For in the Creed the words "the communion of saints" are to be understood as being in apposition to the words "the Holy Christian (Catholic) Church," and are therefore a definition of the Church. The word saint is used here in the Scrip-

---

[1] At this point the old dogmaticians usually treat of the Three Estates—the Church, the Family and the State. But the discussion of the Family and the State belongs rather to ethics than to dogmatics.

[2] Art. VII.

359

tural sense in which it denotes a believer, and not in the sense
of a perfect person or of a person who has been canonized.
This definition of the Church is implied in Paul's first letter to
the Corinthians, in which he addresses the Church at Corinth as
those that "are sanctified in Christ Jesus" (1 Cor. 1:2).

Since, however, the assemblies of believers which gather
around the Word and Sacrament are never composed of true
believers alone, but include some persons who only pretend to
be believers, an additional definition of the Church is needed,
which, while emphasizing the essential nature of the Church,
takes account of the fact that on earth it always appears empiri-
cally in a mixed form, and never in a pure form.

In this improper or mixed sense the Church is to be defined
as the fellowship of true believers gathered, along with pretended believers, around the Word and Sacraments, which have
been intrusted to the believers' administration for the nourish-
ment of their own spiritual life and for the evangelization
of the world.

In reality the Church is composed only of those persons who
are true believers. But in their assemblies on earth, there are
always tares among the wheat. God alone can accurately distinguish between them. He alone knows who actually does and
who does not comprise a part of His Church. The line of demarcation between true and pretended believers is invisible to
the human eye. The attempt to form an assembly from which
all but true believers should be excluded would be wrong and
futile (Matt. 13:24 seq.).

From the Protestant standpoint the distinction between the
Church in the proper sense as composed of true believers only
and the Church in the improper or empirical sense as composed
of believers among whom unbelievers are mingled is fundamental. The Church is essentially of a spiritual nature, and is
a fellowship of faith, though it has outward marks in the Word

and the Sacraments.[3] Unbelieving and impenitent persons, though nominally members of the Church, are not actually members. The Church is composed of those persons who have been spiritually regenerated; and it is that regeneration, and not external organizations, rites or ceremonies, which marks the members of the actual Church. The Church is the living body of Christ.[4] This conception of the Church as a spiritual fellowship stands in opposition to the Roman Catholic teaching that the Church is the external Roman hierarchical organization.[5]

The Terms Visible and Invisible. The use of the terms "visible Church" and "invisible Church" has become established in Protestant circles. By the latter of these terms is meant the actual Church which is composed of true believers in Christ. By the former is meant the Church as it appears on earth as an

---

[3] Apology, 162, 5.   [4] *Ibid.,* 162 seq.

[5] The Roman Catholic teaching concerning the Church is, that it is the visible communion of all Christians under the pope as the vicar of Christ. Only Roman Catholics are members of it. The pope is by divine right the successor of St. Peter. Matt. 16:18 refers to Peter and his primacy. Bishops are the successors of the apostles, with apostolic authority. Ordination confers a *character indelibilis,* and makes the priests members of a privileged order. Priests offer a real sacrifice in the Mass, and are mediators between God and men. Since 1870 the pope, according to the decree of the Vatican Council, is declared to be infallible when he speaks *ex cathedra.* The way to obtain salvation is to be obedient to the laws and regulations of the Church, that is, of the hierarchy. The doctrine of the Church is thus the regulative doctrine of Rome.

In opposition to the pope's claim of the primacy Hollazius (1293-7; Schmid, 602) presents the following: " 1. Neither from necessity nor from Christ's free will and appointment are we to recognize in addition to Christ any other head of the Church who in Christ's stead visibly governs the Church universal. 2. Christ never appointed the apostle Peter the general head of His Church, neither did He grant to him primacy of power and jurisdiction over the Catholic Church. 3. The pope of Rome is neither the successor of Peter in the episcopate nor the head and monarch of the Catholic Church. The meaning of Matt. 16:18 is, "Thou art Peter, a man made of rock, standing upon thy confession just as upon a rock or most firm *petra,* and upon this rock I will build my Church, so that it may be made of rock, immovable and impregnable as long as it will stand upon this confession of doctrine, as upon an immovable rock. Christ gave the keys to Peter, not as a prince, but as a minister and steward. Now, not only Peter but the rest of the apostles were appointed stewards by Christ (1 Cor. 4:1). Therefore the keys here promised to Peter were likewise given to the rest of the apostles."

assembly in which unbelievers are mingled with believers. The terms are likely to remain in use. But they are not accurate; for there are not two Churches, one visible and the other invisible; and the terms refer to two aspects of the same entity, one to its inner reality, and the other to its empirical manifestation upon earth.[6] The so-called invisible Church is not really invisible, since the persons who compose it have bodies and are seen, and the place where the Church is can be known from the presence of the Word and Sacraments.

Its Founding. While in Old Testament times there were those who believed the promise of coming redemption and were counted as God's people, and they are sometimes spoken of as the Old Testament Church, the Church as we now understand the term came into existence on the day of Pentecost. The Church exists where the Word is rightly preached and the Sacraments are rightly administered; and it was not till the day of Pentecost, when the Holy Spirit was poured out on the apostles, that the first Gospel sermon concerning the crucified and risen Savior was preached and the first Christian baptisms were administered. The Church was actually founded, therefore, on the day of Pentecost.

Its Members. The Church, which in its essence consists of the fellowship of believers, includes all those persons and only those persons who from the heart believe in Jesus Christ as their personal Savior. No matter where those persons live, or what may be their race, color, sex, age or rank, or to what particular external organization of professed believers they may belong, if they are true believers they belong to Christ's Church. On the other hand, no matter to what external organization of professed believers they may belong, and no matter in what external activities ostensibly in Christ's cause they may engage, if

---

[6] The Reformed Church, which lacks the Lutheran conception of the Means of Grace as the bond of unity between the "visible" and the "invisible" Church, regards the visible and the invisible Church as practically two entities.

they are not humble, contrite believers in Christ as their
Savior, they are not recognized by Christ as His and do not
belong to His Church (Matt. 7:21-23).

Membership in the Church means the spiritual fellowship of
faith—spiritual union with Christ and through Him with all
fellow believers. Christ is the Head and the Church is His Body
(Eph. 1:22). He is the vine and the believers are the branches
(John 15:6). The Christians are those who are in Him. As the
body has many members, each with its own office, so the Church,
the Body of Christ, has many members, each with his own
office (Eph. 4:4; 1 Cor. 12:12 seq.; Rom. 12:4). But all are
united in Christ the Head (Col. 1:18; Eph. 2:13) and form a
holy temple in the Lord (Eph. 2:21). They are the temple of
God, and God dwells in them (1 Cor. 3:16). They are a
chosen generation, a royal priesthood, a peculiar people (1 Pet.
2:8) ; and the bride of Christ (2 Cor. 11:2; Eph. 5:23).

The Church and the Kingdom of God. As the fellowship of
believers the Church is identical with the kingdom of God on
earth. That kingdom existed in the Old Testament times in a
provisional form which pointed toward its full establishment
by Christ, and comprised all those persons who believed the
promise of coming redemption. With the coming of Christ
that Kingdom was at hand, and with His death and resurrection
it was established. It is a kingdom of grace in which Christ is
the King, and in which those who believe in Him are the subjects. It is not an outward visible kingdom of this world, but is
a kingdom in the heart. It is established there and Christ's reign
begins there, when He is accepted as Savior and Lord.

For entrance into that kingdom there is necessary on man's
part an entirely new attitude toward God and the things of
God, which is variously termed a change of mind, a conversion,
and a new birth or regeneration. Its members must be humble, and the humblest in it are the greatest (Mark 9:34; Luke

9:46). As subjects they must be obedient and not only say Lord, Lord, but do His will (Matt. 7:21; Luke 6:46; 13:25 seq.). In its various aspects the Kingdom is described in such parables as that of the Sower, the Mustard Seed, the Leaven, the Treasure Hid in a Field, the Pearl of Great Price, the Lost Sheep, the Lost Coin, the Lost or Prodigal Son, the Great Supper, the Wedding of the King's Son, the Ten Virgins, the Pounds, the Talents, the Net, the Wheat and the Tares. If the Church is regarded only from the standpoint of its existence in this world, then the idea of the Kingdom is more comprehensive than that of the Church; but if the Church is regarded as including the believers both on earth and in heaven, then the Church and the Kingdom of God are practically identical as the communion of saints or the fellowship of believers. In the world to come the Church becomes the Church Triumphant, and the Kingdom becomes the Kingdom of Glory.

Militant and Triumphant. When considered in its entire scope as existing through all time and all eternity, the Church is composed of those believers who are still alive on earth and of those who have gone to their eternal reward in heaven. On earth it is called the Church Militant, because it is here composed of those who are still fighting the good fight of faith. In heaven it is called the Church Triumphant, because it is composed of those who have gained the victory. It is essentially the same Church on earth and in heaven, and is one Body with one Head. The entrance into the Church Triumphant is through the Church Militant. The congregation of the saints in heaven is composed of those who have been saints or believers on earth. Here on earth the believers are in a state of imperfect sanctification; there they are transformed and glorified into the likeness of Christ their Savior.

Attributes of the Church. The attributes ascribed to the

Church are Unity, Holiness, Catholicity, Apostolicity, and Perpetuity. They are ascribed to the Church in the proper sense of the term as the communion of saints or the fellowship of believers, but not to the Church in the improper or empirical sense as an external assembly composed of both believers and unbelievers.

Unity. The Church is one in the sense of being a unit, and also in the sense of being only one.[7] Though its members live in all parts of the world, speak many different languages, and have many divergent customs, they are all united in one Body of which Christ is the Head, and are one living unitary spiritual organism. Though outwardly the Church is divided and split into many different churches, denominations and sects, there is only one Church of Christ, and it is composed of the true believers in all the various Christian assemblies and congregations. There are many different folds, but only one flock and one Shepherd (John 10:16. R.V.). Outwardly they are separated by distance, by forms of organization, and even by divergence in doctrines. But they are all spiritually bound to Christ and to one another by a common faith in Him as their Savior. The Church comprises all those who are Christians at heart, and includes all adults who have been baptized and believe and all baptized infants.

Holiness. The Church is holy because it is composed of all those persons in whom the Holy Spirit has wrought His gracious and holy effects, and in whom He continues to work. Its members are by no means perfect and sinless in this world (1 John 1:8, 9). They are subject to many temptations, hampered by much weakness, and fall far short of the ideal of holiness which they have set before themselves in the law of God and in the example of Christ. But they are striving to reach the ideal, and

[7] *Unus et unicus.*

are daily, though often very slowly, growing in holiness of heart and life.[8]

Catholicity. The Church is Catholic or Universal. It includes all true believers everywhere, and is meant to include all men. It is subject to no limitations of time, space, race, tribe or language. The Jewish religion was national, and many heathen religions are national also. But the Church is catholic and includes all nations. It comprises one universal spiritual fellowship of all the believers belonging to particular churches, assemblies or communities at different times and in different lands. The Catholic Epistles of the New Testament are so called because they are addressed to all Christian believers everywhere.[9]

Apostolicity. The Church is apostolic because it rests upon and proclaims the revelation of God in Christ which was proclaimed by the apostles. The term is not to be understood as an apostolic succession of office, including the primacy of Peter, as Rome claims. The apostolicity of the Church is an apostolicity of teaching or doctrine.

Perpetuity. The Church will endure perpetually through all the ages of this world and to all eternity. Until the end of time there will remain on the earth those who truly believe in Christ and testify for Him. Many individuals will fall away from the faith, particularly in the last times; and churches once prosperous in certain parts of the world, as for example those of North Africa, may disappear. But the Church as such will abide

---

[8] Because this holiness seemed to be contradicted by the actual moral condition in the external Church, the Montanists, the Novatians and the Donatists sought to bring about this holiness by discipline. This necessitated a distinction between the real and the professed members of the Church.

[9] The terms Roman Catholic and Greek Catholic as designations of a particular part of the Church contain a contradiction. For a Church cannot be Roman or Greek and at the same time be universal. On the other hand, when the members of those Churches simply call themselves Catholic, they are seeking to monopolize a name which belongs to the Church as a whole.

to the end of the world. The gates of hell shall not prevail against it (Matt. 16:18). It shall not be destroyed by persecution or error. Its course in history has been undulating, with alternate periods of prosperity and adversity. But the truth has never lacked and never will lack confessors. False philosophies may assail the Church, rationalistic critics may seek to undermine her, and waves of worldliness may threaten to engulf her. But she shall endure because Christ says, "Lo, I am with you always, even unto the end of the world" (Matt. 28:20).

The Church and Salvation. Membership in the Church is necessary to salvation; and if the membership be enduring, it gives certainty of salvation. For to be a member of the Church means to be a believer in Christ; and to believe in Christ means to be saved. The membership here referred to is not that of an outward organization but of the spiritual fellowship of believers. The statement that outside of the Church there is no salvation [10] is true when the reference is to the Church in the proper sense as the communion of saints. But it is not true that there is no salvation outside of some one particular Church or denomination.

The Marks of the Church. As the Augsburg Confession declares,[11] "the Church is the congregation of saints in which the Gospel is rightly taught and the sacraments are rightly administered." The marks of the Church are thus the pure preaching of the Gospel and the right administration of the Sacraments. Where these are found, there is the Church. It is not necessary that there shall be found there certain human rites, traditions or ceremonies. These are *adiaphora.* "To the true unity of the Church it is sufficient to agree concerning the doctrine of the Gospel and the administration of the Sacraments." [12]

---

[10] *Extra ecclesiam nulla salus.* The Roman Catholic Church interprets this maxim to mean that there is no salvation outside the Church of Rome.
[11] Art. VII.   [12] *Ibid.*

By the pure preaching of the Gospel as a mark of the Church is meant a preaching by which persons can be and are led to faith in Christ as their Savior, and thus become members of the fellowship of believers. Errors which subvert the foundations of the Christian religion and prevent the hearer from coming to true and saving faith in Christ mark an assembly as not being part of the Church. In deciding concerning the purity of the Gospel proclaimed in any particular branch of the Church, judgment is to be made not simply according to the preaching of an individual here and there, but according to the official doctrinal position of the body. The degree of purity with which the Gospel is preached in various Churches varies from the clear and full proclamation of the whole counsel of God, on the one hand, to a proclamation so honeycombed with error, on the other, that only by the narrowest margin can the hearer obtain enough of the true Gospel to be brought to faith and be saved.

By the right administration of the sacraments is meant their administration in accordance with their institution. This has reference, not to possible variations in the formulas used or to additional rites and ceremonies added or omitted in the administration, but to the observance of the essentials of the sacrament in its consecration and administration.

The truth or falsity of a Church is to be judged solely by the marks mentioned above. In condemning other Churches on the basis of those marks, it is to be borne in mind that the condemnation is not aimed at the persons belonging to those Churches, but at the false doctrines which are set forth and proclaimed.

A Church is as old as its doctrines. If it sets forth the same doctrines which were preached by the apostles, then, no matter when a name by which it is now known may have first been employed to designate it, it is the ancient apostolic Church of

Christ. For the true Church is found wherever the Gospel is purely preached and the sacraments are rightly administered.[13]

Organization. Believers band themselves together in local congregations for the administration of the Means of Grace, for common worship, common strengthening of their faith, a common testimony before men, and common efforts for the extension of the Church's work. These local congregations are then banded together in larger organizations. The form which these organizations are to take and the mode of Church government are not prescribed in the New Testament, but are left to the judgment of the Church itself.

In these local congregations, and hence in the larger organizations also, there are always, as we have already seen, some persons who are true believers, and some who are not. It will always be so. It is the Lord's will that no violent effort be made to eliminate from the congregation all who are not believers at heart, but are only professed believers. The wheat and the tares are to be left to grow together till the harvest, which is the end of the world, when they will be separated and each be sent to the proper eternal destiny.

It is the duty of the Church to have that form of government which will best lend itself to the accomplishment of the purposes for which the Church exists. Rejecting the "apostolical succession of bishops" as lacking all Scriptural basis, and recognizing the identity of the office of bishop and presbyter in the New Testament (Tit. 1:5, 7), the Lutheran Church does not

[13] The fifteen marks of the true Church given by Rome are, according to Hollazius (p. 1311, VI, the following: 1. The Name Catholic. 2. Antiquity. 3. Long Duration. 4. Largeness, or Multitude of Believers. 5. Succession of Bishops in the Roman Church, from the Apostles down. 6. Agreement in Doctrine with the Ancient Church. 7. Union of the Members with one another and with the Head, namely, with the Roman Pope. 8. Holiness of Doctrine. 9. Efficacy of Doctrine. 10. Holiness of the Life of the Early Fathers of the True Religion. 11. The Glory of Miracles. 12. Prophetic Light. 13 Confession of Adversaries 14. Unhappy End of Enemies. 15. Temporal Happiness of those who defended the Church. But without the true doctrine these marks do not count.

regard the episcopal form of government as essential, though acknowledging it as a possible form. Luther and the other reformers would have kept the bishops, if these had sanctioned the preaching of the pure Gospel. When they refused to do so, the princes took the place of the bishops in the oversight of the Church in their dominions. This was followed by the consistorial form of government. On account of the union of Church and State in Europe the Church there never attained that full measure of self-government which it has attained in America.

In this country the Church, unhampered by any union with the state, was able to apply without hindrance the principles of Church government which she believed to be most evangelical and best adapted to the circumstances in which she found herself. At the basis of her organization lies the local congregation, consisting of pastor and laity, which potentially possesses all the rights and duties committed to and enjoined upon the Church. The pastor, chosen by the congregation, is the person charged both with the official administration of the Means of Grace and with the spiritual leadership in the congregation. All the local affairs of the congregation are administered under his leadership. A Church Council consisting of a definite number of deacons [14] is elected to assist the pastor in the direction of the affairs of the congregation.

Synods and General Bodies. For the doing of the work of the Church which lies beyond the local sphere, the congregations are united in synods. The work of education, missions, mercy and other general activities of the Church cannot be performed by individual congregations acting separately, but is performed by the congregations acting together in a synodical

---

[14] The number varies according to the constitutional provisions. Properly the Church Council consists of the pastor and the deacons. The so-called elders in some congregations are only deacons under another name, and it is better to drop the other name. So, too, it is better to have the whole church council constitutionally designated as the Board of Trustees than to elect special officers to be the trustees.

organization. The synod derives its powers from the congregations which have united to constitute it, on the principle that the government derives all its just powers from the governed. It lawfully possesses and should exercise those powers and those only which the congregations have expressly delegated to it. But within the limits of the synodical constitution to which it has agreed, the congregation must regard itself as bound by the decisions of synod. While the synod ought naturally to be in a better position to decide doctrinal questions than the individual congregation, because it represents a number of congregations, the congregation nevertheless retains the right to judge whether the actions of synod are in harmony with the Scriptures and with the confessions of the Church.

When the synods unite in a larger general body, the same fundamental principles which obtain in the relation of the congregation to the synod obtain also in the relation of the synod to the larger body. The synod delegates certain of its rights and the performance of certain of its duties to the larger body. This larger body lawfully possesses and should exercise those powers and those only which the synods have delegated to it in the constitution to which they have agreed. And while in doctrinal matters the larger body ought naturally to be in a better position to speak for the Church than the synod, the synod nevertheless retains its right to judge whether the actions of the general body are in harmony with the Scriptures and with the confessions of the Church. In so far as the decisions of general bodies concern purely practical matters and pertain to those things which have been delegated to them by the synods, and in so far as the doctrinal decisions conform to the Scriptures and the confessions, their decisions are to be accepted by the synods. In general the way of safety and prosperity for the Church lies in a happy medium between a highly centralized form of government on the one hand, and a loose form on the other. It is of the utmost importance for the peace and the prosperity of the Church that the rights of the general bodies, of the synods, and of the congregations be clearly distinguished and observed.

Church Discipline. The proper exercise of Church discipline is necessary for the purity of the Church in doctrine and life. She must see to it that her pastors preach the pure Gospel, that the Word is taught in its purity in her schools, and that pastors and laity lead Christian lives.

The fact that the pastor is the head of the congregation and is charged with the administration of the Word and Sacraments and with the giving of an example of Christian living puts the minister in a class by himself as regards the matter of discipline. He has responsibilities which, if not properly met, expose him to discipline from which as a layman he would be free. A pastor may be disciplined by a synod for preaching false doctrine or for conduct unbecoming a minister of the Gospel. The penalties are reproof and admonition, or suspension from office, or deposition from it. Before charges of any kind against a minister should be entertained, they should be substantiated by at least two or three reliable witnesses. The minister is entitled to a fair trial, with every reasonable opportunity for defense. The penalty, if he is found guilty, is to be inflicted by the president of the synod as its executive officer.

In addition to this discipline which is exercised by the synod in the case of a minister, and which has to do particularly with the matter of the official administration of the Word and Sacraments, there is committed to the Church and exercised by the congregation the Power of the Keys (Matt. 18:15-18). It is the power of binding and loosing, or of retaining or forgiving sins. This power must, of course, be exercised only in accordance with Christ's will. The forgiveness of sins is contingent upon repentance, and the retention of sins upon impenitence. If the binding and loosing be wrongly exercised, it is not valid before God; but if it is exercised in accordance with His directions, what is bound or loosed on earth is bound or loosed in heaven.

In a general way this power of the keys is exercised by the Church through the pastor in the Public Confession and Absolution. In a more direct way it is exercised in Private Absolution. In its disciplinary form, the exercise of this power involves the penalty of admonition and reproof to gross offenders against Christian morality, and, in case of persistence in the offense, of exclusion from the Lord's Supper for a time or of excommunication from the Church. The extreme form of the penalty must never be inflicted upon any but gross, persistent and incorrigible offenders.

The course of procedure is outlined by Christ, and involves three steps (Matt. 18:15-18): *first,* private admonition and reproof; *secondly,* admonition and reproof in the presence of one or two witnesses; and *thirdly,* the summoning of the offender before the congregation, and the establishment in proper form of his guilt or innocence. If the accused is found guilty, the penalty is to be pronounced by the pastor in the name of the congregation. The object of this procedure is, first of all, "to gain the brother," as Christ expressly says; and secondly, to maintain order and discipline in the Church, and to testify against error and sin.

A distinction must be made between those offenses which are more or less private and unknown to the public and those which are public and flagrant. Christ evidently refers in his directions to offenses which are more or less private. In the case of one whose offense has become a public scandal, the first two steps of the procedure which He outlines seem to be uncalled for. But even in many of those cases in which the offense has become publicly known, a private interview with the offender by a member of the Church and especially by the pastor may do much to save the individual and to shield the Church. In all cases it must be borne in mind that the salvation of a soul is at stake, and that what is spoken in the way of admonition and reproof must be spoken in love. The reproof is meant chiefly for the good of the offender. The excommunication is chiefly meant for the preservation of the good name of the Church. Yet even in the case of excommunication the penalty is inflicted in the hope that the offender may come to repentance and be reinstated.

The Church's Work. The task which the Lord has laid upon the Church is that of evangelizing the world. For the accomplishment of this purpose she has been entrusted with the preaching of the Word and the administration of the Sacraments. The Word and Sacraments are, indeed, the Means of Grace through which the Holy Spirit, and not the Church, regenerates and sanctifies the sinner. But the Holy Spirit uses the Church as His human agency in administering the means through which He works. According to God's own appointment, therefore, the evangelization of the world is hastened or retarded according as the Church is earnest and devoted or not in the fulfillment of the task which Christ has given her to do. The magnitude of her task is stupendous, and means the organizing and maintaining of much ecclesiastical machinery in the field of education, missionary operations and merciful ministrations. But it is a work which Christ has given her to do, and she dare not shirk it. It is her business to do all that lies in her power to hasten the time "when at the name of Jesus every knee shall bow of things in heaven and things in earth, and things under the earth," and when "every tongue shall confess that Jesus Christ is Lord, to the glory of God the Father" (Phil. 2:10, 11).

CHAPTER XXXII

THE MINISTRY

THE Ministry is the office through which the Church administers the Word and Sacraments, which Christ has committed to her for the evangelization of the world.

Its Necessity. While the evangelization of the world is a work laid upon the whole Church, it is not intended by the Lord that every Christian shall be an actual preacher of the Gospel. The gift of the Word and Sacraments carries with it the divine will for their proper administration. The New Testament shows that while ordinary members of the Church sometimes preached the Gospel (Acts 8:4; 11:19), and the deacons Stephen and Philip were active in preaching the Word (Acts 6:9 seq.; 8:5 seq.), the office of the ministry of the Word was one which was regarded as specifically placed in the hands of certain individuals (Acts 6:4). These individuals were first of all the apostles (Matt. 10; Luke 6:12 seq.; Acts 2:14). But while the ministry of the Word was included in the apostleship, the office of a minister of the Word was never identical with the office of an apostle. The work assigned to the apostles was larger and more comprehensive than simply preaching the Word. They were to lay the foundation of the Church through their personal testimony concerning Christ as eyewitnesses of His life, death and resurrection (Matt. 16:18; John 15:27; Acts 1:22). They were, therefore, during a period of three years, specially trained and prepared for the work by Christ, and endowed with the gift of the Holy Ghost on Pentecost.

They were personal witnesses of the facts of the Gospel which they proclaimed; they possessed an inspired knowledge of the Gospel truth; they promulgated the basic and normative teaching concerning Christ; they performed miracles in proof of their divine commission; and their parish was the world. They had and could have no successors in the apostolic office, because no other persons had or could have the same qualifications.

But while there could be no addition to the apostolate, it is manifest that the apostles needed and received the help of others in the preaching of the Word and the guidance of the Church. Paul was accompanied and assisted on his missionary journeys by Timothy, Titus, Barnabas, John, Mark, Silas and others. And when he himself removed from a certain place, men were appointed to continue the work. Lists of the offices which sprang up in the Church for the furtherance of the cause of the Gospel are given by St. Paul (1 Cor. 12:28; Eph. 4:11); and these offices are declared by him to be the result of God's will. They had to do with all the varied work of the Church, preaching and teaching, evangelistic and pastoral work, works of mercy, government and the like. It is evident from Paul's letter to Timothy that the outstanding and most important offices came to be those of the bishop and the deacon (1 Tim. 3). The office of an elder or presbyter was identical with that of a bishop, only under another name.[1] These offices were filled, not by an immediate call from God, but through appointment by an apostle, or election by the congregation, or both.

No ecclesiastical constitution was framed by inspiration and handed down for the guidance of the Church in later years. The New Testament offices were the outgrowth of the peculiar circumstances and needs of those days. The Church has the right to add other offices from time to time, if the exigencies of the work demand it. But the fundamental office of the ministry

---

[1] In Tit. 1:5, 7 the names bishop and elder are applied to the same official.

of the Word and Sacraments must remain (Rom. 10:14, 15). The Means of Grace must be furnished with individuals specially set apart for their administration. As pastor of the congregation the minister of to-day engages in the activities of a number of offices, such as preacher, teacher, elder, evangelist, pastor, and head of the congregation, which seem to have been distinct in apostolic times, but which were all given "for the perfecting of the saints, for the work of the ministry, for the edifying of the body of Christ" (Eph. 4:12).

Nature of the Ministry. The ministry, as already pointed out, is not identical with the apostolate, but is the office of the Word and Sacraments. The parish of the minister is not the world, as it was for the apostles, but a certain definite and circumscribed field of labor to which he is called.

The ministry is not an order into which the selected individual is admitted and in which he is endowed with certain prerogatives not enjoyed by other Christians. As a man and a Christian he remains on a par with his fellow believers, and has no preëminence or special privileges. He is not a lord over God's heritage, but a servant of Christ, and for His sake a servant of all. But by virtue of his office he wields certain powers, bears certain responsibilities, and is entitled to a certain respect and honor. He is an ambassador for Christ, through whom God beseeches men and who prays men in Christ's stead to be reconciled to God (1 Cor. 5:20). In the services in God's house he is alternately the representative of God declaring His will to the people, and the spokesman of the congregation in offering up thanksgiving, petitions and intercessions. In the latter case he is included in the congregation, and speaks in behalf of all.[2]

---

[2] In liturgical language, the part of the service in which the minister declares God's will is called the sacramental, and the other part is called the sacrificial element in worship. Where high liturgical forms prevail, the pastor faces the congregation in the former case, and the altar in the latter.

The ministry is not a priesthood. The only priesthoods remaining in the New Testament are the high priesthood of Christ and the spiritual priesthood of all believers (1 Pet. 2:5, 9). The latter is shared by the minister with all his fellow Christians. He offers no sacrifices to God except the sacrifices of praise and thanksgiving, and these he offers in common with the congregation.[3]

The ministry is an office in the Church, intrusted to certain individuals who have been specially prepared and trained for it, and who have been solemnly set apart for its duties. It is often called, and very suitably, the office of the Word and Sacraments. But there belongs to it also the Office of the Keys.

The ministry is an office given with the Word and Sacraments and indispensable for their proper and efficient administration. Though the obligation to employ the Means of Grace for the evangelization of the world rests on the whole Church, the obligation and the right to administer them does not belong to each individual as such, but to the congregation as a whole. The calling of a pastor is, therefore, not an agreement among the members of a congregation to transfer to one individual the personal rights inherent in each member to administer the Means of Grace, but the appointment of a person to fill an office which belongs to the whole congregation of believers.[4]

Since, as we have seen, the office of bishop and presbyter is identical in the New Testament, there is no episcopate existing by divine right,[5] and no apostolic succession of bishops. The adoption of an episcopal or non-episcopal form of government is entirely a matter of expediency; and where the Church pos-

[3] In the Roman Catholic Church the minister is regarded as an actual priest who offers a real sacrifice to God in the Mass.

[4] The United States possesses the office of president, and each citizen has a right to vote for an incumbent for that office. But each voter is not really a president who transfers his office to one particular person to administer for him.

[5] De jure divino.

sesses the episcopate, it does so by human right,[6] and not by divine command.

The Call. The ministry is an office to which men must be called, and which they must not otherwise undertake to exercise.[7] Being an office in which the incumbent is God's representative and spokesman, it must be filled in accordance with the divine will. In the past this will has sometimes been expressed directly to the individual, as in the case of Moses, the prophets and the apostles. The call which came thus directly from God was an immediate one.[8] The call which comes through the Church, and which is now the only kind that is given, is a mediate call.

There is no inner call to the ministry, but only the external call of the Church. There is, however, an inner conviction of the individual that he ought to become a minister, which is wrought by the Holy Ghost through the Word and which is sometimes spoken of as an inner call. But this is a mistaken use of the word "call," and is calculated to lead to confusion. An inner call in the true sense of the word would have to be an immediate one; and no immediate calls are any longer given. Men have sometimes imagined that they had an "inner call" when it was painfully evident to every one else that they had neither the requisite natural gifts nor the proper training for the office.

It is the duty of the Church carefully to select and train men for the holy office of the ministry, and she should not set men apart for it without due consideration of their physical, mental and spiritual qualifications. She is to lay hands suddenly on no

[6] *De jure humano.* Forms of government are *adiaphora.* Thus, the Lutheran Church has bishops in Sweden, but none in America.

[7] Augs. Conf. XIV, "No man should publicly in the Church teach or administer the sacraments except he be rightly called."

[8] Aaron was called through Moses by divine direction. This was really a variation of the immediate call, and needs no separate classification.

man (1 Tim. 5:22), but is to see to it that only those are admitted to the office who have the requisite natural gifts, common sense, and Christian faith and piety; and who have received the necessary academic and theological training. Ordinarily this training ought to include a full course in college or university and in a theological seminary. Few exceptions, and those only for the best of reasons, should be made. The demand for quality in the ministry to-day is very great. The Lord not only needs men for the ministry, but He needs gifted and well-trained men.

The man who sets out to prepare for the Gospel ministry should have an inner conviction that the Lord needs and desires him for the work, and a determination to give his life and strength to it. This conviction and determination may be simply the result of his own reflection and prayers. Perhaps the desire of parents and the influence of pastors, teachers and others may have had a share in shaping his decision. Special providential dispensations may have turned his mind to the ministry.

Ordination. The congregation elects, but the synod approves or disapproves of the chosen individual as a proper man for the Christian ministry. He is subjected to a careful examination as to his mental and spiritual fitness for the work, and if approved he is ordained. This ordination is usually performed by the clerical officers of synod, but may be performed by any minister or ministers authorized by the synod.

Ordination is not a sacrament, and conveys no special gift through the laying on of hands. It is a rite or ceremony in which the Church sets its approval upon the man as fitted for the office to which he has been called, and solemnly sets him apart for it, praying that God may give him the grace and strength needed to perform his work faithfully and well. The spiritual benefit comes in answer to the prayer, and not as a result of the laying on of hands.

The installation takes place when the chosen pastor takes charge of his parish, or soon after. Since ordination is not admission into an order, but a certification that the individual has been properly called to a definite work, usually in a parish, there is in essence not a very great deal of difference between ordination and installation. There is bound to be much similarity in the formulas used. The difference in the effect of the two acts may, however, be described in this way, that ordination certifies to the Church and the State that the individual is duly authorized to preach, administer the sacraments, and perform other ministerial acts, including marriage, which has a legal as well as an ecclesiastical side; while installation, on the other hand, certifies to the members of a definite parish that this particular person is their duly elected and authorized pastor, who now formally accepts the weighty obligation of caring for their spiritual wants, and to whom, therefore, they owe all honor, respect and obedience in the Lord.

Important as ordination and installation are as a matter of Christian order, it is conceivable that, in emergencies, when no minister can be secured to perform the ordination and installation, a man who has been properly called as pastor by a congregation or congregations might assume charge without ordination, and perform all ministerial acts except marriage,[9] or that he might be ordained by laymen appointed by the congregation. It is the call, and not the ordination, which makes the man a minister in the sight of God.

Since the call really makes a man a minister, it is not proper to ordain a man who has not received a regular call to some definite work. To ordain without a call carries with it the notion that the ministry is an order into which the individual is admitted. Since, however, synods and other general bodies

[9] On account of its legal side the marriage ceremony dare be performed only by one who has been properly empowered by the state to do so.

are the Church in a collective and representative capacity, they have a right to call, as well as congregations. But it must be a call to a definite work, and not a call to go forth and preach anywhere in general and nowhere in particular.

Whether a man should be reordained when he comes from another communion and desires to serve in our Church is a question of expediency, whose answer depends to a large extent on the nature of the Church from which he comes. If it is a Church which is sound on the great fundamental doctrines of Scripture, a confession of the Lutheran faith on those doctrines on which the other Church differs from us would seem to be sufficient without reordination. But if it is a Church which repudiates doctrines fundamental to salvation, or one which like the Roman Catholic differs radically in its whole view of Christianity, it is better to reordain on the strength of a call from some Lutheran parish.

The administration of the Word and sacraments must not be undertaken without a regular call.[10] Teachers in Sunday school and other schools of the Church are to be regarded as the pastor's assistants in the instruction of the young. While a layman may and should privately make known and teach the Word among his friends and acquaintances, he should not ordinarily preach or administer the sacraments. Baptism in case of emergency is an exception. Preaching by a theological student or other layman in response to an invitation from a congregation or from an administrative officer of synod is not to be regarded as preaching without a call, but as preaching in response to a call for special service.

Sphere of Work. The minister's sphere of work is found in the particular field to which he has been called. That is the place where he is to administer the Word and sacraments. This does not mean that he may not, in response to special calls,

---

[10] Augs. Conf. Art. XIV.

administer the Means of Grace anywhere else, but that his own field and not the world is his parish. His work is among the people to whom God has called him to minister, and includes first of all the members who belong to his congregation or congregations. But it also includes an obligation to the community which his parish may reasonably be supposed to cover. To confine his work to the routine administration of Word and sacraments among the members of his flock is to fail to realize the breadth of his mission and the greatness of his opportunity and responsibility. Christ wills that the world shall be evangelized; and the world includes the indifferent, impenitent, unbelieving and hostile at home as well as the heathen in darkest Africa. Christ's command is to go into the highways and hedges and compel them to come in. The adult catechetical class should be a standing institution in every parish, and constant efforts should be made to persuade those outside of the Church to attend. The pastor's efforts should be directed to meeting the needs of his own people and of the unchurched, and not to proselyting from other Churches.

Administering Word and Sacraments. The chief duty of ministers is that of preaching the Word, and they are to preach it in season and out of season (2 Tim. 4:2). As ambassadors for Christ they are to beseech men to be reconciled to God, and are to be instruments in the hands of the Holy Spirit for the conversion and sanctification of souls. While it is not human learning, skill or eloquence that converts men, but the power of God, that power must come through the Word which the minister proclaims. If, therefore, his proclamation is weak, unclear, confused or unsound, how can the Holy Spirit through it convert and sanctify? It is the truth which converts and saves. But it will and can do this, not magically but by the pressure of the truth clearly, intelligibly and forcefully presented to the mind. The minister must seek, therefore, to be an efficient instrument of the Holy Ghost, and to present the truth soundly and intelligibly. He must rightly divide the Word of truth, presenting it according to the needs of the people, and particularly proclaiming Law and Gospel in due proportions. He must declare the whole counsel of God, withhold nothing, and add nothing. He must seek to convert the sinners and to edify the saints. At the basis of his preaching should lie a true psychology. He must aim to enlighten the intellect, move the feelings and persuade the will. If he aims only at enlightening the intellect, he delivers an essay, and not a sermon.

He must administer the sacraments in accordance with their institution, and do so in a proper spirit of reverence, and not in a perfunctory manner. He should emphasize the importance and meaning of the sacraments; urge upon parents the necessity of having their children baptized in early infancy; and set forth the importance and blessedness of participation in the Lord's Supper.

Demitting the Ministry. Since ordination does not confer an indelible character, and it need not be said that "once a minister always a minister," a man who has been ordained may under certain circumstances cease to be a minister. This is the case if he voluntarily demits the ministry and devotes himself to a secular pursuit. It is also the case, if the Church in the exercise of its disciplinary power deposes him from the office. But it is a mistake to suppose that a man has ceased to be a minister because he is temporarily without a parish, or is forced to retire from active service by age or ill-health, or accepts some more general office in the Church such as secretary or superintendent of missions and the like, or teaches theology. In all these cases he still has authority to administer the Word and Sacraments, and does so from time to time in answer to calls for temporary service. But on the other hand it is wrong for a man to give up the actual work of the ministry and devote himself to secular pursuits without giving up the name and title of minister.

Deacons and Deaconesses. The other offices which have come down to us in name and essential features from apostolic times are those of the deacon and the deaconess. Deacons were chosen in the early days of the apostolic Church, in order to relieve the apostles from the necessity of serving tables and to enable them to devote themselves more completely to the preaching of the Word (Acts 6). Essentially the same purpose is served by deacons now. They are chosen by the congregation to assist the pastor in every needful way and particularly to attend to the temporal affairs of the Church. They should be men of discretion and of sound Christian character. They should be duly and solemnly installed in office and be made acquainted with the duties and obligations which rest upon them.

The office of deaconess, which existed in the early Church, has in its modern form been developed into a helpful agency in the Church's work of mercy. To a large extent deaconesses have found a place in hospitals; but they have also proved themselves valuable assistants to the pastors in congregational work, when assigned to that task.

PART IV

THE LAST THINGS OR THE CONSUMMATION OF REDEMPTION

CHAPTER XXXIII

THE STATE AFTER DEATH

THE purposes of God with respect to men will not be completely accomplished in this world, but await the world to come. Eschatology, or the doctrine of The Last Things, deals with the final consummation of Christ's kingdom with respect to the individual, the Church and the world. It includes all those events which have to do with man's transition into eternity, the end of the present order of the world, and the condition of men in the world to come. The subjects to be treated under this head are: 1. The State after Death; 2. The Second Coming of Christ; 3. The Resurrection of the Body; 4. The Judgment and the End of the World; 5. Eternal Death; 6. Eternal Life.

Bodily Death. Temporal or bodily death puts an end to the earthly career of saint and sinner. It is the result of the fall into sin, and has passed upon all men, because all have sinned (Rom. 5:12). It is not a natural thing, but is part of that penalty of death which man incurred by his transgression, and which includes both spiritual and bodily death as a result of separation from God. Bodily death dissolves the intimate union between soul and body, and sends the soul forth into eternity, while the body disintegrates and returns to the earth from which it was taken. This death came upon men as a punishment, and is still to be regarded as such for the unbeliever. But it is not to be regarded as a punishment in the case of the believer, because the believer has been freely forgiven for Christ's sake, and there exists no punishment for him any more

389

(Rom. 8:1). It is in his case a means to a blessed end. It is the door through which he enters upon his eternal inheritance. It is also the method through which he receives, in the resurrection which follows, a new and glorified body fitted to be the eternal habitation of the regenerated and glorified soul. In place of the natural body which he had on earth, he will receive a spiritual body (1 Cor. 15:44). Those who are alive at the second coming of Christ will not undergo the bodily death; but their bodies will in a moment, in the twinkling of an eye, undergo the same change which the others have undergone through death and the resurrection (1 Cor. 15:51, 52). The full purpose of redemption will have been completely accomplished only when both soul and body have been regenerated and perfected, and when the believer, glorified both in body and soul, has entered upon his eternal inheritance.

The Immortality of the Soul. The soul is immortal. The belief in its immortality has been practically universal. The existence of God and of the immortality of the soul are innate beliefs of mankind. Man's consciousness that he is a person and is meant for communion with God gives him the hope if not the conviction that he will survive the death of the body and live beyond the grave. This natural belief is corroborated and confirmed by the certainty of faith based on the supernatural revelation of God. The Christian is certain that while death means separation from the body, it also means for him the transition to a glorified state with Christ in heaven (Phil. 1:23).

Numerous attempts have been made to establish philosophically the proof of the immortality of the soul. The Metaphysical proof argues that since death is the breaking up of existence into its constituent elements, the soul, which is immaterial, simple and indivisible, cannot die. The Teleological proof argues from the endless possibilities of development in the human spirit, that since this life neither satisfies its aspirations nor fully develops its powers and capacities, its life must extend beyond the grave. The Analogical proof argues that as there is no annihilation in nature and new life emerges from the death of the old, so the soul must be imperishable. The Moral proof argues that since virtue and vice by no means receive their just rewards in this world, there must follow another world in which there will be consistence between virtue and happiness. The Theological proof argues that a being constituted as man is for communion with God must be meant to partake of that communion beyond the grave. The Historical proof argues that a belief as universal as that in the immortality of the soul must be grounded in the very nature of man as a person, and must therefore be true. Where there is no religious conviction of any kind as a basis, these arguments may, however, fail to convince men.

The Teaching of Scripture. The immortality of the soul underlies all the teaching of Holy Scripture. On this point, however, as on others, divine revelation was progressive. The teaching of the Old Testament is not as clear and definite as that of the New. The dead depart into Sheol, which is not identical with the grave, but is the place of departed spirits. It is related to the heathen idea of Hades as the dwelling place of shadow-like but real souls. Sheol is a shadowy realm which stands in striking contrast to the activity of the present life (Ps. 6:5; 20:9; 88:11-13; 115:17; Job 10:21, 22). It is a place of darkness and of silence far from men and from the wondrous works of God. Back of this conception of Sheol, however, lies the certainty of life after death.[1] The dead are gathered to their fathers,[2] and this cannot refer to their graves, because their interment was in widely separated places. The

[1] See Ps. 17:15; 73:24; 111:15; Eccl. 11:9; 12:7; Hos. 13:14; Isa. 26:19; Dan. 12:12; Job 19:25 seq.
[2] See Gen. 15:15; 28:8; 35:29; 49:33; Numb. 20:24; 27:13; Deut. 32:50.

translations of Enoch and of Elijah imply personal continuance beyond this world.

In the New Testament the immortality of the soul is everywhere taken for granted. Men can kill the body, but they cannot kill the soul (Matt. 10:28). The gain of the whole world will not compensate for the loss of the soul (Luke 9:25). Christ declares that the God of Abraham, Isaac and Jacob is a God of the living and not of the dead, and that therefore those patriarchs are living (Matt. 22:32). Moses and Elijah are present at the transfiguration of Jesus (Luke 9:30). The Old Testament idea of Hades appears in the New Testament in a more developed form, with two divisions or compartments separated by a great gulf, one for the blessed and one for the lost (Luke 16:22 seq.). When Christ died His soul went to the part of Hades called paradise, and the repentant thief was with Him there (Luke 23:43). Lazarus was carried into Abraham's bosom, and the rich man awoke in hell (Luke 16:22, 23). Since Christ's resurrection the departed believers no longer enter Hades, but as perfected spirits enter into blessedness in heaven (Heb. 12:23) with Christ (2 Cor. 5:6, 8; Phil. 1:23), and enjoy eternal rest (Rev. 7:9). Believers on earth are at home in the body, but after death they are absent from the body and present with the Lord (2 Cor. 5:6-8). Their disembodied souls shall receive back their bodies at the resurrection (John 5:25; 6:40; 11:23 seq.); for the resurrection of Christ is a guarantee of their resurrection (1 Cor. 15:12). The nature of that resurrection is described at some length by St. Paul (1 Cor. 15:35 seq.).

Preliminary Judgment. At death the soul goes to its reward, as seen in the case of the rich man and Lazarus. God knows exactly the state of each heart, and passes preliminary judgment at death. The soul of the believer enters upon a state of happiness, and the soul of the unbeliever upon a state of misery.

These states are provisional, inasmuch as the souls are without their bodies, and the general judgment has not yet taken place. With the resurrection and the judgment, the respective states of the saved and of the lost will be fixed forever.

The intermediate states of happiness or misery are a matter of condition rather than of place. Souls are not limited to spacial relations. But the conditions of our earthly existence compel us to think in terms of space; and so we conceive of the departed spirits of the saved and of the lost as existing respectively in a place of happiness and a place of misery. Where this place is we have no means of knowing. The believers are with Christ; the unbelievers are excluded from His presence. There will be no opportunity for repentance on the part of those who have refused to repent here; for the day of salvation is now (2 Cor. 6:2; Heb. 9:27).

The psychological condition of the soul after death is to a large extent shrouded in a mystery which revelation has not chosen to remove. But there are certain facts which stand out as Scripture teaching or as reasonable deductions from it. It is the soul, the real self, the person, which passes into eternity at death. It is conscious. In this world it lived in the body; but in the intermediate state it lives without a body. In this world the body was the organ of speech as well as of all external actions. The disembodied souls are able to converse with one another without the use of the bodily organs of speech, as we see from the conversation of the rich man in hell with Abraham in Paradise. The mode of that speech must be analogous to that of the angels who are purely spiritual beings. The soul after death is in possession of all its faculties, and capable of supreme happiness or of utter misery. The departed will not revisit the earth nor hold communication with those who are still in the flesh (Luke 16:27 seq.). There is no reason to believe that in the intermediate state the souls have any knowledge of what is taking place on earth.

The Scripture teaching concerning the intermediate state is incompatible with such theories as the annihilation of the wicked, the unconscious slumber of the dead until the resurrection, the heathen theory of the transmigration of souls, and the Roman Catholic doctrine of a purgatory,[3] with which the practice of saying masses and offering prayers for the dead is connected.[4]

[3] The Roman Catholic Church teaches that there are five places to which departed spirits go: Heaven, Purgatory, Hell, the Limbus Infantum (for unbaptized children) and the Limbus Patrum (to which the patriarchs and other Old Testament saints were assigned, but which is vacant since the resurrection of Christ).

According to its teaching, "purgatory is a fire in which the souls of the pious by suffering for a definite period expiate their sins, so that entrance may be opened for them into the eternal home into which nothing unclean shall enter" (Cat. Rom. Part I, Art. V, 4). Through this fire they are to be finally purified from those sins for which they have not done adequate penance on earth. Connected with this doctrine is the practice of saying mass and offering prayers for the dead, so that their stay in purgatory may be shortened. The attempt is made to prove the existence of purgatory from such passages as 1 Cor. 3:11-15; Matt. 5:26; 12:32; Luke 12:10; 16:9; 1 John 5:16-17; Mal. 3:2, and the Apocryphal passage, Macc. 12:39-46. Not only does the doctrine of a purgatory have no basis in Scripture, but it is in conflict with the doctrine of salvation by faith alone and with that of the sufficiency of Christ's atoning merit. It implies that God has forgiven some sins, but not others, while in reality forgiveness is the forgiveness of the person, and is either complete or non-existent.

[4] Concerning the prayers for the dead Luther says, "We have no command from God to pray for the dead; hence it is no sin not to pray for them. For what God has not commanded nor forbidden is something with respect to which no man can sin. On the other hand, since God has not more clearly made known to us what the condition of the departed is . . . it is not a sin if you pray for them. But it must be in such a way that you leave it uncertain and speak on this wise: 'Lord, if the soul is in such a state that it can yet be helped, I pray Thee to be gracious to it.' And when you have done this once or twice, let it go at that, and commend them to God." Kirchenpostille, First Sunday after Trinity. St. Louis ed. p. 1206.

CHAPTER XXXIV

THE SECOND COMING OF CHRIST

WHEN the present age, or the dispensation of grace, has reached its close, Christ will come to earth a second time. He Himself clearly and unequivocally predicted His second advent. In contrast with His first coming, which was in all humility and lowliness, He will come the second time with power and great majesty. He shall be seen and recognized as the Lord by all. He will set up His judgment seat, and summon all the children of men before Him to judgment. The believers shall then enter into eternal glory, and the unbelievers shall be cast into outer darkness.

The Time. The exact time when Christ will come again is unknown to us. It is a coming which is constantly imminent, and the believers are warned against permitting themselves to become careless or indifferent in their spiritual life, lest the day come upon them unawares (Luke 21:34). It will come suddenly and unexpectedly like a flash of lightning, like a thief in the night, and like the flood in the days of Noah (Matt. 24:27-41). It is so vividly described as imminent that the apostles and the early Church expected it to take place in their day, and believers in every generation since then have realized that it may come at any moment. That the apostles did not know when Christ would come and expected Him to appear in their lifetime is not an evidence of the lack of inspiration on their part; for this is a point on which Christ said beforehand that they would remain ignorant. The time of His coming

395

would not be revealed to any man, and even the Son of Man according to His human nature knew not when it would be (Matt. 24:35; Mark 13:32; Luke 12:40, 46). The fact that He has been constantly expected throughout the centuries and has not yet come has caused many to mock at the prediction of His advent, just as some in the apostle's time mocked at it (2 Pet. 3:4). But a thousand years with God are as one day, and one day as a thousand years. The era of grace is prolonged, in order that men may have opportunity to repent and be saved (2 Pet. 3:9). As in the case of the first advent Christ came when the fullness of time had come, so in the second advent He will come when God's time is at hand.

Numerous attempts have been made, frequently on the basis of mathematical calculations from numbers mentioned in the Old Testament and in the book of Revelation, to set a date for Christ's appearance. But such predictions, as was to be expected, have always proved to be false. The time of His coming is meant to remain unknown, and will remain unknown until He actually appears. He will come unexpectedly, and not on any date set by men.

Signs. There are certain signs, mentioned in the Scriptures, which shall precede Christ's second coming. First, the Gospel of the kingdom shall be preached in all the world for a witness (Matt. 24:14). Only after this has been done shall the end come. *Secondly,* the Jews shall be converted to Christ (Rom. 11:25, 26). This does not necessarily mean that every individual Jew shall by that time have become a true Christian, but that the Jews as a whole shall have been turned from their unbelief to faith in Christ as the Messiah. A city or nation is said to be converted to Christianity, even though individuals belonging to it remain in impenitence and unbelief.[1] *Thirdly,* there shall be extraordinary events in human history. There

---

[1] This is the position of most of the Lutheran exegetes and dogmaticians, though a few, like Hunnius, Hafenreffer, Calixtus and others have taken an opposite view.

shall be wars and rumors of wars, a clashing of nations, pestilence and famine (Matt. 24:6, 7; Mark 13:8; Luke 21:9). The history of mankind shows at least a partial fulfillment of this sign in the many bloody wars since Christ's time, and notably in the Great World War. To-day men's hearts fail them for fear when, in view of modern instruments of destruction, they contemplate the possibility of further wars among the nations. *Fourthly,* there shall be extraordinary phenomena in nature; in the heavens above a darkening of the sun and of the moon and the departure of stars from their places, and on the earth beneath tidal waves, earthquakes, upheavals, and shifting of great spaces (Rev. 6:12 seq.)—all of which may or may not be explained by men on the basis of natural causes, but which are nevertheless among the signs which shall precede Christ's coming. *Fifthly,* the Church will be put to the severest tests in the last times. False prophets will arise and deceive many; fierce persecution of Christians will break out; there will be a great apostasy, and many will turn away from Christ. *Sixthly,* Antichrist, the man of sin, will be revealed. Even in the apostles' time there were many Antichrists (1 John 2:18); and there have been many Antichrists since their day. But there will come an individual in whom all the antichristian forces will center, the man of sin, the son of perdition, who will exalt himself above all that is called God, or that is worshiped, and will claim divine worship for himself (2 Thess. 2:1-11).[2]

[2] Various persons have from time to time been regarded by different persons as the Antichrist, on account of their opposition to the truth or their persecutions of the Christians. The members of the Ancient Church thought that Antichrist was revealed in Nero; the Middle Ages, in Mohammed; the sects of the Middle Ages and the early Protestants, in the pope (Cf. *Book of Concord,* 320, 10; 345, 39; 220, 18). While we can readily understand why the Reformers regarded the pope as the Antichrist, when we remember the bitterness with which the papacy withstood the truth of the Gospel which the Reformers proclaimed, the papacy does not present the marks of the final Antichrist. The Antichrist is declared to be a person, not an institution. He will deny that Christ is God, and the papacy acknowledges it. He will make himself God, while the pope is satisfied to call himself the vicar of Christ. Antichrist will lead men into a total denial of Christianity; but many of the adherents of the papacy are still Christians in spite of their many errors. Scripture teaches

Purpose. The second coming of Christ with the accompanying resurrection of the dead and the judgment will bring the great consummation of Christ's mediatorial work. He will come in order to gather His own unto Himself (1 Thess. 4:16, 17). He will come to deliver them from their sufferings and persecutions, and to give them their eternal inheritance (Matt. 25:34). This will necessarily include the rejection of the unbelieving, and hence the public judgment and condemnation of the wicked. Because of this purpose of His coming the believers are told to look up and take courage at the signs of His coming (Luke 21:28). He will come visibly and in majesty, and every eye shall behold Him; they also that pierced Him (Rev. 1:7). When He comes the unbelieving will be filled with fear and dismay, and will cry out to the mountains and the rocks to cover and hide them from the wrath of the Lamb (Rev. 6:16-17).

The End of the World. The second coming of the Lord will usher in the end of the world, the resurrection, and the final judgment. "He will come again to judge the quick and the dead." With His coming the era of grace will be past, the opportunity for repentance will be gone, and man's fate will be decided forever. The Scriptures know nothing of a twofold future coming of Christ, and the establishment of a reign of Christ on earth for a thousand years before the end of the world. The Augsburg Confession rejects Chiliasm or Premillennialism as a Jewish opinion.[3] The New Testament knows only the present age and the age to come—the temporal era of

that there will be an Antichrist; but it does not teach that this or that individual who has so far appeared in human history is he.

[3] Art. XVII. "They condemn others also who now scatter Jewish opinions, that before the resurrection of the dead the godly shall occupy the kingdom of the world, the wicked being everywhere suppressed." This was aimed particularly at the Anabaptists. Comp. Melanchthon's Var. Ed., "They condemn the Anabaptists who now scatter Jewish opinions." The old dogmaticians reject Chiliasm of every kind.

grace in which the Church is commanded to evangelize the
world through the Means of Grace committed to her, and the
eternal era inaugurated by the second coming of Christ, the
resurrection of the dead, the final judgment, the administration
of eternal rewards and punishments, and the passing away of
the old cosmic order to make way for new heavens and a new
earth wherein dwelleth righteousness.[4]

[4] Pre-millennialists are far from agreeing among themselves, and there are
many different kinds of pre-millennialism. In general it may be said that their
tenets include the following: Christ will come before His final coming to judgment, and will establish His kingdom visibly upon the earth. The conversion of
men will then proceed very rapidly. Satan will be bound during that period.
There will be a twofold resurrection: a first resurrection of the just at His
coming to establish His kingdom, and a final resurrection of all the dead at the
end of the world. The living Christians and those raised from the dead at the
first resurrection shall reign with Christ on earth for a thousand years. The
Jews shall be converted, and take a large place in the kingdom.
    This supposed reign of Christ on earth for a thousand years is based by the
Pre-millennialists on Rev. 20:1 seq., and on a number of other passages interpreted in the light of Rev. 20. But in thus interpreting Scripture they do not
follow the analogy of faith by interpreting the dark passages of Scripture in
the light of the clear passages. On the contrary, they take a dark and figurative
passage as the norm of interpretation.
    Against the pre-millennial position the following is to be urged. Christ
nowhere speaks of a millennium, nor does any passage of Scripture except Rev.
20 speak of a reign of a thousand years. Christ expressly declares that His
kingdom is not of this world (John 18:36; 6:16), and that it cometh not with
observation (Luke 17:20). The separation of the wheat and the tares shall
not take place at a preliminary coming of the Lord but at the harvest which
is the end of the world (Matt. 5:11, 12). The apostles regarded the end of
the world as near at hand, and give no hint of an intervening millennium (1 Pet.
4:7; 1 John 2:18). Pre-millennial theories look for the conversion of the world
through the visible appearance and reign of Christ on earth, while the Scriptures
teach that the world is to be converted by the Holy Spirit through the Means
of Grace which have been committed to the Church for that purpose.
    Were it not for the dark and highly figurative passage in Rev. 20 there
would quite certainly be no pre-millennialists. What then does that passage
mean? The thousand years ought not and certainly need not be taken literally
in so figurative a book as Revelation. The thousand years in which Christ and
His saints reign and in which Satan is bound may properly be taken as
standing for a long period of time. That period is the New Testament era of
the Gospel during which Satan is bound and can no longer deceive the
nations so freely as he did before the coming of the Gospel. The loosing of the
devil for a little while at the end of that period most probably refers to the
final effort of Satan through Antichrist to destroy Christ's kingdom. The passage does not teach a first and second *bodily* resurrection. It is not souls
reunited with bodies by a resurrection who reign with Christ, but simply souls
(Rev. 20:4). The passage in 1 Thess. 4:16, 17 which is often quoted in

support of a first and second bodily resurrection does not teach such a doctrine. "The dead in Christ shall rise first" does not mean that they shall rise before the unbelieving dead shall rise, but that they shall rise before those who are alive at Christ's coming shall be caught up with Him in the air. The purpose of the apostle is not to teach that there are two bodily resurrections, but to assure the Thessalonians that their friends who have died will rise from the dead and share with the living the joy of being caught up with Christ.

The *first* resurrection mentioned in Rev. 20:5, 6 is not the bodily resurrection, but the spiritual resurrection, the being raised from the death of sin (Eph. 2:6; Rom. 6:13). Those who are thus spiritually raised from the dead and pass into eternity are souls that reign with Christ during the Gospel era. The statement that the rest of the dead lived not till the thousand years were finished (v. 5) means that they lived not at all. Compare similar language in Matt. 5:26; 18:34; 2 Sam. 6:23. There is no mention in Rev. 20 of a second or bodily resurrection, and no mention of a first or bodily death. These are taken for granted. Those raised from the first death (that of sin) through spiritual regeneration are persons on whom the second death has no power (v. 6). The first resurrection evidently refers back to the *souls* mentioned in v. 4. If there were two future advents of Christ, then the second one ought to be mentioned in verse 9 after the devil has been loosed for a little while.

Summing up this interpretation of Rev. 20, which in essence was already given by Augustine (City of God, Book 20, Chs. 8 seq.), the passage means: 1. The term "a thousand years" in so figurative a book as Revelation is to be taken as representing a long period of time. 2. The thousand years in which Satan is bound are the Gospel era in which he cannot so unrestrictedly deceive the nations as He did before the proclamation of the Gospel. It includes the entire period between Christ's coming to redeem men and His coming to judge the world. 3. The loosing of the devil for a little season refers to the great apostasy and the days of the Antichrist immediately before Christ's second advent. 4. The souls of the martyrs and of the other saints are with Christ immediately after bodily death, and live and reign with Him during the Gospel era. 5. The rest of the dead, namely those who are not raised from the death of sin, do not live during the Gospel era, and hence do not live at all. 6. Those who have part in the first or spiritual resurrection (from the death of sin) escape the second or eternal death. They live and reign with Christ till the Mediatorial kingdom is finished.

Post-millennialists hold that the thousand years refer to a period of extraordinary prosperity of the Church before Christ's second coming. Some have endeavored to place this supposed millennium in the past, others place it in the future.

CHAPTER XXXV

THE RESURRECTION OF THE BODY

THE separation which takes place at death between the soul and the body is not permanent. There shall be a resurrection of the dead on the last day, and the soul and the body shall be reunited. The resurrection of the body is absolutely necessary, if man is not to spend eternity in a bodiless and hence incomplete state of humanity.

The doctrine of the resurrection of the body is purely a Scriptural one, and cannot be established philosophically, like the immortality of the soul. It was denied by many in the days of the apostles (Acts 17:32; 1 Cor. 15:12), and is denied by many to-day. But it is a doctrine clearly and definitely taught in the Scriptures.

Teaching of Scripture. The declaration of God to Moses that He is the God of Abraham, Isaac and Jacob is interpreted by Christ to imply the resurrection of the dead (Exod. 3:6; Matt. 22:31, 32; Mark 12:26, 27; Luke 20:37, 38). Isaiah said that the dead shall live (Isa. 26:19), and Daniel declared that many of them that sleep in the earth shall awake, some to everlasting life and some to shame and everlasting contempt (Dan. 12:2). The belief in the resurrection of the dead was common among the Jews, though the sect of the Sadducees denied the doctrine.

The force of the Old Testament teaching on the resurrection can be fully appreciated only in the light of the New Testament. Christ said to the Jews, that the hour is coming in which all that are in the graves shall hear the voice of the Son of

God, and shall come forth: they that have done good unto the resurrection of life, and they that have done evil unto the resurrection of damnation (John 5:25-29). To Martha, who was mourning over the death of her brother Lazarus, Christ said, "I am the resurrection and the life; he that believeth in me, though he were dead, yet shall he live; and whoever liveth and believeth in me shall never die" (John 11:25, 26). There shall be a resurrection of the just and of the unjust, at which time the godly shall be recompensed (Luke 14:14). Those who are raised from the dead shall neither marry nor die any more, and shall be equal unto the angels (Luke 20:35, 36).

The reality of the resurrection of the dead is frequently emphasized by the apostles.[1] And St. Paul declares not only that the resurrection of Christ is a guarantee of ours (1 Cor. 15:12 seq.), but that our bodies shall be fashioned like unto His glorious body (Phil. 3:21).

The raising of the daughter of Jairus, of the young man at Nain, and of Lazarus by Christ, and the raising of Tabitha or Dorcas by St. Peter, are not examples of the resurrection on the last day, but were a restoration to this present life, and were followed again in due time by bodily death.

The resurrection on the last day will include the bodies of all the dead, both of the just and of the unjust. The former will be raised to eternal life, and the latter to eternal condemnation. There will not be a long interval between the resurrection of the believers and that of the unbelievers, as the pre-millennialists hold, but the resurrection of both will take place at the second coming of Christ, which will usher in the end of the world.[2]

[1] See Acts 4:2; 17:18, 31; 23:6; 24:15; 26:8, 23; Rom. 8:11, 23; 1 Cor. 6:14; 2 Cor. 4:14; Phil. 3:21; 1 John 3:2; 1 Cor. 15; 2 Cor. 5:1-10; 1 Thess. 4:13-16.

[2] 1 Thess. 4:16, "the dead in Christ shall rise first" has no reference to a pre-millennial resurrection of the believers, but declares that the dead in Christ shall rise before the living believers shall at Christ's coming be caught up in the clouds with Him.

The resurrection of the dead will be followed immediately by the general judgment, in which all the living and all the dead, raised to life again, shall appear before Christ's judgment seat.

Nature of the Resurrection. The resurrection of the dead on the last day will be a real resurrection of the body. Such a bodily resurrection is necessary in order that believers and unbelievers may, as complete human beings, with body and soul, receive the award of eternal life or eternal death at the judgment. It will not be due to any properties inherent in the human body, or to the natural survival of any life principle in it, but to the direct will and action of God. It is ascribed in the Scriptures to God as such, as all the *opera ad extra* are ascribed to God as such, that is, to the Triune God (1 Cor. 15:38). But it is also ascribed to the Father (John 5:21; 2 Cor. 4:14), to the Holy Ghost (Rom. 8:11), and especially to the Son (John 5:25; 6:40; 1 Thess. 4:14).

The Nature of the Body. What the nature of the resurrection body will be is to be learned from the example of the risen body of our Lord, in whose likeness ours shall be fashioned, and from the description of the resurrection body given by the apostle Paul. It will be our own body, so that we and others recognize it as our own; but it will have new properties and powers. This does not necessarily imply that every particle of matter that composed the body at death will compose it at the resurrection. In this life we recognize our body as our own and as the same body we always had, although we know that it is undergoing constant change and that at the end of every seven years it consists of entirely new particles of matter. In like manner it is possible for the resurrection body to be the same body as we had on earth, even though the particles composing it should be entirely different ones.

The body of Christ after His resurrection was His own body, and was recognized by His disciples as such; but it possessed new attributes and powers. It was freed from the limitations of space, could pass through closed doors, and could appear and disappear as He willed. Being a spiritual body, it had qualities similar to those pertaining to the spirit world, and was freed from the weaknesses and limitations of the natural body. The denial by some that there can be such a spiritual body rests on the assumption that matter will always have the qualities or properties which we now attribute to it, and is incapable of existing without them. But this assumption is unwarranted; for even now we know that a material thing like the X-ray can pass through matter; and science assumes that the ether penetrates and permeates everything without meeting with any resistance. God will give to man such a body as pleases Him (1 Cor. 15:38). It will be a spiritual body, endowed with new and marvelous powers. It will not be dependent on food and drink. The fact that Christ ate and drank after His resurrection, to prove to His disciples that it was He Himself and not a spirit, is to be ascribed to the exceptional need of the circumstances, and probably also to the fact that His exaltation was not yet completed (John 20:27).

St. Paul tells us that the body which dies is corruptible, but that it shall be raised incorruptible; it is sown in dishonor and weakness, but it shall be raised in glory and power; it is sown a natural or psychical body, but it is raised a spiritual body. The present body is of the earth, earthy; but the resurrection body will be heavenly (1 Cor. 15:47-49). Such a change in the qualities of the body is necessary, because flesh and blood cannot inherit the kingdom of God, neither doth corruption inherit incorruption. For this reason, the believer, though forgiven, dies nevertheless in order that through death and the resurrection a new body may be brought forth from the grave. Just so the grain of wheat is sown into the ground and decays, but is raised up with a new body. For the same reason, also, the bodies of those who are alive at Christ's second coming shall

be changed in a moment, in the twinkling of an eye at the last
trump, in order that those persons, though they escape bodily
death, may nevertheless have a spiritual body. For this corruptible must put on incorruption; and this mortal must put on
immortality (1 Cor. 15:51-53). The bodies of all the saints
shall be made fit tabernacles for their redeemed, regenerated
and glorified souls.

The resurrection bodies will thus have the following attributes. They will be immortal and incorruptible. They will be
glorious, perfect and powerful, free from all the ailments,
afflictions and defects of the earthly body. They will be spiritual, and thus not only be freed from the limitations of matter
as we now know it, but endowed with spiritual qualities which
will make them perfect organs of the glorified souls that are to
inhabit them forever.

The bodies of the unbelievers shall also be changed, and
become immortal and incorruptible, so that body and soul may
be united throughout eternity. But as the unbelievers are
doomed to eternal destruction, their bodies will lack the glorious properties which will belong to those of the believers.

The question as to what will be the bodily stature of each
person in the world to come, and whether infants will ever
reach maturity, is one on which the Scriptures give us no information. It has been maintained by some that the bodies of all
the saints will be conformed to the stature of Christ; by others
that the stature of each will be that which he had or would have
had at youthful maturity; by others that each will have the age
and stature which was his at death. Some even maintain that
the women will become men, in order to be conformed to the
image of Christ. But all these things belong to the realm of
speculation. Of this we may be sure, however, that each saint
in heaven will have a perfect body, and that each will be satisfied and happy in the possession of the new body which God has
given him.

CHAPTER XXXVI

THE FINAL JUDGMENT

THE Final Judgment will follow immediately upon the second coming of Christ and the resurrection of the dead. Christ will come in glory and majesty to judge the living and the dead, and all the nations of the earth shall be brought before His throne to judgment. For we must all appear before the judgment seat of Christ, that everyone may receive according to the deeds which he has done in the body (2 Cor. 5:10).

Preliminary Judgment at Death. Since God is constantly aware of all men's thoughts and words and deeds, and nothing is hidden from Him, He is in a sense constantly judging men during their lifetime upon earth. This judgment of God during men's lifetime is subject to reversal by a change in men's attitude toward God and His grace. But there is a definite and decisive judgment of God upon men at death; for then the period of grace allotted to them in this world is passed, their character is fixed forever, and the record of their life is completed. It is appointed unto men once to die, but after this the judgment (Heb. 9:27). The judgment which follows upon their death is twofold; namely, a preliminary secret judgment at death, and a final public judgment at the second coming of Christ.

The preliminary judgment which God passes upon men at death is absolutely accurate and infallible, and will not be altered in the least by the public judgment which follows. For God knows without any possibility of error whether those who

406

die are true believers or not. And when at death he admits the believer to eternal life and condemns the unbeliever to eternal death, their destiny is fixed forever. No public examination of the life and deeds of the believer or of the unbeliever is necessary in order to show God to which class men belong. A final public judgment is not at all necessary so far as God's knowledge of men's character and works or of the eternal fate to which they are to be consigned is concerned. Such a public judgment is necessary only from the standpoint of man, in order to take from the condemned one every semblance of a pretext for complaining that he was treated unjustly in being assigned to hell. The wicked and unbelieving man will be given a public trial, and will have every opportunity to defend himself if he can. But those who in this world have planned to argue their case before God and to show that they have not justly deserved condemnation will be stricken with dumbness and confusion when they are confronted with the record of their transgressions and unbelief (Matt. 22:12). That final judgment will be a public vindication of the righteousness of God as exhibited in the preliminary judgment which assigned men to eternal life or to eternal death.

Christ the Judge. The final judgment is ascribed to God as such, that is to the Triune God (Heb. 11:23; Acts 17:31; Rom. 2:5). But it is the peculiar office of the Son, the Mediator, to be the judge at the end of the mediatorial era (Matt. 25:31 seq.; John 5:22 seq.) The judging of the living and of the dead will be the concluding act of His reign in the mediatorial kingdom. After that He will deliver up the kingdom to God, even the Father, and God shall be all in all (1 Cor. 15:24 seq.; John 5:27; Acts 17:31). It will be a judgment by Christ the God-man. He who was crucified for men's sins will then appear as the Exalted One, with power and great glory, visible to all, and recognized as the King of kings and the Lord of lords

(Acts 1:11; Matt. 21:30; 25:31; Luke 21:27), and He will require a reckoning of men as to how they have treated His grace. He will be accompanied by the angels, whose office it will be to announce His coming, to gather all the living and all the dead before His throne, to separate the believers from the unbelievers, and to cast out the condemned into everlasting torment (Matt. 25:31; 1 Thess. 4:16). When it is said that the saints shall share with Christ in the judgment, this does not mean that they shall have independent power of judging, but that they shall witness and approve the judgment of Christ.

The judgment will be universal as well as final. There will be summoned before Christ's judgment seat all men, good and bad, great and small, from all the nations and tribes of the earth. And the judgment will decide their fate forever.

The Norm of Judgment. The norm of judgment will be the Gospel of redemption (Phil 3:9). The decisive question will be, how men have treated the grace of God which was offered them in Christ Jesus. They will be assigned to eternal life or to eternal death according as they have accepted or rejected that grace, and possess or do not possess the righteousness of Christ. Both the believers and the unbelievers will be found to have broken God's holy law and to have deserved eternal punishment. But the believers will be accounted righteous on account of the merit of Christ in whom they believe, and will receive eternal life as the reward of grace. The unbelievers, on the other hand, having rejected the grace of God which freely offered them the forgiveness of sins and a robe of righteousness for Christ's sake, will have nothing with which to appear before the judgment but their own record of sin; and that will utterly condemn them. Having refused to be saved by grace from the condemnation of the law, they will have nothing but the law to appeal to; and that will brand them guilty and deserving of eternal death.

An Accounting Demanded. The descriptions of the final judgment show that the record of men's sins will be exhibited (1 Cor. 3:13; 4:5). Every thought, word and deed that has been in conflict with God's holy law will be laid bare. Every secret sin will be revealed. Men will be asked to give an account of every idle and useless word (Matt. 12:36). Called before that tribunal men will not be able to answer one question out of a thousand.

This publishing of the record of sin together with the demand for an accounting will take place in the case of all the wicked and unbelieving, so that their guilt and their well-deserved punishment may be plain to themselves and to all others. But such an accounting for their sins will not be required of the believers. The handwriting that was against them has been blotted out with the blood of Christ (Col. 2:14). Having been fully and freely forgiven for all their sins, their transgressions are no longer remembered. The forgiveness of their sins for Christ's sake implies that they no longer need to render an account for them. Christ has already accounted for all their sins by His sufferings and death. There is no possibility of condemnation for those who in this life have been and have remained in Christ (Rom. 8:1). It is not the sins, but the good works of the believers which will be published (Matt. 25:35, 36).

According to Works. The judgment of all men will be according to their works (Rom. 2:6 seq.). This does not mean that they will receive reward or retribution on account of their works. If this were the case, even the believers would be condemned; for they have merited no reward but only punishment by their deeds. The reward is altogether of grace and not of works. But the works are the outward index of the state of heart, and show whether faith is present or not. They exhibit the moral activity of men either as that of souls who are justified by faith or as that of souls who are unjustified by reason of unbelief. These works will be viewed not simply as external works; for externally the works of believers and of unbelievers often look very much alike. But they will be viewed according to their real inner quality and with respect to the motive from which they have sprung (1 Cor. 4:5). The works, including the motive back of them, are evidence of the presence or absence of living faith. Hence the judgment will be according to the works. Those who are found to have been true believers will be told to inherit the kingdom prepared for them from the foundation of the world; and those who are found to have been unbelievers will be told to depart into everlasting fire prepared for the devil and his angels (Matt. 25:31). The former, being clothed with the righteousness of Christ put on by faith (Phil. 3:9), will be awarded eternal life; the latter, having nothing in which to appear before the judgment except their own sin and unrighteousness, will be condemned to eternal death.

Hell not Prepared for Men. It is to be noted that while Christ says that the kingdom which the believers shall inherit was prepared for them from the foundation of the world, He does not say that the everlasting fire into which the unbelieving will be cast was prepared for them. On the contrary, He says that it was prepared for the devil and his angels. For men God has prepared an eternal kingdom and mansions of glory; and He has done and is now doing all that lies within His power to bring men into the possession of the blessedness which He has prepared. But if by their persistent sin and unbelief men prevent Him from fitting them for the eternal inheritance which He has prepared, there remains nothing else for Him to do with such persons but to exclude them from heaven and to cast them out into the everlasting fire which was prepared for the devil and his angels. For that place becomes the only possible one for those who have spurned and rejected the grace which sought to save them.

The reference to the books which will be opened so that judgment may be rendered according to what is written in them is an anthropomorphism. God does not need to keep books of account nor to have written records made of what men have done during their lifetime. All things are present to His mind.

The End of the World. Immediately after the judgment and the assignment of men to their eternal destiny, the world will come to an end. There shall be new heavens and a new earth wherein dwelleth righteousness (2 Pet. 3:13). As the theater in which man's sin was developed, and as a creature which has become cursed and contaminated by sin, so that even the brutes living on it have suffered bondage on account of man's sin (Rom. 8:19 seq.), the earth must pass away (1 Cor. 7:31) to make room for a new, perfect and glorious earth. The destruction of the present order of things will take place through a cataclysm of some kind, and the world shall be burned up (2 Pet. 3:7, 10). The destruction of the world and its replacement by a new world was taken by the old dogmaticians to mean the total annihilation of the earth, and the creation of an entirely new one to take its place. But it is probably better to understand the destruction of the earth as meaning a transformation and purification by fire, so that while the substance of it remains the quality is completely changed. Luther said that the world now has on its working-day clothes, but will then have on its Sunday clothes.

The world is said to have perished in the flood (2 Pet. 3:6), though its substance remained. The soul is a new creature when it has been regenerated, though the change in it is a qualitative and not a substantial one. And so by parity of reasoning it is quite possible, and even likely, that by the destruction of the world of which the Scriptures speak there is to be understood not its annihilation, but its transformation and perfecting, so that every vestige of the effects of sin is removed, and so that it shall be perfectly adapted to the recreated soul and body of man.

CHAPTER XXXVII

ETERNAL DEATH

THE final judgment will effect an eternal separation between the good and the bad, between the believers and the unbelievers. The former will be told to inherit the kingdom prepared for them from the foundation of the world (Matt. 25:34), and the latter will be told to depart into everlasting fire prepared for the devil and his angels (Matt. 25:41). The eternal abode of the believers will be heaven; the eternal abode of the unbelievers will be hell.

Definition. Eternal death is the eternal continuance of the spiritual death incurred by sin. It becomes the lot or fate of all those persons in whom grace in this world does not succeed in replacing spiritual death with spiritual life. It involves eternal persistence in enmity and antagonism against God, and hence eternal separation from Him and exclusion from His presence, together with the eternal endurance of the consequence of that separation and exclusion; namely, an eternal abiding in that condition and place in which there is an utter absence of light and love and a constant presence of indescribable darkness, hatred, raging passions, unutterable woe, and endless despair. Those who become the subjects of eternal death are described as the victims of the fire that never is quenched, of the gnawing of the worm that never dieth (Mark 9:44), and as spending eternity in the lake of fire (Rev. 21:8), in outer darkness, and amid weeping and gnashing of teeth (Matt. 8:12).

413

The Lost. Those who are condemned to eternal death are spoken of as the lost. They consist of all those persons who on the day of judgment are found wanting the righteousness of Christ put on by faith. Only those who are reconciled to God through Christ shall enter heaven. All others, being still in their natural state of enmity to God, will be excluded from heaven and cast out into hell. Since redemption from the transgressions of the law has been provided by Christ, the sin which actually condemns men on the day of judgment is unbelief. Hence the lost will include all those who are lacking in true faith in Christ—the openly and defiantly wicked (1 Cor. 6:9, 10), the self-righteous (Gal. 3:10), the hypocrites (Matt. 23:14), those who have neglected the Gospel (Heb. 2:3), and even many who profess to have done much service in Christ's cause but who have been in reality impenitent and unbelieving (Matt. 7:22, 23). All who have failed to accept the grace of God in Christ, whether it be through active hostility to the Gospel, indifference to its appeals, or sheer neglect of the grace which it offers, will be lost. Lacking the one essential for heaven, they will find their eternal home in hell.

The lost have chosen to remain enemies of God and have permanently aligned themselves against Him. They have refused to permit divine grace to bring their minds and hearts into harmony with Him, and hence must be excluded from heaven, and cast into hell. Were it possible that those whose mind is set in enmity against God should somehow gain temporary admittance into heaven, they would not only be utterly out of place but would be unhappy even there, because there is nothing in their attitude which would enable them to appreciate the holiness of heaven. Miserable as they will be in hell, they will be more at home in their surroundings there than they could ever be in heaven. For in hell there is on all sides of them that same bitter antagonism to God which fills their own hearts.

God will not cast into hell any human beings whom He can possibly by His grace make fit to enter and enjoy heaven. But there is a meetness or fitness which is essential for entrance into heaven and for the enjoyment of its blessedness (Col. 1:12). This fitness is wrought through justification, regeneration and sanctification. Those in whom it is not wrought have only themselves to blame when, because of their persistent enmity to God, they find themselves shut out into outer darkness. They refused to let God change their minds and hearts, and justify them through Christ; and as those who have been found permanently unsalvable they will be left by God to the fate which they have chosen.

God desires to save all. But He will not and cannot save any by compulsion. He cannot have any persons in heaven who would be there against their will. Through the Means of Grace He is constantly seeking to make men willing. But as personal beings men have the power persistently to refuse His grace and to persevere in an attitude of hostility to Him. Those who do so exclude themselves from heaven. For heaven is a condition and place of harmony with God, and those whose will has not been brought into harmony with His cannot enter.

Hell as the place of eternal punishment must be distinguished from Sheol and Hades, which in some places are translated by the term hell, but which in reality mean the place of departed spirits. The place where hell is has not been revealed to us. Though we realize that hell is fundamentally a condition and not a locality, and that hell may be anywhere where the required conditions of hell are present, we are unable in this world to think either of heaven or hell totally apart from the idea of location. The fact that the lost as well as the saved will have bodies after the resurrection requires that we shall conceive of both heaven and hell as existing in some actual place. But the location of the place we do not know.

Nature of Punishment. The misery of the lost will be so

complete and unutterable, that human language lacks terms
adequate to describe it. What is involved in the misery is
partly negative and partly positive. The negative pains and
woes of hell are exclusion from the presence of God who is the
source of all light and love, and from the society of all those
who love God and do His will. The positive woes of hell are
found in the society of the devils and the most wicked of men,
and in the darkness, hatred, bitterness, lamentations and hopeless despair. There will be the rage of unbridled passions which
can find no outlet, the hatred against God which is utterly
futile, the anguish of conscience which never ceases for wrongs
done and opportunities neglected, and the bitter never-ending
consciousness of the lost that they might be in heaven, but are
in hell by their own choice. For this reason they are described
as the victims of the worm that never dieth and of the fire that
never is quenched—constantly burning, yet never consumed.

Figurative Descriptions. The descriptions of hell are frequently in terms of fire. Is this fire to be understood as a literal,
physical fire? When we remember that the rich man in hell is
said to have been tormented in the flames of hell at a time when
only his soul or spirit was there, while his body was still on
earth, the flames referred to cannot have been physical. How
could a physical fire burn a mind, soul, or spirit? Evidently hell
is pictured as a place of torment through fire, because the
agonizing pain inflicted by fire is familiar to men, and is one of
the most terrible known to them. The object of Holy Scripture evidently is to paint hell in as terrible colors as human
language will permit; for the simple reason that even then the
descriptions of its pains and woes will fall far short of reality.
For no human words can picture adequately the miserable state
of one who by his own fault is utterly forsaken by God forever, and is cast out eternally into a condition and place of
darkness, hatred and despair.

Punishment not Arbitrary. A proper conception of the nature and effects of sin will clear the mind of the notion that God needs to add or does add anything to the punishment which is involved in leaving men to the control and horror of the sins to which they have clung. Having refused to let God save them, the lost are left to reap what they have sown, to eat the bitter fruit of their own enmity against God, to be the helpless and desperate victims of their own pampered lusts, to be subjected to the constant and unending horrors of an accusing conscience, to grope in indescribable darkness, to hear the hissings of hatred, and to be themselves a part of that unutterable horror which is called hell. No worm that gnaws unceasingly and no fire that burns unquenched can furnish an adequate illustration of the utter misery and despair that reign in that place of eternal death and destruction. To that unspeakable wretchedness God need not and does not add any additional woes or torments arbitrarily inflicted. He has built no hell for men; He takes no pleasure in the pains which they suffer there. But He is obliged to put them there, because they have refused to let Him fit them for heaven and its blessedness.

Degrees of Punishment. It is plainly the teaching of Scripture that there will be degrees in the misery of the lost. The greater the wickedness and the greater the opportunities for salvation which have been despised, the deeper will be the woe and anguish of that place of woe. The misery of all the lost will be indescribable, because it is the misery of hopeless and endless separation from God and from all that is good. But there will nevertheless be degrees of suffering. The servant who knew his master's will and nevertheless did it not shall be beaten with more stripes than he who can plead a measure of ignorance (Luke 12:47, 48) It shall be more tolerable for Sodom and Gomorrah in the day of judgment than for the city which refuses to hear and heed the preaching of the Gospel

(Matt. 10:15). It shall be more tolerable for Tyre and Sidon on that day than for Chorazin and Bethsaida, which beheld Christ's mighty works and yet persisted in unbelief (Matt. 11:21). The greatest pangs of the lost will without doubt be due to the consciousness that, if they had only repented in time, they might have escaped their horrible fate. The greater the light which they had and despised in this world, the more terrible will be their self-accusations.

Eternal. The misery of the lost will be eternal. The opportunity for reconciliation with God and for a relation of mutual love with Him was given to them in this life. But if the grace of God proved ineffective in bringing them to repentance in this world, there will be no opportunity in the world to come. The doors of heaven will be shut against them, and it will be too late. They are separated from God by their love of sin; and where divine grace has failed to remove the separation and replace it with union and fellowship, there is no other means of accomplishing that end. The teaching of Scripture clearly is that the punishment of the lost will be eternal. The wrath of God remains on them (2 Thess. 1:8, 9). The smoke of their torment ascendeth forever (Rev. 14:11). Their worm dieth not, and the fire is not quenched (Mark 9:44). The same word which is used to describe the future life as eternal is used to describe the future death as eternal (Matt. 25:46). By parity of reasoning, therefore, if eternal death did not mean eternal, but a punishment which will at some time end, eternal life would have to mean a life which would also at some time end. In the very nature of the case the punishment is and must be eternal, because the antagonism to God which brings on the punishment is an antagonism which the grace of God was unable to remove, and which therefore will last forever.

Objections. Numerous objections have been urged against the doctrine of eternal punishment. It is contended by some that the doctrine is in conflict with the Scripture's teaching concerning the love and goodness of God. If He Himself is love, how can He bear to punish men eternally? In reply, it must be borne in mind that God does not inflict any arbitrary punishment on the lost, but simply leaves them to the sin and enmity from which they persistently refused to let Him separate them. His love prompted Him to redeem men through the incarnation and death of His only Son, and to prepare a home in heaven for those who accept the salvation which He has provided. But what will or can even a loving God do with those who refuse to be saved? He cannot take them into heaven by force and against their will. As personal beings they must be willing and desirous to go there. If He took them there against their will, they would be unhappy and out of sympathy with their heavenly environment, and would defile heaven itself by their enmity against God, and their hatred and malice toward every person and thing that is good. He must do something with them. Since He cannot take them into heaven, He leaves them outside. And outside of heaven is hell. The trouble lies not in any lack of love on God's part, but in the despising of God's love on man's part.

Another objection that is urged is that the lost might repent in hell if they had the opportunity, and that they will have the opportunity. Then, when they have repented, they will escape from hell. But how will they repent in hell? In this world men are brought to repentance by the grace of God, and not simply by experiencing the consequences of sin. And if in this world the grace of God has labored with men in vain, the same grace would fail to save them in the world to come. It will not be offered. But if it were, it would be rejected by the same obduracy which rejected it here.

It is urged that the saved will be unhappy in heaven at the thought that some of their friends and relatives are in hell.

To our human way of thinking, and in accordance with our earthly experience, this objection seems to have some weight. For here the consciousness that friends are in trouble and distress robs us of our peace of mind and happiness. But we cannot judge of conditions in the next world by our experience here. There will be perfect accord between the believer in heaven and God, and absolute assurance on the part of the saints that everything which God does is in accordance with the dictates of love and righteousness.

It is contended by some that the doctrine of an eternal dualism of good and evil in the universe is inconsistent with the dignity of God, and that He will annihilate the devils and the wicked men, so that there will not be a spot anywhere where the good does not prevail. This objection is best met by simply resting on the plain teaching of God's Word. If God finds it in accordance with His dignity to permit devils and wicked men to exist eternally in a state of antagonism to Him, we need not worry about His dignity. In any case those spirits and wicked men will be placed where they can never again harm anyone but themselves.

Underlying nearly all these objections is the fallacy that punishment is arbitrarily inflicted by God and can be arbitrarily abridged, and the failure to realize that the eternal punishment of the lost is directly traceable to their unalterable hostility to God.

CHAPTER XXXVIII

ETERNAL LIFE

WHEN the judgment has been completed the believers shall enter upon the enjoyment of eternal life. They shall inherit the kingdom prepared for them from the foundation of the world (Matt. 25:34). They shall receive an inheritance incorruptible, and undefiled and that fadeth not away (1 Pet. 1:4). They shall be with Christ, where He is, and behold His glory (John 17:24). They shall inherit the mansions which Christ has gone to prepare for them (John 14:23). They shall see God and enjoy His favor and blessing forever (Matt. 5:8; 1 Cor. 13:13; 1 John 3:2; Rev. 22:4). They shall have a glory revealed in them with which the sufferings of this present time are not worthy to be compared (Rom. 8:18).

Definition. Eternal life is the ineffable blessedness which the believers, perfected and glorified in body and soul, and freed from all sin and from all the consequences of sin, shall enjoy forever in the presence of God in heaven.

There is a very true sense in which the believer has eternal life even here in this world (1 John 5:12; John 3:36; 6:47). For having been regenerated by the grace of the Holy Spirit, he has been rescued from the spiritual death which sin brought upon him, and has received a new, spiritual life. He is a new creature in Christ. He has been reunited with God who is the source of all life, and now lives in Him. The eternal life of the world to come is in reality only the eternally continued and perfected spiritual life which the believer possesses here. The

421

believer does not at death receive a new life; but being alive in Christ he passes into eternity in the possession of that life, which thereupon is denominated eternal life in the special sense in which the word is used in this chapter. The difference between the eternal life possessed by the believer here on earth and that possessed by him in the world to come is simply the difference in the degree to which that life is developed and perfected. Here the believer is united with God through Christ; but his love is imperfect, his life fails to measure up to his ideal, and his pathway is made wearisome by many physical, mental and spiritual burdens and trials. But in the world to come the sin which hampers the Christian on earth will be gone, his love will glow with ceaseless fervor, and his life will be one continuous and unending praise and service of God. In that perfect service of God in heaven the believer will find eternal happiness. His spiritual life will there have reached its full development and expression. In thought and feeling and will he will be in absolute harmony with God.

The eternal life upon which the believer enters after the final judgment is the full consummation of his redemption. In the intermediate state after death he enjoys blessedness also; but he is then still in an incomplete condition, because he lacks a body. But at the resurrection he will receive back his body in a new, glorified and perfect state; and then as a complete man, with glorified soul and glorified body, he will enjoy eternal life in the highest sense. All the joys which God has prepared for His own shall then be his forever.

The Blessed. Those who will receive eternal life are those who by faith in Christ have become reconciled to God, and have received forgiveness of sins and a new heart. By faith they have obtained a perfect righteousness which entitles them to stand acquitted before God, and they possess through the divine grace which produced that faith a new attitude of love for God and the things of God. They have, therefore, the fitness for the inheritance of the saints in light of which the apostle speaks (Col. 1:12-14). They are entitled to enter into heaven for the sake of Christ's merit and righteousness, and, being regenerated and sanctified by divine grace, they are spiritually minded and able to appreciate the holy joy and blessedness of heaven. They are God's children through Christ; and since children heirs (John 1:17; Rom. 8:17), and their inheritance is life eternal.

In no sense do the godly enter into heaven on account of any merit in themselves. The thief on the cross who died before he had an opportunity to do any good work except to reprove his fellow thief, and St. Paul, whose life was spent in labors and sufferings in Christ's cause, shall both enter heaven solely on account of the merit of Christ (Phil. 3:9.), and not at all on account of any merit of their own. It is the blood and righteousness of Christ put on by faith, and that alone, which entitles any man to enter heaven.

Happiness of Heaven. The joys and happiness of heaven are such as human language is not adequate to express. The words of our language are dependent on our experience; and the world to come will transcend all real or possible experience in this world. St. Paul was exalted to the third heaven (2 Cor. 12:2-4); but what he saw and experienced there it was not lawful or possible for him to express in the language of earth. The blessedness of heaven is far above all that we can conceive or imagine. It embraces the blessedness which an almighty and loving Father has prepared for His children.

Because of the poverty of human language, the descriptions of heaven which are given in the Scriptures are largely of a negative or of a figurative character. In attempting to picture the ineffable joy and blessedness of heaven, the holy writers were to a large extent reduced to the necessity of describing them in a negative way, namely, by removing from our conception of that heavenly life all those things which come upon men here on earth on account of sin, and which make of this world at best a vale of tears.

There will be no sin there. All the believers will be perfected and freed from every vestige of sin and evil. All desire and all temptation to sin will be removed; and the believer will there be able to do and will actually do what he already on earth desired to do but was not able to do perfectly, namely, to love and serve God in every thought and word and deed. No smallest remnant of sin will be found there. Into that place will enter nothing that is unclean and nothing that defileth (Rev. 21:27). All those whose hearts are still inclined to sin and set in antagonism to God will be excluded from the divine abode.

There will be no consequences of sin there. All the damage that sin has done in this world to the souls and bodies of the believers will have been repaired. With a regenerated and glorified body and soul they will dwell in a new heaven and a new earth wherein dwelleth righteousness. There will be no more death, neither sorrow nor crying, neither will there be any more pain, because the former things are passed away (Rev. 21:4). The saved will never hunger nor thirst, nor suffer from cold or heat, or from weariness or want (Rev. 7:16, 17). They will sit at the wedding-feast of the King's Son; and Christ will present them to Himself a glorious Church not having spot or wrinkle or any such thing (Eph. 5:27).

St. John, in the twenty-first chapter of the book of Revelation, describes the glory of the heavenly city, the new Jerusalem, the abode of the saints. His language is taken from the glory and splendor of earth, because the actual glory of heaven cannot be pictured in human words. The length and breadth and height of the city are equal, and measure twelve thousand furlongs each. It has a great and high wall made of jasper. It has twelve gates, three on each side, each made of one great pearl. The streets are of gold, and present the appearance of transparent glass. There is no temple in that heavenly city, because the Lord God Almighty and the Lamb are the temple of it. The city has no need of the sun or of the moon to shine in it; for the glory of God lightens it, and the Lamb is the lamp thereof. Its gates shall never be shut, and there shall be no night there (Rev. 21). While this description is given in terms of earth, it serves to indicate that the glories of the heavenly home are beyond our highest powers of conception.

From the positive standpoint the blessedness of heaven is described in various ways. The believers shall be present with the Lord (John 14:3; 17:24; Phil. 1:23) in the company of the angels (Heb. 12:22) and of their fellow believers (Matt. 8:11; Heb. 12:23) and in mansions prepared for them (John 14:3). They shall see God,[1] know him with a fullness which is impossible in this world, and find eternal joy and blessedness in the knowledge of His love, wisdom, holiness and power (1 John 3:2; 1 Cor. 13:12). The things which were dark, mysterious and incomprehensible to them in nature and in God's dealings with men will then become plain. And in company with their fellow saints and the angels they will admire, worship and serve God forever, and find in the loving activities of heaven endless delight and happiness.

The rest which is spoken of as belonging to the saints in heaven (Heb. 4:9) does not mean inactivity. It simply means rest from all those things which distress, burden and pain men here on earth. Where there is life there is always activity, and the saved will doubtless have work to do which will fill their hearts with constant delight. They will not simply sing or play on the heavenly harps, but will each find some avenue of service in which their perfect love to God will find expression. What

---

[1] This seeing God is sometimes called the Beatific Vision.

each will be given to do will doubtless be dependent on the capacity with which he has been endowed and the degree in which his spiritual life on earth was developed (Luke 19:16-19).

Degrees of Glory. All the saved will be unspeakably happy. But as there is one glory of the sun and another glory of the moon and another glory of the stars, and one star differeth from another star in glory, so there will be ranks and gradations in heaven with corresponding duties and responsibilities. As large and small vessels may all be filled to overflowing and each be as full as it can be, so all the saved will be filled to overflowing with happiness, while at the same time some of them as vessels of grace will have capacity for a greater content of glory than others. The parable of the Pounds shows that along with the favor of the Master there went in one case a higher position and greater responsibility than in another. The thief on the cross and St. Paul the apostle will equally inherit eternal life, and each be perfectly happy in heaven. But the capacity for eternal glory in the case of the apostle who labored and suffered so much for the extension of Christ's kingdom will be greater than that of the thief. In any case, however, the measure of glory will be vastly in excess of the labors and sufferings (Rom. 8:18), and will be a reward of grace and not of merit.

The Place of Heaven. Heaven is, of course, first of all a condition—a state of perfect harmony and accord with God. Where this harmony exists, there is heaven. But since man shall receive his body again at the resurrection, and we think of the body in terms of space, the question as to the whereabouts of heaven presents itself. We think of heaven as upward; but we know that those who live at the antipodes point in an opposite direction from ourselves when they point upward. In any case our modern knowledge of astronomy clothes the idea of the location of heaven as upward with extreme vagueness. It has been held by Luther and others on the basis of certain passages of Scripture (2 Pet. 3:13; Rev. 21:2) that heaven will ultimately be upon the earth. There is much to recommend this view. God made the earth for man's abode in the first place. Here man might have dwelt in holiness and happiness. But he sinned and brought suffering and death upon himself as a consequence. And along with the personal consequences of sin he brought a curse upon the earth. In His mercy God set into operation a plan of redemption by which all the damage wrought by sin should be repaired and man be raised by divine grace to a higher level than he would have attained had he never sinned at all. For by faith we now become the children of God, with Christ the Son of God in a true sense our brother. This redemption provides regeneration and sanctification and ultimate glorification for the soul. It also provides for the resurrection, perfecting and glorification of the body. And we are assured that the earth itself shall according to God's plan undergo a purification by fire, and that there shall be a new and glorified earth. And when this has come to pass, what would be more natural than that the earth, which was originally intended for man, should in its regenerated and glorified state become the eternal home of the believer. With the new powers and properties belonging to his spiritual body he would not necessarily be confined to the earth, and might in his work of loving service and ever-growing knowledge of God travel to the farthest spheres of the universe. But the new earth would be his home.

The location of heaven is purely a matter of speculation, because the Scriptures do not tell us where it will be. But the condition of the saved as one of everlasting glory and happiness is a clear teaching of Scripture. Perfect in body and soul, they will dwell with Christ for ever and ever.

BIBLIOGRAPHY

Creeds and Confessions

J. T. Müller: Symbolische Bücher der evangelisch-lutherischen Kirche, Gütersloh, 1882. Einl. von Kolde, 11 ed., 1912.

Bente and Dau: Concordia Triglotta (German, Latin and English). St. Louis, 1921.

H. E. Jacobs: The Book of Concord; or Symbolical Books of the Evangelical Lutheran Church. 2 vols. Phila., 1882.

Ph. Schaff: The Creeds of Christendom. 3 vols. New York, 1877.

C. Fabricius: Corpus Confessionum. Die Bekenntnisse der Christenheit. Berlin and Leipzig, 1928 seq. To be completed in about 20 vols.

Sixteenth and Seventeenth Century Dogmatics

Ph. Melanchthon: Loci Communes. 1521. Ed. by Kolde. Leipzig, 1900.

M. Chemnitz: De Coena Domini. 1560.

—— Examen Concilii Tridentini. 4 vols. 1565-73. Ed. by Preuss, Berlin, 1861. German (in part), St. Louis, 1875.

—— De Duabus Naturis. 1570.

—— Loci Theologici. 1591.

Aeg. Hunnius: De Persona Christi. 1585.

J. Heerbrand: Compendium Theologicum. 1573.

M. Hafenreffer: Loci Theologici. 1609.

L. Hutter: Compendium Locorum Theologicorum. 1610. Trans. by H. E. Jacobs and G. F. Spieker. Phila., 1881.

—— Loci Communes Theologici. 1619.

J. Gerhard: Loci Theologici. 1610-25. Ed. Cotta, 22 vols., 1762-81. In 9 vols. with indexes, Leipzig, 1864-75.

A. Calovius: Systema Locorum Theologicorum. 12 vols. 1655-77.

J. F. König: Theologia Positiva Acroamatica. 1661, 1669, 1690.

J. A. Quenstedt: Theologia Didactico-Polemica. 1685.

J. W. Baier: Compendium Theologiae Positivae. 1685. Ed. by Preuss, Berlin, 1864. Ed. by C. F. W. Walther, St. Louis, 1879.

D. Hollazius: Examen Theologicum Acroamaticum. 1707.

C. Löber: Evangelisch-lutherische Dogmatik. Altenburg, 1711. Mit einem Vorwort von C. F. W. Walther, St. Louis, 1893.

Nineteenth and Twentieth Century Dogmatics

J. T. Beck: Einleitung in das System der christlichen Lehre. Stuttgart, 1838, 1870.

K. Hase: Evangelische Dogmatik. Leipzig, 1850 (Rationalistic).

R. Rothe: Dogmatik. Herausgegeben von D. Schenkel. 3 vols. Heidelberg, 1870 (Speculative and mediating).

A. Ritschl: Christliche Lehre von der Rechtfertigung und Versöhnung. 3 vols. Bonn, 1870, 1888, 4 ed. 1895.

W. Herrmann: The Communion of the Christian with God. From the 4th German ed. of 1893. Trans. by R. W. Stewart, New York, 1930 (Ritschlian).

Lipsius: Lehrbuch der evang. prot. Dogmatik. Braunschweig, 1876, 1879, 3 ed. 1893.

Th. Haering: Der christliche Glaube (Dogmatik). Calw und Stuttgart, 1906. Eng. Trans., The Christian Faith, a System of Dogmatics. 2 vols. by J. Dickie and C. Ferries. London and New York, 1915 (Ritschlian).

K. Hase: Hutterus Redivivus. Leipzig, 1828.

H. Martensen: Christian Dogmatics. Trans. by W. Urwick. Edinburgh, 1866.

E. Sartorius: The Doctrine of Divine Love. Trans. by Sophia Taylor. Edinburgh, 1884.

G. Thomasius: Christi Person und Werk. 3 ed. by F. J. Winter. 2 vols. Erlangen, 1886.

F. A. Philippi: Kirchliche Glaubenslehre. 3 ed. 6 vols., Gütersloh, 1883.

J. C. K. Hofmann: Der Schriftbeweis. Ein theologischer Versuch. 3 Teile. Nördlingen, 1852-55, 1857-60.

K. F. A. Kahnis: Die lutherische Dogmatik historisch-genetisch dargestellt. 2 vols. 2 ed. Leipzig, 1874.

A. F. C. Vilmar: Dogmatik. Gütersloh, 1874.

H. Voigt: Fundamental Dogmatik. Gotha, 1874.

F. H. R. Frank: System der christlichen Wahrheit. 3 ed. Erlangen and Leipzig, 1894.

M. Kähler: Die Wissenschaft der christlichen Lehre. 3 ed. Leipzig, 1905.

H. Cremer and O. Zöckler: Principienlehre und System der Glaubenslehre. In Zöckler's Handbuch der theol. Wissenschaften, Vol. III. München, 1890.

A. von Oettingen: Lutherische Dogmatik. 3 vols. München, 1897.

C. E. Luthardt: Kompendium der Dogmatik. 10 ed. Leipzig, 1900. 11 ed. by Winter, 1914.

—— Christliche Glaubenslehre gemeinverständlich dargestellt. Leipzig, 1906.

W. Rohnert: Die Dogmatik der evangelisch-lutherischen Kirche. Braunschweig and Leipzig, 1902.

O. Kirn: Grundriss der Evang. Dogmatik. 3 ed. Leipzig, 1910. 7 ed., 1921.

K. Girgensohn: Grundriss der Dogmatik. Leipzig, 1924.

R. H. Grützmacher: Textbuch der system. Theologie und ihrer Geschichte. 2 ed. Leipzig, 1923.

L. Ihmels: Centralfragen der Dogmatik in der Gegenwart. 4 ed. Leipzig, 1921.

R. Seeberg: Christliche Dogmatik. 2 vols. Erlangen and Leipzig, 1924-25.

H. Schmid: Doctrinal Theology of the Evang. Lutheran Church. Trans. by C. A. Hay and H. E. Jacobs. Phila., 1876.

A. L. Graebner: Outlines of Doctrinal Theology. St. Louis, 1898.

M. Valentine. Christian Theology. 2 vols. Phila., 1906.

H. E. Jacobs: A Summary of the Christian Faith. Phila., 1905.

R. F. Weidner: Dogmatic Theology. Based on Luthardt and Krauth. 8 vols. 1888-1915.

A. G. Voigt: Biblical Dogmatics. Columbia, S. C., 1917. 2 ed., Between God and Man, *Ibid.*, 1926.

C. E. Lindberg: Christian Dogmatics. Rock Island, Ill., 1922.

F. Pieper: Christliche Dogmatik. 3 vols. St. Louis, 1924.

J. A. Singmaster: A Handbook of Christian Theology. Phila., 1927.

W. Elert: An Outline of Christian Doctrine. Trans. by C. M. Jacobs. Phila., 1927.

W. Hove: Christian Doctrine. Minneapolis, 1930.

P. L. Mellenbruch: The Doctrines of Christianity. New York and Chicago, 1931.

Reformed Dogmatics

Calvin: Institutes of the Christian Religion. 1536. Eng. trans. by John Allen, London, 1813. 2 vols. Phila., no date.

A. Kuyper: Calvinism. New York, 1900.

F. Schleiermacher: Der christliche Glaube. 1821-22. In Bibliothek theol. Klassiker. 4 vols. Gotha, 1889.

A. Schweizer: Die Glaubenslehre der evangelisch-reformierten Kirche. Zurich, 1844-47.

H. Heppe: Die Dogmatik der evangelisch-reformierten Kirche. Elberfeld, 1861.

J. H. A. Ebrard: Christliche Dogmatik. Königsberg, 1863.

I. A. Dorner: System der christlichen Glaubenslehre. 2 vols. Berlin, 1879, 1886, 1887. Eng. trans. A System of Christian Doctrine. 4 vols. Edinburgh, 1888.

W. G. T. Shedd: Dogmatic Theology. New York, 1888.

C. Hodge: Systematic Theology. 3 vols. New York, 1877.

J. J. Van Osterzee: Christian Dogmatics. Eng. trans. London, 1874.

H. B. Smith: System of Christian Theology. New York, 1885.

A. H. Strong: Systematic Theology. 3 vols. Phila., 1907.

L. Berkhof: Reformed Dogmatics. 2 vols. Grand Rapids, 1931.

D. A. Goodsell, J. B. Hingeley, J. M. Buckley: The Doctrine

and Discipline of the Methodist Episcopal Church. Cin-
cincinnati, 1908.

History of Dogmatics and Theology

W. Gass: Geschichte der prot. Dogmatik. 4 vols. Berlin,
1854-67.

I. A. Dorner: Geschichte der prot. Theologie. München,
1867. Eng. trans. Edinburgh, 1871.

K. F. A. Kahnis: Der innere Gang des deutschen Protestan-
tismus seit Mitte des vorigen Jahrhunderts. 2 Teile. 3 ed.
Leipzig, 1874. Trans., Internal History of German Protestantism, Edinburgh, 1856.

F. H. R. Frank: Geschichte und Kritik der neueren Theologie,
insbesondere der systematischen, seit Schleiermacher.
Erlangen and Leipzig, 1898.

History of Doctrine and Symbolics

A. Harnack: History of Dogma. Trans. from the third German ed. by N. Buchanan. 7 vols. London, 1905.

G. P. Fisher: History of Christian Doctrine. New York,
1896.

R. Seeberg: Text-book of the History of Doctrine. Trans. by
C. E. Hay. 2 vols. Phila., 1905.

F. Loofs: Symbolik oder christliche Konfessionskunde. Tübingen, 1902.

G. Thomasius: Dogmengeschichte. Herausgeben von R. Seeberg. 2 vols. Erlangen and Leipzig, 1889.

M. Schneckenburger: Vergleichende Darstellung des luth.
und ref. Lehrbegriffs. 2 vols. Stuttgart, 1855.

F. Kattenbusch: Lehrbuch der vergleichenden Religionskunde.
Freiburg I. B., 1892.

W. Walther: Lehrbuch der Symbolik. Leipzig and Erlangen,
1924.

J. A. Moehler: Symbolism, or Exposition of Doctrinal Differences between Catholics and Protestants. Trans. by J. A.
Robertson. London, 1906.

E. H. Klotsche: Christian Symbolics. Burlington, Ia., 1929.

J. L. Neve: Introduction to Lutheran Symbolics. Burlington,
Ia., 1917.

W. H. Lyon: A Study of the Christian Sects. 13 ed. Boston, 1926.

C. P. Krauth: The Augsburg Confession. Phila., 1868.

M. Loy: The Augsburg Confession. Columbus, O., 1908.

F. H. R. Frank: Die Theologie der Konkordienformel. 4 vols. Leipzig, 1858-65.

C. P. Krauth: The Conservative Reformation and Its Theology. Phila., 1885.

T. E. Schmauk and C. T. Benze: The Confessional Principle and the Confessions. Phila., 1911.

J. Köstlin: The Theology of Luther in Its Historical Development and Inner Harmony. Trans. by C. E. Hay. 2 vols. Phila., 1897.

Fundamentals of Christianity

J. A. W. Haas: The Unity of Faith and Knowledge. New York, 1926.

E. H. Johnson: Christian Agnosticism. Phila., 1907.

T. Christlieb: Modern Doubt and Christian Belief. Trans. by W. U. Weitbrecht. Ed. by T. L. Kingsbury. Edinburgh, 1874.

W. H. Turton: The Truth of Christianity. 9 ed. London, 1919.

F. L. Patton: Fundamental Christianity. New York, 1926.

R. Seeberg: Die Grundwahrheiten der christlichen Religion. Leipzig, 1902. 7 ed. 1921.

C. E. Luthardt: Saving Truths of Christianity. Trans. from the second German ed. by S. Taylor. Edinburgh, 1868.

F. Hamilton: The Basis of the Christian Faith. New York, 1927.

Liberalism

W. Walther: Ad. Harnacks Wesen des Christentums für die christliche Gemeinde geprüft. 3 Aufl. Leipzig, 1901.

H. Cremer: Reply to Harnack on the Essence of Christianity. Trans. from the third German ed. by B. Pick. New York, 1903.

O. Hallesby: The Main Differences between Positive and Liberal Theology. Trans. by G. T. Rygh. Minneapolis, 1923.

P. H. Buehring: Modernism. A Pagan Movement in the Christian Church. Columbus, O., 1928.

L. S. Keyser: The Conflict of Fundamentalism and Modernism. Burlington, Ia.

J. G. Machen: Christianity and Liberalism. New York, 1923.

J. Horsch: Modern Religious Liberalism. Scottdale, Pa., 1921.

E. Gordon: The Leaven of the Sadducees. Chicago, 1926.

J. A. Faulkner: Modernism and the Christian Faith. New York and Cincinnati, 1921.

W. Burggraaf: Rise and Development of Liberal Theology in America. New York, 1928.

J. H. Snowden: Old Faith and New Knowledge. New York, 1928.

W. H. Johnson: The Christian Faith under Modern Searchlights. New York, 1916.

C. Gore: The New Theology and the Old Religion. New York, 1907.

E. Y. Mullins: Christianity at the Cross Roads. New York, 1924.

G. B. Smith: Religious Thought in the Last Quarter Century. Chicago, 1927.

—— Current Christian Thinking. Chicago, 1928.

J. A. W. Haas: Trends of Thought and Christian Truth. Boston, 1915.

W. P. King: Behaviorism; A Battle Line. Nashville, 1930.

—— Humanism; Another Battle Line. Nashville, 1931.

F. H. R. Frank: System der christlichen Gewissheit. 2 Teile. Erlangen, 1884.

L. F. Stearns: The Evidence of Christian Experience. New York, 1890, 1916.

Early Christianity

E. Hatch: The Influence of Greek Ideas and Usages upon the Christian Church. 1890. London, 1914.

G. Uhlhorn: The Conflict of Christianity with Heathenism. Trans. from the third German ed. by E. C. Smyth and C. J. H. Ropes. New York, rev. ed., 1891.

B. F. Cocker: Christianity and Greek Philosophy. New York, 1870.

E. de Pressensé: The Ancient World and Christianity. Trans.
by A. H. Holmden. New York, no date.
T. R. Glover: The World of the New Testament. New York,
1931.
E. von Dobschütz: Christian Life in the Primitive Church.
Trans. by G. Bremner and W. D. Morrison. London and
New York, 1904.
D. S. Schaff: Our Fathers' Faith and Ours. New York, 1928.

Barthianism

K. Barth: The Word of God and the Word of Man. Trans.
by D. Horton. Boston, 1928.
H. E. Brunner: The Theology of Crisis. New York and
London, 1930.
R. B. Hoyle: The Teaching of Karl Barth. New York, 1930.
J. McConnachie: The Significance of Karl Barth. New York,
1931.
E. Brunner: The Word and the World. New York, 1931.
W. Pauck: Karl Barth, Prophet of a New Christianity? New
York, 1931.

The Doctrine of God

S. Harris: The Philosophical Basis of Theism. New York,
1890.
B. P. Bowne: Theism. New York, 1902.
J. Iverach: Theism in the Light of Present Science and Phi-
losophy. New York, 1899.
A. S. Eddington: Science and the Unseen World. New York,
1929.
B. P. Bowne: Personalism. Boston and New York, 1908.
A. C. Knudson: The Philosophy of Personalism. 1927.
C. C. J. Webb: God and Personality. London and New York,
1919.
J. H. Snowden: The Personality of God. New York, 1920.
R. M. Vaughan: The Significance of Personality. New York,
1930.
J. R. Illingworth: Personality, Human and Divine. London
and New York, 1894.
—— Divine Transcendence. London, 1911.

—— Divine Immanence. New York and London, 1898.

Pringle-Pattison: The Idea of God. New York, 1920.

Wobbermin: Der Christl. Gottesglaube in seinem Verhältniss zur heutigen Philosophie und Wissenschaft. 2 ed. Berlin, 1907.

Gwatkin: The Knowledge of God. Edinburgh, 1906.

Hocking: The Meaning of God in Human Experience. New Haven, 1912.

E. H. Reeman: Do We Need a New Idea of God? Phila., 1917.

L. F. Gruber: The Theory of a Finite and Developing Deity Examined. 1918.

S. Mathews: The Growth of the Idea of God. New York, 1931.

J. Fiske: The Idea of God as Affected by Modern Knowledge. Boston and New York, 1886.

R. Otto: The Idea of the Holy. Trans. by J. W. Harvey. London, 1926.

W. F. Tillett: The Paths That Lead to God. New York, 1924.

W. J. Moulton: The Certainty of God. New York, no date.

E. S. Brightman: The Problem of God. New York, 1930.

W. A. Brown: Pathways to Certainty. New York and London, 1930.

R. M. Jones: Pathways to the Reality of God. New York, 1931.

R. L. Swain: What and Where is God. New York, 1921.

J. E. Turner: The Revelation of Deity. New York, 1931.

J. Iverach: Is God Knowable? London, 1874.

A. C. Knudson: The Doctrine of God. New York, 1930.

The Trinity

E. H. Bickersteth: The Rock of Ages, or Scriptural Testimony to the One Eternal Godhead of the Father and of the Son and of the Holy Ghost. New York, 1861.

P. H. Steenstra: The Being of God as Unity and Trinity. New York, 1891.

R. N. Davies: Doctrine of the Trinity. The Biblical Evidence. Cincinnati, 1891.

R. Rocholl: Der christliche Gottesbegriff. Göttingen, 1900.
R. F. Horton: The Trinity. London, 1901.
G. Krüger: Das Dogma von der Dreieinigkeit und der Gott-
menschheit. Tübingen, 1905.
S. B. McKinney: Revelation of the Trinity. London, 1906.
J. R. Illingworth: Doctrine of the Trinity Apologetically Con-
sidered. London and New York, 1907.
A. F. W. Ingram: The Love of the Trinity. New York, 1908.
L. G. Mylne: The Holy Trinity. New York, 1916.

Predestination

L. Boettner: The Reformed Doctrine of Predestination. Grand
Rapids, 1932.
A. Pfeiffer: Anti-Calvinism. Trans. by E. Pfeiffer. Colum-
bus, 1881.

Creation. Evolution

L. F. Gruber: Creation ex Nihilo. Boston, 1918.
A. Fairhurst: Organic Evolution Considered. Cincinnati. 2
ed. 1918.
H. H. Lane: Evolution and Christian Faith. Princeton, 1923.
A. C. Zerbe: Christianity and False Evolutionism. Cleveland,
1925.
Th. Graebner: Evolution; an Investigation and a Criticism.
Milwaukee, 1922.
A. W. McCann: God or Gorilla. New York, 1922.
H. C. Morton: The Bankruptcy of Evolution. London, Edin-
burgh and New York, no date.
A. Patterson: The Other Side of Evolution. Chicago, 1903.
W. A. Williams: Evolution Disproved. Camden, N. J., 1925.
E. Dennert: At the Death-bed of Darwinism. Trans. from
the German. Burlington, Ia., 1904.
P. Mauro: Evolution at the Bar. New York, 1922.
L. S. Keyser: The Problem of Origins. Burlington, Ia., 1926.
G. M. Price: Q. E. D., or New Light on the Doctrine of
Creation. New York, 1917.
B. G. O'Toole: The Case against Evolution. New York,
1929.
G. M. Price: The Phantom of Organic Evolution. New York,
1924.

W. H. C. Thomas: Evolution and the Supernatural. Phila., no date.

Providence

W. F. Tillett: Providence, Prayer and Power. Nashville, 1926.

Sir R. Anderson: The Silence of God. London, Glasgow and Edinburgh, no date.

M. J. Savage: Life's Dark Problems. New York and London, 1905.

E. Petavel: The Extinction of Evil. Trans. by C. H. Oliphant. Boston, 1889.

W. Schmidt: Die göttliche Vorsehung und das Selbstleben der Welt. Berlin, 1887.

—— Der Kampf der Weltanschauungen. Berlin, 1904.

C. E. Luthardt: Die modernen Weltanschauungen. 3 ed. Leipzig, 1891.

J. Orr: The Christian View of God and the World. New York, 1897.

E. Stange: Christentum und moderne Weltanschauung. Leipzig, 1914.

A. M. Fairbairn: The Philosophy of the Christian Religion. New York and London, 1902.

O. Kirn: Vorsehungsglaube und Naturwissenschaft. Berlin, 1903.

R. Otto: Naturalism and Religion. Trans. from the German. New York, 1907.

O. Dewey: The Problem of Human Destiny; or the end of Providence in the World and Man. 5 ed. New York, 1866.

A. B. Bruce: The Providential Order of the World. New York, 1897.

—— The Moral Order of the World. New York, 1899.

Man and Sin

O. Zöckler: Die Lehre vom Urstand des Menschen, geschichtlich und dogmatisch-apologetisch untersucht. Gütersloh, 1886.

Klaiber: Die neutestamentliche Lehre von der Sünde und dem Erlöser. 1836.

Umbreit: Die Sünde. Gotha, 1853.

Ernesti: Ursprung der Sünde nach paulinischem Lehrgehalt. 2 vols. 1862.

J. Müller: The Christian Doctrine of Sin. 2 vols. Trans. from the German. Edinburgh, 1877.

A. Tholuck: Die Lehre von der Sünde und vom Versöhner. 9 ed. Gotha, 1871. Eng. trans. Edinburgh, 1877.

J. Tulloch: The Christian Doctrine of Sin. New York, 1876.

R. Mackintosh: Christianity and Sin. New York, 1914.

F. R. Tennant: Origin and Propagation of Sin. 2 ed. London, 1906.

J. Orr: God's Image in Man and Its Defacement. New York, 1906.

W. E. Orchard: Modern Theories of Sin. London, 1909.

H. H. Horne: Free Will and Human Responsibility. New York, 1912.

C. E. Luthardt: Die Lehre von dem freien Willen in seinem Verhältniss zur Gnade in ihrer geschichtlichen Entwickelung dargestellt. Leipzig, 1866.

The Person and Work of Christ

E. Sartorius: Die Lehre von Christi Person und Werk. 7 Aufl. Gotha, 1870. Trans., The Doctrine of the Person and Work of Christ. London, 1838.

M. Schneckenburger: Zur christlichen Christologie. 1848.

A. W. Dieckhoff: Die Menschwerdung des Sohnes Gottes. 1882 (against Ritschlianism).

A. C. Garrett: The Philosophy of the Incarnation. New York, 1891.

A. Aall: Der Logos. Geschichte seiner Entwickelung in der griechischen Philosophie und der christl. Literatur. Leipzig, 1896.

R. L. Ottley: The Doctrine of the Incarnation. 2 vols. London, 1896.

C. Gore: Lux Mundi: Studies in the Religion of the Incarnation. New York, no date.

—— The Incarnation of the Son of God. New York, 1891.

—— Dissertations on Subjects connected with the Incarnation. New York, 1895.

J. H. Seeley: Ecce Homo. London, 1865. New York, 1908.

Anon: Ecce Deus. Essays on the Life and Doctrine of Jesus Christ. Boston, 1867.

W. L. Walker: The Spirit and the Incarnation. Edinburgh, 1899.

H. C. Minton: The Cosmos and the Logos. Phila., 1902.

H. C. Powell: The Principle of the Incarnation. London and New York, 1896.

Guthrie, Epler, Thorp: The Significance of the Personality of Christ. Boston, 1907.

H. M. Relton: A Study in Christology. London, 1917.

J. Stalker: The Christology of Jesus. Being His Teaching concerning Himself according to the Synoptic Gospels. New York, 1899.

R. J. Knowling: The Testimony of St. Paul to Christ. London and New York. 3 ed. 1911.

R. J. Cooke: Did Paul know of the Virgin Birth. New York, 1926.

J. G. Machen: The Virgin Birth of Christ. New York and London, 1930.

H. P. Liddon: The Divinity of Our Lord and Saviour Jesus Christ. London and Oxford, 1882.

Ph. Schaff: The Person of Christ. The Perfection of His Humanity Viewed as a Proof of His Divinity. New York, 1880.

G. S. Streatfeild: The Self-Interpretation of Jesus Christ. A Study of the Messianic Consciousness as Reflected in the Synoptics. Cincinnati, no date.

P. T. Forsyth: The Person and Place of Jesus Christ. Phila., 1910.

R. Seeberg: Christi Person und Werk nach der Lehre seiner Jünger. 2 ed. Leipzig, 1910.

A. B. Bruce: The Humiliation of Christ. 2 ed. New York, no date.

R. Whately: The Kingdom of Christ. London, 1892.

E. F. Scott: The Kingdom of God in the New Testament. New York, 1931.

C. E. Raven: Jesus and the Gospel of Love. New York, 1931.

T. Kagawa: The Religion of Jesus and Love the Law of Life. Phila., 1931.

C. F. W. Walther: The Proper Distinction between Law and Gospel. Trans. by W. H. T. Dau. St. Louis, 1929.

The Atonement

Anselm: Cur Deus homo? Ed. by Lämmer. Berlin, 1857. Eng. trans. in Ancient and Modern Library of Theol. Lit. London. Also Chicago, 1903.

J. Denney: The Death of Christ. Its Place and Interpretation in the New Testament. Cincinnati and New York, no date.

—— The Atonement and the Modern Mind. New York, 1903.

A. A. Hodge: The Atonement. Phila., 1867.

J. Miley: The Atonement in Christ. New York and Cincinnati, 1879, 1907.

J. B. Reimensnyder: The Atonement and Modern Thought. Phila., 1905.

H. C. Mabie: The Divine Reason of the Cross. New York, 1911.

M. Kähler: Die Versöhnung durch Christum und ihre Bedeutung für christl. Glauben und Leben. 2 ed. Leipzig, 1907.

H. Mandel: Christl. Versöhnungslehre. Leipzig, 1916.

M. Kähler: Das Kreuz, Grund und Mass fur die Christologie. Gütersloh, 1911.

P. Bachmann: Die Bedeutung des Sühnetodes für das christl. Gewissen. Leipzig, 1907.

S. Mathews: The Atonement and the Social Process. New York, 1930.

The Holy Spirit and His Work

J. Owen: Of the Holy Spirit. London, 1684, 1826.

J. C. Pfeiffer: De Divinitate Spiritus Sancti. Jena, 1740.

K. F. A. Kahnis: Die Lehre vom Heiligen Geiste. 1 Teil. Halle, 1847.

J. C. Hare: Mission of the Comforter. Boston, 1854.

J. P. Coyle: The Holy Spirit in Literature and Life. Boston, 1855.

J. Buchanan: Office and Work of the Holy Spirit. Edinburgh, 1856.

G. Smeaton: Doctrine of the Holy Spirit. 1882.

H. Gunkel: Die Wirkungen des Heiligen Geistes. Göttingen, 1888.

K. von Lechler: Die biblische Lehre vom Heiligen Geiste. 3 vols. Gütersloh, 1899.

J. Robson: The Holy Spirit, the Paraclete. Aberdeen, 1893.

A. J. Gordon: The Ministry of the Holy Spirit. New York, 1894.

C. I. Schofield: Plain Papers on the Holy Spirit. New York and London, 1899.

W. Kölling: Pneumatologie, oder die Lehre von der Person des Heiligen Geistes. Gütersloh, 1894.

F. Nösgen: Geschichte der Lehre vom Heiligen Geiste. Gütersloh, 1899.

—— Das Wesen und Wirken des Heiligen Geistes. Berlin, 1907.

A. Kuyper: The Work of the Holy Spirit. Trans. by H. De Vries. New York and London, 1900.

J. E. C. Welldon: The Revelation of the Holy Spirit. London, 1902.

I. Wood: The Spirit of God in Biblical Literature. 1904.

L. B. Crane: Teachings of Jesus concerning the Holy Spirit. New York, 1906.

J. H. B. Masterman: "I Believe in the Holy Ghost." A Study of the Doctrine of the Holy Spirit in the Light of Modern Thought. London, 1907.

A. C. A. Hall: The Work of the Holy Spirit. Milwaukee, 1907.

J. D. Folsom: The Holy Spirit our Helper. New York, 1907.

G. F. Holden: The Holy Ghost, the Comforter. New York, 1908.

F. C. Porter: The Spirit of God and the Word of God in Modern Theology. New York, 1908.

E. W. Winstanley: The Spirit in the New Testament. New York, 1908.

Swete: The Holy Spirit in the New Testament. 1909.

R. A. Torrey: The Person and Work of the Holy Spirit. New York, 1910.

J. N. Kildahl: Misconceptions of the Word and Work of the Holy Spirit. Minneapolis, 1927.

W. T. Davison: The Indwelling Spirit. London and New York, 1911.

H. W. Robinson: The Christian Experience of the Holy Spirit. New York and London, 1928.

J. Moffatt: Grace in the New Testament. New York, 1932.

Faith

Musaeus: De Fide. Jena, 1677.

Calovius: De natura et officiis fidei in actu justificationis. Wittenberg, 1699.

P. J. Spener: Wahrer seligmachender Glaube, dessen eigentliche Art und Beschaffenheit. Frankfurt, 1696.

Reiche: Von dem seligmachenden Glauben und dessen Vorstellungsart. Berlin, 1774.

D. Schultz: Die christliche Lehre vom Glauben. Ein biblischer Entwurf. Leipzig, 1830, 1834.

J. Köstlin: Der Glaube und seine Bedeutung für Erkenntniss, Leben und Kirche. Göttingen, 1859.

A. Schlatter: Der Glaube in Neuen Testament. Leiden, 1885. Calw und Stuttgart, 1896.

J. G. Machen: What Is Faith? New York, 1925.

E. König: Der Glaubensakt des Christen. Leipzig, 1891.

Skovgaard-Petersen: Faith and Certainty. Trans. from the Danish. 1920.

K. Thieme: Die sittliche Triebkraft des Glaubens. Leipzig, 1895.

L. Ihmels: Fides implicita und der evangelische Heilsglaube. Leipzig, 1912.

Justification

N. Selnecker: De justificatione hominis coram Deo et de bonis operibus. Leipzig, 1570.

P. J. Spener: Evang. Glaubensgerechtigkeit. Frankfurt, 1684.

Fresenius: Abhandlung uber die Rechtfertigung eines armen Sünders vor Gott. Göttingen, 1717, 1776. New ed. by Vilmar, Marburg, 1857.

P. D. Burk: Rechtfertigung und Versicherung. Neu in Auszug herausg. von Kern. Stuttgart, 1854.

Koopman: Die Rechtfertigung allein aus Glauben. Kiel, 1870.

Anon: Die lutherische Lehre von der Rechtfertigung. Ein Referat. St. Louis, 1880.

M. Loy: The Doctrine of Justification. Columbus, 1869. 2 and rev. ed. 1882.

Conversion, Repentance, Regeneration

Hollazius: Gnadenordnung. Neu herausg. Basel, 1866.

Musaeus: Tract. theol. de conversione hominis peccatoris ad Deum. Jena, 1666, 1706.

E. Wacker: Wiedergeburt und Bekehrung in ihrem gegenseitigen Verhältniss nach her Heiligen Schrift. Gütersloh, 1908.

J. Herzog: Der Begriff der Bekehrung. Giessen, 1903.

P. Feine: Bekehrung in Neuen Testament und in der Gegenwart. Leipzig, 1908.

P. Gennrich: Die Lehre von der Wiedergeburt. Leipzig, 1907.

F. Pieper: Conversion and Election. A Plea for a United Lutheranism in America. St. Louis, 1913.

L. S. Keyser: Election and Conversion. 1914 (a reply to Pieper's book).

T. Walden: The Great Meaning of Metanoia. New York, 1896.

G. H. Gerberding: New Testament Conversions. Phila., 1889.

G. Jackson: The Fact of Conversion. London, 1908.

N. H. Marshall: Conversion, or the New Birth. London, 1909.

H. Begbie: Twice-born Men. A Clinic in Regeneration. New York, London and Edinburgh, 1909.

H. E. Monroe: Twice-born Men in America. 1914.

Psychology of Religion

W. R. Inge: Faith and Its Psychology. New York, 1913.

G. S. Hall: Adolescence. New York, 1904.

E. D. Starbuck: The Psychology of Religion. New York, 1899.

W. James: Varieties of Religious Experience. New York, 1902.

G. A. Coe: The Spiritual Life. New York, 1900.

—— The Religion of a Mature Mind. New York, 1902.

—— The Psychology of Religion. Chicago, 1916.

J. B. Pratt: The Psychology of Religious Belief. New York, 1907. 3 ed. 1916.

—— The Religious Consciousness. New York, 1921.

E. S. Ames: The Psychology of Religious Experience. Boston, 1910.

J. H. Leuba: A Psychological Study of Religion. 1912.

S. F. Fletcher: The Psychology of the New Testament. London and New York, 1912.

G. Steven: The Psychology of the Christian Soul. London and New York, 1911.

B. M. Stratton: Psychology of the Religious Life. New York, 1911.

D. A. Murray: Christian Faith and the New Psychology. New York, 1911.

J. Stalker: Christian Psychology. New York, 1914.

H. E. Warner: The Psychology of the Christian Life. New York, 1910.

T. W. Pym: Psychology and the Christian Life. New York, 1910.

—— More Psychology and the Christian Life. New York, 1925.

H. C. McComas: The Psychology of Religious Sects. New York, 1912.

E. L. House: The Psychology of Orthodoxy. New York, 1913.

P. H. Heisey: Psychological Studies in Lutheranism. Burlington, Ia., 1916.

C. E. Ellis: The Religion of Religious Psychology. Phila., 1922.

Word of God, Scriptures, Inspiration

P. Gennrich: Der Kampf um die Schrift. Berlin, 1898 (contains a full bibliography of nineteenth-century works on the subject).

W. Rohnert: Die Inspiration der heiligen Schrift und ihre Bestreiter. Leipzig, 1889.

Walther: Was lehren die neuen orthodox sein wollenden Theologen von der Inspiration. Dresden, 1871.

Kübel: Ist die Bibel Gottes Wort? 2 ed. 1879.

—— Luther und die Bibel. 1883.

Schlatter: Schrift, Glaube und Erfahrung. 1896.

H. Ebeling: Die Bibel Gottes Wort und des Glaubens einzige Quelle. 2 ed. Zwickau, 1897.

Krug: Der gottmenschliche Ursprung und Inhalt der heiligen Schrift. Elberfeld, 1847.

A. W. Dieckhoff: Das gepredigte Wort Gottes und die heilige Schrift. Rostock, 1887.

Hassenkamp: Die Herrlichkeit der Bibel gegenüber den Angriffen ihrer Kritiker. Gotha, 1888.

K. Walz: Die Lehre der Kirche von der heiligen Schrift nach der Schrift selbst geprüft. Leiden, 1884.

W. Sanday: The Oracles of God. London, 1891.

M. Kähler: Unser Streit um die Bibel. Leipzig, 1895.

H. Cremer: Glaube, Schrift und heilige Geschichte. Gütersloh, 1896.

A. B. Bruce: The Chief End of Revelation. London, 1881, 1887.

J. H. A. Ebrard: Revelation; Its Nature and Record. Edinburgh, 1884.

H. Rogers: The Superhuman Origin of the Bible. London, 1884.

G. P. Fisher: The Nature and Method of Revelation. New York, 1890.

S. J. Andrews: God's Revelation of Himself to Men. New York, 1901.

J. R. Illingworth: Reason and Revelation. London, 1902, 1908.

W. E. Gladstone: The Impregnable Rock of Holy Scripture. Rev. and enl. Phila., 1891.

J. Orr: The Bible under Trial. London, Edinburgh and New York, no date.

F. Bettex: The Bible the Word of God. Trans. from the third German ed. Cincinnati, 1904.

—— The Word of Truth. Trans. by A. Bard. Burlington, Ia., 1914.

Henderson: The Bible a Revelation from God. Edinburgh, 1910.

H. Mackensen: Revelation in the Light of History and Experience. With an Intro. by H. Offerman. Boston, 1926.

H. Schultz: Die Stellung des christlichen Glaubens zur heiligen Schrift. Braunschweig, 1877.

Th. Harnack: Uber den Kanon und die Inspiration der heiligen Schrift. Dorpat, 1885.

R. Grützmacher: Wort und Geist. Leipzig, 1902.

W. Rohnert: Was lehrt Luther von der Inspiration der heiligen Schrift. Leipzig, 1890.

Romberg: Die Lehre Luthers von der heiligen Schrift. Wittenberg, 1868.

L. Gaussen: Theopneustie. Paris, 1862. Eng. trans., London, 1888.

F. L. Patton: The Inspiration of the Scriptures. Phila., 1869.

E. Elliot: Inspiration of the Holy Scriptures. Edinburgh, 1877.

W. E. Atwell: The Pauline Theory of Inspiration. London, 1878.

J. G. W. Herrmann: Die Bedeutung der Inspirationslehre. Halle, 1882.

F. W. Farrar, J. Cairns et al.: Inspiration; a Clerical Symposium. London, 1884.

C. Wordsworth: On the Inspiration of Holy Scripture. London, 1867.

B. F. Westcott: Introduction to the Study of the Gospels. London, 1888. New York, 1902.

R. Seeberg: Offenbarung und Inspiration. Gross Lichterfelde, 1908.

J. Orr: Revelation and Inspiration. New York, 1910.

J. M. Gibson: Inspiration and Authority of Holy Scripture. London, 1908.

R. F. Horton: Inspiration of the Bible. London, 1906.

J. Urquhart: The Inspiration and Accuracy of the Holy Scriptures. New York, 1904.

A. W. Dieckhoff: Die Inspiration und Irrtumslosigkeit der heiligen Schrift. Leipzig, 1891.

Baptism

J. W. F. Höfling: Das Sakrament der Taufe. Dogmatisch, historisch, liturgisch dargestellt. 2 vols. Erlangen, 1859.

C. D. Day: Baptizing, Biblical and Classical. Cincinnati and New York, 1907.

Gerhard: Ausführliche schriftmassige Erklärung der beiden Artikel von der heiligen Taufe und von dem heiligen Abendmahl. Jena, 1610. Stuttgart, 1662. Berlin, 1868.

Martensen: Die christliche Taufe und die bapt. Frage. Gotha, 1843, 1860.

Wetzel: Die Kindertaufe in ihrer Schriftmässigkeit. Berlin, 1865.

Kemmler: Der Kindertaufe Recht und Kraft. Stuttgart, 1890.

C. P. Krauth: Baptism; the Doctrine set forth in Holy Scripture and taught in the Evang. Lutheran Church. Gettysburg, 1866.

E. Greenwald: Sprinkling the True Mode of Baptism. Phila., 1876.

—— The Baptism of Children. Phila., 1881.

J. E. Whittaker: Baptism. 1893.

J. A. Seiss: The Baptist System Examined. 1858, 1917.

J. B. Mozley: Review of the Baptismal Controversy. 2 ed. 1895.

W. Good: The Doctrine of the Church of England as to the Effects of Baptism in the Case of Infants. 1848.

The Lord's Supper

K. F. A. Kahnis: Die Lehre vom Abendmahl. Leipzig, 1851.

J. W. F. Höfling: Die Lehre der ältesten Kirche vom Opfer im Leben und Kultur der Christen. Erlangen, 1851.

Meier: Geschichte der Transubstantiation. Heidelberg, 1832.

Dieckhoff: Die evang. Abendmahlslehre im Reformations-Zeitalter. Göttingen, 1854.

H. Schmid: Der Kampf der lutherischen Kirche um Luthers Lehre vom Abendmahl im Reformationszeitalter. 2 ed. Leipzig, 1873.

C. P. Krauth: The Person of Our Lord and His Sacramental Presence. The Evang. Luth. and Ref. Doctrines Compared. Gettysburg, 1867.

W. Ockham: De Sacramento Altaris. Trans. and ed. by T. B. Birch. Latin and Eng. text. Burlington, Ia.

The Church

Hönig: Der kathol. und prot. Kirchenbegriff in ihrer geschichtlichen Entwickelung. Berlin, 1894.

J. Köstlin: Das Wesen der Kirche. Stuttgart, 1854. 2 ed. 1872.

A. W. Dieckhoff: Luthers Lehre von der kirchlichen Gewalt. 1860, 1865.

—— Staat und Kirche. 1872.

Delitzsch: Vier Bücher von der Kirche. Dresden, 1847.

Kliefoth: Acht Bücher von der Kirche. Schwerin, 1854.

W. Loehe: Three Books concerning the Church. Trans. by E. T. Horn. Reading, Pa., 1908.

E. Greenwald: The True Church, Its Way of Justification and Its Holy Communion. Phila., 1876.

M. Loy: The Christian Church in Its Foundation, Essence, Appearance and Work. Columbus, O.

J. A. Seiss: Ecclesia Lutherana. Phila., 1867, 1871.

C. H. L. Schuette: The State, the Church and the School. Columbus, 1883.

C. Zollman: Church and School in American Law. 1918.

The Ministry

W. Löhe: Aphorismen uber die neutestamentl. Aemter. Nürnberg, 1849.

C. F. W. Walther: Die Stimme unserer Kirche in der Frage von Kirche und Amt. Erlangen, 2 ed., 1875.

G. C. A. Harless: Kirche und Amt nach lutherischer Lehre. Stuttgart, 1853.

Vilmar: Die Lehre vom geistlichen Amte. Marburg, 1870.

Münchmeyer: Das Amt des Neuen Testaments. Nach der Lehre der Schrift und nach den luth. Bekenntnissen. Osterode, 1852.

K. Lechler: Die neutestamentliche Lehre vom heiligen Amte. Stuttgart, 1857.

Preger: Die Geschichte der Lehre vom geistl. Amt. Nördlingen, 1857.

Th. Harnack: Die Kirche, ihr Amt, ihr Regiment. Nürnberg, 1862.

C. P. Krauth: Theses on the Ministry of the Gospel.

J. C. Mattes: The Significance of Ordination.

The Last Things

C. E. Luthardt: Die Lehre von den letzten Dingen. Leipzig, 1861, 1885.

F. Richter: Die Lehre von den letzten Dingen. 2 vols. Breslau, 1843-44.

Kliefoth: Christliche Eschatologie. Leipzig, 1885.

H. Karsten: Die letzten Dinge. Hamburg, 1885.

Flörke: Die letzten Dinge. Rostock, 1866.

S. Lee: Eschatology. Boston, 1858.

G. T. Cooperrider: The Last Things, Death and the Future Life. Columbus, O., 1911.

J. A. Spencer: Five Last Things. New York, 1887.

N. West: Studies in Eschatology. New York, 1889.

L. A. Muirhead: The Eschatology of Jesus. London, 1906.

Käbisch: Die Eschatologie des Apostel Paulus. Göttingen, 1892.

G. Hoffmann: Das Problem der letzten Dinge in der neueren evang. Theologie. Göttingen, 1929.

L. Atzberger: Geschichte der christlichen Eschatology. Freiberg, 1896.

J. T. Beck: Die Vollendung des Reiches Gottes. By Lindenmeyer. Gütersloh, 1885.

J. Telfer: The Coming Kingdom of God. London, 1902.

Schöberlein: Zeit und Ewigkeit, Himmel und Erde. Heidelberg, 1874.

The Life After Death

W. Menzel: Die vorchristliche Unsterblichkeit. 2 vols. Leipzig, 1870.

Spiess: Entwickelungsgeschichte der Vorstellungen vom Zustand nach dem Tode. Jena, 1877.

Kattenbusch: Der christliche Unsterblichkeitsglaube. Darmstadt, 1881.

Schumann: Die Unsterblichkeitslehre des Alten und Neuen Testaments. Berlin, 1847.

H. Schultz: Die Voraussetzungen der christl. Lehre von der Unsterblichkeit. Göttingen, 1861.

Stade: Alttestamentliche Vorstellungen vom Zustand nach dem Tode. Leipzig, 1877.

Oertel: Hades. Leipzig, 1863.

Splittgerber: Tod, Fortleben und Auferstehung. 1862. 3 ed. Halle, 1885.

Fechner: Das Büchlein vom Leben nach dem Tode. 3 ed. Hamburg, 1885.

S. D. F. Salmond: The Christian Doctrine of Immortality. Edinburgh, 1901.

H. Cremer: Ueber den Zustand nach dem Tode. Gütersloh, 1910.

J. Huber: Die Idee der Unsterblichkeit. 3 ed. München, 1878.

J. Strong: The Doctrine of a Future Life. New York, 1891.

J. Fyfe: The Hereafter. Edinburgh, 1890.

G. S. Barrett: The Intermediate State and the Last Things. London, 1896.

Löscher: Auserlesene Sammlung der besten und neueren Schriften vom Zustand der Seele nach dem Tode. Dresden, 1735.

Schwally: Leben nach dem Tode. Giessen, 1892.

P. Feine: Das Leben nach dem Tode. 2 ed. Leipzig, 1919.

W. Smyth: Dorner on the Future State. New York, 1883.

J. H. Snowden: The Christian Belief in Immortality. In the Light of Modern Thought. 1925.

E. Abbot: The Literature of the Doctrine of a Future Life.
New York, 1874.

The Second Coming of Christ

Bautz: Weltgericht und Weltende. Mainz, 1866.
J. A. Seiss: Last Times. Phila., 1856, 1878.
W. E. B.: Jesus Is Coming. New York and Chicago, 1908.
G. Duffield: Millennarianism Defended. New York, 1843.
S. Hopkins: A Treatise on the Millennium. Boston, 1811.
S. Waldegrave: New Testament Millennarianism. London,
1855.
E. Storrow: The Millennium. London, 1886.
A. T. Pierson: The Coming of the Lord. New York, 1896.
D. Bosworth: The Millenium and Related Events. New
York, 1899.
D. Heagle: That Blessed Hope, the Second Coming of Christ.
Phila., 1907.
D. Brown: Christ's Second Coming. Will It Be Pre-Millen-
nial? Edinburgh, 1849.
J. F. Berg: The Second Advent of Jesus Christ not Pre-mil-
lennial. Phila., 1859.
J. H. Snowden: The Coming of the Lord. Will It Be Pre-
millennial? New York, 1922.
H. Corrodi: Kritische Geschichte des Chiliasmus. 4 vols.
Zurich, 1704.
Hebart: Die zweite sichtbare Zukunft Christi. Darstellung
der gesammten Eschatologie. Erlangen, 1850.
F. Philippi: Die biblische und kirchliche Lehre vom Anti-
christ. Gütersloh, 1877.
G. Calixtus: De supremo judicio. Helmstadt, 1658.

The Resurrection of the Dead

A. H. Cremer: Die Auferstehung der Toten. Barmen, 1870.
G. Calixtus: De immortalite animae et resurrectione carnis.
Helmstadt, 1661.
Bautz: Die Lehre von der Auferstehung nach ihrer positiven
und spekulativen Seite dargestellt. Paderborn, 1877.
E. Wolfsdorf: Die Auferstehung der Toten. Bamberg,
1904.

J. Hall: How are the Dead raised up, and with what Body
do they come? Hartford, 1875.

W. Milligan: The Resurrection of the Dead. Edinburgh,
1894.

C. S. Gerhard: Death and the Resurrection. Phila., 1895.

W. F. Whitehouse: The Redemption of the Body. London,
1895.

E. Huntingford: The Resurrection of the Body. London,
1897.

J. Maynard: The Resurrection of the Dead. London, 1897.

J. Hughes-Games: On the Nature of the Resurrection Body.
London, 1898.

J. G. Björklund: Death and the Resurrection from the Point
of View of the Cell Theory. Chicago, 1910.

C. K. Staudt: The Idea of the Resurrection in the Ante-
Nicene Period. Chicago, 1910.

Heaven and Hell

Bautz: Die Hölle. 1881.

Falke: Die Lehre von der ewigen Verdammniss. Eisenach,
1892.

J. B. Reimensnyder: Doom Eternal. The Bible and Church
Doctrine of Eternal Punishment. Phila., 1880.

W. G. T. Shedd: The Doctrine of Endless Punishment. 1886.

Chytraeus: De morte et vita aeterna. Wittenberg, 1581,
Rostock, 1590.

H. Harbaugh: Heaven; an Earnest and Spiritual Inquiry into
the Abode of the Sainted Dead. 3 vols. Phila., 1853.

J. E. Schubert: Vernunft- und Schriftgemässe Gedanken vom
ewigen Leben. Jena, 1742 and often.

Löscher: De glorioso animarum coelo. Wittenberg, 1692.

Storr: De vita beata. Tübingen, 1785.

I. C. Craddock: The Heaven of the Bible. Phila., 1897.

R. Winterbotham: The Kingdom of Heaven Here and Hereafter. New York, 1898.

General Works

On the various topics of dogmatics see also the respective
articles in the following encyclopedias:

J. Orr: International Standard Bible Encyclopedia. 5 vols. Chicago, 1915, 1930.

J. Hastings: Encyclopedia of Religion and Ethics. 12 vols. New York and Edinburgh, 1912.

S. Mathews and G. B. Smith: A Dictionary of Religion and Ethics. New York, 1921.

Schaff-Herzog: New Encyclopedia of Religious Knowledge. 12 vols. and Index. New York and London, 1912.

A. Hauck: Real Encyclopädie für prot. Theologie und Kirche. 3 ed. 24 vols. Leipzig, 1896, seq.

C. Meusel: Kirchliches Handlexikon. 7 vols. Leipzig.

Jacobs and Haas: The Lutheran Cyclopedia. New York, 1899.

Fuerbringer, Engelder and Kretzmann: The Concordia Cyclopedia. St. Louis, 1927.

INDEX

A

Absolute, 6, 35.
Absolution, private, 270.
Active principle, 282.
Adam, the sin of, 109.
Adiaphora, 357, 367.
Agnosticism, 36, 38.
Alexandrinus, 107.
Ambrose, 101.
Anabaptists, 334.
Analogy of faith, 23.
Angels, 88ff.; good and bad, 90.
Anhypostasia, 146.
Annihilation, of the wicked, 394.
Anselm, 195.
Antichrist, 397.
Antinomianism, 311.
Apocryphal books, 313-4.
Apollinaris, 147.
Apology of Augs. Conf., 222, 234, 253, 261, 264, 270, 272, 295.
Apostolate, 375-6.
Arianism, 57-8.
Aristotle, 100.
Arminians, 12, 120.
Ascension, of Christ, 178.
Assent, 210.
Athanasian Creed, 56, 151.
Athanasius, 58.
Atheism, 1, 36, 38.
Atonement, 187ff.; sufficiency of, 193; objections to doctrine of, 195ff.; Anselmic theory of, 195; false theories of, 196-7.
Attributes, of God, 38-42.
Attributive genus, 156.
Augsburg Confession, 115, 117, 121, 234, 291, 299, 308, 344, 367, 379, 382, 398.
Augustine, 2, 206, 209, 235, 342, 400.
Awakening, 235, 242ff.

B

Baier, 15, 342.
Baptism, 329ff.; definition of, 329; a sacrament, 330; O. T. type of, 330; of John, 330; divine command concerning, 331; the Word and, 331; the water in, 331; modes of, 331-4; of adults and children, 334; reasons for infant, 335-6; the heavenly gift in, 336; purpose of, 336; faith and, 337; a permanent covenant, 337; administration of, 338; lay, 338; validity of, 339; effect of, 339; formulas of, 339; sponsors in, 338; filial attitude in, 341; regeneration in, 342; necessity of, 344; secondary purposes of, 345.
Baptists, 334.
Beginning, the, 64.
Benevolence, the, of God, 121ff.
Bible, the Word of God, 22; contains the Word of God, 22.
Birth, of Christ, 169, virgin, 142.
Bishop, 376, 378.
Blessed, the, 422-3.
Blumenbach, 102.
Body, the, 100; resurrection of the, 401ff.
Brentz, 100.
Buffon, 102.

C

Calixtus, 100.
Call, the, 235; definition of, 236; purpose of, 238; through the Gospel, 239; serious and earnest, 239; sufficient and efficacious, 240; universal, 240; to the ministry, 379, 381-2.
Calvin, 12, 15, 132.
Calvinism, determining principle of, 12.
Capernaitic, 352.
Chaos, 65.
Chalcedon, Creed of, 152.
Change of Mind, 235, 250, 265ff.; necessity of, 266; definition of, 267.

457

Donum superadditum, 104, 120.
Dorner, 151.
Duality of natures, in Christ, 142.
Dynamistic, 57.

E

Earth, smallness of, 68.
Ebionites, 144.
Elder, 376.
Election, 134; a free act of grace, 135; eternal, 135; not absolute, 136; in view of faith, 136; categorical, 137; particular, 137; immutable, 137.
End, of the world, 398, 411.
Enhypostasia, 147.
Eternal death, 110, 413ff.
Eternal life, 421ff.
Eternity, of God, 41.
Ethics, and dogmatics, 15.
Eutychians, 151.
Evangelical counsel, 286.
Evil, origin of, 73.
Evolution, 68, 69, 100, 113, 120.
Exaltation, of Christ, 162, 170.
Exinanitio, 195.
Ex opere operato, 298, 301, 326, 334, 343.
Expiation, 195.

F

Faith, 9, 205, 207ff., 235; definition of, 209; cause of, 211; value of, 212; grace and, 212; two-fold effect of, 214; two-fold activity of, 214; and good works, 215; degrees of, 216; gives certainty, 216; joy of, 217; knowing that we have, 218; as a state, 219; loss and restoration of, 219; necessity of, 220; theological distinctions with regard to, 220; human, 220; divine, 220; direct and discursive, 220; explicit and implicit, 221; crude, 221; general and special, 221; righteousness of, 232; of infants, 342-3.
Fall, the, into sin, 106; consequences of, 111.
Fatalism, 85.
Feelings, change in the, 268.
Fichte, 100.
Filiation, 58.
Filioque, 58.
Final judgment, 406ff.; norm of, 408; according to works, 409-10.

First sin, the, 106; punishment of, 109; of Adam, 109.
Forgiveness, 227. *See* Justification.
Formula of Concord, 22, 102, 252, 257, 261, 264, 265, 272, 296, 313, 353.
Freedom, loss of, 120.
Free will, 206.
Fundamental articles of faith, 18.

G

Generation, 58, 59.
Generationism, 101.
Genus Idiomaticum, 156.
Genus Majestaticum, 156, 163.
Genus Apotelesmaticum, 156, 159, 161.
Gerhard, 308, 315, 340, 342, 356.
Gess, 165.
Giessen, theologians of, 167.
Glory, degrees of, 426.
God, being and attributes of, 31ff.; natural knowledge of, 31; proofs of existence of, 32; supernatural knowledge of, 32; definition of, 32; absoluteness of, 33; names of, 38; attributes of, 38.
God-man, the, 142, 190.
Goodness, of God, 43.
Good works, 225-6, 284; the fruit of faith, 285; nature of, 385; do not justify, 286; reward of, 288.
Gospel, law and, 245, 304; is promise of forgiveness, 311, 312.
Government, providential, 82.
Governmental theory, 197.
Grace, 43; saving, 127ff., 205ff.; efficacious but not irresistible, 259; kingdom of, 201; the believer is under, 310; Means of, 283-4, 289ff.
Greek language, 128.

H

Hades, 171.
Harless, 99.
Harnack, 7.
Heaven, 423-7.
Hegel, 107.
Heidelberg Catechism, 172.
Hell, 413ff.; not prepared for man, 410.
Helplessness of man, 127.
High Priest, 189.
Hindrance, providential, 182.
Historical proof, 33.